LOW CARB CREATIONS
From Lauri's Kitchen

Recipes for your Carb Conscious Lifestyle

by
Lauri Ann Randolph

Published by:

Avalon Enterprises, Inc.
P.O. Box 1044
Golden, CO 80402-1044
AvalonLowCarb@cs.com

LOW CARB CREATIONS
From Lauri's Kitchen
Recipes for your Carb Conscious Lifestyle

By Lauri Ann Randolph

 Avalon Enterprises, Inc.
P.O. Box 1044
Golden, CO 80402-1044
AvalonLowCarb@cs.com

ISBN 0-9667963-3-0

Cover design and many book illustrations by Lauri Ann Randolph

Printed in U.S.A by:

Eastwood Printing
2901 Blake Street
Denver, Colorado 80205

A wonderful company which has a warm, personal touch.
Thanks for everything, Peggy. It is a pleasure doing business with you.

With Gratitude

I dedicate this book to my friends & family who have
been so invaluable with recipe testing, recipe ideas and their
unwavering encouragement for me to continue in this line of work.
You know who you are. I offer my deepest appreciation to you all.

I also dedicate this book to every person who purchased my first book,
Lauri's Low-Carb Cookbook: Rapid Weight Loss with Satisfying Meals,
without whom it would have been impossible for me to complete the shift
from engineer to cookbook author. Again, you know who you are.
Thank you for contributing to my opportunity to work with my
passion for cooking. I am so very grateful to each of you.
May Sacred Spirit also bless your life with prosperity
and the satisfaction of joyful livelihood.

TABLE OF CONTENTS

~Introduction ~

Welcome to the low carb world! You may be a long time proponent of the low carb lifestyle or this may be your very first low carb cookbook. In any case, I am grateful to you for choosing this cookbook and trust that I can provide you with some good basic information and plenty of fabulous recipes to enhance your low carb experience.

I wish I had an extra dollar for every time someone has said to me, "Oh, you mean that meat and cheese diet" or "that heart attack waiting to happen diet." Such silliness! Although there is a tremendous amount of information available regarding the low carb diets, many people are alarmingly misinformed. I was too for the longest time. I paid little attention to the distinctions between healthy low carbs and not so good low carbs or essential fats versus toxic fats. But then I started reading and learning more about nutrition and began to better understand why the low carb diets work and how they could be approached to obtain optimal health.

I have no vested interest in which type of low carb plan you have chosen for yourself. It is a personal choice and some plans might resonate with you better than others. I will refer to the Akins plan in this book frequently only because it is the one that got me initially involved with the low carb lifestyle and is the one with which I am most familiar. Also the Atkins plan has more universal awareness; just about everyone familiar with a low carb diet is also familiar with Atkins. But the vast majority of the information in this cookbook will be applicable to any of the current low carb diets.

Although Dr. Atkins introduced the low carb diet several decades ago, it has only been a handful of years since it has become widely popular. It took a long time for the general public to believe the claims that were being made by Dr. Atkins, let alone the medical community. Many so called "nutrition experts" continue to disparage the low carb diet. But I find their arguments to be ill-informed and narrow-minded as they attack just one single aspect or another without looking at the entire program. Certainly if one assumes that the entire low carb plan looks like a lifetime of eating only that which is recommended for the initial two week induction period then yes, I too would agree that this would be an unhealthy way to live. But the Dr. Atkins plan is more complex and more thorough than just eating bacon and eggs for breakfast and grilled meat for lunch and dinner. The Atkins diet progresses in stages. It is a fast way to lose weight and it is a life long plan to stay healthy. This is being demonstrated by countless dieters, nutritionists and doctors.

Today there are many spin-offs and variations to the basic Atkins diet, all of which are generally the same, although they typically use different terminology and perhaps offer a different emphasis or spin here and there. The South Beach diet seems to be the most popular diet of 2004. It utilizes the glycemic index (GI) and glycemic load (GL) approach which is sometimes used by people with diabetes. This approach sounds good on paper, but it is a bit complicated and not without some controversy. Both methods have the same intended goal, they are just utilizing a different technique. In time, the GI/GL approach may develop to the point where it proves to be more useful but for now it is much easier to find carbohydrate information for food items than it is to find GI information. As research in the area of carbohydrate metabolism progresses, they may find new and improved ways of measuring the blood sugar and insulin response to food.

If you really intend to live the low carb lifestyle then I highly recommend that you read several of the how-to-books. But at a minimum, please read *Dr. Atkins' New Diet Revolution* or *Atkins for Life* and at least one other low carb "how to" book (The South Beach Diet, The Carbohydrate Addict's Diet, Protein Power, Sugar Busters, etc.). I believe that it is important to have a basic understanding of how the diet works and some of the variations presented by the different low carb programs. Each low carb diet is a little bit different and you will obtain the best success by following a specific plan "to the letter" at least for a few months. So find the one that resonates best with you. There are many "how to" low carb books available at every bookstore and library, you will surely find one that you like.

The science underlying a low carb weight loss program is the same regardless of who has packaged and labeled it. It is about putting your body into a state of lipolysis ketosis (ketosis for short) which is a specific metabolic mechanism for burning stored body fat. This is a safe biological process not to be confused with ketoacidosis which is a serious concern for some diabetics, but ketosis is the exact opposite metabolic state.

Ketosis in the most effective way to burn stored fat and has many advantages over a low fat diet or simply reducing calories. (But hey, I am not knocking these diets. Some people are more suited to a low fat or low cal diet. Everyone is different and must find what works best for themselves.) During ketosis our body will prefer to use stored fat as the primary fuel source and generally will not also breakdown the protein in our muscle mass as it would if we just reduced calories. And since we will be eating plenty of protein at the same time, then we can actually be able to simultaneously build muscle mass if we engage in appropriate exercise. Having additional muscle mass also helps make our bodies become better fat burners (this is one reason why men typically lose weight easier than women; they generally have more muscle mass). Ketosis naturally curbs the appetite (after about 48 hours) so we are not plagued by pangs of hunger and will generally desire less food. In fact, most people will feel quite energized; which is far different than the effects that many people experience on low fat or low calorie diets. Another by-product of the ketosis process is the formation of ketone bodies; which is superior brain food. The brain actually prefers ketones over glucose (its normal food source), so you may experience enhanced brain function such as sharper memory, heighten ability to focus and a general sense of wellbeing. The most effective way to get our body into ketosis is by dramatically reducing carbohydrates.

But the low carb diets are not only about reducing carbs in general, they are about eliminating refined carbohydrates, reducing starchy carbs while increasing the good carbs and eating the good fats and nutrient-rich foods that assist the weight loss process while promoting optimal health. If you take all of the low carb diet books and distilled them down to some basic concepts regarding nutrition, they will all point to the same things:

- Refined carbohydrates are not healthy and can make you fat
- Carbs from fresh fruits and vegetables are healthy and slimming
- Carbohydrates from *whole* grains are healthy
- Some fats are essential and healthy (e.g., omega 3)
- Saturated fats should be consumed in moderation
- Trans fatty acids (partially hydrogenated fats) are detrimental to your health and should be avoided

Most books on general nutrient will say pretty much the same things too. This is intellectually pretty simple stuff. The concept of the low carb diet is rather straight forward. The challenge is breaking the old habits that got us fat/unhealthy in the first place. Old habits die hard, but so will we if we are not committed to eating in the most healthy way that we are able to devise for our personal lifestyles. We each get to choose where we want to put our focus in life and where we are willing to make sacrifices. The way I see things, if I am taking the time to cook, then why not cook good, nutritious, healthy food; it is really just as easy.

Eating is a creative act where we choose the raw materials from the world around us that will integrate and transform to become our bodies. From a simple biological point of view, every part of our body (cells, organs, bones, tissue, etc.) is assembled from just a few basic forms of energy; food, sunshine, air and water. That is it! Since these are the building blocks for life, then the formula for good health would merely entail consuming the purest forms of these vital life forming energies. Conversely the pathway to disease and other health troubles is to expose ourselves to poor quality or contaminated sources of food, sunshine, air and water. So doesn't it seem reasonable that we would want to partake in the purest forms of these components as possible? Some cultures don't have a lot of choices about where they acquire these essential ingredients of life. But many of us do. Many of us are in a position to choose fresh, whole foods over processed foods anytime we want. It is merely a matter of priorities.

Most overweight people are not lazy or undisciplined as some people would like to portray us. The vast majority of people in America who are overweight are actually suffering from being alarmingly undernourished. This seems astonishing since Americans have more access to exceptional nutritional products than most of the population on the planet. But the research is extremely convincing; the typical American is malnourished.

Most convenience foods and prepackaged foods have plenty of calories to sustain life but so many of them have very little nutritional value to create a healthy life. Many of the basic essential ingredients for good health such as vitamins, minerals and other nutrients are too often grossly deficient or are simply not present. These empty calories leave us feeling hungry even when our bellies are full. Our bodies are constantly craving more and more food, unconsciously looking for more adequate nourishment. This can create a pattern of overeating.

However, being overweight has never been solely about food or even inadequate food quality. It is a symptom of a complex human mechanism that has fallen out of balance. We certainly need more nutrients in the foods that we eat but many of us also need more nourishment from our daily activities. So many people are not satisfied with the life they are leading: if only I had a better job, I need more money, I wish I had a better life partner, there's not enough time in the day, etc. The correlation between life dissatisfaction and weight problems (obesity and anorexia to name the extremes) has not gone unnoticed. However, rarely do we find diets or nutritional programs that talk about the whole person.

Who knows what the name of the next big diet trend will be, but I predict that the premise of the diet will be more holistic, factoring in one's entire lifestyle and not just focused on the foods we eat (the mind/body/soul approach). It may be something along the line of:

- Eat mostly whole foods,
- Avoid processed foods whenever possible,
- Drink plenty of pure, clean water and breathe clean air
- Get ample rest and plenty of exercise,
- Have meaningful and satisfying work to do,
- Laugh and be playful whenever possible, and
- Develop deep love and gratitude for god, nature, family and friends.

This has been the intent of my approach to life since leaving Corporate America in 1997 (an interesting story but for another type of book) and embarking on the low carb journey. Sometimes it unfolds effortlessly and other days I loose my way and my priorities get all screwed up. But my motivation for staying with the low carb lifestyle is one of healthy living much more than one of weight loss. Oh yes, I have had some success with weight loss (at the time of this writing, I am 60 pounds lighter than my heaviest pre-Atkins weight seven years ago) but more importantly I am far more healthy now than I have for years. Even though I really should shed quite a few more pounds (just let me finish testing all these yummy recipes first - too much of a good thing is not necessarily a good thing); my medical check-ups no longer show the typical symptoms associated with an overweight person (with the exception of some wear on my 50 year old knees). The customary markers of general health (cholesterol, blood pressure, blood sugar, etc.) have all returned to normal and healthy levels since I began my carb conscious way of eating.

Most of the media attention about the low carb lifestyle has narrowly been focused on just the weight loss aspects. Most everyone who has tried cutting carbs has had some level of success losing weight and everyone loves a dramatic weight loss story. Yet I suspect that over the next few years the spotlight will start to shift towards highlighting the low carb way of eating (as laid out by the leading low carb doctors) as a remarkably healthy way to live in addition to being an effective weight loss program.

So welcome again to the low carb lifestyle. May your road to weight loss and wellness unfold with ease and grace. Thank you for acquiring this cookbook and I trust that it will enhance your journey. I bid you health, happiness and immense success in everything which you endeavor to do.

Happy Cooking,

Me and my boys; Barkley and Spencer

Disclaimer:
I tried the best I could to find and present accurate and up-to-date information in this book. Since I have no formal education in nutrition, I have relied on the wisdom of others and have gathered information from many different sources. I have sorted through plenty of contradictory information and have used my own intuition to decipher, compile and present herein that which seemed the most valid and appropriate. The nutritional suggestions presented in this book are simply the results of my personal search for meaning in the world of nutrition and should not be given precedence over the recommendations and advice of your medical doctors, nutritional counselors and your own intuition. Everyone has different nutritional needs. My research has focused on those topics which are most important to me, so consequently I have probably formulated a bias in certain areas and have placed more emphasis on some issues while remaining silent on others. That is just how it has unfolded for me.

My formal education and background is engineering (encompassing more than 25 years of blood, sweat and tears developing renewable energy power facilities) a far cry from nutrition. But that scientific training makes it rather easy for me to understand and assimilate the nutritional information that I have read. And my engineering knowledge comes in quite handy in the kitchen; cooking is a science as well as an art form. I have an insatiable thirst for knowledge, particularly in the areas of spirituality, science, nutrition, health, cooking, gardening, art, psychology, ecology, renewable energy, ... okay, many diverse things. But the point is this; I am merely an opinionated cookbook author who loves to share constructive information and various tidbits of wisdom I have gathered along my journey. I apologize if you find any of my commentary annoying in anyway or contrary to your beliefs. My intention is to be helpful. Nevertheless, I trust that you will adore all my yummy recipes as they are the purpose and focus for this cookbook. As author and publisher, I expressly disclaim responsibility for any adverse effects arising from the use or application of any information contained in this book. (Yep, a lawyer had a hand in that last sentence!)

~ LOW CARB STAGES ~

Most of the low carb diet programs present three or more stages of dieting. In this book, I will also use the three stage approach, slightly modifying the Atkins terminology. The first stage, is called the Induction phase, designed to rid your body of starches and sugars, kick start your metabolism by shifting you into ketosis (see Dr. Atkins' book for an explanation), reduce your hunger and abate your cravings for carbohydrates. The second stage is the Weight Loss phase, where you concentrate on losing weight by wisely managing your carbohydrates and creating a healthy eating program that is deliciously enjoyable. The third stage is the Maintenance program where the emphasis is on eating a life long, healthy balance of whole foods while maintaining your desired weight.

The recipes in this cookbook are divided into these three categories. There are many Induction recipes even though this stage will typically only last for 2 weeks, because these recipes are to be incorporated into all three stages. The majority of the recipes fall into the Weight Loss category. These are the types of recipes that are the foundation of the low carb way of eating for both the weight loss phase as well as your maintenance program. Additionally, I have included numerous recipes for things that you will want to begin to introduce into your lifestyle during your maintenance program. These maintenance recipes are not intended to be the primary types of recipes for your new low carb lifestyle but are extra things that are to be included at a moderate level in order for you to maintain your desired weight and to optimize your health and well being.

Induction Phase

If you are following the Dr. Atkins plan, then your induction phase will last for two weeks. If you are new to the low carb world, then two weeks is certainly recommended. However if you have been generally following a low carb diet but are now ready to initiate a new weight loss phase, then it is recommended that you start off with the induction phase for at least four or five days so that ketosis is fully kicked in and reducing your appetite and carb cravings.

Each individual will have a different threshold of carbohydrate intake depending upon age, average activity level, general metabolic rate, gender and other considerations. The Atkins program recommends keeping your carb count under 20 grams per day. For those who are metabolically resistive (that would be me) then you may need to keep carbs closer to 10 grams for the first several days. The best way to determine what works best for you is utilizing ketosis strips (KetoStix or one of the other brands) , also called lipolysis testing strips. These handy ketone-detecting strips (which you can purchase at any pharmacy) are passed through your urine stream and measure excess ketones indicating how much body fat is being burned (see Dr. Atkins books for further explanation). If your ketosis strips become dark purple you are doing great. If they are just a little bit pink then reduce your carbs even more.

The Induction phase of the program is the most difficult not only because you are eating such a restricted diet but also because your system will be clearing toxins and that can make you feel rather unwell. Headaches, irritability, and digestive troubles are very common. Howeve,r with perseverance you can break through and overcome the symptoms in a relatively short time (the human physiology is amazing). Lots of pure water (bottled or filtered and no additives, not even a slice of lemon) is the best anecdote for 90% of the Induction phase symptoms. Stay positive, believe in yourself and trust the process.

If you are able to stay in the induction phase for the full two weeks then Congratulations: you probably lost 10 to 15 pounds! But do not be fooled into thinking that if you continue the induction phase for another two weeks that you will experience another 10 to 15 pounds of weight loss. It will very rarely happen. Besides it would not be healthy to try and do so. Our bodies can only handle a sustained weight loss rate of about 2 to 3 pounds per week, so you might as well move into the weight loss phase and start eating more enjoyable foods right away.

This cookbook contains a variety of recipes that are suitable for the induction phase. In general, I have assumed that recipes under 3g net carbs per serving are classified as Induction. But everyone is different. You may be able to easily tolerate recipes that are in the 4 – 7g net carb range during your Induction phase. I've just tired to create a general guideline. As you plan your menus with this cookbook, you might want to look through the weight loss recipes too, I have provided a few variations for some of them that will make the recipe suitable for the induction phase. These are also listed in the index under "Induction Variations."

Weight Loss Phase
The weight loss phase is the primary focus of the recipes in this cookbook. These are also the foundation of the maintenance program as well. I have designated the recipes that are less than 10 grams net carbs per serving as those recipes which are most applicable to the weight loss phase. But this does not mean that most people will be able to regularly eat meals that include an entrée, salad, vegetable, and dessert each containing 10g net carbs and still expect to see a weight loss. You must determine for yourself what is appropriate for you. I am merely providing a general guideline and a reasonable approach to organizing the recipes.

Each individual will need to determine for themselves how many carbs they can typically eat in a day and still lose weight. The range can be as low as 10g and perhaps as high as 60g, but more typically 30 to 40 grams per day works well for most people. Again the ketosis strips are very helpful in establishing the appropriate carb level for you. But it is not just the number of carbs that count. The types of carbs are important too. If the majority of your carbs are coming from low carb vegetables, then you might be able to eat substantially more carbs and still lose weight. But if you have a tendency to consume carbs from processed foods or an abundance of high calorie, low carb foods (e.g. nuts, cheese, sour cream, mayo, low carb ice cream, etc.) then you may need to shoot for a lower daily carb count. You will also need to be mindful of foods that have a high total carb count even though their stated net carb may be minimal. For example, sweet treats made with sugar-alcohols (see page 29.) may indicate a very low net carb but this can be deceiving. The packaging of these types of foods indicates that the carbohydrates associated with sugar-alcohols can be entirely subtracted from the total carbohydrates. But this is not true for everyone; most people will actually digests a portion of the sugar-alcohols, thereby significantly increasing the carb count.

If you are metabolically resistive due to medications or some medical condition and your ketosis strips won't turn even to the first shade of pink, don't give up. Read Dr. Atkins book as he discusses some approaches for this situation.

If you have a lot of weight to lose, then you may want to take a break from dieting from time to time. But please do not go off the diet completely (you don't want to start gaining); just shift to the maintenance phase for awhile and enjoy a greater variety of food while you maintain your weight. When you are ready again to initiate additional weight loss, then be sure to start with the induction phase again for at least four or five days before moving back into the weight loss phase.

Maintenance Phase
Congratulations you are at your desired weight! Yippee! Way to go! You rock! Give yourself the biggest form of acknowledgement that you can imagine. Your dedication has paid off (with interest and major dividends). You are well on your way to a long and healthy life.

Or perhaps you haven't yet reached your goals; maybe you just need a break from dieting. Maybe you are seriously missing oatmeal for breakfast or maybe you have a holiday or special occasion where you don't want to feel quite as restricted. Great! Don't worry about it, just shift to the maintenance plan for awhile and enjoy it. Then when you are ready, just step back into your weight loss phase. It took years to put on all that weight, right? So there is nothing wrong with taking years to melt it away. (Or perhaps this point of view is merely self-justification. Tee, hee! You decide.)

There are a number of food items that you can now start introducing into your diet. Of particular interest to many will be grains. Yes, whole grains are allowed on the low carb plan; they are actually encouraged by most low carb experts. It is just that they are eaten differently than what is customary for many. Grains become side dishes and additives to other dishes. Portion control is the key. And then there are fruits! The almighty apple can be added to your routine as well as other fruits. But an apple pie from McDonalds is NOT a maintenance item. Your apples should be served without the sugar, refined flour, trans fatty acids and preservatives offered by fast food chains. Try a delicious Waldorf Salad (page 164) or the scrumptious Apple Crumble (page 416).

I've indicated recipes that are 10g net carbs per serving or above as those more appropriate for the maintenance phase. But these recipes can be included from time to time during the weight loss phase as long as your total carb count for the day stays under your target. I have created a few maintenance specialty recipes that use grains and some of the fruits that are normally restricted from the weight loss phase. Again, moderation and portion control is the key.

~ BUSTING A PLATEAU ~

Weight loss plateaus are extremely common. You will likely experience them every now and then. The weight has been melting off, everything is good, then all of a sudden a plateau – days or weeks of no weight loss despite eating well and exercising. Do not fret, just figure it out. There is a reasonable explanation and a solution to the situation. Here are some things to consider.

1. More often than not, additional carbs are finding their way into your diet. Start writing down every carb you eat for a few days and see if you can decipher where you need to tighten up. No need to lie to yourself; every carb counts.

2. What about calories? Even if your carbs are on target, you may be getting too many calories. Watch out for some of those low carb sweet treats, the carbs may be low but typically they have a high caloric value.

3. Are you drinking enough water? Your body can have troubles flushing out excess fat when it is not sufficiently hydrated. Think about washing a greasy plate, a tiny trickle of water does not work nearly as well as a blast of water.

4. What about exercise? Has your body gotten use to your daily/weekly routine? Is it time to take your exercise program to the next level?

5. Have you lost a lot of weight already and so now your body requires even less food? Is it time to start reducing some calories too?

6. Have you starting taking a new medication or supplement? Some medicines can interfere with our metabolic functions. Consult your physician; perhaps there is an alternate formula that is appropriate for your situation.

7. All of the above are fine, so what else can it be? Well sometimes the body just stops losing weight. Dr. Atkins talks about this in his book. He suggests doing a reverse diet at this point. For a day (or two at the most) you should eat carbs. Yep that's right, eat carbs! It is just a day or two so eat whatever you like, pasta, potato, basmati rice (oh yum), whatever you desire (although refined sugar is still discouraged). Obviously, whole grains will be your best choice, but so are sweet potatoes, winter squash, and beans. Be sure to drink plenty of water. Then after a day or two get back to your low carb plan and increase your exercise level for the next few days.

If the weight does not start to melt away within a few days of making your adjustments, then I recommend starting at the induction phase once again. Stay as low carb as possible and use the lipolysis testing strips. If you are not able to get ketone indication after a few days, then you really should contact your health care provider to determine the cause of the problem.

~ STRAYING FROM THE PATH ~

I prefer not to use too much terminology that triggers guilty or other negative emotions, so I'd rather not talk about "cheating" or "falling off the wagon" or other such catch phases. I try to be a bit more compassionate with myself when I deviate from my food program. It is going to happen, (let me repeat; it is going to happen) so I recommend that you devise a few strategies that can help guide you back to your chosen path. Devise these strategies when you are feeling good about your life.

For me there are two major situations where I find myself eating foods that are not aligned with my intended eating program. The first is the easiest to deal with; unexpected social pressure. A good friend is having a party, I brought some food to share that works for my diet, so all is good. But my friend has just proudly made a certain something loaded with refined sugars and/or other carbs that are no longer part of my lifestyle. However, I feel that I must politely try this certain something. I tell myself, "Go ahead, try it, enjoy it, but truly experience it. Be extremely conscious of the choice and allow the body to feel whatever it feels." When I am truly able to give myself this permission, I generally realize that I don't really like that sugar thing nearly as much as I thought I would. I politely say "this is so delicious" and then I revel with glee in the knowingness that I truly no longer want such things! These are great and happy moments! But maybe it is not just one item, but it is the entire meal. Perhaps it is a special occasion or just an ordinary day gone awry. I try not to view these situations as "blowing it" as much as taking a time out; as long as I do it with full consciousness. That way it will be much easier to get back to my low carb path without dragging along some feelings of guilt (which can again trigger overeating). The goal is to consistently make wise and healthy choices; perfection is overrated and unnecessary.

The second situation is when I am having emotional difficulties about something. I may be acutely aware of what the situation is about or I might not have any idea what it is regarding, I just know that I am craving junk food and allowing myself to indulge. These occasions might be for just a couple of hours, but it might drag out for days, or weeks or even months. The worst thing about emotional eating is that eating unhealthy food makes me feel even more unhealthy which just deepens the emotional drag and then the snowball effect is put in place: the worse I feel, the worse I eat which makes me feel even worse, and so on. I use to have all sorts of ugly, negative labels for this situation, but now I try to just say, "Oh no, I have strayed from the path again. So let's set a new course. My past choices are history, no regrets. I now have the opportunity to make new and different choices in this very moment." Sometimes it can be challenging for me to know how to set the course back to the path when I have become particularly lost. So I believe that it is important to have a plan. To devise one or more strategies to be used as a guide or compass when we have become lost. My approach is by creating what I call "maps". My maps are predetermined plans for getting me oriented in the desired direction. They are a list of steps to take to get me back to my preferred path, my preferred way of living. I've discovered that I need a couple of different strategic maps because there are a couple of different places where I can get lost and I've not found a single map that works for all situations. Each of my maps are basically a list of activities; things that I know will help me shift and adjust my perceptions so that I can find my way back to living the carb conscious life I truly wish to lead.

My maps focus mostly on things that have nothing to do with food. But they all have certain components in common, something physical, something spiritual and something that shifts my attention to gratitude. Only the last steps involve a food plan. The physical component is usually first. Depending on the circumstances, I generally need to either increase my physical activity or decrease it. The activities include things like getting more rest (e.g., nap, slowly brush out the dogs, casually chat on the phone with a friend, go to bed early, etc.) or the opposite of getting more active (take a rigorous hike, dance, scrub the floor, sing, do some sit-ups, tend to that yard work, etc.). The spiritual component can look like prayer, reading, meditation, chanting, etc. It can be anything that consciously brings me back in touch with the source energy (I call it Spirit, but for you it may be God or nature or a higher power).

The gratitude aspect is the most common to all my maps. Making a gratitude list is always one of the components. Not just physically writing down things for which I am grateful, but really taking the time to feel each one as deeply and completely as I can under the circumstances. My goal is to feel each so deeply that I shiver with awe or cry with joy. I use to only make my "G List" at night just before bed. But my friend Eryn DeFoort, who is a weight management coach (www.theGaiaCenter.com), recently gave me an incredible yet simple suggestion: immediately after dinner, make a list of at least 5 things for which I am deeply grateful and 5 things for which I can acknowledge myself. Not only does this new gratitude and acknowledgement list address my map item but it also delays the time between dinner and the time I would normally be fixing something for dessert. This extra 10 to 20 minutes allows my body to completely feel how full I really am after dinner, allowing me to choose a smaller dessert portion (and sometimes I choose a healthier dessert). This has been an extremely powerful tool for me. Perhaps it could be a benefit to you too. Thanks Eryn!

The last component of my map is the food plan. The basic approach is baby steps; slow and easy transition back to the path. If it is a short term situation and I merely binged on something, then the activity might be about getting in touch with how my body is truly feeling in response to the situation. I bless the food which I overate, become grateful that I had a choice and then I forgive myself for making that particular choice. Then last, I vow to eat something incredibly healthy at my next meal. But if I've been lost for awhile and I am just awakening to that realization, then the food issue component may be more involved. I might not commence the food plan for a couple of days until I've come into closer alignment with the physical, spiritual and emotional things first. Then when I am ready to address the food, I might start off with having a healthy salad before eating that "comfort food" which I know I'm going to eat anyway. Then the next day, perhaps I'll prepare one meal that is completely low carb and healthy, and so on. With comfortable baby steps, I can find my way back to the path. For others, perhaps going "cold turkey" might work better. Simply choose a moment and then eat only health food, no exceptions. If that works for you then great! Go for it! But for me that challenge generally creates a boomerang effect and I'm back to junk food in no time as a rebellious response to such rigid discipline.

We are all different in this regard and I encourage you to devise your own plans of how you are going to handle the times when you stray from your intended path. I use "maps", but you may find some other type of plan or strategy that works better for you. However, the plan must be formulated in advanced when you are feeling relatively good about things. Waiting until you are lost before you start to try and figure out an approach is tragically ineffectual. Albert Einstein taught us that the solutions to problems do not exist in the same field as the problems; we must go outside of the field of problems to discover the solutions.

~ PREPACKAGED LOW CARB FOODS ~

In early 2004, prepackaged low carb food items exploded into the marketplace. Where there use to be just a small shelf of a few items dedicated to low carb things, now grocery stores have the low carb items on the same shelves as their mainstream counterparts. Low carb or sugar-free ketchup use to be a challenge to find (even at a good health food store) and now *Carb Options*™ *Ketchup* is sitting on the same shelf as the regular *Heinz 57!*

At first I was extremely excited about this emerging trend. But as I started to read key ingredients on the labels I became discouraged. There were just too many products that were simply following a hot, new, marketing trend with little or no regard for the health-conscious, carb-conscious, dieter. Some low carb products contain inappropriate, unhealthy ingredients. We've seen a similar thing in the low-fat industry as well, where manufacturers load their products with refined sugars in order to make their low fat products more palatable. People are given a false sense of healthiness, because they are actually consuming high amounts of sugar which metabolizes directly into saturated fat if it is not immediately used for energetic activities. Fat-free does not mean that it is not fattening. Many fat-free foods are far more fattening than their customary counterparts. This high sugar, low fat trend has persisted for many years now and surprisingly has not been properly exposed to the general public. I fear a similar trend with the prepackaged low carb food products. I am finding that many of these early low carb products contain partially hydrogenated fats (a toxic substance that most experts say to avoid at all costs), particularly from the large, well-known food manufacturers. What a shame! However, some of the smaller manufacturers are actually dedicated to a healthy low carb lifestyle and not just jumping on a new market bandwagon. Many are using relatively healthy ingredients in their prepackaged mixes and food items. But look at those price tags, yikes. This is not price gouging however. It is more costly per unit to manufacture products on a smaller scale. As low carb items become more popular we should see some price relief.

Now don't get me wrong folks, I'm no purist. I've tried almost all of the low carb prepackaged products available today (research for this book - yeah right). There is a lot of crap out there (low carb pasta anyone?) but there are some really delicious products too, like Carb Options™ Original Barbecue Sauce, supplied to us by *Lawry's*™ (oh so yum and convenient!). I also have a particular weakness for Carb Fit™ Almond Cookies (by Hain Celestial Group, Inc.), even if I can't pronounce one or two of the ingredients. And what about some of those low carb ice creams! Shazam! Lately, I've been expressing gratitude for these on a daily basis. My favorite at the moment is called Carb Solutions™ Butter Pecan Ice Cream! Oh my god! I find that the Carb Solutions™ ice creams taste better than most and are much more economical than most of the other brands (so far).

I love ice cream; perhaps I am even addicted to it. If so, it is an addiction that I have never desired to abate. I once heard Dee Pak Chopra jokingly proclaim that ice cream isn't in any of the major food groups because it is actually medicine! Yeah, he dah man! More than any other single substance, ice cream has been my pitfall on every diet that I have tried. Regular ice cream has too much fat for the low-fat diet, too much sugar for the low carb diet and too many calories for any diet. Once I even tried the ice cream diet (it didn't work for me, but I enjoyed trying). But now, thanks to Splenda® (see page 27) I can enjoy a little bit of low carb ice cream on a daily basis without much guilt and tons of pleasure. Yippee! I must be careful about serving size however (½ cup is not much), and I've had more than a couple of binges on the stuff (especially when they first became available). But when I can limit myself to 1/2 cup which has only 3g net carbs, I can more easily justify the 160 calories and 14 grams of fat. And with Carb Solution™ I can even pronounce all of the ingredients! I'm in heaven!

As for low carb pasta, I don't really care for them so you will find only a handful of recipes in this cookbook utilizing them. They are made mostly from soy and wheat gluten so they are products which I rarely use. The pasta recipes that are included in this book uses the Carb Fit Rotini type but there are several different brands so experiment and find the one which you like the most. For best results, cook them exactly as how stated on their package and do not overcook.

Undercooking isn't much better. Also use low carb pasta mostly with heavy, flavorful sauces. You'll probably be disappointed if you try to make the pasta itself the main ingredient. *DreamFields* has several pasta products which claim to have only 5g digestible carbs per serving. It tastes truly wonderful: too wonderful, however! I just don't follow their rational for subtracting so many carbs as it is made with typical pasta flour (refined durum wheat semolina). My attempts to contact them, has not provided sufficient information for me to believe that it is actually as low in net carbs as they profess. I deeply hope that through <u>independent</u> research that their assertion of 5g effective carbs will be validated. That will open up a huge culinary arena to create even more low carb recipes! But until then; if it seems too good to be true … well, I advise caution.

There are a number of low carb prepackage foods that I have included in this cookbook. I may refer to some generically while others I may state a specific brand. I do have my preferences but I am not endorsing any particular brand or product per se, unless specifically noted otherwise in the recipe. Use the brands that you prefer. I have not been paid to include any particular products (unlike some other cookbook authors); I choose not be influenced that way. My opinions have been swayed only by my own personal preferences. The following are some of the low carb specialty products that you will come across in my recipes. Those in italics are specific brands otherwise they are generic.

Carb Options™ Original Barbecue Sauce
Carb Options™ Ketchup (simply the best!)
Carb Solutions™ Ice Cream (assorted flavors)
Dannon's Carb Control™ yogurt (assorted flavors)
Hood's Carb Countdown™ Dairy Beverage (2% and the chocolate flavor)
Joseph's Sugar-Free Maple Syrup
La Tortilla Factory low carb tortillas (whole wheat & green onion)
Low carb marinades
Low carb pasta
Low carb salad dressings
Splenda®

For most of my recipes you can substitute the brands that you prefer. Although, there are a few recipes where I caution against certain products whose usage will greatly alter the results of the recipe. However, if your preferred product is not extremely similar then you may need to do some label comparisons and make the appropriate adjustments to the nutritional analysis for that recipe.

Other Specialty Products
There are a few other products that you will see specified in my recipes on a frequent basis which you may not already have in your pantry. The following is a list of some of the ones which you will probably want to acquire in order to make full use of this cookbook..

Almond Meal

You will notice that I use quite a lot of almond meal. This is simply ground up almonds (typically blanched). You may also find it under the name of almond flour. Not only is it high in fiber and omega 3 fatty acids, it is also a great substitute for flour and other ingredients for certain types of recipes, particularly baked goods such as muffin, cookies and pie crusts. Bob's Red Mill® is a quality provider of almond meal and is the brand which I used to develop the recipes in this cookbook. It is readily available in both health food stores and many ordinary grocery stores. Please note that it should be refrigerated once opened if it will not be used up within about 2 or 3 months. Use can substitute other ground nuts in many of the recipes for variations and to suit your tastes.

Flax Seed Meal

Flax seed is a nutrient-dense product containing protein, fiber, minerals, vitamins and a host of other micronutrients. It is the best known source of the omega-3, essential fatty acid, alpha-linoleic acid and is very high in fiber. (See page 33 for more information). In addition to health considerations, it is also a valuable ingredient to add texture and flavor in several of my recipes. I love its mild nutty taste and the way it adds bulk and flavor to recipes like pancakes and muffins. Although it is available in any health food store, only purchase the ones kept in the refrigerated sections and not the ones on the ordinary shelves unless you are buying the whole seed and intend to grind them yourself. Whole flax seeds can not be broken down in our digestive track so it must be ground first in order to be bioavailable. Whole seeds have an excellent shelf life (years). But once it is ground it can become rancid easily so it must be stored in the refrigerator (for up to 3 months).

Guar Gum

I use guar gum as a thickening agent for sauces and soups. It is a soluble fiber that comes from the guar bean grown primarily in India. It has 8 times the thickening power as cornstarch but without the net carbs. Its primary advantage over other thickeners is that it dissolves easily in either hot or cold water. You still must stir vigorously to assure that it does not lump, but it is far less susceptible to this than most other thickeners. Its only disadvantage is that it does have a little bit of a taste to it. Although the taste is rather mild, it can be noticed when used in recipes with delicate flavors. Be cautious when adapting your other recipes, it is easy to add too much. I recommend no more than 1/2 tsp of guar gum to each cup of liquid (less if your liquid is cream based). It is slow to come to its full thickening power (about 5 minutes) but heating will expedite this somewhat. You can find guar gum at most health food stores as it is mostly used as a fiber supplement.

Just Whites

This product is powdered egg whites. There are many other brands and they are all about the same. I also use Bob's Red Mill® powdered eggs whites. This is a product of convenience. I like that it needs no refrigeration and that I don't have to figure out what to do with those extra egg yolks. It dissolves in water but you have to be patient about this as it takes a little while.

Kitchen Bouquet
This product is caramel based and is used to add color and flavor to sauces and gravies. It is not a low carb product (3g carbs per teaspoon) but generally you need only a small amount of it. Most grocery stores carry this product either where they have canned or instant gravy or somewhere near the steak sauces.

Nellie & Joe's Key West Lime Juice
I use quite a lot of this product. I much prefer the taste of lime to that of lemon. Besides, it is easier to pour out a tablespoon from the bottle than squeezing a lime or two every time I want some citrus flavor. I wish someone would come up with an equivalent product for lemon juice (the stuff in that little yellow, lemon shaped plastic bottle doesn't taste like lemons to me).

Whey Protein Powder
Whey is a highly nutritious milk protein that is formed in the cheese-making process. You know, separating the curds and whey. Once it was simply a discarded by-product. But now whey protein is concentrated into a powder and used in a variety of shakes, protein bars and other manufactured goods as well as a stand alone product. Whey protein powder is an excellent source of protein which is very easy to digest. You have undoubtedly seen flavored whey protein powder mixes used for breakfast and sport drinks. This is not the stuff that I use. It is too expensive and has too many other ingredients including sweeteners (however, this is generally the type of whey protein power which is specified in other low carb cookbooks).

The product which I use in the recipes contained in this cookbook is whey powder concentrate that has at least 74% whey protein (the higher the protein content the better). It is reasonably priced and works wonderfully as a flour substitute in things like cookies and muffins. Since it is mostly protein it is very low carb with only about 1g per cup. You can also find whey protein powders that have lower concentrations of protein and are cheaper but they do not perform as well in my recipes. You should be able to find the high protein whey concentrate at any good health food store. I prefer the type from New Zealand which uses a low temperature filtration process and has no chemical residues.

Whey protein isolates are also available on the market, which have whey protein concentrations of 90-95%. This product is great for smoothies and such, but it doesn't bake as well as the high protein concentrate which I use. The isolates are also twice as expensive.

Soy Products
You may have already noticed that I specify very few soy products in my recipes except for soy sauce. My primary reason for this is that soy contains a very large amount of phytoestrogens (natural, plant-based estrogens). This is one reason why some women purposefully include soy in their diets. But for me, I need to

limit soy products as I had an estrogen-related cancer about a dozen years ago. There are many sources of phytoestrogens (many are considered to be in safe concentrations) but soy is especially high in plant-based estrogens and therefore is not a wise choice for me.

Many low carb products are soy based. I caution about consuming too much (particularly men and anyone woman who has a family history of breast, ovarian or uterine cancer). Talk with your health care provider to determine if you have a need to limit your soy products. Exercise moderation in all things, my friends. Yes, yes easier said than done; but it is still an admirable goal.

~ THE NUTRITIONAL ANALYSIS ~

For each recipe I have provided the total calories, fat, carbohydrates and dietary fiber per serving. Additionally, I have shown the calculation for the "net carbs" (also known as effective carbs) per serving. Generally, the net carbs equals the total carbs minus the total dietary fiber. Fiber is a type of carbohydrate that is not metabolized by the body and therefore does not cause a rise in insulin and blood sugar levels (in fact it can actually lower them). So the general convention of today is to subtract the total dietary fiber from the total carbohydrates to obtain the net carb effect of foods. Polyol sweeteners (also known as sugar-alcohol; see next section) are also a type of carbohydrate which many people subtract from the total carbs. However, polyols are actually metabolized to some extent depending on the type of polyol and the general metabolism of the individual consuming them. I believe that this practice of subtracting all of the polyol grams to arrive at net carbs will be short-lived because the percentage that does get digested has a significant metabolic effect. Research is showing that the percent which is metabolized varies from about 10% to as much as 50% for some individuals. I have very few recipes which use any type of polyol sweeteners. But for those recipes that do include polyols, I have subtracted only 70% of the associated grams to arrive at the net carbs. This assumes 30% absorption which is simply the mid point of what is being indicated by research. However, each individual will have a different absorption rate.

The nutritional analysis of the recipes in this cookbook primarily comes from a computer program that is based on data from the United States Department of Agriculture (USDA). I have also obtained certain nutritional information from manufacturers for specific products and a few analyses simply come from product labels.

I have compared the USDA data with other sources (on the internet, carb counter books, and other computer programs) and have found some deviations from time to time particularly with carbohydrates. Also different manufacturers of the same basic product often indicate different numbers on their labels. This may be due to a different formulation of the product (e.g., one uses more vinegar than another), but even with the exact same formulation the labeling could still be a little different because of their particular method for determining the nutritional content. So don't worry if you find different numbers from different sources – it is difficult to be exact particularly when specifying ingredients utilizing inexact quantities. With my program, stating "3 tomatoes" gives the same analysis as 7/8 of a pound of tomatoes. But certainly not every group of 3 tomatoes will weight exactly that amount. The vast majority of the recipe analyses are based on average sized items, so if you grow a mega zucchini it will obviously have a higher carb count than what I'll provide when I simply indicate, "one zucchini".

Don't sweat the small stuff. Try not to get too carried away with counting carbs past the decimal point. This is a tendency for people during the Induction phase and it can drive you crazy. But on the other hand you can't completely dismiss certain food items that have less than 1 gram carb as having zero carbs (which might subsequently make you think that you can eat as much as you want). There are very few zero carb foods so don't believe all those crazy labels. If the food is less than 0.5g carbohydrate per serving then the manufacturers are allowed to say zero. Similarly if the food item is 0.9g they are permitted to write less than 1g. So unless it is unprocessed meat, poultry or fish, then assume 0.5g carbs per serving when it says zero and count 1g per serving for packages that say less than 1 gram. There are many hidden carbs lingering around too that catch some people by surprised, particularly during the Induction phase. An average egg has 0.5g of carbs, as does a typical 12oz diet soda. It doesn't sound like much but it can add up. An area of particular concern is with regards to products which use any of the polyol sweeteners (see the next section); these can be disastrous for some people. But with all that being said, try not to get too weird with this stuff. If you simply round up to the nearest whole gram of carbs, then you'll be fine.

~ Regarding Sweeteners ~

One of the hardest things for me to do when dieting is to avoid or just cut back on sweets. Even low carb sweets can sometimes trigger unwanted responses of craving certain carbohydrates, an urge to overeat, a desire to procrastinate, etc. How and why the consumptions of sweets can sometimes impair our judgment is still a mystery to me. Even though that "sugar dazed" syndrome is more often associated with refined sugar, I have experienced it with all different types of sweeteners; even with simple fruit. Nevertheless, I love sweets. I have had a sweet tooth all my life. Although the degree of desire for sweets is significantly reduced when I am eating strictly low carb; I still enjoy having something sweet everyday, particularly after my evening meal. You will find many satisfying sweet treats in the dessert section of this cookbook.

In my first book, *Lauri's Low-Carb Cookbook*, I used only Sweet'n Low® as an added sweetener to recipes. I received a fair amount of criticism for this. However, it was the only low carb sweetener that I could tolerate at that time. In this cookbook, I use primarily Splenda; as it is easy to cook with, tastes great and is widely available. Though I'm sure I will be criticized for this too. But please refrain from sending me mail if you have an objection to Splenda®, just substitute whatever you feel is most appropriate for the recipe and for your personal tastes. (The 3rd Edition of *Lauri's Low-Carb Cookbook* should be available sometime in 2005 and will have revised recipes using Splenda® instead of the Sweet'n Low®.)

Sweeteners are a very controversial subject. All of them seem to have health risks to some degree or another, but it varies from sweetener to sweetener and from person to person too. Some people seem to be able to tolerate refined white sugar; while it is absolute poison for others. Please don't think that I am trying to claim that Splenda® is a healthy sweetener just because I use it ubiquitously in this cookbook. It is simply the sweetener which I have preferred lately and it is the easiest to use when creating recipes. New sweeteners are continually being developed, so my next cookbook may highlight something else.

When using other people's cookbooks which simply states "sugar substitute," you may want to contact them and determine which sweeteners they actually use the most. Especially if you are having troubles with a particular recipe that you would like to have in your repertoire. I had a friend who made one of my desserts from *Lauri's Low-Carb Cookbook* using Equal instead of the Sweet'n Low® and the results were dreadful. Each sweetener behaves a bit differently in the presence of other ingredients and when heated. To me, specifying "sugar substitute" is a cop-out; it is virtually impossible to develop recipes that will work for every type of sugar substitute.

The following is a brief discussion of a few sweeteners. I will not include aspartame (also known as Equal and Nutrasweet) as I feel it is more harmful to people than refined sugar.

Splenda®
You may find other cookbooks or nutrition labels which list sucralose as a sweetener. Well that's the same thing as Splenda®. I prefer to use the brand name Splenda® as it is less likely to be confused with sucrose, which is ordinary sugar. Splenda® is a non-nutritive sweetener; which means that it has no nutritional value including no calories and no carbs. It is chemically derived from sugar and is mixed with dextrose and maltodextrin to give it volume. It is the "fillers" that provide the carbs in Splenda® (about 24g/cup, 1.5g/Tbsp and 0.5g/tsp). Pure sucralose is not yet available to the American consumer, but I look forward to the day when it is. Even though sucralose is made from sugar, it passes right through the body without being metabolized. The FDA considers Splenda® to be a safe product (no warning label is required). I found no research which shows harmful side effects from the use of Splenda®; unlike aspartame which typically causes headaches and weight gain as well as a multitude of other symptoms and disorders.

The flavor of Splenda® is very close to that of white sugar and it measures cup for cup the same as sugar with regard to sweetening power. This makes it a particularly useful sweetener when adapting traditional recipes to low carb recipes. However, Splenda® does not have all the same characteristics as ordinary sugar. The crystalline structure is different so it will not produce some of the special features such as the brittle topping on crème brulee nor will it brown or make caramel. But this does not diminish its usefulness in the low carb kitchen.

Splenda® is rather expensive, as of today. I have seen those large "economy"10 oz bags (equivalent to 1 lb of sugar) priced as high as $8.99! And the smaller boxes and individual packets are even more expensive on a per ounce basis. However, if you have access to Costco, then you can get a box containing 2 of the large bags for about the same price as a single bag in the ordinary grocery stores. There is no worry about the shelf life so buy in bulk when you can.

As demand for this product increases, the price should come down. There will be manufacturing savings when large batches are produced and hopefully fair market competition will also drive the price down once other manufacturers start to produce it (although they will need to use a name other than Splenda®).

Stevia

This sweetener comes from an herb which has been used for centuries and is popular today in many cultures from South American to Japan. Stevia is a zero-carb and zero-calorie sweetener yet it contains various micronutrients (depending upon the brand). Some people call it "the healthy sweetener" and various healing properties have been attributed to it. But the FDA has not yet approved it as a sweetener (only as a dietary supplement). Perhaps this is due to some politics with the sugar industry. I don't know for sure; I'm just guessing. Once it becomes approved by the FDA as a food additive then we will be seeing Stevia in many food products.

I think that Stevia is probably one of the healthiest sweeteners available today, low carb or otherwise. But the taste does not appeal to me very much except in rather small quantities (I love it in green tea) and depending upon the brand. However, the biggest problem with Stevia is trying to write recipes for it. Each brand is different regarding amount of sweetening power, bitterness, after taste, and the type of fillers used. Even when I have used the same brand consistently for awhile, all of a sudden I get a batch that tastes different to me. So until there is more consistency in this product, it is too unpredictable for me to try and develop recipes for a cookbook using Stevia.

But experiment with Stevia at home and see if there are some foods (coffee, tea, cereal, etc.) where it works for you. Also you can blend it with Splenda®; they work together well making an extra sweet combination. If you do this, then you can reduce the amount of Splenda® stated in the recipes.

Like Splenda®, the powdered forms of Stevia generally contain fillers (typically maltodextrin) to bulk it up for more convenient usage. Most fillers have some carbs. The liquid forms generally have no carbs, but it is hard to control the number of drops used. NuNaturals brand has a zero carb Stevia powder that uses erythritol (one of the better polyols) as the filler. This product is a bit difficult to find; check with their website (www.nunaturals.com). However, I suspect that this low carb version will become much more popular as time goes by.

Blackstrap Molasses

I have a couple of recipes that call for this thick, black, delicious by-product of the sugar refining processing. It is definitely not a low carb sweetener as it has 10.5g per tablespoon (3.5g/tsp). But I use it in very small quantities; not for its sweetening power but for its distinctive flavor when making things like my Ginger Pecan Cookies (page 400) which are a wonderful cross between a ginger bread and ginger snap cookie. Blackstrap molasses (as opposed to regular molasses) is loaded with minerals; which helps me to rationalize its usage.

Fructose

Although fructose occurs naturally in fruits, this does not mean that it is a healthy or appropriate sweetener. It is a pure carbohydrate, just like sucrose. If you are counting carbs then you will naturally avoid food products with added fructose sweeteners, because the carb counts will be too high. However, if you are using the glycemic index (GI) approach, then watch out! Fructose has a low GI but it is nothing short of fattening and will counteract any efforts to lose weight.

As researchers look for where to place the blame on America's weight problem, fructose keeps showing up at or near the top of the list. Unnatural concentrations of fructose in manufactured foods will not only add significant calories but has been shown to elevate cholesterol and can cause diabetes, obesity and other health concerns. These problems are most prevalent with high fructose corn syrup; the primary sweetener in non-diet sodas. Fructose in its natural form (fresh fruit) is fine. But if you see a food product that has added any type of fructose, then stay away from it: even if it looks like healthy food, such as yogurt.

Polyols

This class of sweeteners is also known as sugar alcohols. But they are neither sugar nor alcohol so this has been a confusing name (although it makes sense to chemists). Any sweetener whose name ends in "ol" is typically a polyol; such as erythritol, lactitol, maltitol, mannitol, sorbitol, etc.

Most polyols occur naturally in fruits and vegetables, but most of the ones used in food products have been synthesized and have not been extracted from their natural sources. Many of the polyols have been used for decades in various medicinal and food products. But the low carb craze has greatly increased their usage.

Although polyols are carbohydrates, they are metabolized differently than sugars and starches and mostly passed through the body without being absorbed; but not completely. There is a portion of the polyols that is absorbed and has an insulin response in the body. Low carb food product are indicating on their packaging a zero carb impact for the polyol content and subtracting 100% of these carbs to arrive at the net carbs. This is wrong and I hope that this practice comes to an end soon; because a percentage of the polyols are metabolized by the body. So only the portion which is not absorbed can be subtracted from the total carbohydrates to determine the net carbs. But how much is that? Research is showing that the absorption rate varies between the different types of polyols and from person to person and can range from about 10% to as much as 50% for some individuals. This is the dilemma.

I have very few recipes which specify products containing any type of polyol sweeteners. But for those recipes that do include polyols, I have subtracted only 70% of the associated grams to arrive at the net carbs. This assumes 30% absorption which is simply the mid point of what is being indicated by research. However, each individual will have a different absorption rate.

So this is good news and it is bad news. We don't want our bodies to absorb the polyols, because we don't want the carbs or the rise in insulin or blood sugar. But that which is not absorbed, ferments in our intestines and causes gas and generally also has a laxative effect. For some people this is just a minor amount and for others it can cause extreme discomfort. Erythritol has been demonstrated to have the least effect for most people. Some claim that with time our colonic flora will adapt to the polyols and our digestive tolerance will improve. But this may not be true for everyone. Do not take *Beano* or other similar products to combat these symptoms as you will then be digesting more of the polyols and will then need to account for more of the carbs to your daily totals, negating the reason why you chose the polyol sweetened treat in the first place.

When experimenting with sweet treats containing polyols, go slowly. It can take 2 to 10 hours for you to notice the intestinal effects, and the symptoms typically last for many, many hours. As each person with have a different tolerance for the different types, it is recommend that you try just one type of polyol for awhile and see how it goes. Read the labels. Most products will specify which polyol is being used. If the label merely states polyol or sugar alcohol, then typically they are using a blend of polyols.

~ Regarding Fiber ~

It is important to assure that you get adequate fiber in your diet. All of the nutritional experts agreed on this point. Some types of diets, like a macrobiotic diet, are high in fiber no matter how it is approached. Other diets have to work a bit more consciously to keep their fiber intake up to par. Some individuals, who are new to the low carb way of eating, often find themselves eating way too little fiber which can ultimately lead to many health problems. One of the first signs of low fiber when starting a low carb diet is constipation. This situation is easily alleviated with drinking more water and eating higher fiber foods, particularly dark leaf greens. Fortunately there are many low carb foods that are also high in fiber. Be advised that if you are not accustomed to eating a high fiber diet then you may experience some flatulence at first. So increase your fiber intake slowly over a several week period; your body will adjust and you will be on your way to a healthier life. Be sure to significantly increase the amount of water that you drink as you increase your fiber intake.

Fiber is indigestible carbohydrates; that's why we get to subtract them from the total carb count to get the net carbs or effective carbs. There are two types of dietary fiber; soluble and insoluble. We need both kinds and fortunately most natural sources of fiber contain both kinds, although in varying amounts. Too much insoluble fiber without the balance of the soluble kind can be irritating to our system.

Insoluble fiber such as cellulose and lignin do not dissolve in water and is what some people call "roughage". Cellulose is like a broom which sweeps out the system, gives us a feeling of fullness and bulks up our stools which reduces constipation and hemorrhoids. Lignins have anti-viral, anti-bacterial, and anti-cancer properties. Insoluble fiber is said to reduce irritable bowel syndrome, colon cancer and diverticulosis. Sources high in insoluble fiber include; berries, most vegetables, flax seed meal, wheat bran, seeds, brown rice and other whole grains.

Soluble fiber such as gum and pectin, dissolves in water and forms a gel–like mucilage which soothes our intestinal tract and makes bowel movements easier. Soluble fiber absorbs many times its volume in water and helps remove bile acids and transports toxins out of our body. This type of fiber will slow our digestion and reduces blood sugar and cholesterol. Sources high in soluble fiber includes flax seed meal, oats and oat bran, barley, psyllium, citrus fruits, legumes and many vegetables particularly okra.

As mentioned before, both types of fiber are typically provided by most vegetables, fruits and grains. So you generally do not need to differentiate which type of fiber you are getting from your foods. Fiber tends to be concentrated in the skin and membrane of most vegetables so leave them on if you are trying to increase your fiber.

The recommended daily intake of dietary fiber varies a bit from source to source. Typically for women the range is 20–25 grams per day and about 30–35 grams per day for men. Some nutritionists claim that these amounts should actually be minimal daily requirements. The typical American diet generally has less than 1/2 of these amounts. If you are not use to paying attention to your dietary fiber intake then I suggest that you keep track by writing it down for about a week and see how you are doing and then make adjustments from there.

Some people insist on taking drug store fiber products to get their daily requirement. There is nothing wrong with this approach especially if you find it to be a challenge to get sufficient fiber from your diet. Although with drugstore fiber supplements you are not getting the other nutrients that you would also be getting from natural food sources high in fiber. Also be sure that you are getting both types of fiber in these products. I feel that the simplest and most satisfying way to achieve adequate fiber intake is by eating plenty of leafy green vegetables and other high fiber vegetables, and to find creative ways to include bran, seeds and nuts to our daily diets. Flax seed meal is my preferred way to add extra fiber to my diet for it has many other healthy benefits in addition to fiber. Try my breakfast recipe for Hot Cereal (page 84); it has 12g of fiber per serving and only 6g net carbs! Fruit, especially those delicious berries, are also high in fiber (see page 385).

Fortunate for us, most of the low carb veggies are also fairly high in fiber. A vegetable is considered to be a good source of fiber if it has at least 2.5 grams of fiber per serving. But all vegetables contain some fiber and every little bit helps, so don't avoid a particular vegetable just because it maybe a bit lower in fiber for it will certainly have many other beneficial nutrients. The following table is a list of some the high-fiber, low-carb vegetables. See page 170 for the fiber content of other vegetables and page 127 for the leafy salad greens. The fiber information for fruits and nut begins on page 385.

High-Fiber Low-Carb Vegetables

Vegetable 1 cup	Carbs grams	Fiber grams	Net Carbs grams
Asparagus	6.0	2.8	3.2
Broccoli	4.6	2.6	2.0
Brussels sprouts	7.8	3.3	4.5
Bell pepper	9.5	2.6	6.9
Cauliflower	5.3	2.5	2.8
Crookneck squash	5.3	2.5	2.8
Green beans	7.9	3.8	4.1
Jicama	10.6	5.9	4.7
Okra	7.6	3.3	4.4
Snow pea pods	7.4	2.5	4.9
Turnip	8.1	2.4	5.7

One serving of vegetables is considered to be 1 cup of the raw vegetable. But you'll notice that one cup of sturdy veggies like broccoli will generally cook down to 2/3 to 3/4 of a cup where as leafy greens like spinach can cook down to less than 1/4 cup. So when looking at tables of fiber content in foods it is important to notice the amounts specified and whether or not the food is in its raw form or it is cooked.

Another good source for fiber is bran and seeds. Since these are generally used in small quantities (1 serving typically equals 1 tablespoon) they pack quite a fiber punch relative to their volume, particularly flax seed meal and psyllium husks. Most types of bran are a good source of vitamin B and a few minerals. Seeds, on the other hand, are loaded with nutrients. Nature packed each seed with a vast array of micronutrients including vitamins, minerals as well as various antioxidants and other beneficial phytonutrients. Seeds and bran are easy additions to many dishes. They can be a featured ingredient, or just sprinkled on top of a salad, vegetable, etc. as a garnish. Also grab a handful of pumpkin seeds or sunflower seeds as a quick and easy snack. The following are some of the more popular seeds and brans that are used as sources of fiber.

High-Fiber Seeds & Bran

Brans & Seeds 1 Tbsp	Carbs grams	Fiber grams	Net Carbs grams
Flaxseed Meal	5.6	3.7	1.9
Oat Bran	3.9	0.9	3.0
Psyllium Husks	4.5	3.5	2.0
Pumpkin Seeds	2.1	0.6	1.5
Rice Bran	3.7	1.6	2.1
Sesame Seeds	2.1	1.1	1.0
Sunflower Seeds	1.7	0.9	0.8
Wheat Bran	2.3	1.6	0.7

Flax Seed Meal

Flax seed is an incredibly nutrient-dense food source, containing protein, fiber, minerals, vitamins and a host of other micronutrients. You simply can't beat flax seed meal as one of the easiest ways to add fiber to your diet. It contains a high percentage of both types of fiber, soluble and insoluble. Flax seed meal contains lignin and is one of the best known sources of this fiber. Lignins have anti-viral, anti-bacterial, and anti-cancer properties.

Whole flax seeds can not be broken down in our digestive track so it must be ground first in order to become bioavailable. Whole seeds have an excellent shelf life (years). But once it is ground it can become rancid easily so it must be stored in the refrigerator (but only for up to 3 months). When purchasing flax seed meal, look for it in the refrigerator sections of your health food store. If your store only keeps it on the regular shelves, find a new health food store or purchase the whole seeds and grind them yourself.

Flax seed is the highest known source of the omega-3, essential fatty acid, alpha-linoleic acid. This type of omega-3 is found in very few foods and when it is present it is often in small amounts. Alpha-linoleic acid is an essential nutrient not only for optimum health but for sustaining life itself. Sadly, most Americans are alarmingly low in this essential fatty acid. But it can be easily provided by incorporating flax seed meal into our daily diet, thereby getting not only the essential omega-3 fatty acids but also some omega-6 fatty acids, both types of fiber, and many other nutrients.

The taste of flax seed meal is mildly nutty and generally is a good compliment to most baked goods (cookies, muffins, etc. as well as casseroles). Some of the recipes in this cookbook specifically calls for flax seed meal, but please feel free to add it to almost anything. Experiment and find the places that you enjoy it the most (breakfast cereals, smoothies, tuna fish salad, salad dressings, sprinkled over vegetables, with peanut butter, on yogurt, etc.) You can also sprout the seeds and use them in salads. One tablespoon of flax seed meal supplies almost 4 grams of dietary fiber but with only 2 grams of net carbs impact.

Psyllium Husks are also a popular form of fiber and is the primary product in many drugstore fiber supplements. It has approximately the same amount of carbs and fiber as flax seed meal but no where near the other nutrients and health benefits that are offered by flax seed meal. It is practically devoid of essential fatty acids. The advantage of psyllium is that it has a good shelf life and it is far less expensive than flax seed meal.

~Regarding Fats and Oils ~

Much of the misplaced criticism of the low carb diets is directed towards the fact that the diet allows for the consumption of fat in rather generous quantities. Who hasn't heard the generalities of fat makes you fat or fat causes cardiovascular disease and so on. Much of the disparaging comments come from the low fat industry who have a vested interest in the public continuing to choose their low fat products. But the general public has been duped by advertising campaigns that fat is bad. The truth is: yes, there are bad fats but many fats are good.

Different types of fats and oils have different flavors, properties, benefits and disadvantages from a cooking point of view as well as a health point of view. It is a complex subject which is all too often simplified into good fats and bad fats; such as olive oil is good, animal fat is bad. But it is not that simple. Although I would love to write a full dissertation on the topic of fats and oils, I trust that this overview will be informative enough to assist you in choosing the types and quantities of fats and oils that you would like to include in your diet. Or perhaps it will inspire you to conduct your own research on the topic.

In recent years, the general public has become more and more aware that there are some fats that are vital to our health. A fair amount of attention is being given to the omega-3 and omega-6 essential fatty acids and rightfully so. But there are many types of fats and oils and they all have their role to play. Fat is a major component of the human body, second only to water. Every cell in our body requires some form of fat in order to function properly. Fat is a basic nutrient providing energy, protecting internal organs and insulating the body. Fats are vital for normal brain development and function and perform a vast array of other critical duties.

Fats and oils are technically fatty acids. If the fatty acid tends to be a liquid at room temperature, then we call it an oil and if it tends to be more solid (like butter) then we call it a fat. But this is not a hard and fast rule as tropical "oils" tend to be solid at room temperature. There are three major classifications of fatty acids, saturated fatty acids (SFA), monounsaturated fatty acids (MUFA) and polyunsaturated fatty acids PUFA). All fats and oils are a mixture of these fatty acids and the type that holds the highest percentage is how that particular fat or oil is classified. For example, butter is considered a saturated fat, but it is actually only ~55% saturated fatty acids and is 30% MUFA. Extra virgin olive oil is considered a monounsaturated oil because it is 77% MUFA but it also 14% saturated fats. Flax seed oil is 73% polyunsaturated and it has 18% and 9% MUFA and SFA, respectively.

Fatty acids break down, oxidize and turn rancid when exposed to heat, air and light. This process creates several by-products which are extremely harmful to our bodies including free radicals and trans fatty acids. Free radicals are oxidized molecules that are highly reactive. They can cause extensive damage by degrading the integrity of our DNA and cellular structure as well as compromise our immune system. Free radicals cause premature aging and contribute to various diseases including arterial disease and cancer. Antioxidants (as in vitamin E, blueberries, tomatoes, broccoli, spinach, garlic, etc.) scavenge and destroy free radicals but they generally can not repair the damage caused by them. This is why it is important to use fresh fats and oils and protect them from conditions that cause deterioration.

Saturated Fatty Acids (SFA)
The conventional impression is that saturated fatty acids are the bad guys. But just like people, they are basically good although they are known to behave quite badly when residing in unhealthy environments.

People have been living off of saturated fats for thousands of years. They are an excellent source of energy. In fact, they are the source of fats which our bodies most prefer to burn for energy and will convert other fats into saturated fats when needed. Our bodies also converts excess carbohydrates and sugar (that which is not immediately needed as fuel) into saturated fats which are then stored as body fat for future use. Saturated fats are also used to improve cell membrane vitality and other important functions.

Saturated fats from natural sources (e.g., meat, poultry, fish, milk, butter, etc.) are not the culprits that they have been made out to be. Typically, natural sources of saturated fats contain within that same food source many of the necessary nutrients to assist with the breakdown and assimilation of the fats. On the other hand, unnatural (man-made) sources of saturated fats (i.e., hydrogenated oils) are the super sticky guys which clog arteries and lead to many health problems. They are completely devoid of nutrients and require our bodies to work over-time to try and metabolize them.

As with anything, it is the excess of saturated fatty acids that is the primary cause of health problems, particularly from the unnatural sources. Excessive SFA have been shown to increase cholesterol and are associated with atherosclerosis and certain kinds of cancer. Studies show that this is particularly a problem with diets that are also high in carbohydrates, particularly refined carbohydrates such as white flour and white sugar. But if we eat a nutrient-rich diet, avoid refined carbohydrates and are active enough to use most of the saturated fats that we consume as fuel, then SFA are not a particular problem.

Many low carb dieters consume a fair amount of saturated fats. But much of this SFA intake is from natural sources. However, in order to minimize the potential ill effects of saturated fats, it is important to have adequate and balanced levels of essential fatty acids (omega-3 and omega-6) in our diets. This can be achieved through eating foods which are high in omega-3 and omega-6 and by using supplements. The essential fatty acids work to protect and reverse the effects of SFA. Adequate intake of omega-3 and omega-6 will allow us to be well equipped to deal with the saturated fats that we consume as well as a moderate excess, without worries.

Sources of saturated fats include animal fat, butter, cheese, coconut oil, palm oil, and palm kernel oil. Man-made source of SFA include hydrogenated oils and partially hydrogenated oils also known as vegetable shortening. Saturated fats are very stable and do not breakdown very easily. This property makes them very suitable for most cooking methods used in the home kitchen. See page 42 for a further discussion.

Monounsaturated Fatty Acids (MUFA)

Monounsaturated fats are also a good source of energy for the body. MUFA helps lower LDL cholesterol and triglycerides (the bad guys; when in excessive amounts) and keeps our arteries supple, thereby improving atherosclerosis. They also have properties which improve skin condition and they offer some protection from the sun. Extra virgin olive oil is the Champion of the monounsaturated fats. It also has other constituents that have a synergist effect providing additional health benefits. See page 46 for a further discussion.

Sources of monounsaturated fats include extra virgin olive oil, canola oil, walnuts and walnut oil, peanuts and peanut oil as well as avocados, cashews, macadamia nuts, pistachios and pumpkin seeds. MUFA are not as stable as SFA and breakdown when heated and with exposure to air and light. But they are substantially more stable than the polyunsaturated fats.

Polyunsaturated Fatty Acids (PUFA)

Polyunsaturated fats are a large category of fatty acids including the essential fatty acids which are vital to sustain life, other fats that are crucial to good health and the trans fatty acids which are highly toxic. Natural forms of polyunsaturated fats (not the trans fatty acids) are known to lower cholesterol. But unlike the MUFA which primarily lowers the LDL and triglycerides, many of the PUFA slightly lowers the HDL components of cholesterol as well (the good guys). The PUFA are inherently unstable and breakdown quickly in the presence of heat, air and light. This is especially true for oils rich in essential fatty acids (typically 100 times more unstable than MUFA). Nuts and seeds containing high levels of PUFA are reasonable stable in their raw form (particularly when still in their shell) but once they have been toasted and/or ground they start to breakdown much more easily.

Essential fatty acids (EFA) are called "essential" because these fats are required in order to sustain life and are critical nutrients that can not be manufactured within the human body; therefore, they must to be supplied by the foods we eat. There are two EFA; alpha-linolenic acid (ALA) which is an omega-3 EFA and linoleic acid (LA) which is an omega-6 EFA. Other fatty acids are also necessary nutrients for optimal health but they can be synthesized by our bodies (if the proper precursor nutrients are also available to do so) or they can be acquired from food sources.

Omega-3 is a family of fatty acids in the polyunsaturated fatty acid category. The mamma bear of the omega-3 family is alpha-linolenic acid (ALA), an essential fatty acid which produces life energy from food, increases metabolic rate, assists in the regulation of blood sugar, produces smooth skin, increases stamina, enhances immune system and vitality, and brings a feeling of calmness. ALA reduces inflammation, water retention, platelet stickiness and blood pressure. ALA is the precursor of prostaglandins (which regulate all body function at a cellular level). Omega-3 makes us feel energized which allows us to exercise more easily. It also increases metabolism which helps us to burn up stored body fat.

In a healthy body, ALA can produce all of the other omega-3 offspring that are required for good health. Of particular interest are eicosapentaenoic acid (EPA) and docosahexaenoic acid (DHA) which are critical to optimum health. EPA and DHA are abundantly present in brain cells as well as other vital tissue and are crucial to supporting optimal function of the brain. The body's ability to convert ALA to EPA and DHA is challenged by many factors including deficiency in certain vitamins and minerals, diets high in trans fatty acids and saturated fats as well as genetics. These omega-3 oils are most plentifully supplied by certain fish and fish oils.

It is interesting to note that a percentage of the population is genetically unable to make this conversion from ALA to the other forms of omega-3 fatty acids especially EPA and DHA and therefore must acquire these forms of omega-3 from food sources. The affected cultures are those whose diets have historically relied upon cold water marine life, including the Inuit, Irish, Scottish, Welsh and Scandinavian cultures. These people and those with ancestry of 25% or more would be well advised to eat cold water fish 3 to 4 times per week or take fish oil supplements on a daily basis so as to assure that they provide their bodies with sufficient EPA and DHA.

Sources of omega-3: Flax seed oil is the most abundant source of the essential fatty acid, alpha-linolenic acid (ALA). Cold water fish and marine animals (particularly salmon, trout, tuna, mackerel, sardines and herring) are rich sources of EPA and DHA. Other sources of omega-3 include hemp seed oil, canola oil, walnuts and walnut oils, dark green leafy vegetables, pumpkin seeds, soybeans and soybean oil.

Sadly, the typical American diet is alarmingly deficient in the omega-3 essential fatty acid. But this is a complicated story. Just taking omega-3 supplements such as flax seed oil and fish oil is not sufficient. There must be a good balance of both the omega-3 and the omega-6 EFA and there must be sufficient additional nutrients to allow the EFAs to metabolize and perform their essential functions in the body (particularly vitamins E, C, B_3, B_6, A in additional to magnesium and zinc).

Omega-6 is another important family of fatty acids in the polyunsaturated fatty acid category. The mamma bear of the omega-6 family is linoleic acid (LA), an essential fatty acid which must work in concert with the omega-3 family. LA supports the immune system, kidneys, liver and sexual organs and reverses cardiovascular problems. LA helps to produce hemoglobin, reduces risk of cancer and is also a precursor of prostaglandins. The body can make all the other necessary omega-6 fatty acids from LA, but these can also be supplied by food sources. One of the omega-6 family members is particularly important to those on a weight loss program; this is gamma-linolenic Acid (GLA) which lowers cholesterol, increases fat metabolism, and increases metabolic rate by supporting thyroid function.

Sources of omega-6: The best source for the essential fatty acid linoleic acid (LA) is unrefined safflower oil, followed by sunflower seeds and their oil, walnut and walnut oil, pumpkin seeds, sesame seed and sesame oil, and flax seed oil. The best source or GLA is borage oil but also black currant seed oil and evening primrose oil. Other source of omega-6 include poultry, eggs, butter, nuts & seeds (and their oils), grape seed oil, corn oil, soybeans and soy bean oil.

The ratio of omega-3 to omega-6 is rather important, but no one seems to agree on the proper balance and the recommendations range dramatically from 4:1 to 1:10 of omega-3 to omega-6. However, the majority of the sources I have come across recommend a ratio of 1:1 or 2:1; that is an even balance or twice as much omega 3 as omega 6. A couple of sources indicated that a 3:1 ratio of omega-3 to omega-6 was particularly beneficial while dieting. Several reports claimed that the typical American diet has a 1:20 ratio of omega-3 to omegas-6 particularly for those who routinely eat fried foods (fast-food fries being a major culprit). This imbalance has been cited as the primary cause of certain health problems such as atherosclerosis, diabetes, learning disabilities and some mental illness. Flax seed oil is our richest source for the omega-3 essential fatty acid. Unrefined safflower oil is an excellent source of omega-6. But moderation in everything; remember it is a balancing act.

Having adequate levels of properly balanced essential fatty acids counteract most of the problems associated with eating saturated fats and therefore are essential for anyone that eats a substantial quantity of meats. Some experts recommend that we consume twice as much EFA as saturated fats. Ideally, essential fatty acids should be about one third of our total fat consumption from all sources of fat.

Trans Fatty Acids (TFA)

We usually think of polyunsaturated fats as healthy fats and advertising certainly has reinforced this thinking. However, only the natural polyunsaturated fats are healthy. Some fats are processed in such a manner as to form trans fatty acids. These are the really bad guys, yet they are also classified as PUFA. Margarine is traditionally composed primarily of partially hydrogenated oils (which are extremely high in TFA) and some of the margarine packaging may advertise "High in Polyunsaturated Fats" trying to make consumers think that this is a good thing. But it is the wrong kind of PUFA. Trans fatty acids are associated with a host of health problems; and in my opinion should be prohibited from commercial use. TFA increases cholesterol (dramatically raising LDL and lowering HDL – a double whammy), damages cell membranes, interferes with the immune system and promotes cardiovascular disease, atherosclerosis and cancer. They also disrupt the functioning of the liver, sexual organs and insulin as well as inhibit the vital performance of the essential fatty acids. The primary source of trans fatty acids is from partially hydrogenation oils. But TFA can also be formed during the refining process of some oils and by cooking oils at high temperatures.

Hydrogenation artificially saturates oil by processing them with high heat, under pressure utilizing hydrogen gas. When oils are in the process of being hydrogenated they form trans fatty acids. But once the hydrogenation process is completed the oils have become mostly saturated fats and act accordingly. Hydrogenated fats are very stable, chemically inert and can be used for frying foods without increasing its toxicity. However they are not health promoting oils as they provide no nutrients other than calories, but they also do not become more harmful when heated to temperatures used for cooking.

But when the hydrogenated process is not completed, partially hydrogenated oil is formed and that is our highest source of trans fatty acids. Food manufacturers love partially hydrogenated oil because it has a good shelf life, has properties to make things smooth and tasty but mostly because it is inexpensive for them to use. But there is little else on our grocery store shelves that is as toxic and disease promoting as partially hydrogenated oils.

The FDA has been extremely slow to respond to the research which demonstrates the dangerous effects of trans fatty acids. For years, health proponents have tried to get the FDA to require that food labeling include the TFA content as well as a health warning label. But this has been thwarted by influence from certain food manufacturers. However, in July 2004 the FDA finally made it mandatory that the TFA content be specified on labels; although this will not go into effect until January 2006. Hopefully by that time manufacturers will find a more suitable way to make their products, so they won't have to advertise how harmful their products have been.

Recommended Fat Intake

This topic is a very controversial subject and I couldn't help but laugh as I sorted through all the data I had compiled on this topic. The experts are all over the map on the matter of what constitutes the optimum daily fat intake. The low fat industry recognizes that some fats are vital for optimum health but obviously target the requirements on the low end suggesting 10-15% of total caloric consumption and recommends keeping saturated fats under 5%. At the other extreme is the Inuit way of eating for which fat calories can comprise up to 75% of the diet, much of which is saturated fat and yet these are remarkably healthy people (due to the high percentage of essential fatty acids in their diet).

The typical American obtains 40-60% of their total daily calories from various sources of fat. Considering that fat calories (~9 cal/gram) add up much faster than calories from protein or carbohydrates (~4 cal/gram), it is easy to see why these percentages are so high. A typical fast food cheeseburger has about 800 calories and 49 grams of fat; which is ~55% of the total calories. The fat content of pizza and French fries also comes in at about 50% of the total calories.

The majority of the well known sources which I researched (e.g., the USDA, the American Dietetic Association, National Cholesterol Education Program, and others) have recommended fat consumption that falls somewhere in the range of 25-35% of total caloric intake. In addition, some sources recommend keeping saturated fats under 10% of total daily calories. The Zone and South Beach diets both recommend about 30% of calories be obtained from fat sources.

The Atkins plan does not specify a recommended percentage of fat in the diet, and it places no stigma on saturated fats. Although, it stipulates that fats should come from a variety of sources (except for trans fatty acids which should be completely avoided). Dr. Atkins (and other nutritional experts) postulates that the health problems that have been associated with saturated fats are mostly a problem when in the presence of excess carbohydrates. The Atkins plan emphasizes getting adequate essential fatty acids and stresses the importance of getting individual nutritional counseling. The general Atkins guideline for daily essential fatty acids supplementation is 2 grams each of flax seed oil, fish oil and borage oil.

After sorting through a plethora of main-stream expert opinions, and reading cutting-edge research papers as well as popular books on fats and oils; my personal belief is that the percentage of total fat intake is not definitively meaningful. There are so many other things going on that to isolate the effects of total fat consumption without regarding to type and other nutrients present, is a complex issue not readily reduced to simple answers. The human body is very complex and adaptable to varying diets and conditions. Legitimate arguments can be made for reducing over-all fat intake but on the other hand, there are just as valid reasons for increasing fat intake (particularly the fats and oils consumed through natural food sources when in the presence of other nutrients necessary for fat metabolism). But all things considered for the American way of life, a range of 25-35% seems like an appropriate goal. Based on a diet of 2000 calories per day (the average for maintaining weight for western cultures) this would translate to 56-78 grams of fat per day. To keep saturated fats below 10% total caloric consumption, then 22 grams per day of saturated fat would be the limit.

Much of the data which I came across, strongly suggests that the type of fats and their ratio to each other in conjunction with the presence of other micro and macro nutrients (vitamins, minerals, carbohydrates, proteins, etc.) are vastly more important considerations than the total number of fat grams consumed per day. I believe that a low carb diet emphasizing whole, natural foods (including natural sources of fats), supplemented with a good multi-vitamin and adequate essential fatty acids is an exceptionally healthy approach to fat consumption and nutrition in general.

~ Fats & Oils in the Kitchen ~

Fats and oils are important ingredients in cooking. They provide flavor and texture as well as a means for heat distribution and for browning. Their emulsifying properties are imperative in certain sauces and some oils are also used as preservatives. Different fats and oils have different characteristics and different roles to play in the kitchen. Eggs cooked in bacon fat convey that certain down-home taste and aroma, while extra virgin olive oil is indispensable in creating a Mediterranean flavor.

Unrefined versus Refined Oils

As mentioned previously, the refining process can create trans fatty acids and it can also deplete oils of their nutrients. Refining oils has the advantage of increasing shelf life and the stability of the oils allowing them to be used at higher temperatures. Refined oils create less additional toxins when heated than the healthiest oils do. So when cooking with oils at medium-high temperatures, refined oils are the most suitable. However, refined oils generally have been stripped of most of their nutrients so they are not typically health promoting oils. The healthiest refined oils are canola oil, olive oil and sesame oil. If you use quite a bit of refined oils you should be mindful to get plenty of vitamin E, which has wonderful antioxidant properties to combat many of the by-products of the refining process as well as being important in the metabolism of fats.

Unrefined oils are typically rich in micronutrients and provide a plethora of health benefits when consumed fresh. But they are inherently unstable and are sensitive to light, air and of course, heat. Even moderate temperatures can cause them to breakdown into an array of dangerous substances including the dreaded trans fatty acids and free radicals. So keep your unrefined oils fresh by storing them away from air, light and heat and use them up quickly.

Unrefined oils should be purchased in small enough quantities to be used up within about 2 months and ideally should be kept in the refrigerator after opening. You should select dark colored bottles or purchase then in cans. If you can't find them in light-resistant containers then you can transfer then into old wine or beer bottles when you get home (sterilize them in boiling water first). Pour slowly so as not to mix in too many air bubbles. Be sure to label the bottles and re-sterilize them before refilling with new fresh oil.

If the label does not specifically state "unrefined" then it has unquestionably been refined. The exception to this is olive oil. Unrefined olive oil is called virgin or extra virgin which by definition means unrefined. Rarely do you see the term virgin or extra virgin with other types of oils, but if you should, then it too is unrefined and should be treated as such.

Unrefined oils can be used for cooking with low heat, generally staying under 250°F (e.g., boiling, poaching, braising, etc.) but are best used without heating (e.g., making salad dressings, dipping sauces, etc.). I think that making your own salad dressings is the best way to incorporate unrefined oils into your diet. You can even use unrefined flax seed oil for dressings and enjoy its mild nutty flavor. But it is extremely unstable so again purchase in small quantities. Most commercial salad dressings use refined oils and offer very little health benefits.

Cooking with Fats and Oils
If it is too hot then get out of the kitchen! Cooking with fats and oils can create harmful substances if the fats and oils are not matched up properly with the specific cooking method. The healthy, unrefined oils (especially those rich in essential fatty acids) become particularly toxic when exposed to heat, forming trans fatty acids and other harmful by-products. We have heard many chefs say that we should never put extra virgin olive oil into a fry pan, but they rarely say why. So now you know; it becomes hazardous to your health. Save your good stuff (unrefined oils) for salad dressings and drizzling over foods after they have been cooked. It is not a matter of economics; it is a matter of health.

Heat breaks down fats and oils in varying degrees depending on the particular fat or oil, the amount of heat and the duration in which heat is applied. The more stable the fat, the less effected it is by the heat of cooking. The most stable are the saturated fats both the natural forms (like butter and tropical oils) and the man-made hydrogenated oils. The natural monounsaturated fats are moderately stable but become more stable once they have been refined (canola, peanut, olive and sesame). Natural, unrefined polyunsaturated fats are the least stable and the most harmful when heated (e.g., avocado, corn, cottonseed, grape seed, soy and walnut).

Smoking point is a term which means the temperature at which a fat or oil begins to smoke. But this is a point beyond when toxins have started to form. If you ever heat oil in a fry pan to the point where it is smoking, then it is best to discard it and start over again with fresh oil. I am shocked when I see TV chefs on cooking shows letting their oils heat-up to the smoking point and then continue cooking with it while saying "don't ever let your oils get that hot." I don't get it! It takes little time to pour it out, wipe down the skillet and add fresh oil. Then sometimes these TV chefs are shown eating this harmful food or even worse, feeding it to their studio audience! What's up with that? They really should know better ... but perhaps their producers don't.

Grilling and Broiling creates an extreme temperature environment, sometimes reaching 500 to 550°F. Few fats can withstand such temperatures for any amount of time. Those which hold up the best are the natural fats in meats. Fortunately, we do not usually grill or broil at the extreme temperatures for more than just a few minutes. The best oils to use at high temperatures are the tropical oils and the refined versions of peanut oil, grape seed oil, as well as the high oleic safflower and sunflower oils (but not regular safflower and sunflower oils). Refined grape seed oil can be heated to 475°F before damage starts to occur, but its taste is not agreeable to everyone.

Deep-Frying is not as popular in today's home cooking as it has been in the past, but we still enjoy a few deep-fried foods from time to time. The typical temperature range for deep-frying is about 355-385°F. The most typical oils for home use are corn, soy and peanut oils as their smoke points are typical about 440-450°F. Many restaurants use hydrogenated oils. But the best oil to use at home is refined peanut oil. Only use the oil one time; as prolonged and repeated heating is harmful.

Pan-Frying, sautéing and stir-frying can occur at fairly high heat as well and sometimes for prolonged periods such as when pan-frying chicken. For chicken it is best to simply leave the skin on and use no additional fats or oils. For high heat settings, use refined peanut oil, grape seed oil, soy bean oil or sesame oil. But do not let them get near the smoke point. For cooking at temperatures up to medium-high, your best choice is butter, then the tropical oils. Refined olive oil and canola oil can withstand temperature up to 375°F and so are useful for stir-frying (especially with vegetables with high water content which help keep temperatures down). Garlic and onions are excellent free radical scavengers, so add them frequently and generously when pan-frying, sautéing and stir-frying. But make allowance for the carbs of the onions and garlic or leave them on your plate and don't eat many of them.

Baking and roasting is less destructive than frying because the temperatures are typically lower. Butter and tropical oils are still preferred particularly when greasing a baking sheet or casserole dish, as if they do burn they are the least detrimental. But any of the vegetable oils can withstand most baking temperature. I typically use canola oil if I'm not going to use butter. Be careful when browning the top of a cheesy casserole or the out side of a roast; those yummy brown bits are actually slightly toxic. The lighter the brown color the fewer toxins are present.

Boiling is the safest cooking method when using fats and oils. The boiling temperature of water and most other cooking liquids is capped at 212°F (or closer to 201°F at 6,200 feet elevation here at my home in Colorado). No matter how much heat you put under a pot of water it will not rise above 212°F (unless you use a pressure cooker or some other devise to build the surface pressure above atmospheric). Although fats and oils can reach much higher temperatures, when they are surrounded by water (and water based liquids such as stock, etc.) their temperatures equalize to the water temperature. At these lower temperatures, even unrefined oils and the oils rich in essential fatty acids (EFA) can be safely utilized. Boiling also refers to braising, stewing, poaching and steaming. Home pressure cooking is included as well since typical temperatures are still less than 250°F.

So what if you don't cook enough to have a half a dozen different types of oils in your kitchen? What are the best choices overall? Here's my recommendation:

- For most cooking purposes, butter and canola oil are best.
- For non-heat applications (salad dressing, drizzling over cooked foods, some sauces, etc.) use extra-virgin olive or use an unrefined nut oil which is high in essential fatty acids (like walnut oil). Find one that has a taste which you love, so you will use it up quickly.
- For deep-frying use refined peanut oil.

Butter is better. Believe it or not butter is one of our best choices for most home cooking methods. It is very stable and lets us know quickly when it has reached its limit – it turns brown. Most other fats and oils do not let us know so noticeably when they have become a health risk until they have already started to smoke and by then they are very toxic. But even browned butter is quite low in harmful substances especially compared to over-heating other natural oils. You may even find cookbooks with recipes which specifically call for browned butter.

Butter is a natural product which has been minimally processed. You could easily make it at home if you were so inclined. It is about 55% saturated fat, 30% monounsaturated fat, 4% polyunsaturated fat and the remaining 12% is primarily water and milk solids. A major component of the saturated fat in butter is stearic acid, which is a saturated fatty acids that does not raise cholesterol.

Butter comes both salted and unsalted. Salt is added for flavor and as a preservative. Sometimes annatto food coloring is added, although I can not recommend those brands. If you can find organic butter, this is a much healthier choice, as it will not contain residual antibiotics or pesticides. Costco sells organic butter at a price cheaper than the generic grocery store brand butter. Butter has many micronutrients including essential fatty acids but the levels are all rather low providing little if any extra nutritional value. However, butter is the most easily digestible of the fats and oils and has exceptionally good flavor.

Clarified butter is also known as ghee or butter fat. I prefer the Indian name ghee. Separating the butter fat from the milk solids (clarifying) makes butter even more stable, more easily digestible and allows it to be used at higher temperatures. I mostly use ghee when sautéing and regular butter when baking. Any recipe in this cookbook which specifies the use of butter in a skillet is a suitable place to use ghee. The main reason most people don't use ghee very often is that it requires your full attention while making it and it is fairly expensive to purchase ready-made ghee at a store.

To make ghee:
1. Heat one pound unsalted butter over low heat until completely melted.
2. Raise temperature to medium. Skim off and discard foam as it develops.
3. Once it comes to a full boil (but don't rush it by turning up the heat), lower the heat and simmer for about 10 minutes allow all the water to cook off and the milk solids to settle to the bottom. Do not stir. But watch it carefully because it can go from "nothing seems to be happening" to burnt in just a few seconds.
4. As soon as you notice the milk solids turning a light golden brown, immediately remove from the heat and allow it to cool (uncovered) to room temperature. Do not stir; you want the solids to remain on the bottom.
5. Carefully pour the butter fat into a jar or bowl leaving behind the milk solids.

Ghee will last for several weeks without refrigeration. If refrigerated, it will last indefinitely. Ghee no longer has that creamy buttery taste. It behaves much more like an oil.

Canola oil comes from rape seeds and is generally only used as a refined oil. I believe that it is the best refined oil on the market today. Unlike most refined oils, Canola oil actually still contains some of its nutrients including omega-3 fatty acids. Fresh oil will have from 1 to 1.3 grams of omega-3 per tablespoon. Although it has a very high smoke point it is not suitable for deep-frying and is best when used at 375°F or lower temperatures. This is the temperature where the omega-3 breakdown. Of the oils appropriate for cooking, canola oil has the lowest percentage of saturated fats. It is composed of approximately 62% MUFA, 31% PUFA and only 6% SFA. Another advantage of using canola oil is that it has no taste of its own so it does not compete with the other flavors in a recipe. We have our Canadian friends to thank for this very valuable oil.

Coconut oil (unrefined) and the other tropical oils are just starting to regain some popularity in the US after having been erroneously accused of increasing cholesterol and triglycerides (the hydrogenated forms has this characteristic but not the unrefined forms). Studies conducted in other countries which predominately use unrefined tropical oils show that they moderately decrease cholesterol levels. Coconut oil is extremely high in saturated fats (~77% SFA, 6% MUFA and 2% PUFA, the remainder is mostly water and solids) and therefore is very stable and can withstand high temperatures. Coconut oil is a rich source of vitamin E which is a powerful antioxidant. It can typically be used in pan-frying, sautéing and stir-fry without breaking down. Although many claim it has no taste, the brand which I use (*Spectrum Naturals*) has a very mild but distinctive coconut taste. I especially like to use it when I am cooking with coconut anyway.

Extra virgin olive oil is relatively low in the essential fatty acids (contrary to popular belief) but it has a multitude of other components shown to be health promoting. It is 77% monounsaturated fatty acids and as with other MUFA it is known to lower the LDL component of cholesterol. Extensive research has been conducted on extra-virgin olive oil and the health benefits are numerous including, protecting cell membrane, and improving cell formation and differentiation. Extra-virgin olive oil is anti-mutagenic which means that it protects our DNA from being damaged. Various types of Polyphenols (the stuff that makes red wine healthy) are present in extra-virgin olive oil and have antioxidant properties helping to make the oil more stable.

Extra virgin olive oil is best used in salad dressing, sauces which are not heated and as a finishing oil poured over meats or vegetables after they have been cooked. It is the most easily obtainable unrefined oil in our stores today. As mentioned previously, be sure to buy it or any other unrefined oil in dark colored glass or in tins. Purchase in small enough quantities to be used up in a couple of months (otherwise store it in the refrigerator). Although the flavor of extra virgin olive oil varies depending upon where the olives were grown, it has a very distinctive taste that does not appeal to everyone. I personally only like it in a few things that typically have strong enough flavors to overshadow the flavor of the oil.

Walnut oil (unrefined) is also an excellent oil for salad dressings and is typically used in the same manner as extra virgin olive oil. I like its mild nutty taste so much better, but it is rather expensive. Unlike extra virgin olive oil, walnut oil is a good source of omega-3 fatty acids and to a lesser extent omega-6. The omega-3 content of unrefined walnut oil varies between 2 and 3 grams per tablespoon. Once it has been refined, the omega-3 content drops to about 1.5 grams per tablespoon (which is still pretty darn good). Unrefined walnut oil has many micronutrients and antioxidants which makes it a very healthy oil. It is composed of 56% PUFA, 28% MUFA and 16% SFA.

Other nuts oils such as hazelnut, almond, cashews, pistachios, etc. are very similar to walnut oil, as are their uses. Nut oils taste much like the nut that they came from and can be used in baked goods imparting their distinctive flavor with out adding the carbohydrates of the nuts.

~ REGARDING HERBS & SPICES ~

Since the low carb diet can appear limiting at times, the use of herbs and spices is essential for creating not only variety but also a depth of flavor to your cooking. A big burst of flavor is the perfect thing when you are tempted to stray from the diet. If you enjoy cooking, then experimenting with herbs and spices can provide endless diversity and enjoyment to your culinary adventures.

So which is it: an herb or a spice? Herbs consist primarily of leaves and are used both fresh and dried. Spices are any other botanical part except leaves including seeds, flowers, berries, roots, pods, bark and fruit which are used mostly in their dried form (with just a few exceptions).

Fresh versus Dried

I use both fresh and dried herbs. The convenience of dried herbs makes them indispensable in any kitchen, although the flavor of fresh herbs is much superior. The presentation of most dishes is enhanced with the look of the fresh herbs whether they are in a sauce, a stew, a rub, or used as a garnish.

A portion of my garden is dedicated to growing culinary herbs, both annuals and perennials. The luxury of stepping out to the garden a few minutes before I need a particular herb is downright exhilarating; although fleeting as our growing season in Colorado is very short. Fortunately, many fresh herbs are available in the markets today all year around. They are not much more expensive than dried herbs, but they do have a much shorter shelf life. I have some solutions for this as you will see in the following pages.

Some herbs and spices taste pretty much the same whether they are fresh or dried, such as rosemary, oregano and thyme; while others taste completely different when they have been dried. Let's look at ginger. Fresh ginger and dried ground ginger are so dissimilar to me that it is hard to believe that they come from the same plant. Garlic is another example of this. Fresh garlic and garlic powder taste are very different to me. I use them both quite a lot and I interchange them in recipes all the time, but the results are rather different. And what about those bottles of chopped garlic? These are very handy indeed! Yet these products have even another taste all together. Sometimes I don't really care and other times the choice is essential; it is about what is most appropriate in the moment; enhanced taste or convenience.

Shelf Life

Spices that have been dried and left in their original form (berries, seeds, pod, etc.) can be kept for years and years (perhaps decades) if they are kept away from air, heat and light. But once they have been ground, they start to loose their potency. The more pungent the spice the longer the shelf-life; although you might need to increase the quantities stated in a recipe by a little bit if you have had them for well over a year. Herbs are more delicate than spices and can have a very short shelf life, but again the more robust, the better it does. Rosemary and bay leaves are fine for a year or so. But most others need to be used up more quickly, generally within 6 months.

There are a few herbs, in my opinion, that are just hardly worth using in a dried form unless they have been very freshly dried; these include basil, chives, cilantro, and parsley. These delicate herbs loose their flavor quickly. Smelling them in the bottle may indicate some flavor but they may not have enough flavor to offer anything of value to your recipe. If you have any of these herbs that are older than just a few months, then I suggest using them up right away in a rich stew or when making a stock or simply throw them away. But wait - save those bottles! Wild Oats and most other health food stores carry herbs in bulk. You can buy just a little bit at a time, enough for filling 1/4 to 1/3 of a bottle and then use it up in the next couple of months. I purchase almost all of my herbs this way. A bottle of herbs at the grocery store can cost $3 to $6 each! But I can refill a bottle of most herbs and spices for about $1. Wild Oats has fast turn over of their inventory of herb and spices so I know that they are fresh. But I try to only buy as much as I need for the next season or so. I tend to use different herbs at different times of the year. For example I generally use more dill in the summer and more rosemary in the winter months.

Adjusting Recipes

It can be difficult to adjust recipes when they call for fresh herbs and all you have is dried herbs. Or when you prefer to use fresh but the recipe calls for dried. There really are no reliable formulas to convert from one to the other since the same dried herb could be left somewhat leafy or might be finely ground. Sage is a good example of this. Most dried sage is found either rubbed or ground. You'll need about twice more rubbed than ground.

Most herbs reduce in volume by 2 or 3 times when dried and as much as 10 times when dried and ground. So you'll need to use your own judgment. This will become easier with practice. But let me give some examples. If the recipe calls for 1 teaspoon of ground oregano then you might want to use 3 tsp (1 tablespoon) of dried leafy looking oregano or use 6 teaspoons (2 tablespoon) of fresh oregano (chopped). When substituting fresh rosemary for dried, use only about 50% more than what the recipe calls for, as this is a pungent herb and doesn't shrink all that much when dried. For example, the recipe states 2 tsp of dried rosemary, then use about 3 tsp (1 tablespoon) of fresh rosemary. However, taste testing is generally the best method for making the conversion – add a little, let the flavor develop for a few minutes, then taste and add more if desired.

When cooking with dried herbs and spices they should generally be added at the beginning of the recipe, which helps to fully reconstitute them and extract the most flavor. Fresh herbs on the other hand are best when added at the last stage of a recipe particularly for stews, soups and sauces. But a fresh sprig of rosemary (and other woody herbs) placed in the cavity of poultry prior to roasting is a noted exception. Fresh herbs generally need to be cut or bruised in some way in order to fully release the flavor and aroma.

Storing Fresh Herbs

If you do not grow your own herbs, but prefer to use the fresh herbs available from the markets, then here are some helpful hints to extend their use, since most fresh herbs come in quantities that are larger than a single recipe.

For woody herbs, such as rosemary, oregano, marjoram, thyme, summer savory, etc. they do best if wrapped in a lightly dampened paper towel (feels almost dry) and placed in a plastic bag then put in the refrigerator. But they will not last long that way (perhaps 5 days or so if you purchased them shortly after they were harvested). You can also make herb paste out of them. But it is easier to throw them into a zip-lock freezer bag and freeze them. Then when you are ready to use some, all you have to do is break off the leaves you need for the recipe.

Do not throw away the stems from your fresh herbs. The stems are great to add when making stock. If you will not be using them soon, then simply freeze the stems until you are ready to use them. Be sure to label the freezer bag (such as "rosemary stems for stock" or "mixed herb stems for stock") since specific herb stems are hard to identify once frozen.

For leafy herbs, such as basil, parsley, cilantro, tarragon, dill, mint, etc. place them in a small vase, glass or cup with fresh water just up to but not covering the first set of leaves. Change the water every other day, and the herbs should last for one or three weeks (depending on how soon they are put in water after harvesting). Parsley, cilantro and basil respond exceptionally well to this method. I think they look lovely sitting on the kitchen counter and talk about conveniently located for cooking! Pull leaves from the bottom first and discard any portions that start to decay. You know the saying, "One bad apple spoils the whole bunch"; well that is true for herbs as well. If the herbs look a bit droopy when you buy them, then trim the stems a little before you put them in the water, loosely cover the herbs with a baggy and place them in the refrigerator. Hopefully they will start to perk up a bit. They can be left in the refrigerator (for a longer life) but I generally need that space for other things. Don't bother trying to freeze leafy herbs, unless you make a paste out of them first

If you have more fresh herbs than you can use up in the next week or so, then you have several options. You can make herb paste, herb vinegars, herb oils, herb butter, etc. These are all relatively easy.

Herb Paste
Making an herb paste out of left over fresh herbs is a simple way to keep them for many more weeks. Simply pull off the leaves and put them in a food processor with only enough oil to form a paste. Then put the paste in a jar (squish out any air pockets) and pour about 1/4 - 1/3 of an inch of oil on top to keep the air out, then refrigerate or freeze. When you want some of that herb, spoon away the oil which is on top, spoon out some of the herb paste and then replace the oil (the same oil or fresh new oil). I generally use canola for making herb pastes since it does not have much taste of its own and will not complete with the herb flavor. Herb paste is the foundation of pesto: basil pesto being the most common type.

Herb Vinegar
Making herb vinegar is so easy and is a great way to use up your extra fresh herbs and is much more economical then buying those fancy bottles of herb vinegar. Specialty herb vinegars can cost $5 - $10 for a 10 oz jar. But you can

make twice that much for just a few dollars. You can use any type of vinegar that you prefer as well as any type of herbs. Experiment with new combinations, as you please. The vinegar will change the color of most herbs to a grayish color, but do not let this discourage you. It is the flavor that you are going for.

The basics are simple.

1. Use no more than one ounce of herbs to every 4 ounces of vinegar. This will assure that the vinegar will preserve the herbs (assuming that the vinegar acid is at least 5%).

2. Sterilize a glass jar (do not use plastic) in boiling water, especially if the jar was previously used for other food items. The jar should have either a plastic lid or a tight fitting cork. Metal tops will corrode and change the flavor of the vinegar. If your metal lids are coated (as for canning) then these are fine to use.

3. Thoroughly rinse the herbs and pat dry with a paper towel. (If you grew the herbs yourself, then immerse them in ice cold water for a few minutes to chase away any bugs, then pat dry.)

4. Heat your choice of vinegar to 180°F. Do not boil.

5. Place the herbs in a sterile jar; cover the herbs completely with the heated vinegar. Sealed the jar and store it (away from the sun) for 2-4 weeks.

6. You can use the vinegar directly from the jar it was stored in if you plan to use it all within 2 more weeks. Otherwise you should strain it to remove the herbs. I will usually add a small fresh sprig of the herbs used. This will add a tiny bit more flavor over time but mostly I do it to remember what herbs I used in that particular blend (a label is a good idea too).

I use herbs with their stems so that they stand tall in the jar. This provides an attractive display when using nice clear glass jars. But you will need to either push the herbs down or remove them once the vinegar is used to the extent that it no longer covers the herbs. Once opened, I recommend using all of the vinegar within six to eight weeks, unless you have strained out the herbs or kept it tightly sealed. Due to the organic content, the vinegar may appear cloudy after the jar has been poured. This is perfectly okay and quite natural. The cloudiness should settle out after the jar has sat still for several hours.

Various other things can be added to the herbal vinegar for additional flavor and variety. Try adding lemon zest (the yellow portion of the peel), chili peppers (dried or blanched), cloves, peppercorns, dill seeds, anise seeds, allspice, roasted garlic, etc. I do not recommend fresh garlic since it may rot (unless it is removed after 1 or 2 days). Dried garlic works great.

Here are a few combinations that I like.

1. **Herbal Blend Vinegar**: Apple cider vinegar (16 oz) with 3 tall sprigs of rosemary, a sprig or two of oregano, 1 teaspoon dried garlic, 1 dried whole chili peppers (seeds intact) and 3 - 5 peppercorns. After 2 weeks, I strain it,

then add a small sprig of fresh rosemary and oregano and two cocktail onions. This vinegar is great for making salad dressings or drizzled over stemmed vegetables such as cabbage, cauliflower, broccoli or spinach.

2. **Tarragon Vinegar.** White wine vinegar (16 oz) with 6 or 8 tall sprigs of French tarragon, the zest of $\frac{1}{2}$ lemon, 2 whole cloves, and 1 whole allspice berry. I strain it after 2 weeks and then add just a single sprig of fresh tarragon and a bit of lemon zest (making a spiral adds visual appeal). This vinegar is indispensable for making hollandaise sauce. I also like it sprinkled over cucumber and sliced tomatoes, as well as on white fish instead of lemon.

3. **Basil/Garlic Balsamic Vinegar.** Balsamic vinegar (1 cup/8 oz) heated to a simmer with 6 to 8 cloves of garlic (coarsely chopped) and a $\frac{1}{2}$ cup of basil leaves. Remove from heat and put in a tightly seal jar. Once cooled, place in a cool dark place for a week or two. Strain the vinegar into a sterile jar and add another cup of balsamic vinegar. This vinegar is excellent in salad dressings and marinades.

Herb Butter

I simply love herbal butter. I usually have a jar in the refrigerator at all times. It is a fast and easy way to dress up vegetables or baste poultry or fish. Just about any fresh herbs can be used, by themselves or in combinations.

1. Remove butter from refrigerator and slice into $\frac{1}{2}$ tablespoon chucks.
2. Rinse and thoroughly dry fresh herbs. If you grew the herbs yourself, immerse them in ice cold water for a few minutes to chase away any bugs.
3. Remove leaves from stem and mince leaves.
4. Place herbs in a small saucepan. Add enough cooking oil (any kind) to cover the bottom. Heat herbs and oil, over medium heat stirring frequently for 1 or 2 minutes (before the herbs begin to darken). If using basil add it in at the last 2 seconds. Immediately remove from heat.
5. Add butter and stir well.
6. Refrigerate or use right away.

The addition of oil to the butter gives the spread a nice creamy texture, even minutes after removing from the refrigerator. I like to use olive oil when using Mediterranean herbs and sesame oil when using Asian herbs. But mostly I use canola oil since it has no particular taste of its own to compete with the butter and herb tastes. I use no more than 1 part oil to 8 parts butter – in other words 1 tablespoon oil to 1 stick of butter.

Dried herbs can also be used to make herbal butters, but the appearance and taste is dramatically inferior in many cases. If using dried herbs then prepare the butter at least one day in advance to using it. Stir it frequently throughout the day. This will allow the flavors to meld.

The following are a few herb butters which I like and use the most:

1. **Lemon-Sage Butter**. Heat 1 teaspoon of canola oil with 10 to 12 leaves of fresh sage (minced finely) for 1 or 2 minutes. Remove from heat and add 1/2 stick of butter and 1/4 teaspoon of lemon extract. Mix well. This butter is wonderful on fish or poultry.

2. **Mixed Herb Butter**. Use finely chopped fresh herb leaves; 1 tablespoon each of rosemary, chives, oregano, Italian flat parsley and basil (an extra tablespoon of basil, optional). Finely mince 1 clove of garlic. Heat 1 or 2 tablespoons of olive oil, add the garlic, stir and remove from heat. Add the herbs and stir. Then add 2 sticks of sliced butter (at room temperature). Mix well and refrigerate for at least 1 hour before using. This butter is very versatile and is great for coating any type of poultry prior to roasting, baking or grilling. It is also excellent for any type of steam vegetables, especially summer squashes and then a sprinkle of parmesan cheese (yum!).

3. **Cumin-Chili-Cilantro Butter**. Heat 1 scant tablespoon of canola oil with 1/4 teaspoon of cumin and 1/4 teaspoon of chili powder heat over medium heat for 1 or 2 minutes. [Love garlic? Add a minced clove or two.] Then add 2 tablespoons of fresh cilantro (minced finely) for about 30 seconds. Remove from heat and add 1 stick of butter and mix well. This butter is wonderful on grilled meats, poultry or fish (add a teaspoon of lime juice if you like). Or butter up some veggies that you are serving with southwestern or Mexican entrees.

Herb Oil

Fresh herbs can also be used to flavor cooking oils. As with the herb butters; a single herb can be used or a combination of herbs. Different oils add different flavors. There are two basic approaches. One is to heat the herbs in the oil on medium heat for about 20 minutes (don't let it smoke) and then strain off the herbs. Refined oils (particularly canola oil) are best with this method. If the oil is stored at room temperature try to use it up with in two month (up to 6 month if refrigerated). Dried herbs can also be used with this heating method. The second method is to blend the fresh herbs with the oil in a food processor or blender and store the oils in the refrigerator for up to three weeks for unrefined oils (e.g., extra virgin olive oil) or up to 2 months for refined oil. If you strain out the herbs after a week or two, then the oil will last longer. The ratio of herbs to oil is subject to taste and use. I blend herbs with just enough oil to form a paste (like pesto) to use as a rub for meats and poultry. Other times I add more oil to use as a sauce for drizzling over vegetables or making vinaigrettes.

Herb Blends

You can purchase all sorts of specialty blends of herbs and spices. They are very convenient to have on hand. Compare brands when shopping as many include quite a lot of salt – why pay those kinds of prices for salt. But there are many salt free type and these are the ones which I recommend. I call for various blends from time to time in this cookbook. I generally purchase blends, but sometimes I run out and need to improvise. Here are a few that you might want to mix-up for yourself. Simply put the ingredients in an air tight container (empty spice bottles or tins work great) and shake them up. Now they are ready when you want them. Having blends makes cooking faster, but also can inhibit the creative process of cooking. You can add salt to your blends if you'd like, but I generally don't. I prefer to salt food separately. I am very sensitive to salty foods and have a tendency too little salt sometimes. If you like salty food, then you'll probably need to add additional salt to the majority of my recipes.

Cajun Seasoning

2	tsp	paprika
2	tsp	garlic powder
1	tsp	black pepper
1	tsp	cayenne pepper
1	tsp	chili powder
1	tsp	onion powder
1	tsp	oregano
1	tsp	thyme

Curry Powder

2	Tbsp	coriander
2	tsp	cumin
2	tsp	mustard seeds
2	tsp	turmeric
1	tsp	ginger
1	tsp	black pepper
1	tsp	chili powder
1/2	tsp	cinnamon

Herbs de Provence

1	Tbsp	thyme
2	tsp	marjoram
2	tsp	savory
2	tsp	rosemary
1	tsp	oregano
1	tsp	sage
1	tsp	lavender

Poultry Seasoning

1	Tbsp	oregano
1	Tbsp	thyme
1	tsp	black pepper
1	tsp	celery salt
1	tsp	garlic powder
1	tsp	rosemary
1	tsp	sage

Crab Boil Seasoning

1	Tbsp	celery seeds
1	Tbsp	paprika
1		bay leaf, crumbled
1	tsp	allspice
1	tsp	black pepper
1	tsp	dry mustard
1/2	tsp	cardamom
1/4	tsp	ground cloves

Garam Masala

2	Tbsp	coriander
1	Tbsp	black pepper
2	tsp	cumin
1	tsp	cardamom
1	tsp	cinnamon
1	tsp	allspice
1	tsp	turmeric
1/2	tsp	ground cloves

Steak & Chop Seasoning

1	Tbsp	black pepper
2	tsp	lemon pepper
2	tsp	garlic powder
1	tsp	chili powder
1	tsp	dry mustard
1	tsp	marjoram
1	tsp	oregano
1/2	tsp	allspice

Pumpkin Pie Blend

1	Tbsp	cinnamon
1	tsp	ground ginger
1	tsp	allspice
1/2	tsp	cardamom
1/2	tsp	ground cloves

~ COOKING WITH ALCOHOL ~

I rarely drink alcohol; it's just not suited to who I am. However, I occasionally enjoy a good glass of wine with a special dinner on a special occasion but that turns out to be about 6 glasses a year. Maybe I'll have a vodka tonic once or twice a year just for kicks. But if you saw my kitchen you might think I had a drinking problem. I have a reasonably well stocked liquor cabinet, plus a nice selection of fortified wines (more on these later) and I will have low carb beer in my refrigerator from time to time. All of this is because I love to cook with alcohol! The depth and complexity of flavor certain liquors can develop in a sauce is another layer of culinary delight for me.

Have you heard it said that all the alcohol evaporates when you cook with it? Well this is a myth. Most of the alcohol certainly cooks off but rarely all of it. The residual amounts of alcohol are generally quite small however if used in limited quantities and the recipe is at a boil for a few minutes. This is the manner in which I generally use alcohol in cooking (with very few exceptions). You will find a significant number of recipes calling for alcohol particularly fortified wines. In some cases it can be eliminated with just a moderate loss of flavor. For other recipes the flavor of the alcohol is essential to the dish. The Chicken Marsala, for example, requires a fair amount of marsala wine. You could make the same recipe using just chicken stock, but it would be a different dish. For some recipes where I specify a fortified wine, you can substitute wine vinegar or apple cider vinegar (although use only half the amount or so). But if there is a significant amount of alcohol called for (more than just a few tablespoons) and you choose not to cook with alcohol, then maybe you should just skip that particular recipe altogether.

I'm sure you have seen those small bottles of "cooking wine" in the grocery store. I simply cannot recommend them; they are higher in sugar than a table wine and their flavor is, well, unacceptable in my opinion. When cooking with wine you really want to use something that you would enjoy drinking. Table wine is an excellent cooking liquid. Red wines typically have about 0.5g carbs per ounce (2 tablespoons) where as white wines are generally closer to 0.2g carbs per ounce. Making a sauce with a few tablespoons and then serving the same wine with dinner is a very practical approach for many. But table wines do not store well after they have been opened, so if you do not intend to consume the whole bottle that day, you might not want to waste a good bottle of wine just for a few tablespoons worth in the kitchen. But there is an alternative: fortified wines!

Fortified Wines

Fortified wines have been prepared with brandy and are fermented differently than table wines (although I do not know the particulars). I much prefer to cook with fortified wines than ordinary table wines not only for their distinct flavor but mostly because of their exceptional shelf life. A bottle of table wine should be consumed within 24 hours after opening it, where as the typical fortified wine can last up to a year after opening without refrigeration. This quality makes these wines very popular in my kitchen. For low carb cooking you will want to use only the "dry" versions of each wine which generally have less than 0.5g carbs per ounce (2 tablespoons). Port is a noted exception; it is much sweeter and should be used sparingly if at all. Fortified wines that are labeled dry have been fermented to the point that all the sugar has converted to alcohol and this keeps the carbs down. The following are the more popular types of fortified wines.

Madeira – this wine is from the Portuguese island of Madeira. The dry type is sometimes called *sercial* and has a pale golden color. This is a delightful wine if you can find it (your mom & pop shop probably will not carry it). It can be a little pricy too but it is excellent in poaching liquids and sauces.

Marsala – this wine is from Sicily, Italy and gets its name from the Mediterranean town of Marsala which produces it. This one is just a bit drier (0.2g carbs per ounce) than the madeira and has a mild flavor. It is essential for making Chicken Marsala and is a nice addition to sauces and marinades.

Port – this sweet wine originated in the Douro region of Portugal and acquired its name from the town of Oporto where it was first aged and bottled. Port is now produced in many different locales. Port is typically too sweet for low carb cooking in my opinion at 3.5g carbs per ounce.

Sherry – this wine originally came from an area near Andalusia, Spain. But today, it can refer to any number of wines that come from Spain as well as elsewhere. Sherry comes in many varieties ranging from the very sweet (2.5g carbs per ounce) to the very dry (0.3g carbs per ounce). The dry and extra dry are the most useful in your low carb kitchen. I use sherry the most as it is very economical, easy to find and has a nice flavor.

Vermouth – this fortified wine is flavored with various aromatic herbs and spices. It gets its name from the German word "wermut" or wormwood, which was the primary flavoring herb before it was discovered to be poisonous. The blend of aromatic herbs is what makes this fortified wine stand out from the others. Again you will want the dry or extra dry vermouth for your low carb cooking. This fortified wine is even easier to find than the dry sherry since a dry martini is still a very popular drink. I feel that vermouth is best with red meat dishes, but that's just my taste.

Other Alcohol

I use very little of the "hard" liquors such as vodka, gin, tequila, rum, etc. but they are nice from time to time mostly to provide variation. They are particularly good in marinades and added to poaching or braising liquids. There are only a couple of recipes in this cook book specifying any type of hard liquor.

You really can't live in Golden, Colorado without knowing one or two recipes using beer, even if it is simply grilled bratwurst finished off in a beer bath. This is Coors country; yet I am told that there are also many wonderful micro breweries nearby. But I support the company that provides much vitality to this small, lovely, charming town; so I stick with Coors. I can get it fresh, fresh, fresh (and cheap)! Lucky me! Coors has a low carb light lager which they call Aspen Edge with only 2.6g carbs per 12 oz bottle (about 10g less than an average beer). It is excellent beer for cooking. I am sure that there are many other low carb brands of beer, but my loyalty makes them invisible to me. You will find a couple of recipes in this cookbook calling for Aspen Edge beer.

~COOKING AS A RITUAL ~

I am sure that all of us have our own rituals when it comes to cooking. For some, the morning breakfast ritual is a highly synchronized and fairly predictable chain of events. The push to get the coffee or tea brewed, the eggs scrambled or the cereal poured and get to work on time is a well practiced routine for many. Over the years, I have developed more & more food rituals such that now cooking has become a spiritual practice for me.

Just about everything involving food has become some form of spiritual ritual in my life. A significant portion of each day revolves around food in some manner or another and I am always looking for more ways to deepen my spirituality, so the combination was a natural blending for me. Grocery shopping, gardening, cooking and eating are all ceremonies that I thoroughly enjoy. Some of my greatest pleasures in life are associated with food. I get immense satisfaction from cooking a meal for others and taking the time to eat slowly as we share stories (inspiring humor, wisdom and compassion) and relax into the unique presence of everyone that has gathered together for that meal. This is a common Thanksgiving practice for many American families, but such consciousness need not be restricted to a few seasonal events. It can be every day and every meal; whether alone or in a group. It is purely a choice. For me, it does not matter if the meal is merely zapping leftovers in the microwave, I can make it into a sacred moment for myself with a simple intention.

I absolutely love to cook. I love everything about it; well, except for doing the dishes afterwards. I love the creative process of choosing a menu keeping in mind the preferences of those for whom I am cooking, the season and the occasion. I enjoy selecting the ingredients from the pantry and the refrigerator and gathering them on the counter. I can get almost giddy as my senses become heightened with all of the luxurious colors, textures, tastes and smells. The process of slicing and dicing and mixing things together feels like an exciting science experiment to me. I can even enjoy the forced impromptu changes I need to make as I discover that I am low on a particular ingredient that is necessary for the meal I have planned. Such happy accidents are the source of many new recipes for me; what luck! I also enjoy food presentation and choosing plates, serving platters and other items which complement the colors or theme of the meal. And then all of these joyful moments culminate into the final product – a delicious meal! Cooking is a pleasure, a divine experience, particularly when I have the opportunity to cook for others.

Although I greatly enjoy preparing meals for other people, I very much prefer to do the actual cooking portion alone. So if someone is coming over for dinner, I will generally do all of the prep work and as much of the cooking as I can before hand. When I cook alone, I simply love that I can openly talk to myself and to the ingredients that I am using without feeling weird or self-conscious. I can select any type of music and play it at whatever volume I desire. One of my quirkiest rituals is when I am making muffins or cupcakes. For some reason these items make me feel particularly playful, so I generally choose some dance music, like reggae, and do my "muffin dance" while I am preparing them and while they cook. It is so fun and makes me smile, but I would feel terribly silly if anyone were around to observe this.

I enjoy using the time in the kitchen preparing meals as part of my daily spiritual practice. Before I begin, I like to consciously shift my awareness to one of reverent gratitude. As I choose each individual ingredient, I like to give thanks to its nutrients, flavor or other special qualities. I bless each chicken (and other meats) for its life of service providing protein to humans and other animals. I try to consciously put into each meal the intention for health and wellness. Okay, I realized that this may be overly woo woo for some of you, but certain spiritual leaders claim that food will pick up whatever energies are in the kitchen, particularly those of the person who is preparing the food. And then as others eat the food they ingest these energies as well as the nutrients of the actual food. I happen to believe in this philosophy. As such I try to remain conscious of my thoughts and feelings particularly when I am cooking for others.

I am aware of the fact that I am a good cook. Over many years, I have developed notable skills around food selection and preparation. However, I believe that the secret ingredient which makes my meals worthy of complements is the fact that I try to prepare them with a consciousness of love, gratitude and joy. It is this conscious intention that makes my cooking special. But these types of nutrients are difficult to specify in a recipe. I had thought about providing commentary suggesting music for certain recipes, thoughts and feelings for the preparation time and listing specific ingredients such as a dash of love, a pinch of joy and a bunch of gratitude. However, this seemed a bit silly and could easily have been overdone and distracting.

You may find this far-fetched, but I guarantee that if you practice an attitude of gratitude while you are preparing your meals that you will find that you have become an amazing cook. I'd wager that your family and friends will notice a difference too. Are you up for the challenge of this experiment? Give love and gratitude to your food and your food will multiply it and give it back to you and your family.

At a minimum, consider reviving the tradition of saying a blessing before each meal. It is not really about religion (although it can be if you desire to place the focus there). It is purely about gratitude. Let everyday be one of giving thanks, not just the last Thursday in November.

Kitchen Hygiene Ritual

You may choose to ignore the ingredients of consciousness and intentions while you are cooking, but I have another kitchen ritual which I highly encourage that you practice since it has more emphasis on hygiene than spirituality. As you know, it is vitally important to thoroughly wash your hands, knives and working surfaces after handling raw poultry, pork, and other meats before you touch anything else. A quick rinse even with a touch of anti-bacterial soap is not nearly adequate. Experts recommend that we vigorously rub our hands together with soap for 30 seconds or longer before rinsing with warm water. Well, this is about as much time as it takes to sing the happy birthday song, or to say the Lord's Prayer or state the Pledge of Allegiance. So you might as well put that time to additional good use. I encourage you to devise your own song, prayer or affirmation to utilize each and every time that you wash your hands in the kitchen so that you will consistently wash for the full 30 seconds. It is just too easy to get rushed and take short cuts here.

Also, each time you wipe down your knife and working surface after handling raw meats (particularly poultry), then pop that wet sponge or dish rag into the microwave for one full minute before using it again to clean up any other part of the kitchen. This one minute microwave (highest setting) will kill more germs than any antibacterial soap that you can find at a grocery store. At the end of each day, zap that sponge again for good measure; even if you have not prepared meats or poultry that day. Hygiene experts also recommend that we replace our sponges monthly. So on the first day of every month (or each full moon or other specific day of the month that would work well for you) throw away that nasty sponge and replace it with a new one! It may look perfectly fine but it is actually a housing development for all sorts of yucky stuff. If you use a dish rag be sure to launder them frequently using the hottest water setting that you have (a little Clorox helps too). Why make our bodies fight off those extra germs when it could be using that energy to create a greater state of health and wellness.

BREAKFAST

BREAKFAST

~ REGARDING EGGS ~

Ah, the almighty egg. Eggs play so many different roles in cooking that they are indispensable in the kitchen. I will not attempt to provide a complete overview of eggs but there are a few basic items that I would like to cover. First of all eggs are not a zero carb food, as some people may claim. There are very low however at only about 0.5g carbohydrates each. This will probably be a concern to you only during the Induction Phase when every half gram of carbs makes a difference.

For most people during the Induction phase, breakfast will consist of some type of eggs with or without meat. But if you do not like eggs then simply have typical lunch or dinner items for breakfast. There is no rule that says grilled chicken can not be eaten for breakfast. Once you get past the Induction phase then you can enjoy smoothies, muffins, pancakes and such.

Eggs come in a variety of sizes and colors. Contrary to popular opinion, the color of the egg shell has no bearing on the quality or nutritional value. It is merely a function of the breed of chicken which laid the egg. In addition to the common white and brown eggs found in the grocery stores, you can find a variety of colors at the farmers market including green, blue, gray, spotted, etc. There are standards for sizing eggs from pee wee to Jumbo. However, all of my recipes are for large eggs; the most common size. Some experts say it is best to store eggs on a shelf in the refrigerator rather than in the door compartment, as this will provide a more stable temperature environment and they will not be jostled every time the door is opened and closed. But I prefer the convenience of the door where the carton is less likely to be buried under other things. Very fresh eggs are best for frying, poaching or baking whole (in other words, not beaten first). Older eggs are best for cooking in their shells. Eggs that will be beaten can be fresh or older without any noticeable differences. However eggs that will have the whites and yolks beaten separately, as for a soufflé, or making meringues, will produce the best results from very fresh eggs.

Powdered Egg Whites
You will see, particularly in the dessert section, that I sometimes use powdered egg whites. The brands that I use the most are *Just Whites* and *Bob's Red Mill*, but there are several other brands that are widely available. In most cases you can substitute fresh egg whites or use the eggs whites that come in those refrigerated containers which look like small milk cartons. I like the powdered eggs whites because they have a greater shelf life, but mostly because I don't end up with extra egg yolks.

The Perfect Hardboiled Egg
Why are they called "hardboiled" when the last thing we want is to let them cook in boiling water? But that's what we call them. They are actually eggs which have been poached in their shells; but "poached eggs" refers to another technique all together.

Are your hardboiled eggs difficult to peel? Then they were probably too fresh. Ever get a green layer on your egg yolks? Then they were cooked too long. Are your egg whites ever rubbery? They were probably cooked in boiling water.

The best eggs to use for hardboiled eggs are the older ones; close to their expiration date. These will be easier to peel and it will be easier to center the egg yolks (important in some recipes, like deviled eggs). Eggs are generally stored with the large end in the upright position. To get centered egg yolks, try to remember to lay them on their side for about 24 hours before cooking them. But don't worry if you forget to do this, you can still twirl the eggs. This is accomplished by spinning each egg with a spoon while the water comes to the boil. Be sure the pot is large enough to maneuver the eggs this way without cracking them. But I've gotten ahead of myself. Here are the steps for hardboiled eggs.

1. Lay eggs on their sides 24 hours in advance
2. Remove eggs from refrigerator 5 minutes before cooking.
3. Place eggs in a pot so that there is only one layer off eggs. Fill a pot with enough cold tap water to cover the eggs plus 1 to 2 inches more. Add approximately1/2 tsp of salt for every cup of water (so if there are minor cracks in the shells, then the salt will help cook the leaking whites more quickly thereby sealing the cracks). Turn heat to the highest setting and bring just to the boiling point. (If centering the egg yolk, twirl continuously until the water reaches the boil).
4. Turn of heat, cover and let sit for 12 minutes (15 minutes if higher than 4000 feet elevation).
5. Drain and rinse with plenty of cold water or plunge into a bowl of iced water to stop the cooking process.
6. Peeling is easiest if done as soon as the eggs have cooled (but you can store them with the shells on if you prefer; they'll pick up less "refrigerator tastes" that way). Crack the eggs all over and peel under water. Some people do this under the faucet with running water, but I don't like bits of shell going down the drain so I do it using a large bowl of water.

That's it; the perfect hardboiled egg! Slice them, dice them or serve them whole. Or best of all; stuff them, making your own creation of deviled eggs.

Scrambled Eggs
Scrambled eggs are probably the easiest way to prepare eggs and are well suited to cooking for one or for a crowd. There are a few tricks you may not know.

First of all it is best to use a non-stick skillet that is in good condition (no pits or scratches) or a well seasoned pan (also without pits or scratches).

1. Heat the skillet over medium heat for 1 or 2 minutes before adding butter or oil. This allows any tiny pores to close up and helps keep the eggs from sticking to the pan. This step is also advisable for fried eggs, omelets and frittatas.

2. If you are including veggies, add them to the skillet next with some butter or oil. Let them cook until about 75% done before adding the eggs.
3. Beat the eggs (room temperature is best) with a pinch of salt and up to 1 tablespoon of liquid for every 2 eggs. I like to use cream, but low carb milk or even just a splash of water is fine too. The salt and liquid helps break down the albumin (the whites) to create a more homogeneous mixture.
4. Let the eggs cook without too much stirring on your part. Try scraping and folding instead. Gently move the cooked portions to the side so that the runny parts can get to the bottom of the pan.
5. Add cheese or cooked meats before the eggs are completely set. Fold and remove from the heat when they are just 30 seconds from being completely set. Let the eggs finish cooking on the plate.

This method for scrambling eggs should yield fluffy, melt in your mouth eggs. You don't want to cook too slowly but you also don't want too high of heat. Both of these create hard nodules (but if you prefer your eggs that way, then stir the eggs while they are cooking too).

Omelets

I rarely make omelets. They are more temperamental than most other methods and I prefer to either scramble the eggs or make frittatas. You'll need to use a pan that is the desired size of the omelet and has a nicely slopped edge so that you can slip the omelet out of the pan without the need to lift it.

The approach to omelets is similar to the scramble and the frittata. The fold is the tricky part. It sounds simple but for me, it doesn't always work out.

1. Follow steps 1 and 3 from the scrambled eggs (skipping step 2).
2. As the eggs are cooking, tilt the pan a little while raising up the edges of the cooking eggs with a spatula to allow the runny portions to flow under and make contact with the bottom of the pan.
3. Once there are no more runny parts but the eggs are still not completely set, add your desired filling (veggies and meats should have been sautéed in another pan).
4. Folding is the trick. Lift up one half and fold it onto the other half forming a half moon shape and then slide it out of the skillet and onto a plate. Again, let the eggs finish cooking on the plate using their own heat.

Frittatas

A frittata is basically an open faced omelet that is finished under the broiler. Frittatas are fun and are easier to make than omelets. The trick with these is having the right size and type of skillet. The size needs to be such that the eggs can fill it completely and be at least $1/2$ inch thick or up to about $1 1/2$ inches thick. The handle of the skillet is a concern as the skillet will be put under the broiler. My skillets can withstand this heat. If your skillet handle is plastic or wood, you'll need to wrap it with damp paper towels before putting the skillet under the broiler. In any case the handle should be propping open the broiler door as far from the heat source as you can manage. You must use a mitt when removing the skillet from the broiler regardless of the type of handle (even the "cool handle" designs).

1. Follow steps 1 through 3 for the scrambled eggs.
2. Preheat broiler with rack about 5-6 inches from the heat.
3. As the eggs are cooking, tilt the pan a little while raising up the edges of the cooking eggs with a spatula to allow the runny portions to flow under and make contact with the bottom of the pan (as with an omelet).
4. Once there are no more runny parts but the eggs are still not completely set, add your desired topping or merely add a handful of cheese.
5. Move the skillet to under the broiler for about 3 minutes allowing the cheese to brown but not burn. Use a mitt to remove from the boiler

Slice into pie shaped wedges. You can bring the whole skillet to the table or serve up the slices individually.

Breakfast Squares

These are egg casseroles and one of my preferred ways to prepare eggs. They can be simple or quite elaborate. They are awesome fresh out of the oven, but what I like best is the convenience of the left-overs. I'll make a batch on the weekend and then have the left-overs for breakfast the following mornings. They are also great as a quick snack, an appetizer, served as a side dish or as a main course for lunch or even dinner. You can include any type of veggies, meat and cheese. Combinations are limited only by your imagination. I typically use an 8x8 baking dish and then cut them into six pieces. But you can always cut them into smaller pieces if you need more portion control or serving as a side dish or appetizer. Here's how to cut a square pan into different numbers of servings.

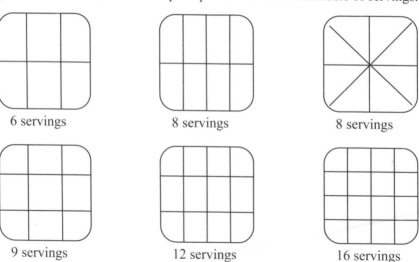

| 6 servings | 8 servings | 8 servings |
| 9 servings | 12 servings | 16 servings |

~ Regarding Milk, Cream and Yogurt ~

Milk and cream products are almost as invaluable in the kitchen as eggs. The low carb dieter should probably avoid regular milk (regardless of fat content) as they are all particularly high in carbohydrates (about 12g carbs per cup). But for you milk lovers, there are now low carb milk products available that taste exactly like regular milk to me. I use the Hood Carb Countdown™ Dairy Beverage in both the 2% and the chocolate flavored as they have only 3g and 2g carbs respectively (yep, the chocolate is lower!). There are other brands available too but watch for variations in carb count when making the substitutions. Some brands of soy milk (which is not truly a dairy product) are also low in carbs (1.2g net carbs per cup). But check the labels and avoided the flavored types which generally contain sugar.

Yogurt is a wonderful food with many health benefits. The unique aspects of yogurt are the live active cultures which helps keep a healthy balance of bacteria in our digestive track. When buying yogurt for your low carb diet, you'll want to be diligent in reading labels. The flavored non-fat yogurts generally add quite a lot of sugar products pushing carbohydrates up over 20g per cup. Plain, whole milk yogurt is a better choice (typically 10g carbs per cup) and then you can add fruits and sweeteners in a controlled fashion to your liking. You also want to look for live active cultures. The best ones are those that list many types of cultures (e.g., L. acidophilus, B. bifidus, S. thermophilus, L. bulgaricus, l. casei) and the amounts of each culture. If the label does not specify the details then it probably only contains L. acidophilus at the minimum level allowed and still able to carry the live active culture labeling.

Grams of Carbs for Milk, Cream and Yogurt

Product, 1 cup	Carbs	Fiber	Net Carbs
Hood Carb Countdown™ , 2%	3.0	0	3.0
Hood Carb Countdown™ , chocolate	3.0	1.0	2.0
Milk (whole, 2%, skim & non-fat)	~11.7	0	~11.7
Half and half	10.4	0	10.4
Table cream	8.8	0	8.8
Heavy whipping cream	6.6	0	6.6
Sour cream	9.8	0	9.8
Soy Milk	4.4	3.2	1.2
Yogurt, Dannon's Carb Control, low-fat	6.0	0	6.0
Yogurt, whole milk, plain	10.5	0	10.5
Yogurt, low-fat, plain	16.0	0	16.0
Yogurt, non-fat, plain	17.0	0	17.0

Dannon has come out with yogurt products specifically designed for the low carb diet which are called *Carb Control*™ and are available in a variety of flavors. These are quite delicious although they do not specify the amounts or types of live active cultures contained in their product. I've seen ads on TV for low carb yogurt products made by *Hood*. These products are not yet available in my area, but I truly look forward to trying them as I love their milk products.

As time goes by, hopefully there will be a variety of new milk, cream and yogurt products aimed specifically for the low carb diets. I know my journey has been greatly enhanced by what is available so far.

~ REGARDING CHEESE ~

Cheese is a great low carb snack as well as an invaluable ingredient for enhancing the flavor of a variety of recipes, both savory and sweet. Cheese typically has slightly less than 1g carbs per once. One ounce of cheese is the size of one of those string cheese packages, which is a great serving size whether for a snack or grated on top of an omelet or other dish. Cheese has no fiber. There are several types of cheese that are very low in carbs including brie, camembert, gruyere and limburger which have only 0.1g of carbs per ounce. If you are accustomed to eating Velveeta, I recommend that you reconsider this choice. Not only does it have 5.3g of carbs per ounce but jt is loaded with preservatives. Besides, it is not really cheese.

Grams of Carbs per Ounce of Cheese

American	0.4	Gouda	0.6
Blue	0.7	Gruyere	0.1
Brie	0.1	Limburger	0.1
Camembert	0.1	Monterey Jack	0.2
Cheddar	0.4	Mozzarella	0.7
Colby	0.7	Muenster	0.3
Cottage Cheese	1.0	Neufchatel	0.8
Cream Cheese	0.8	Parmesan	1.0
Edam	0.4	Pepper Jack	1.0
Feta	1.2	Provolone	0.6
Fontina	0.4	Ricotta	0.9
Goat – soft type	0.6	Romano	1.0
Gorgonzola	1.0	Swiss	0.9

Cheese is fairly high in fat, varying from 6-9 grams of fat per ounce. Typically the lower the carbs, the higher the fat content. Most cheeses have a fat breakdown of 50-70% saturated fat, 20-35% monounsaturated fat and the remainder is polyunsaturated fats.

Breakfast Sausage

Most packaged sausage meats have a bit of sweetener in them;
so here's a zero carb way to make your own.

1	lb	ground pork
1		egg
1	tsp	dried sage -- crumbled
1/2	tsp	dried thyme -- crumbled
1/2	tsp	onion salt
1/4	tsp	ground black pepper
1/4	tsp	chili powder

Induction

6 Servings
0g Net Carbs

1. Beat the egg well. Add the sage, thyme, garlic powder, salt, pepper and cayenne. Beat again. Add the ground pork and squish it all together with your hands.

2. Form into 6 patties. Pan fry for 3 - 4 minutes per side.

Serve with eggs. Refrigerate left-overs and reheat in the microwave.

Per Serving: 211 Calories; 17g Fat; 14g Protein; trace Carbs; trace Dietary Fiber

Ham & Swiss Egg Cup

An easy breakfast for one or make it for many.

1/2	cup	ham -- cooked & diced
1	oz	Swiss cheese -- shredded
2	Tbsps	heavy cream
2		eggs
1	Tbsp	parmesan cheese
1	dash	nutmeg

Induction

1 Serving
3g Net Carbs

I make this often for myself when I have left over ham.

Preheat oven to 350°F. Grease one 8 oz ramekin with butter or canola oil.

1. Toss the ham and Swiss cheese together and place in the bottom of the ramekin. If your cheese is sliced instead of shredded then layer the ham and cheese in a couple of layers.

2. Whip together the eggs, cream and nutmeg.

3. Pour eggs into the ramekin. Top with the parmesan cheese.

4. Bake for 20 minutes or until eggs are set.

Although this recipe is for one, it's a great way to serve many people all at once. If you have more than 4 ramekins on a cookie sheet to be baked, then add a few more minutes to the cooking time. Or try using a buttered non-stick muffin tin.

Per Serving: 635 Calories; 50g Fat; 42g Protein; 3g Carbs; trace Dietary Fiber

Jicama Hash Browns

These low carb hash browns are awesome!

1	cup	jicama -- grated
1	Tbsp	refined peanut oil -- or more if needed
1		scallion -- minced
		salt and pepper -- to taste

Induction

2 Servings
3g Net Carbs

In my first cookbook, *Lauri's Low-Carb Cookbook*, I provided a recipe for hash brown using cauliflower. This recipe is exceptionally good too and has the advantage of looking more like traditional hash browns and having more fiber.

1. Cut off about 1/3 of a jicama and peel it (I think a knife works best) then grate it. This should make about 1 cup depending on the size of your jicama. Mince the scallions.

2. In a fry pan over high heat, add the peanut oil and heat until it begins to quiver (but don't let it smoke). That's the perfect time to add the jicama. Stir fry until they have taken on some color but not too dark. Add the scallions, stir, and immediately transfer to a paper towel and toss with some salt and pepper (it'll need both). Serve with fried, scrambled or poached eggs.

Per Serving: 85 Calories; 7g Fat; 1g Protein; 6g Carbohydrate; 3g Dietary Fiber;

Spicy Broccoli Breakfast Squares

This breakfast casserole is heavenly delicious, spicy and nutritious!

4	cups	broccoli florets -- chopped
4	ozs	Pepper Jack cheese
10		eggs
2	Tbsps	Carb Countdown™ Milk, 2%
1	tsp	mustard
1/4	tsp	chili powder
1/4	tsp	salt and pepper -- each

Induction

6 Servings
2g Net Carbs

Preheat oven to 350ºF. Butter an 8x8 casserole dish (you can lightly dust it with whey powder if you have some handy).

1. Chop the broccoli but not too small. Place in the casserole dish and sprinkle the cheese evenly over the broccoli.

2. In a bowl, add the eggs, milk, mustard, chili powder and the salt & pepper. Beat the eggs well. Pour over the broccoli.

3. Bake at 350ºF for 40 minutes. Let cool for about 5 to 10 minutes before cutting into 6 pieces.

This makes a great side dish too.

Per Serving: 197 Calories; 13g Fat; 15g Protein; 4g Carbohydrate; 2g Dietary Fiber

Steak & Eggs with Chipotle Sauce

This will get your motor running in the morning!
It is also great for lunch or dinner.

2	**sirloin steaks**
2	**eggs -- fried**

Induction	
2 Servings	
1g Net Carbs	

Chipotle Sauce

1/4	cup	**mayonnaise**
1/4	cup	**sour cream**
2		**chipotle chilies -- canned in adobo**
1	pinch	**salt**

1. To make the chipotle sauce you can either mince the chilies (with a bit of the sauce) and stir it in with the mayo and sour cream or you can put all 3 ingredients in a food processor or blender. Taste before you add the salt for it might not need it depending on your brand of Chipotle. If it is too spicy (wait for the heat, it's slow to arrive) then simply add more mayo or sour cream. Of course if you want more heat then add more chipotle (only 0.5g net carbs/Tbsp). Set aside.

2. Fry the steaks and eggs to your liking. I typically pan-fry the steak over medium-high heat in a non-stick skillet (no oil added) for about 4 minutes per side then transfer to an oven proof platter and put into a 250°F oven for 5 to 10 minutes. Then I lightly wipe out the fry pan with a paper towel (leaving just a bit of fat) and fry the eggs.

3. Place one egg on top of each steak and drizzle the sauce over the steak & eggs. Serve immediately.

Per Serving: 537 Calories; 48g Fat; 27g Protein; 2g Carbohydrate; 1g Dietary Fiber

Pancakes

These low carb pancakes are a great way to start the day.
The fiber and coconut variation below are even better!
I personally think that these are better than ordinary pancakes.

1		egg
1	pinch	salt
4	ozs	Dannon's Carb Control™ Yogurt -- peach
3	Tbsps	almond meal
2	Tbsps	whey protein powder
1/4	tsp	baking powder -- *See Note
1	tsp	butter -- or oil for the griddle

Induction

2 Servings
3g Net Carbs

*Note: If you live much below 3000 feet elevation, then use a rounded 1/4 tsp of the baking powder (i.e. as full as your 1/4 tsp can get). Or if you live above 6000 feet, then use a scant 1/4 tsp.

This makes 4 pancakes; just enough for a breakfast for two, when served with the left over yogurt spread on top. You can add 1/4 tsp of any flavor extract or cinnamon with zero carb impact. I prefer the peach yogurt for these pancakes but feel free to substitute any of the other flavors - see the blueberry variation; they are pretty darn good too.

1. In a bowl, beat the egg with a pinch of salt. Add just 2 Tbsps of the yogurt. Mix well. Add the almond meal, whey and baking powder. Stir well. If it is too thick then add a tsp of water at a time.

2. Prepare your griddle with butter or oil as desired. Pour 1/4 of the batter for each pancake. Allow to bubble on the surface some before you sneak a peak underneath. When they develop the color that you like, gently flip. Please resist the urge to press them down with the spatula (unless they are rising out of control) these are best when fluffy.

Serve with the remaining yogurt spread on top of each (that's how the analysis is calculated). Or use a low carb syrup or jam.

Per Serving: 199 Calories; 12g Fat; 19g Protein; 4g Carbohydrate; 1g Dietary Fiber

For some reason the following variations don't really form bubbles like the basic pancakes do (maybe this is just a high altitude phenomenon). In any case, sneak your peak when the edges start to look a bit drier even though the center may still be glistening.

Fiber Variation: These are a lot better than the basic induction pancake, but they push up the carb count. If you can handle the extra carbs go for this one. Add 1 Tbsp of flax seed meal and 1 tsp of Splenda (optional).
5g net carbs; 227 Calories; 12g Fat; 21g Protein; 7g Carbohydrate; 3g Dietary Fiber

Fiber & Coconut Variation: These are even better than the fiber pancake. To the basic recipe add 1 Tbsp of flax seed meal, 2 Tbsps unsweetened coconut flakes and 1 tsp of Splenda (optional).
6g net carbs; 249 Calories; 14g Fat; 21g Protein; 9g Carbohydrate; 3g Dietary Fiber

Blueberry Variation: Substitute blueberry flavored yogurt for the peach, add 1 Tbsp flax seed meal, 1/2 cup of blueberries and 1 tsp Splenda (optional).
8g net carbs; 247 Calories; 13g Fat; 22g Protein; 12g Carbohydrate; 4g Dietary Fiber

Pine Nut & Basil Scramble

This recipe was inspired by my love for basil pesto (which is also good in scrambled eggs). Freshly minced basil is the key.

5	large	eggs
2	Tbsps	Carb Countdown™ Milk, 2%
1	Tbsp	fresh basil leaves -- minced
	dash	salt and pepper -- each
3	Tbsps	pine nut
1/2	Tbsp	butter
1	clove	garlic -- minced
2	Tbsps	parmesan cheese -- shredded

Induction

2 Servings
3g Net Carbs

1. Beat the eggs with the milk and add the minced basil and a dash of salt and pepper. Set aside.

2. In a dry non stick skillet over medium heat add the pine nuts and roast for about 1-2 minutes, just to where they start to take on some color. Add the butter and garlic and sauté for 1 minute.

3. Add the beaten eggs to the skillet and gently scrape and flip frequently with a spatula. Just before the eggs are completely set add the parmesan cheese. Scrape and flip then turn off the heat; letting the heat in the skillet finish off the cooking without over cooking the eggs.

Serve as is or with bacon or sausage.

Per Serving: 293 Calories; 22g Fat; 20g Protein; 4g Carbohydrate; 1g Dietary Fiber

Spinach & Salmon Frittata

This is a wonderful brunch item combining spinach and cream cheese with left-over or canned salmon.

10		eggs
1/4	cup	Carb Countdown™ Milk, 2%
1	tsp	fresh oregano -- $\frac{1}{2}$ tsp if dried
1/4	tsp	garlic powder
1/8	tsp	lemon extract
1/4	tsp	lemon pepper
1/4	tsp	salt
2	cups	spinach leaves
4	ozs	cream cheese
1	cup	salmon, canned -- of left over
1	Tbsp	butter
1/2	cup	parmesan cheese

Induction
4 Servings
3g Net Carbs

The trick with frittatas is having the right pan (see page 63) and having everything prepared before you start to cook.

1. In a small bowl, beat the eggs with the milk, oregano, garlic powder, lemon extract, salt and lemon pepper. Set aside.

2. Coarsely chop spinach and set aside. If you are not using fresh spinach then thaw and drain 1/3 cup frozen spinach. Cut cream cheese into cubes, set aside. Drain the salmon and flake with a fork, set aside. Measure out the parmesan cheese and set aside.

3. Prepare broiler, set rack as close as it can go and preheat.

4. In a skillet over medium heat, melt the butter and sauté the spinach just until wilted. Reduce heat to medium, add the egg mixture and started scraping it up from the bottom and sides (just a bit more gentle then you would for scrambled eggs). When it is about 1/2 way set (still runny) toss in the salmon and the cubes of cream cheese. Immediately remove from heat, smooth out top with your spatula and sprinkle the parmesan cheese evenly over the top.

5. Put under the broiler with the skillet handle propping open the door. Broil until the cheese starts to turn brown. Be sure to use a towel or pot holder to remove the skillet. If you used a non stick skillet it will slide out easily onto a plate where it can be cut into pie wedges to be served.

Per Serving: 425 Calories; 31g Fat; 33g Protein; 3g Carbs; trace Dietary Fiber

Weight Loss Variation: Use 3 minced scallions and sauté with the spinach and use 1 Tbsp fresh lemon juice instead of the lemon extract. Improves the flavor.
4g net carbs; 429 Calories; 31g Fat; 33g Protein; 5g Carbohydrate; 1g Dietary Fiber

Artichoke Breakfast Squares

Artichokes coupled with mushrooms in a creamy egg casserole.
What a yummy, low carb way to start the day!

12	ozs	canned artichoke bottoms
6	ozs	canned mushroom slices
2		scallions -- diced
1/2	cup	Monterey jack cheese -- shredded
1	tsp	fresh oregano – chopped (1/2 tsp if dried)
10		eggs
1/4	cup	heavy cream
1	dash	salt and pepper -- each
1/4	cup	Parmesan cheese -- shredded

Weight Loss
6 Servings
6g Net Carbs

Preheat oven to 350°F

1. Drain and chop the artichoke into small bite sized pieces. Place in a mixing bowl with the mushrooms, scallions, jack cheese and oregano. Toss together.

2. Put the artichoke mixture in a well buttered 8x8 casserole dish.

3. In the original mixing bowl, beat the eggs thoroughly. Add the cream and salt & pepper. Mix again. Pour this mixture over the artichokes. Sprinkle the top with the parmesan cheese.

4. Bake at 350°F for 35 minutes. Let cool for about 5 minutes before cutting into 6 servings.

Per Serving: 224 Calories; 15g Fat; 15g Protein; 7g Carbohydrate; 1g Dietary Fiber

Cauliflower Cashew Breakfast Squares

Cauliflower is a great low carb substitute for potato; so just tell your kids that this is a cashew breakfast casserole and they'll probably gobble it up.

3	cups	cauliflower -- chopped
1/2	cup	bell pepper -- minced
1/3	cup	cashew -- chopped
2		scallion -- minced
1/2	tsp	dried oregano
4	ozs	cheddar cheese -- shredded
8		eggs
2	Tbsps	Carb Countdown™ Milk, 2%
1/4	tsp	salt and pepper -- each
1/2	tsp	paprika

Weight Loss
6 Servings
5g Net Carbs

Preheat oven to 350ºF. Butter a 8x8 casserole dish (you can lightly dust it with whey powder if you have some handy)

1. Chop the cauliflower and cashews. Mince the bell pepper and scallions.

2. In a large bowl, gently toss the cauliflower, cashews, bell pepper, scallions, oregano and about 1/2 of the cheese. Press this into the casserole dish.

3. No need to clean that bowl yet, add the eggs, milk, and the salt & pepper. Beat the eggs well. Pour over the cauliflower mixture. Sprinkle the remaining cheese and dust with the paprika.

4. Bake at 350ºF for 40 minutes. Let cool for about 5 or 10 minutes before cutting into 6 pieces.

Makes a great side dish too.

Per Serving: 226 Calories; 16g Fat; 15g Protein; 7g Carbohydrate; 2g Dietary Fiber

Induction Variation: Leave out the cashews
3g net carbs; 184 Calories; 12g Fat; 14g Protein; 5g Carbohydrate; 2g Dietary Fiber

Green Eggs and Ham Breakfast Squares

Silly name but oh so yummy! This breakfast square is great for any meal of the day. Spinach and broccoli give it its green color.

10		eggs
1	pound	ham – cooked & diced
10	ozs	frozen spinach -- chopped
1	cup	broccoli florets -- minced
2		scallion -- chopped
8	ozs	monterey jack cheese
1/4	cup	heavy cream
2	tsps	mustard
		salt & pepper

Weight Loss

6 Servings
5g Net Carbs

Preheat oven to 350°F

1. In a large sized bowl, thaw the spinach in the microwave. Do not drain off the liquids.

2. Mince the broccoli as finely as you can. A food processor makes this quick work. (Frozen broccoli works fine here too). Add to the spinach. Also add the diced ham and the chopped scallions. Add about 2/3 of the cheese (save the rest for the topping) and toss well.

3. Grease an 8x8 casserole dish with butter or oil. Distribute the spinach/broccoli/ham mixture evenly.

4. In the bowl, whip together the eggs, cream, mustard and a pinch or two of salt and pepper. Pour over the mixture in the casserole dish. Sprinkle the remaining cheese over the top.

5. Bake uncovered at 350°F for 40 minutes. Let cool for about 5 minutes. Cut into 6 servings.

Per Serving: 440 Calories; 31g Fat; 34g Protein; 7g Carbohydrate; 2g Dietary Fiber

Spinach & Crab Breakfast Squares

One of my favorite breakfast items. Left-overs make for a quick
breakfast the next day or a snack anytime.

10	ozs	spinach, frozen
4	ozs	mushrooms, canned -- sliced
6	ozs	crab meat -- canned
1/4	tsp	lemon pepper
4	ozs	parmesan cheese -- shredded
8	ozs	cream cheese
10		eggs
1/4	cup	Carb Countdown™ Milk, 2%
1/4	tsp	lemon extract
1/4	tsp	salt
	dash	paprika

Weight Loss

6 Servings
4g Net Carbs

Preheat oven to 350°F

1. In a microwave safe bowl, place the block of spinach and zap until thawed.

2. Drain the crab (put the juices in a bowl for your cat or dog!) and add the crab to the spinach. Drain the mushrooms and add to the spinach. Add the lemon pepper and half of the parmesan cheese. Toss.

3. Butter an 8x8 non-metallic baking dish on the bottom and the sides. Spread 1/2 of the spinach mixture over the bottom. Using your hands, flatten pieces of cream cheese then lay them on top of the spinach forming a uniform layer. Add the remaining spinach on top of the cream cheese.

4. In the spinach bowl (now empty except for some little bits here and there that you want to keep) add the eggs, milk, extract and salt. Beat with a whisk until well blended. Pour into the baking dish. Sprinkle the remaining cheese on top and garnish with a few sprinkles of paprika (more for the color than the taste).

5. Bake for 35 minutes or just until the center rises slightly above the edges. Cut into 6 servings. Serve at once.

Per Serving: 376 Calories; 27g Fat; 28g Protein; 6g Carbohydrate; 2g Dietary Fiber

Induction Variation: Reduce mushrooms to only 2 ounces and chop them to distribute more evenly.
3g net carbs; 374 Calories; 27g Fat; 28g Protein; 5g Carbohydrate; 2g Dietary Fiber.

Broccoli & Brie Scramble

The Champion low carb vegetable, broccoli, teams up with brie cheese
in this melt in your mouth scrambled eggs.

2	cups	fresh broccoli -- chopped
2		scallion -- chopped
4	ozs	brie cheese
5		eggs
2	Tbsps	Carb Countdown™ Milk, 2%
1	Tbsp	butter
1/4	tsp	garlic powder
		salt and pepper

Weight Loss
2 Servings
5g Net Carbs

1. Chop the broccoli and scallions, keeping them separate. Cut the brie into cubes or thin slices. I like to use some of the rind on the brie, but I also cut some of it away.

2. In a bowl, beat the eggs, cream, garlic power and a pinch of salt and fresh ground pepper. Beat well.

3. In a heavy skillet over medium-high heat, melt the butter and add the chopped broccoli. Stir occasionally. Cook until the broccoli starts to take on some color (about 3 minutes). Then add the chopped scallions and cook another full minute.

4. Add the beaten eggs to the skillet and scrape and flip frequently with a spatula. Just before the eggs are completely set add the brie. Scrape, flip and turn off the heat; letting the heat in the skillet finish off the cooking without over cooking the eggs.

Serve immediately.

Per Servings: 441 Calories; 33g Fat; 29g Protein; 8g Carbs; 3g Dietary Fiber

Induction Variation: Reduce broccoli to 1 cup.
3g net carbs; 428 Calories; 33g Fat; 28g Protein; 5g Carbohydrate; 2g Dietary Fiber;

Cauliflower Bacon Scramble

The cauliflower tastes like hash browns in this dish. Oh so yum!

1	cup	cauliflower -- chopped
2	slices	bacon
1		scallion -- minced
2	Tbsps	bell pepper -- minced
2	ozs	cheddar cheese
5		eggs
2	Tbsps	Carb Countdown™ Milk, 2%
1/4	tsp	garlic powder -- or less
		salt and pepper

Weight Loss

2 Servings
4g Net Carbs

1. Chop the cauliflower. Mince the scallion and bell pepper.

2. In a bowl, beat the eggs, milk, garlic power and a pinch of salt and fresh ground pepper. Beat well.

3. In a heavy skillet over medium-high heat, cook the bacon to a crisp. Remove to a paper towel to drain then crumble. Pour off all but 1 scant Tbsp of fat. Add the cauliflower and sauté until it starts to take on some color (about 3 minutes). Then add the scallions and bell pepper and cook another minute.

4. Add the beaten eggs to the skillet and scrape and flip frequently with a spatula. Just before the eggs are completely set add the cheese. Turn off the heat; letting the heat in the skillet finish off the cooking without over cooking the eggs.

5. Divide between two plates and garnish with the crumbled bacon. Serve immediately.

Per Serving: 339 Calories; 11g Fat; 25g Protein; 6g Carbohydrate; 2g Dietary Fiber

Ricotta Frittata

Asparagus and a nice blend of herbs, garnished with fresh tomato
and a crispy top makes this a crowd pleaser every time.

8		eggs
8	ozs	ricotta cheese
1 ½	cups	asparagus tips
1		shallot -- minced
1	clove	garlic -- minced
1	Tbsp	butter
1	tsp	fresh oregano -- 1/2 tsp if dried
1/4	tsp	salt
1/4	tsp	pepper
1		tomato
1/2	cup	parmesan cheese

Weight Loss

**6 Servings
4g Net Carbs**

The trick with frittatas is having the right pan (see page 63) and having everything prepared before you start to cook.

I use asparagus tips but you can use the whole spears just cut them into bite sized pieces. Set aside.

1. Mince the shallots and garlic, set aside. Slice the tomatoes and set aside. Measure out the parmesan cheese and set aside.

2. In a bowl, beat the eggs with the oregano, salt and pepper. Add the ricotta cheese and whip until mostly incorporated (no lumps bigger than a pea). Let sit for about a couple of minutes.

3. Prepare broiler, set rack as close as it can go and preheat.

4. In a skillet over medium heat, melt the butter and sauté the asparagus, shallots and garlic for about 1 minute. Add the egg mixture and start scraping it up from the bottom and sides (just a bit more gently then you would for scrambled eggs). When it is about 1/2 way set, remove from heat, smooth out top with your spatula, distribute tomato slices on top and sprinkle the cheese evenly over the top.

5. Put under the broiler with the skillet handle propping open the door. Broil until the cheese starts to turn brown. Be sure to use a towel or pot holder to remove the skillet. If you used a non-stick skillet it will slide out easily onto a plate where it can be cut into pie wedges to be served.

Per Serving: 214 Calories; 15g Fat; 15g Protein; 5g Carbohydrate; 1g Dietary Fiber

Turnips & Sausage Frittata

Turnip cubes and sliced sausage links spice up this frittata
for something a bit unusual but incredibly satisfying.

8		eggs
1/4	cup	Carb Countdown™ Milk, 2%
1/2	tsp	brown mustard
1/4	tsp	garlic powder
1/4	tsp	thyme
1/4	tsp	sage -- scant
1/4	tsp	pepper
1/4	tsp	salt
4	ozs	sausage links -- sliced
1	cup	turnip -- cubed
1/2	cup	red and green bell pepper -- diced
2		scallion -- minced
1/2	cup	cheddar cheese -- shredded

Weight Loss
4 Servings
5g Net Carbs

The trick with frittatas is having the right pan (see page 63) and having everything prepared before you start to cook.

1. In a small bowl, beat the eggs with the milk, mustard, thyme, sage, salt and pepper.

2. Slice the sausage links about 1/4 inch thick; set aside. If you are only so-so with turnips you can peel them to reduce that distinctive flavor and make them more like potatoes. Cut into cubes about the same size as the sausage; set aside. Dice the red & green pepper and mince the scallions, set aside. Measure out the cheese and set aside.

3. Prepare broiler, set rack as close as it can go and preheat.

4. In a skillet over medium heat, melt the butter and sauté the sausage and turnips for about 1 minute. Add the peppers and sauté another minute. Add the scallions and sauté another minute. Carefully pour off the fat (use a paper towel to wipe it down even more if desired). Reduce heat to medium, add the egg mixture and started scraping it up from the bottom and sides (just a bit more gently then you would for scrambled eggs). When it is about 1/2 way set (still quite runny) fold in about 1/2 of the cheese and remove from heat. Smooth out top with your spatula and sprinkle the remaining cheese evenly over the top.

5. Put under the broiler with the skillet handle propping open the door. Broil until the cheese starts to turn brown. Be sure to use a towel or pot holder to remove the skillet. If you used a non-stick skillet it will slide out easily onto a plate where it can be cut into pie wedges to be served.

Per Serving: 330 Calories; 25g Fat; 19g Protein; 6g Carbohydrate; 1g Dietary Fiber

Zucchini Ricotta Pancakes

I was going to call this recipe "The Home Gardener's Pancakes" because we are always looking for new ways to cook zucchini. These are great for lunch or dinner too.

1		zucchini
1/2	tsp	salt -- scant
2	Tbsps	Just Whites
4	Tbsps	ricotta cheese
1	tsp	dehydrated onion flakes
1/2	tsp	oregano
1/4	tsp	pepper
1	Tbsp	butter

Weight Loss

2 Servings
4g Net Carbs

Most dishes similar to this, call for squeezing out and discarding the liquids from the zucchini - which of course eliminates some flavor and nutrients. This recipe uses powdered eggs whites and dried herbs which uses the liquid from the zucchini to re-hydrate, thereby retaining all of the good stuff.

1. Slice off the blossom end of the zucchini, grate into a mixing bowl. This should be close to 2 cups (loosely fitting). If your zukes are small then add another one. Add the salt, stir and let sit for about 3 minutes.

2. Squeeze the zucchini releasing some of its liquids into the bowl. Add the powdered egg whites, onion flakes, oregano and pepper, stir and let sit another 3 minutes. Whip with a fork until frothy (1 full minute).

3. Add the ricotta and stir well.

4. On a non-stick pancake griddle or large frying pan, melt a little bit of butter over medium heat. Spoon out 1 rounded Tbsp of batter and flatten with a spatula. Do as many as will fit comfortably allowing room to flip them easily. Let cook until the top loses its sheen. Carefully flip over and cook until nicely browned. Repeat with remaining batter.

Yields 8-12 silver dollar pancakes, depending on how big you make them, with 4-6 pancakes per serving. Serve with your desired breakfast meat: bacon, sausage, ham, etc. This also makes a nice side dish.

Per Serving: 141 Calories; 10g Fat; 9g Protein; 5g Carbohydrate; 1g Dietary Fiber

Brunch Party Variation: make extra small pancakes (try to get 18 or more of them). Cluster three together (overlapping like flower petals) add 1 Tbsp of Tapenade (page366) in the center and keep in a warm oven (~175°F) until ready to serve. Serve with 6 Tbsp of sour cream on the side.

Yields 6 clusters with 1 per serving
3g net carbs, 92 Calories; 7g Fat; 3g Protein; 4g Carbohydrate;1g Dietary Fiber

Southwestern Breakfast Burrito

This low carb breakfast is quick and easy.
This is a tasty breakfast with plenty of protein and fiber.

2		low-carb whole wheat tortillas
4		eggs
2	Tbsps	cream
1	pinch	salt and white pepper
1/4	tsp	cumin powder
1/2	Tbsp	butter
1 ½	Tbsps	salsa -- chunky style
2	ozs	cheddar cheese, shredded

Weight Loss
2 Servings
8g Net Carbs

Take the tortillas out of the refrigerator so that can come to room temperature while you prepare the filling.

1. In a mixing bowl, beat the eggs with the cream, salsa, cumin and a pinch of salt and pepper.

2. In a non stick skillet over medium-high heat, melt the butter and then scramble the eggs. Just before they are set, add the cheese and fold-in until it begins to melt.

3. Lay the tortillas on a flat surface. Divide the eggs equally between the two and place on the bottom third of each tortilla. Fold the bottom third over tucking in. Fold in the two sides and then roll up. Serve.

Per Serving: 391 Calories; 28g Fat; 27g Protein; 22g Carbs; 14g Dietary Fiber

Green Chile Variation: If you are not on the run and can afford a few extra carbs, then try placing these burritos into a casserole dish, spoon 2 tablespoon of *505 Green Chile Sauce* over each and heat in a 350°F oven for about ten minutes. Add a Tbsp of sour cream and serve.
11g net carbs, 419 Calories; 29g Fat; 27g Protein; 25g Carbohydrate; 14g Dietary Fiber

Super Breakfast Burrito

These low carb burritos are cheesy and delicious with 14 grams of fiber.

2		low-carb whole wheat tortillas
4		eggs
2	Tbsps	cream
	pinch	salt and white pepper
1/2	Tbsp	butter
1		scallion
1/2	cup	canadian bacon -- cooked and diced
2	ozs	cheddar cheese, shredded
1	oz	cream cheese -- cubed

Weight Loss

2 Servings
9g Net Carbs

Take the tortillas out of the refrigerator so that they can come to room temp while you prepare the filling.

1. In a mixing bowl, beat the eggs with the cream and a pinch of salt and pepper.

2. In a non-stick skillet over medium high heat, melt the butter and add the Canadian bacon and scallions. Stir fry for about 1 minute. Add the eggs and then scramble the eggs. Just before they are set, add the cubes of cream cheese and stir. Add the cheddar cheese and stir in until it begins to melt.

3. Lay the tortillas on a flat surface. Divide the eggs equally between the two and place on the bottom third of each tortilla. Fold the bottom third over tucking in. Fold in the two sides and then roll up. Serve.

Per Serving: 532 Calories; 37g Fat; 40g Protein; 23g Carbs; 14g Dietary Fiber

Chocolate Raspberry Smoothie

A fast, delicious, low carb breakfast with plenty of protein.

1	cup	Carb Countdown™ milk, chocolate
4	Tbsps	whey protein powder
4	ozs	Dannon's Carb Control™ Yogurt - raspberry flavor

Weight Loss

6 Servings
5g Net Carbs

In a blender or by hand, mix the milk and the whey powder. Add the carton of raspberry yogurt. Blend. You are good to go!

Per Serving: 395 Calories; 11g Fat; 61g Protein; 6g Carbohydrate; 1g Dietary Fiber

Fiber Variation: Add 1 Tbsp of flax seed meal for added fiber.
7g net carbs; 451 Calories; 12g Fat; 66g Protein; 12g Carbohydrate; 5g Dietary Fiber

Other Variations: Try using the other flavors of Dannon's Carb Control™ yogurt. I like using the Peach yogurt with the 2% Carb Countdown milk.

Enhanced Oatmeal

A low carb maintenance must, but also enjoy this occasionally with
your weight loss phase. Enjoy 5 grams of fiber per serving
and all the benefits of whole oats

1/4	cup	rolled oats
4	Tbsps	whey protein powder
2	Tbsps	flax seed meal
1	Tbsp	Splenda®
1/4	tsp	cinnamon
1	cup	water
1/2	cup	carb Countdown™ Milk, 2%
	dash	salt
few	drops	extract -- almond, vanilla, orange or maple flavor

Weight Loss

2 Servings
9g Net Carbs

Do not use instant oatmeal. This cooks up just as fast and has all the nutrients left in it.

1. Stove top: In a sauce pan over medium-high heat, bring to a boil the water, milk and salt. Add the Splenda, cinnamon, and extract. Stir. Stir in the oats, flax and whey. Reduce heat to a simmer and cook for 5 minutes stirring occasionally. If it gets to thick add more water.

2. Microwave: Add all ingredients in a large bowl (big enough for handling the boiling bubbles without spilling over) stir well. Zap for 1 minute (or until it boils) and stir. Zap for another minute then stir. Let sit for 2 minutes then zap again for about 30 seconds. Let it cool a bit before eating.

I love this almost as much as Authentic Oatmeal (page 374). When I'm in weight loss mode, I have to be sure I'm only having this before a long rigorous hike with the dogs or some other strenuous physical activity. Otherwise it can blow my diet for days. However, I'm metabolically resistive so the average dieter should be able to handle this for breakfast more often than I can.

Per Serving: 238 Calories; 5g Fat; 32g Protein; 14g Carbohydrate; 5g Dietary Fiber

Hot Cereal

This low carb cereal is loaded with 12 grams of fiber per serving.

1	cup	wheat bran
1/2	cup	almond meal
1/2	cup	Whey protein powder
1/4	cup	flax seed meal
2	Tbsps	lecithin
1	Tbsp	cinnamon
1	Tbsp	psyllium husks
2	tsps	salt

Weight Loss

5 Servings
6g Net Carbs

Mix all ingredients and store in an air tight container in the refrigerator.

This makes 2 1/2 cups total. Each serving is 1/2 cup.

Per Serving: 284 Calories; 14g Fat; 26g Protein; 18g Carbs; 12g Dietary Fiber

To prepare one serving: In a microwave safe bowl, add 1/2 cup of the dry cereal and 1/2 cup of water. Zap for 1 minute then stir. Zap for one more minute. Stir and let sit for a minute or two. Serve with your choice of sweetener and low carb milk, if desired. (Be sure to add up all those carbs).

Almond Scones

Low carb scones are a great alternative to having eggs for breakfast.
These are quite high in protein containing both whey and almonds.

1	cup	whey protein powder
3	Tbsps	butter -- softened
2		eggs -- beaten
1/3	cup	Splenda®
2	tsps	almond extract
1/3	cup	almond meal
1	Tbsp	flax seed meal
1/4	cup	almonds -- chopped

Weight Loss

**4 Servings
5g Net Carbs**

Preheat oven to 375°F

1. Put the whey powder and butter in a mixing bowl and blend (a pastry cutter is useful here but a big wooden spoon will do the trick too if the butter is soft enough.)

2. Beat the eggs very well with a whisk or hand mixer. Add to the whey & butter mixing well.

3. Add the remaining ingredients and mix by hand.

4. On a parchment paper lined cookie sheet, place 4 heaps of batter. The batter will be quite gooey and will want to spread. Try to heap the batter as high as possible (I prefer log shape) and get them into the preheated oven quickly.

5. Bake at 375°F for 10 minutes. The bottoms will brown some but the tops will be a light buttery color.

I like to serve mine with a dollop of low carb jam (page 360), but cream cheese is really good too.

Put the extras in a plastic storage container. It will keep for about a week.

Yields 4 scones with 1 per serving

Per Serving: 468 Calories; 24g Fat; 52g Protein; 8g Carbohydrate; 3g Dietary Fiber

Pumpkin Spice Muffins

These low carb muffins are dense, moist and rich!
No soy or wheat in these marvels.

1/2	cup	Whey protein powder
1	cup	Splenda®
1	cup	pecans -- finely chopped
2	Tbsps	flax seed meal
1 ½	tsps	baking powder -- *See note
1 ½	tsps	cinnamon
1/2	tsp	ground allspice
1/4	tsp	ground ginger
1/4	tsp	salt
1/2	cup	butter -- melted
1		egg
1/2	tsp	vanilla extract
2/3	cup	canned pumpkin

Weight Loss

8 Servings
6g Net Carbs

* High Altitude cooking use 1 tsp baking powder.

You can buy chopped pecans but they are more course than I like for this recipe so run them through the food processor for a minute.

Preheat oven to 350°F

1. In a mixing bowl, mix together the whey, Splenda, pecans, flax seed, baking powder, cinnamon, ginger, allspice and salt.

2. In a large bowl, beat the egg. Add the pumpkin and vanilla extract. Stir until well incorporated. Add about 1/4 cup of the dry mixture and stir well. Add the melted butter and stir until well incorporated. Add the remaining dry ingredients.

3. Use a lightly buttered non-stick muffin tin (otherwise use parchment muffin cups). Divide the batter between 8 of the cups about 2/3 to 3/4 full. For larger muffins fill only 6, but then each muffin has 8g net carbs instead of 6g.

4. Bake in a 350°F oven for 15 minutes or until the wet gloss has vanished from the top of the muffins and they start to brown. Do not over cook. Let cool for 5 minutes in the tin before turning over to release them.

Turn these into dessert cup cakes by frosting them with Cream Cheese Icing (page 413). This will add 2g carb per cup cake.

Per Serving: 283 Calories; 23g Fat; 14g Protein; 9g Carbohydrate; 3g Dietary Fiber

Pumpkin Spice Cake: You can also make this into a cake by reducing the baking powder by 1/4 tsp and pouring the batter into a greased non-stick cake pan (9 inch round or 8x8 square), lightly dusted with 1 Tbsp of whey powder.

Walnut Muffins

These delicious low-carb muffins contain no flour and no soy!
They are less expensive to make compared to those specialty pre-packaged low-carb muffins mixes."

1/2	cup	Whey protein powder
1/2	cup	walnut -- finely chopped
6	Tbsps	Splenda®
2	Tbsps	flax seed meal
1	tsp	baking powder
1/2	tsp	vanilla extract
1	large	egg
2	Tbsps	walnut oil
1/4	cup	heavy cream
	pinch	salt

Weight Loss
4 Servings
5g Net Carbs

*High Altitude: reduce baking powder to 1/2 tsp.

Preheat oven to 350°F

1. To get 1/2 cup of finely chopped walnuts, put about 2/3 cup of walnut pieces into a food processor until about 1/3 of the walnuts are almost flour and the rest are no bigger than about this – O.

2. In a small bowl beat the egg with a pinch of salt. Add the cream, oil and the extract and beat again.

3. Blend together the whey, walnuts, Splenda, wheat bran and baking soda. Add the egg mixture and stir until well blended.

4. Insert 4 parchment paper baking cups into muffin tin. Spoon batter into the cups dividing evenly. Bake at 350°F for about 12-15 minutes until tops have risen and just started to brown. Do not over cook. Cool for 5-10 minutes before trying to peel the paper off.

Best served warm with butter. Store the extras in a plastic bag after they are completely cooled. Store for up to one week in the refrigerator.

Per Serving: 371 Calories; 25g Fat; 30g Protein; 8g Carbohydrate; 3g Dietary Fiber

Banana Walnut Muffins Variation: substitute banana extract for the vanilla extract. This has the same per serving analysis.

Raspberry Muffins Variation: Add 1/2 cup of raspberries after step 3.
6g net carbs, 379 Calories; 25g Fat; 30g Protein; 10g Carbohydrate; 4g Dietary Fiber

Blueberry Muffins Variation: Add 1/2 cup of blueberries after step 3.
8g net carbs, 381 Calories; 25g Fat; 30g Protein; 11g Carbohydrate; 3g Dietary Fiber

Waffles

These low carb waffles are light and crispy but they are surprisingly filling too.

Dry Mix

3/4	cup	whey protein powder
1/2	cup	almond meal
3	Tbsps	Splenda®
2	Tbsps	flax seed meal
1	Tbsp	wheat bran
1	Tbsp	lecithin -- optional
2	tsps	baking powder -- *See Note
1	tsp	cinnamon
1/2	tsp	salt

2	large	eggs
1/4	cup	water
1/4	cup	heavy cream
1/2	tsp	vanilla extract

<table>
<tr><td>Weight Loss</td></tr>
<tr><td>4 Servings
6g Net Carbs</td></tr>
</table>

*Note: For high altitude baking reduce baking powder to 1 tsp.

1. In a large mixing bowl mix together all the dry mix ingredients until thoroughly mixed.

   This dry mix will keep in an airtight jar for about 1 month if kept in the refrigerator.

2. Whip eggs in a mixing bowl. Add the water, cream and vanilla and whip again.

3. Add the dry mix and blend well.

4. Follow the directions of your waffle machine for preheating. I like to oil mine with butter which adds color and flavor. But it needs to be added just before the batter, so that it doesn't burn. Ladle the batter into the center of each waffle in the waffle iron.

Depending on the individual waffle size of your waffle iron, this should yield 8 to 12 waffles with 2 to 3 waffles per serving.

Serve with Maple Pecan Sauce, commercial low-carb syrup or a low carb jam. They are also good as a dessert with fresh strawberries and whipped cream

Per Serving: 402 Calories; 22g Fat; 42g Protein; 10g Carbs; 4g Dietary Fiber

Maple Pecan Sauce

This is the perfect compliment to your low carb waffles and pancakes.

1	cup	water
4	tsps	Maple flavoring
2/3	cup	Splenda®
1/2	tsp	guar gum
1/4	cup	pecan halves -- chopped
2	Tbsp	butter – optional

Weight Loss
4 Servings
6g Net Carbs

1. In a sauce pan combine the water, maple flavoring, Splenda and the guar gum. Stir until guar gum is completely dissolved.

2. Place the sauce pan over medium-high heat, stirring occasionally until it comes to a boil. Reduce heat to the lowest setting and add the chopped pecans and butter. Cook for 1 or 2 minutes to bring out the flavor of the pecans. Stir occasionally. If it gets too thick then just add some more water, stirring it in vigorously.

This yields ~1½ cups enough for 4 servings of waffles or pancakes.

Per Serving: 141 Calories; 15g Fat; 1g Protein; 7g Carbohydrate; 1g Dietary Fiber;

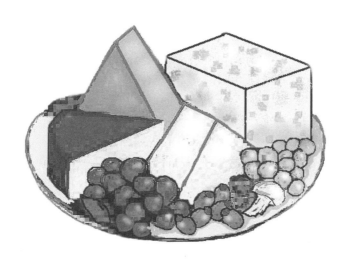

APPETIZERS
& SNACKS

APPEPTIZERS & SNACKS

~ REGARDING APPETIZERS ~

Sometimes we are at a loss to come up with appetizer ideas, particularly for parties and similar gatherings. But truly they are endless, even for the low carb dieter. Some ideas are so simple they do not warrant a recipe and listing variations could be monotonous. For example, celery is a great thing to stuff, but it seems silly to have a recipe that then lists, peanut butter or cream cheese or blue cheese or pimento cheese or hummus or ... well you get the point. So here is a list of things to consider that can be stuffed or that can be used flat to place some other yummy good thing upon. I hope this will help stimulate ides.

Things to Stuff
Artichoke hearts
Baby bell peppers
Belgian endive leaves
Bell pepper squares
Butter lettuce leaves
Celery
Cucumber cups (page 119)
Jalapeno pepper halves
Mushrooms
- Fresh
- Grilled
- Roasted
- Marinated
Pork skin rinds
Radicchio leaves
Strawberries
Tomatoes hallowed out
Zucchini cups (page 110)

Flat Things
Artichoke hearts
Basil leaves
Bell pepper squares
Cheese crackers (page109)
Cheese slices
Cucumber slices
Jicama slices
Lettuce leaves
Pepperoni slices
Strawberry slices
Tomato slices
Turnip slices - grilled
Zucchini slices

And then there are non-edible things that you can use like artichoke leaves, squares of banana leaves, avocado skins, sea shells, tiny saucers, sake cups, and don't forget skewers and toothpicks. Let your imagination soar.

Cajun Crab Boats

Endive leaves stuffed with spicy crab salad.
Omit the jalapeno for a much milder version.

2	heads	Belgian endive
6	oz	canned crab -- drained
1/2	cup	red bell pepper -- minced
2		scallion -- minced
1	stalk	celery -- minced
1		jalapeno -- seeded and minced
2	Tbsp	mayonnaise
2	Tbsp	sour cream
1	Tbsp	lemon juice
1	tsp	Cajun seasoning

Induction
8 Servings
2g Net Carbs

1. Remove the stem and seeds from the jalapeno and mince it as finely as you can. Toss it with the minced bell peppers, celery and scallions. Add the drained crab meat and toss.

2. In a small bowl combine the mayonnaise, sour cream, lemon juice and Cajun seasoning. Mix well and then stir into the crab mixture.

3. Separate the leaves from the endive. You should be able to get 8 or more nice leaves from each head. Spoon a generous portion of the crab mixture onto each leaf. Arrange on a platter and serve.

Yields 16 boats with 2 boats per serving

Per Serving: 82 Calories; 4g Fat; 6g Protein; 6g Carbohydrate; 4g Dietary Fiber

Brie Cheese with Cranberry Chutney

This appetizer is fun for the holidays but it is an
unexpected treat any time of the year.

3/4	cup	Cranberry Chutney -- page 357
12	ozs	brie cheese -- sliced
6		red tip lettuce leaves

Induction
12 Servings
2g Net Carbs

Since the fat in the brie cheese will cut the heat in the chutney you may want to consider adding an additional jalapeno to the chutney or slice a jalapeno paper thin and use as a garnish.

1. Prepare the Cranberry Chutney from page 357. You'll only need half of it for this recipe so you decide if you want left-overs or would like to cut the ingredient portions in half. If making a half batch I recommend keeping the

whole jalapeno and using 2 tablespoons of Splenda (just 1 tsp more than half of 1/3 cup).

2. Rinse and pat dry the lettuce leaves. Remove the base of the rib. Tear or cut into squares which will be the base of each appetizer. You want them big enough so people can grab onto it easily but not so big that it looks weird. Butter lettuce leaves are good for this too, as is radicchio or Belgian endive. But the green leaf is especially appropriate for the holidays.

3. Place 1/2 oz slices on each lettuce square and then top with about 1/2 tablespoon of the chutney.

If you think it needs a garnish consider a thin slice of jalapeno, a walnut or pecan half, a sliver of green bell pepper or a leave of cilantro or mint.

Yields 24 appetizers with 2 per serving

Per Serving: 110 Calories; 8g Fat; 6g Protein; 4g Carbohydrate; 2g Dietary Fiber

Tapenade on Pepper Squares

This olive relish made with fresh herbs is an elegant and delicious appetizer served on squares of bell peppers

1	cup	black olives -- pitted
2	cloves	garlic
1	Tbsp	capers
1	Tbsp	fresh lemon juice
2	tsp	extra virgin olive oil
1/2	tsp	fresh thyme
1/2	tsp	fresh oregano
1/2	tsp	fresh rosemary
2		red bell peppers
4	sprigs	cilantro – for garnish

Induction
8 Servings
3g Net Carbs

1. Place everything except the bell pepper and cilantro into a food processor and pulse a few times until it is a blended chunky relish. Do not over process into a smooth paste.

2. Remove the stems and cut the bell peppers in half. Remove the seeds and membrane. Cut each half into 4 pieces.

3. Spoon about 1 tablespoon of tapenade onto each pepper square. Garnish with 2 or 3 whole leaves of cilantro.

As a variation, use Greek olives and garnish with crumbles of feta cheese.

Yields 16 pepper squares with 2 per serving

Per Serving: 42 Calories; 3g Fat; 1g Protein; 4g Carbohydrate; 1g Dietary Fiber

Turkey Rolls

These fun appetizers look like sushi rolls when presented on a platter. The classic blend of blue cheese and walnuts makes this a favorite.

10	slices	turkey
8	oz	cream cheese
6	oz	blue cheese -- crumbled
8	oz	walnuts -- chopped
1	stalk	celery – finely minced

Induction

10 Servings
3g Net Carbs

Purchasing turkey slices that are perfectly rectangular makes assembly much easier and the presentation more uniform. If the turkey rolls are served whole (instead of cut into fourths) then you can use the higher quality turkey slices from the deli. One pound of sliced turkey usually has about 10 slices so this will make about 40 appetizers (at less than 1 gram each!).

1. Soften the cream cheese by letting it sit out for an hour or by zapping it in the microwave for a few seconds.

2. Dice the walnuts and celery into fairly small bits. You can try using a food processor if yours will actually dice and not puree.

3. Blend together the cream cheese and the blue cheese. Add the walnuts and celery and stir together.

4. Layout some paper towels to work on. Place several slices of turkey on the paper towels. It is easier to make several at a time instead of one after another. At the shorter end of the turkey slices place about 2 heaping tablespoons of the filling in a log shape about the size of a roll of dimes. Be sure the filling goes evenly across the small end.

5. Carefully roll up the turkey slice, spending some time at the beginning to be sure to make a uniform thickness. When each is completely rolled up, check the ends and pack in any filling that is coming out or add more filling to the ends; again to assure uniformity.

6. Cover and refrigerate for at least an hour (or overnight) before slicing. This will make it easier to slice without the filling gushing out.

7. Use a serrated knife and be sure to cut carefully to keep the shape intact. First cut each roll in half then each of those in half. Display the rolls on a platter with the cut ends up.

Yields 40 appetizers with 4 per serving

Per Serving: 327 Calories; 26g Fat; 21g Protein; 4g Carbohydrate; 1g Dietary Fiber

Lunch Variation: These also make a great take-a-long lunch. Make them as above but do not slice them. Put three whole rolls in a baggie and take them to work (9 grams of net carbs).

9g net carbs; 1092 Calories; 88g Fat 70g Protein; 13g Carbohydrate; 4g Dietary Fiber

Cranberry Variation: Add 1/4 cup chopped dried cranberries. The extra carbs depends on the brand that you get. I get unsweetened ones at the health food store and let them soak in 1/4 cup of water mixed with a tablespoon of Splenda. This method will add about 1g net carbs per serving as an appetizer or 2g net carbs for the lunch of 3 rolls.

4g net carbs; 334 Calories; 26g Fat; 21g Protein; 6g Carbohydrate; 2g Dietary Fiber

Salmon Boats

These appetizers are pretty on a tray but they are also good
as a garnish for a simple meat and veggie dinner plate.

4	oz	**smoked salmon lox**
4	oz	**cream cheese**
1	head	**endive**
1	tsp	**lemon juice**
1	oz	**alfalfa sprouts**
1	sprig	**fresh dill**

Induction

8 Servings
1g Net Carbs

1. Soften cream cheese by zapping it in the microwave for a few seconds. Blend in the lemon juice. Using about 80% of the lox (the remainder is used for a garnish) blend into the cream cheese using a fork or spoon. If you would like a brighter pink color add 1/2 tsp (or more) of the Carb Options™ French Dressing.

2. Separate the endive leaves. You should be able to get 8 to 10 good whole leaves.

3. To construct. Place a pinch of sprouts on each endive leaf, all laying the same direction. Use a melon baller or a rounded tablespoon to add a scoop of the cream cheese/salmon mixer. Place a little strip of the lox on top and a tiny bit of dill on top of that.

4. Serve right away or cover and refrigerate until needed.

Yields 8 boats with 1 per serving

Per Serving: 79 Calories; 6g Fat; 5g Protein; 3g Carbohydrate; 2g Dietary Fiber

Fried Green Tomatoes

This Southern delight is primarily for the home gardener, since green tomatoes are rarely found in a market. If you have a friend or neighbor growing tomatoes chances are they have more than they can use and might be willing to give you a few. These can also be used as a vegetable side dish or even as a garnish. Do not try this with ripe tomatoes or you'll end up with mush.

2	large	green tomatoes
1		egg
1/2	cup	parmesan cheese -- grated
1	tsp	garlic powder
1/8	tsp	cayenne pepper – to taste
		canola oil
		salt -- to taste

Induction
6 Servings
3g Net Carbs

1. Rinse tomatoes and remove the stem portion. Cut into slices about 1/3 inch thick. You should be able to get 5 or 6 slices from each tomato. If your tomatoes are small, add a third tomato to the recipe.

2. In a small, flat bowl beat the egg thoroughly. Set aside.

3. On a plate or shallow dish, mix together the parmesan cheese, garlic powder and cayenne pepper.

4. In a frying pan over medium high heat, add enough canola oil to just cover the bottom about a 1/8 inch high or less.

5. Using your left hand, soak a tomato slice in the egg, then place it on the plate with the cheese. Using your right hand, dredge both sides of the tomato through the cheese. Lightly pat it to encourage the cheese to stick. Set aside or place directly in the fry pan. Using separate hands for the wet and dry portions keeps you from getting too messy. Repeat with each slice.

6. Fry the tomato slices until a medium brown. Turn over carefully and fry the other side. Remove the slices to a paper towel and lightly salt them immediately. Serve within a minute or two.

Try changing the spices to compliment your entree. For example, try an Italian spice mix (oregano, thyme, parsley, rosemary and garlic) or a southwestern blend (cumin, garlic, chili powder, cilantro and black pepper). A lemon pepper blend is also good. Use your imagination and have fun with it.

Yields ~ 12 slices with 2 per serving

Per Serving: 57 Calories; 3g Fat; 4g Protein; 4g Carbohydrate; 1g Dietary Fiber

Stuffed Mushrooms

Roasted mushrooms are always a great appetizer.
Here are a few options for the stuffing.

12		mushroom caps
3	ozs	cream cheese
6		olives -- minced
1	pinch	garlic powder

Induction

6 Servings
3g Net Carbs

I like to use crimmi mushrooms, but the white button mushrooms are good too.

1. Remove the caps and place on a foil lined sheet pan (for easy clean-up). The caps should be like domes not bowls so the liquid will not pool up inside. Place under the broiler for about 3 minutes. Remove and let cool.

2. To make the stuffing: soften the cream cheese by zapping in the microwave for a few seconds. Mince the olives and add to the cream cheese along with the garlic power and stir well.

3. Spoon or pipe the cream cheese into each cap.

I like to serve them right away at room temp, but you can cover them and refrigerate them for s few hors ahead of serving time.

Yields 12 mushrooms with 2 per serving

Per Serving: 72 Calories; 6g Fat; 3g Protein; 4g Carbohydrate; 1g Dietary Fiber

There are an infinite number of things that can be stuffed into roasted mushrooms. Here are just a few more ideas.

Roasted Red Pepper Dip: Use 1/2 cup of the Roasted Red Pepper Dip (page 117) and spoon it into each mushroom cap.
4g net carbs; 50 Calories; 3g Fat; 2g Protein; 5g Carbohydrate; 1g Dietary Fiber;

Sausage Stuffing: Cook 1/2 lb turkey sausage with 2 minced scallions. Drain off the fat and stir in 2 Tbsp of Carb Options™ French Dressing. Sprinkle a pinch of Parmesan cheese on top of each. Serve as is or put under the broiler to melt the cheese.
3g net carbs; 195 Calories; 6g Fat; 7g Protein; 4g Carbohydrate; 1g Dietary Fiber

Gorgonzola with Walnuts: Mix together 3 ozs of gorgonzola cheese with 1 tbsp sour cream and 3 Tbsps of chopped walnuts.
3g net carbs; 97 Calories; 8g Fat; 6g Protein; 4g Carbohydrate; 1g Dietary Fiber

Stuffed Jalapeno Peppers

Jalapeno peppers stuffed with a spicy cream cheese mixture. These are similar to poppers but they are not fried. They are crunchy, zesty and are very low carb.

8	large	jalapeno chili peppers
4	ozs	cream cheese
1/4	tsp	garlic powder
1/4	tsp	chili powder

Induction
4 Servings
2g Net Carbs

1. Cut off the stems and cut each pepper in half lengthwise. Cut or scoop out all the seeds and membrane (this where all the heat is and where you get to decide how spicy to make these appetizers). I prefer to discard all the seeds and to finely mince ~1/3 of the membrane to add to the cream cheese.

2. In a small microwave safe bowl, add the cream cheese and pepper membrane (if using). Zap for ~30 seconds or until soft enough to stir. Add the chili power and garlic powder. Stir well. Spoon or pipe the cream cheese mixture into each pepper half.

Serve at once or cover and refrigerate until needed (up to a day in advance).

Yields 16 appetizers with 4 halves per serving.

Per Serving: 108 Calories; 10g Fat; 3g Protein; 3g Carbohydrate; 1g Dietary Fiber

Sliced Peppers with Chipotle Dipping Sauce

Great for a party or to keep in the refrigerator for a quick snack.

3		bell pepper -- green, red, orange
1/2	cup	mayonnaise
1/2	cup	sour cream
3		chipotle chilies -- canned in adobo
1	pinch	salt

Induction
6 Servings
3g Net Carbs

1. To make the chipotle sauce you can either mince the chilies (with a bit of the sauce from the can), stir it into the mayo and sour cream or you can put all 3 ingredients in a food processor or blender. Taste before you add the salt for it might not need it depending on your brand of Chipotle. If it is too spicy (wait for the heat, it is slow to arrive) then simply add more mayo or sour cream. If the heat is right but the sauce is too thick then add a bit of water. Of course if you want more heat then add more chipotle (only 0.5g net carbs/Tbsp). Set aside.

2. Slice the peppers into about 12 strips each.

Yields ~36 pepper slices and ~1 cup dipping sauce. One serving is 6 pepper slices with ~ 3 Tbsps of sauce (or ~ 1 1/2 tsp of sauce for each pepper)

Per Serving: 189 Calories; 20g Fat; 2g Protein; 5g Carbohydrate; 2g Dietary Fiber

Mini Herb Quiche

These mini quiche are always a big hit at parties.

3/4	cup	almond meal
6	Tbsps	Parmesan cheese
1/2	tsp	garlic powder
6	Tbsps	butter -- melted
1	tsp	Just Whites
1	Tbsp	water

8		eggs
1/2	tsp	salt
1/4	cup	heavy cream
1	Tbsp	herbs -- oregano, thyme, rosemary and parsley
2/3	cup	cheddar cheese -- grated

Induction
12 Servings
1g Net Carbs

You will need those mini muffin tins (each mold holds about 2 Tbsp). This recipe makes 2 dozen mini quiche.

Preheat oven to 325°F

1. Mix together the almond meal, parmesan cheese and garlic powder. Mix in the butter.

2. Using a fork or whisk, mix together the water with the powdered egg whites until all dissolved and frothy. Add to the almonds. Mix well.

3. Spoon out 1 tsp of the crust mixture into each of the muffin molds and press down firmly. Bake at 325°F for 5 minutes. Remove and let cool.

4. Meanwhile, beat together the eggs with the salt. Add the cream and the herbs and beat again.

5. Spoon in 1 Tbsp per muffin mold. Top with a pinch of cheddar cheese. Bake at 325°F for 20 minutes or until they have risen above the edges and no longer jiggle. Remove from oven and allow to cool for 15-20 minutes (or until cool enough to handle).

6. Using a thin bladed knife or tooth pick, go around the edge of each mini quiche to loosen it. Turn over onto paper towels. Arrange on a platter and serve.

These are best served warm. If you need to make them in advance you can reheat them in the microwave to serve.

Yields 24 mini quiche with 2 per serving

Per Serving: 189 Calories; 17g Fat; 8g Protein; 2g Carbohydrate; 1g Dietary Fiber

Spicy Chicken Wings

This recipe is for the Jamaican jerk style wings which are extremely hot.
Milder variations are also offered.

3	lbs	chicken wings
1/2	cup	onion -- chopped
1/4	cup	canola oil
2	cloves	garlic
1		Scotch bonnet pepper
1	Tbsp	soy sauce
1	tsp	ground allspice
1	tsp	black pepper
1/2	tsp	dried thyme
1/2	tsp	cinnamon
1/2	tsp	salt
1/4	tsp	nutmeg -- freshly grated

> **Induction**
>
> **6 Servings**
> **2g Net Carbs**

You can use any type of hot peppers that are available to you. The Scotch bonnet peppers are the traditional type used in Jamaica; they are extremely hot. If using jalapeno peppers then use at least two of them. Be sure to remove the seeds since they are typically bitter. The membrane is what adds the most heat and is optional depending upon your tastes.

1. Cut the wings at the joints. Discard the point sections or save them in the freeze for when you next make stock.

2. Add to a food processor or a blender all ingredients except for the chicken wings. Pulse until it forms a paste.

3. Place the chicken wings in a large bowl, pour the marinade over the chicken. Toss until each wing is coated completely. Cover and refrigerate for at least one hour but preferably overnight. Toss the wings a few times while they marinade.

4. Use an oiled rack over a roasting pan. Arrange the wings in a single layer, spoon the marinade over them. Bake them in a preheated 400°F oven for 30 to 35 minutes, or until they are cooked through.

Yields about 36 pieces with 6 per serving

Per Serving: 367 Calories; 29g Fat; 23g Protein; 3g Carbohydrate; 1g Dietary Fiber

The following variations alter the marinade ingredients. Then prepare as above.

Tequila -Lime: 1/2 cup onion, 1/4 cup canola oil, 1/4 cup tequila, 2 T lime juice, 1 tsp chili powder, 1 tsp lemon pepper, 1/2 tsp salt
2g net carbs; 382 Calories; 29g Fat; 23g Protein; 2g Carbohydrate; trace Dietary Fiber

Spicy BBQ: 1/2 cup onion, 1/2 cup Carb Options™ Barbeque Sauce, 1 tsp chili powder, few dashes of Tabasco
3g net carbs; 285 Calories; 20g Fat; 23g Protein; 3g Carbohydrate; trace Dietary Fiber

Spicy Asian: 1/2 cup onion, 1/4 cup sesame oil, 1/4 cup soy sauce, 1 Tbsp freshly grated ginger, 1/4 tsp dry mustard, 1/4 tsp Tabasco sauce, 1/2 tsp salt
2g net carbs; 365 Calories; 29g Fat; 23g Protein; 2g Carbohydrate; trace Dietary Fiber

Parmesan Wings

Are you tired of the same ole spicy wings?
Then try this addictively delicious variation.

2	lb	chicken wings
1/2	cup	Parmesan cheese -- grated
1	tsp	dried oregano
1/2	tsp	paprika
1/2	tsp	garlic powder
1/4	cup	butter (1/2 stick)

Induction

4 Servings
1g Net Carbs

Preheat oven to 350ºF. Prepare one or two cookie sheets by lining them with either aluminum foil or parchment paper.

1. Cut the wings at the joints. Discard the point sections or save them in the freeze for when you next make stock.

2. In a shallow bowl, mix together the parmesan cheese, oregano, paprika and garlic powder.

3. In another bowl, melt the butter by zapping it in the microwave for about 1 minute until completely melted.

4. Dip a few pieces in the butter. Shake off the excess butter and then roll them in the cheese mixture coating them well. Place on the baking sheet. Repeat until all the pieces have been coated. Arrange them on the cookie sheets so that they are not too crowded.

5. Bake for 30 minutes turn them over and bake another 30 minutes. Serve hot.

Yields about 24 pieces with 6 pieces per serving

Per Serving: 285 Calories; 24g Fat; 17g Protein; 1g Carbs; trace Dietary Fiber

Huevos Diablo

These spicy deviled eggs are great as an appetizer or as an accompaniment to a salad. When serving at a party, let people know to expect some heat by garnishing the platter with dried, red chili peppers.

6		eggs -- hard boiled
6	Tbsps	mayonnaise
1	med	chipotle chili canned in adobo
2	tsps	adobo sauce -- or to taste
		salt -- to taste
12	whole	cilantro leaves – as a garnish

Induction

6 Servings
1g Net Carbs

1. See page 61 for how to prepare the hard boiled egg. Peel and slice the eggs into halves. Scoop the yolk out of the whites.

2. Mince the chipotle pepper (with whatever sauce clings to it). In a small bowl, mix together the mayonnaise, egg yolk and chipotle pepper. Taste to test for heat (and does it need salt); it should be quite mild at this point. Add more adobo sauce to taste. I generally need 1 or 2 more teaspoons worth. But feel free to add another chilies if you prefer (only 0.5g net carbs per Tbsp).

3. Spoon or pipe the yolk mixture into the whites. Garnish each with a single, whole cilantro leaf.

Yields 12 appetizers with 2 per serving

Per Serving: 177 Calories; 17g Fat; 6g Protein; 1g Carbs; trace Dietary Fiber

Ham & Swiss Roll Ups

These are perfect for a quick snack or with a salad for lunch

2	slices	Swiss cheese slices
4	slices	deli-style fat free ham slices
1	tsp	mustard
2	tsps	mayonnaise
2	Tbsps	alfalfa sprouts

Induction

1 Servings
2g Net Carbs

The long rectangular slices of cheese works the best here. Let the cheese come to room temperature for ease of rolling.

1. Place the cheese on flat surface, placing two slices of ham onto each slice of cheese. Smear the ham with the mustard and mayo.

2. Put a pinch of sprouts at the end of each and then roll up. Secure with a toothpick if needed.

The mustard and mayonnaise help hold the sprouts in side, but if you are going to eat this on the run then use lettuce instead of sprouts.

Per Serving: 383 Calories; 24g Fat; 37g Protein; 2g Carbs; trace Dietary Fiber

Ham Cubes with Orange Mustard Sauce

Simple and wonderful sauce great for baking a ham
or as a dipping sauce for cooked ham, as presented here

1	lb	ham -- cubed
1	head	cauliflower -- blanched
		lettuce leaves -- as garnish
1/2	cup	brown mustard
1	Tbsp	Splenda®
1	tsp	orange extract

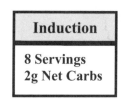

Induction

8 Servings
2g Net Carbs

I love orange mustard! I am so surprised that you can't buy it in a jar. Before I went low carb, I'd just mix orange marmalade with mustard. This is just about as easy and as tasty.

Be cautious of precooked hams; they almost always have some carbs. Check the labels and find a brand that it <1g carbs per serving. The ham can be heated in the microwave or oven or it can be served cold straight out of the refrigerator.

1. Put the Splenda in a bowl, add the orange extract and the mustard and stir.

2. Cut up the head of cauliflower into flowerets and blanch them by immersing them in a big pot of boiling water for 1 minute, drain and then plunge them into iced water to stop the cooking. Drain.

3. Line a platter with whole lettuce leaves. Place the bowl of orange mustard in the center and then evenly distribute the cauliflower flowerets and ham cubes on the lettuce. Place a jar of fancy toothpicks next to the platter.

Yields about 16 cubes of ham & 16 flowerets of cauliflower with 2 pieces of each per serving

Per Serving: 92 Calories; 4g Fat; 12g Protein; 2g Carbohydrate; trace Dietary Fiber

Crab Cakes with Lemon Aioli

These are outstanding appetizer to serve at a party. Very attractive when baked in a sea shell but can be served in traditional cakes too.

Crab Cakes

1	lb	lump crabmeat
1/2	cup	red and green bell pepper
3		scallion
1/4	cup	celery
1		egg
4	Tbsps	mayonnaise
2	tsps	Dijon mustard
1/2	tsp	Worcestershire sauce
1/4	tsp	Old Bay seasoning
1/4	tsp	lemon pepper
1/8	tsp	garlic powder
1/4	cup	parmesan cheese

Induction

10 Servings
2g Net Carbs

Lemon Aioli

1	cup	mayonnaise
2	Tbsps	lemon juice
2	tsps	paprika
1/2	tsp	garlic powder
1/2	tsp	lemon pepper

I have a bunch of clam shells that I frequently use as mini saucers for appetizers. Oyster, mussel or scallops shells are nice too. But you could also serve these on their own individual leaf of lettuce, radicchio or Belgian endive.

Preheat oven to 350°F

1. Make the aioli first. In a small bowl mix together 1 cup of mayonnaise, lemon juice, paprika, garlic powder, and lemon pepper. Taste to see if you want to add any salt. Cover and chill while you make the crab cakes.

2. If the crab meat is canned drain it well. If frozen be sure it is completely thawed and let it drain also.

3. Finely mince the peppers, scallions and celery. Take your time with this; you want the pieces rather small which helps keep the cakes held together.

4. In a mixing bowl add 4 Tbsp of mayonnaise, mustard, Worcestershire sauce, lemon pepper and garlic powder. Mix well. Mix in the peppers, scallions, celery and parmesan cheese. Then fold in the crab meat (try not to break it up too much).

5. To bake on shells be sure that you have sterilized 20 shells first by boiling them for about 5 minutes. If they won't lie flat, then make a bed of rock salt on a sheet pan and twist the shells down until they are flat. Or use aluminum foil and scrunched it up to form cradles for each of the shells. Clam shell usually flay flat so they don't need the salt bed or foil. Arrange 5 rows with 4 shells in each row. Spoon out a bit of the crab mixture into each shell and bake for 8 - 10 minutes (or until golden brown).

6. If you don't use sea shells, then line a sheet pan with parchment paper and spoon out crab mixture and form cakes. Place into 5 rows with 4 crab cakes per row. Bake for 8 - 10 minutes (or until golden brown).

7. Let cool before serving. I usually serve at room temperature. Arrange on a platter. Garnish each crab cake with a dollop of the lemon aioli on top or serve on the side such as in a small bowl in the center of the platter of crab cakes.

Makes 20 crab cakes with 2 per serving.

Per Serving: 260 Calories; 25g Fat; 10g Protein; 2g Carbs; trace Dietary Fiber

Main Course Variation: You can also make this into 8 larger crab cakes and use them as a main course for 2 people (4 cakes each)
7g net carbs; 1299 Calories; 125g Fat; 51g Protein; 9g Carbohydrate; 2g Dietary Fiber.

Cocktail Shrimp on Endive

Belgian endive makes a wonderful, natural, individual
saucer for this shrimp cocktail

1	lb	cocktail shrimp, cooked
2	heads	Belgian endive
1/4	cup	mayonnaise
1/4	cup	sour cream
3	Tbsps	Italian parsley -- or cilantro
2	Tbsps	red bell pepper -- finely minced
1	Tbsp	caper -- chopped
1/2	tsp	dried oregano
1/4	tsp	garlic powder -- to taste

Induction

**8 Servings
1g Net Carbs**

Your shrimp must be cooked. I like to use the tiny shrimp from the grocery store fresh fish department. But you could use frozen or canned just as easily.

1. Finely mince the parsley (or cilantro) and the bell peppers. Rinse and drain the capers then coarsely chop them.

2. In a mixing bowl, add the mayo, sour cream, parsley, peppers, capers, oregano and garlic powder. Mix well. Toss in the shrimp and mix. Cover and refrigerate for at least 1 hour.

3. Separate, rinse and dry the individual endive leaves. You should be able to get 8 - 10 perfect leaves per head. (Use the torn and tiny ones in your next salad). Spoon some of the shrimp into each leaf and arrange on a platter.

This looks best when there are other appetizers on the platter too. Try a relish tray in the middle with roasted bell pepper strips, olives and tiny dill pickles.

Yields 16 appetizers with two per serving

Per Serving: 144 Calories; 8g Fat; 14g Protein; 5g Carbohydrate; 4g Dietary Fiber

Chicken Satay

This traditional Indonesia dish makes a wonderful appetizer.
These will be quite popular so consider making a double batch.

4		chicken breasts -- boned and skinned
24		wooden skewers
2	tsps	coriander -- ground
2	tsps	cumin powder
2	Tbsps	sesame oil
2	cloves	garlic -- crushed
1/2	tsp	chili powder
1/2	cup	peanut butter -- smooth
2	cups	water
1	Tbsp	soy sauce
1	Tbsp	lemon juice
2	Tbsps	Dannon's Carb Control™ Yogurt -- vanilla

> ### Induction
>
> **8 Servings**
> **3g Net Carbs**

Making the Sauce:

1. In a dry pan over medium-high heat, add the coriander and cumin stirring until they are toasted and fragrant (less than a minute).

2. Add sesame oil, garlic and chili powder. Stir for a minute. Then add the peanut butter and stir. Then add the water, soy sauce, and lemon juice. Stir until it boils then reduce heat and simmer until thickens. Remove from heat.

3. Separate the sauce into two equal portions. One is for brushing onto the chicken. The second portion, once it has cooled, is mixed with the yogurt and used for dipping.

Making the Satays:

1. Be sure to soak the skewers before using them, so that they don't burn. Place them in a baking pan and cover with water for at least 30 minutes (but overnight is better).

2. Place 1 boneless chicken breast between two sheets of plastic wrap and using a smooth mallet, pound to flatten the chicken until about 1/4 inch thick. Repeat. Several common items can be used instead of a mallet such as a small cast iron frying pan, the side of a wine bottle, a rolling pin, etc.

3. Slice each chicken breast into thin strips. You should be able to get about 6 strips per breast half.

4. Weave the chicken strips onto the skewers. Try to get at least 4 punctures per strip.

5. Arrange skewers in a single layer in a broiling pan. Brush thoroughly with the brushing sauce. Cover and refrigerate for 20-30 minutes. Brush chicken again just prior to cooking.

6. Preheat either the broiler or the grill.

7. Broil or grill for 1-2 minutes per side.

8. Serve warm with the reserved dipping sauce.

Yields 24 skewers with 3 per serving.

Per Serving: 198 Calories; 13g Fat; 18g Protein; 4g Carbohydrate; 1g Dietary Fiber

Main Course Variation: Serve 4 people with 6 skewers each. Consider serving with Mock Fried Rice (page 179) or Pan Fried Cabbage (page 176).
6g net carbs; 395 Calories; 25g Fat; 36g Protein; 8g Carbohydrate; 2g Dietary Fiber;

Herbal Cheese Crackers

Fried shredded cheese makes wonderful crackers as a snack, as a base for an appetizer or as a garnish for a salad. These are so simple and very low carb.

1	cup	**shredded parmesan cheese**
1	tsp	**oregano**
1/2	tsp	**garlic powder**
1/2	tsp	**thyme**

Induction
4 Servings
1g Net Carbs

Shredded cheese works so much better than grated cheese. The lacy effect is part of the appeal.

1. In a small bowl, toss together the cheese and herbs.

2. Heat a non-stick skillet over medium heat. Sprinkle two or three little circles of the cheese blend, about 1 heaping Tbsp worth. Allow to heat until the edges start to turn a light golden brown, then flip with a spatula. Brown the other side. The transfer to a paper towel and repeat with remain cheese.

3. The cracker is easy to mold as soon as it comes out of the skillet. Lay them on top of spice jars or shot glasses to form a nicely curved cracker great for stuffing.

Yields about 12 crackers with 3 crackers per serving

Per Serving: 86 Calories; 5g Fat; 8g Protein; 1g Carbohydrate; trace Dietary Fiber

Variations are endless! Just change the herbs or eliminate the herbs altogether.
Chive Crackers: Use about 1 Tbsp of fresh snipped chives with the cheese
Spicy Crackers: Replace herbs with 2 tsp Cajun spices
Old Bay Crackers: Replace herbs with 2 tsp of Old Bay Spices (great for seafood appetizers).

Zucchini Barrels with Ravigote

Small zukes cut into barrels, scooped out and filled with an herb and onion relish

4		zucchini
		Ravigote
1/4	cup	red onion -- coarsely chopped
1	Tbsp	capers -- rinsed and drained
1	Tbsp	fresh parsley -- chopped
1	Tbsp	fresh chives -- chopped
1	Tbsp	fresh tarragon -- chopped
1/2	tsp	black pepper -- freshly ground
1/4	tsp	salt -- to taste
2	Tbsps	red wine vinegar
3	Tbsps	extra virgin olive oil

Induction
9 Servings
2g Net Carbs

Try to find zucchini that are long and narrow, as they make the best barrels. Depending on the size you may need a 5th zucchini. Use a mix of green and yellow zucchini for a more interesting presentation.

1. First you'll want to make the ravigote. Be sure to rinse and drain the capers otherwise they are too salty. Mix together the capers with the chopped onions, parsley, chives, tarragon salt and pepper. Toss. Drizzle with the vinegar and oil. Toss. Let sit for about 30 minutes before serving.

1. Meanwhile; slice off the stem and blossom ends of the zucchini. Slice the zukes into 1 inch long segments. You should get 4 to 5 segments per juke. Ideally you will have 18 total. Try to make them as uniform as possible. Cut one and then use it as a guide to cut the rest.

2. Optional step. I like to lightly blanch the zucchini if I will be serving them right away. But if you are making them ahead of time then they can get too soggy. To blanch: bring a pot of water to a boil while you make an ice bath, which is just a huge bowl with ice water with plenty of ice cubes. In two batches, blanch the zukes in the boiling water for 30 seconds, scoop out and put into the ice bath for 30 seconds. Place in a colander to drain.

3. With a spoon or melon baller, scoop out (and discard) some of the zucchini flesh to form a cup to hold the ravigote. Drain the ravigote and spoon out 2 tsp per zucchini cup. Arrange on a platter, cover and chill for 1 hour.

Sprigs of fresh herbs help garnish the platter.

Yields about 18 barrels with 2 barrels per serving

Per Serving: 56 Calories; 5g Fat; 1g Protein; 3g Carbohydrate; 1g Dietary Fiber

Variation: Substitute 3/4 cup of fresh, chunky salsa for the ravigote. Drain off its liquids, then spoon into the zucchini barrels.
3g Net Carbs; 18 Calories; trace Fat; 1g Protein; 4g Carbohydrate; 1g Dietary Fiber.

Baba Ghanoush

This wonderful dip is made with roasted eggplant, tahini, lemon and lots of roasted garlic. Even if you don't usually like eggplant, you just may love this. It is the perfect starter for a Middle Eastern dinner.

1	large	eggplant
1	head	garlic
1	Tbsp	refined olive oil
2	Tbsp	lemon juice
2	Tbsp	tahini
1	tsp	Splenda® -- optional
		salt and pepper -- to taste

Weight Loss

6 Servings
4g Net Carbs

I like to serve this with generous strips of green, red and orange bell peppers for dipping. (Remember that each bell pepper is about 6g net carbs). It is also good stuffed into mushroom, celery or cherry tomatoes.

Preheat the oven to 375°F

1. Pierce the skin of the eggplant in 6 to 10 places with a knife. This will prevent the eggplant from exploding. Place on a roasting pan. Place in a 375°F oven and roast for 30 minutes.

2. With good knife, cut off the top 1/2 inch of the head of garlic exposing the fleshy tops of most of the cloves. Thoroughly coat the garlic with the olive oil and place on the roasting pan next to the eggplant for the last 20 minutes of cooking. Remove eggplant and garlic and let cool.

3. Once the eggplant is cool enough to handle, peel off and discard the skin and place the flesh in a colander and allow it drain for about 10 minutes.

4. Meanwhile, pull apart the garlic cloves. A simple squeeze at the bottom of each clove should easily render the roasted flesh. Set this aside. (You probably won't use all of the roasted garlic for this recipe so store the remainder in a small jar and drizzle olive oil over it. Try to use it up within a few days.)

5. I prefer to mix this in a food processor but it can be done by hand too. Add the eggplant, lemon juice, tahini and about 2 or 3 tsps of the roasted garlic. Blend well. Taste test and add more garlic if desired as well as some salt and pepper. If the eggplant is a little bitter, then add a tsp of Splenda.

Yields ~2 cups with 1/3 cup per serving

Per Serving: 72 Calories; 5g Fat; 2g Protein; 6g Carbohydrate; 2g Dietary Fiber

Blue Cheese Artichoke Dip

Just a little blue cheese adds a wonderful depth of flavor to this traditional dip.
It can be baked for a winter dish or serve cold for a summer dish.

10	ozs	canned artichoke hearts
2	Tbsps	mayonnaise
2/3	cup	sour cream
2	Tbsps	blue cheese -- crumbled
	dash	garlic powder
	dash	black pepper
2	Tbsps	walnut -- chopped, as garnish

Weight Loss
6 Servings
4g Net Carbs

1. Drain the liquids from the artichokes. Finely chop the artichokes and add to a small bowl. If fixing the cold version, then zap the artichokes in the microwave for about 1 minute, stir and then zap another minute. If fixing the baked version then you can skip the microwave zapping.

2. Mix into the artichokes the mayonnaise, sour cream, blue cheese, garlic and pepper. Stir well.

3. If serving cold then refrigerate until needed, garnish with the chopped walnuts (they can be raw or roasted).

4. If serving it baked then place it in a casserole dish and bake at 350°F for 20 minutes. If you would like a crusty top then add 1/3 cup of grated Romano or parmesan cheese before baking. Let cool for 5 minutes then garnish with the chopped walnuts.

Serve with strips of bell pepper, celery sticks or low carb chips (be sure to add in those carbs).

Yields about 2 cups with 1/3 cup per serving

Per Serving: 131 Calories; 12g Fat; 3g Protein; 4g Carbs; trace Dietary Fiber

Cheese Fondue

This is the classic cheese fondue but served with veggies, chicken and ham instead of bread cubes. I keep waiting for the fondue to re-emerge as a popular style for appetizers. They are so much fun for a small gathering.

1	clove	garlic -- cut in half
2	cups	chardonnay
1/2	pound	gruyere cheese
1/2	pound	emmenthal cheese
3	Tbsps	Kirsch
1/8	tsp	guar gum

> **Weight Loss**
>
> 8 Servings
> 5g Net Carbs

2	cups	cauliflower -- blanched
2	cups	broccoli -- blanched
2	cups	asparagus -- blanched
2	cups	chicken pieces -- cooked
2	cups	ham – cooked & cubed

Never prepare the fondue in advance; it does not keep well and loses its distinct flavors quickly. Once your guests are ready and the veggies are prepared then you can begin the fondue. It will take about 15-20 minutes.

1. Vegetables should generally be blanched. Drop veggies into boiling water for 2 minutes; then remove from boiling water and plunge into iced water to stop the cooking and to keep colors crisp.

2. Coarsely grate or chop the cheese. (Unpasturized cheese is best)

3. In a small cup or bowl mix the Kirsch with the guar gum.

4. In a 2 qt. stainless steel sauce pan, rub the garlic onto the bottom and up the sides a little ways. Do the same for whatever you will use as a serving bowl (step 7), then discard garlic.

5. Add the Chardonnay and place over medium high heat. Once small bubbles start to form on the side of the pan, gradually add some cheese. Stir continuously until the fondue is completely finished. Do not let it boil, reduce heat if needed, but things will progress faster with higher heat. Keep adding the cheese in small doses until it is all melted.

6. With your free hand (or a helper) add the Kirsch to the cheese, stirring vigorously for one minute. Do not boil: reduce heat if needed. Keep stirring until thickened; maybe 2-3 more minutes.

7. Transfer to a fondue pot or chaffing dish on low heat. Place the veggies and meat in separate bowls or on a platter. Serve and enjoy.

Per Serving: 432 Calories; 27g Fat; 32g Protein; 7g Carbohydrate; 2g Dietary Fiber

Cheese Quesadilla

These are great as a low carb snack or appetizer. Also consider using them as a garnish for a Southwestern or Mexican main course.

2		low carb, whole wheat tortillas
1/2	cup	cheddar cheese -- shredded
2	Tbsps	salsa

Weight Loss

4 Servings
3g Net Carbs

La Tortilla Factory has large low carb whole wheat tortillas which are highly recommend for this recipe. They have only 5g net carbs each.

Use any type of cheese that you like. Try a blend. I generally use cheddar with Monterey Jack. If you use a pepper Jack cheese then you can skip the salsa (which makes this recipe even easier).

1. Use must have a large nonstick skillet that can hold a tortilla easily. Heat the skillet to medium (or half way to medium high). Add a tortilla and let it get warm (about 1 minute) and remove (remember which side was up). Then warm the second tortilla for one minute and then flip it over.

2. Sprinkle the cheese over the entire tortilla up to about 1/2 inch from the edge. Sprinkle the salsa over the cheese. I like to press out a bit of the liquid from the salsa.

3. Add the second tortilla with warmed side now facing down. Once the bottom tortilla starts to brown, it's time to flip it. If you are skilled you can turn it with just a toss, or you can try a large spatula. But another way is to let it slide off onto a plate held in your hand, then turn the skillet upside down over the plate and then turn them both over and lift the plate out of the skillet and then brown that side of the tortilla a little bit.

4. Using a sharp knife or pizza cutter, cut into 8 pieces. It is best to serve them right away. But if you are going to make extra batches, they can sit in a warm oven for a few minutes. If you plan on doing this then consider using pepper jack cheese and eliminate the salsa or serve the salsa on the side.

Extra salsa, guacamole and sour cream are great additions (but be sure to add-in the extra carbs!).

Yields 8 slices with 2 slices per serving

Per Serving: 42 Calories; 2g Fat; 4g Protein; 10g Carbohydrate; 7g Dietary Fiber

Maintenance Lunch: One serving
11g net carbs; 169 Calories; 6g Fat ; 16g Protein; 40g Carbohydrate; 29g Dietary Fiber

Coconut Shrimp

Lime and coconut pair up with these baked shrimp to make
an appetizer that will be gone in seconds

12		shrimp -- peeled and deveined
1	Tbsp	water
2	tsps	powdered egg white
1	Tbsp	lime juice
1/4	cup	coconut flakes
2	Tbsps	whey protein powder
1	Tbsp	Splenda®
1/2	tsp	salt

Weight Loss

3 Servings
4g Net Carbs

I use medium sized shrimp (30 count) that have been peeled and deveined except for the tip of the tail. Leaving this bit of shell on the tip of the shrimp makes it much easier to handle as the cook and for those enjoying this delicious appetizer.

Preheat oven to 375°F. Line a cookie sheet with parchment paper.

1. In a very small bowl (like a ramekin) mix together the water and powdered egg whites until completely dissolved. This will take awhile. Mix then let sit a couple minutes and then mix again. Add the lime juice and mix again.

2. In a shallow bowl, blend together the coconut, whey, Splenda and salt.

3. Dip each shrimp into the egg wash. Shake off any extra (just so it is not dripping). Then press gently into the coconut mixture and coat on both side. Place on the parchment lined cookie sheet. Repeat with the remaining shrimp.

4. Bake at 375°F for 6-8minutes, just until the shrimp have turned red and the coconut is just starting to brown at the tips ever so slightly.

5. Remove from oven and transfer carefully to serving platter.

If making a double batch, you will not need to double the egg white & lime bath.

You can serve these just the way they are or perhaps place each shrimp on a leaf of radicchio or Belgian endive and garnish with Hawaiian Salsa (page 363)

Yields 12 shrimp with 4 per serving

Per Serving: 95 Calories; 3g Fat; 12g Protein; 4g Carbohydrate; trace Dietary Fiber

Ginger Pumpkin Seeds

This simple mixture is a nutritious and tasty snack. It's also great
to have at a holiday party. Caution it is addictive!

2	cups	pumpkin seeds -- raw
2	Tbsps	butter
2	Tbsps	Splenda®
2	tsps	ground ginger

Weight Loss
16 Servings
4g Net Carbs

Pre heat oven to 275°F

1. In a small bowl mix together the Splenda and ginger.

2. In a medium sized sauce pan over medium heat, melt the butter with 2 tsps of the ginger mixture. Once melted, turn off the heat and add the pumpkin seeds. Stir well to thoroughly coat.

3. Use either nonstick or line a shallow roasting pan with parchment paper. Evenly distribute the pumpkin seeds over the roasting pan. Cook in a 275°F oven for 15 minutes.

4. Stir the pumpkins seeds a couple of times, don't let them brown or pop (reduce heat if necessary). Remove from oven and immediately stir in the remaining sugar/ginger mixture.

5. Once the pumpkin seeds have cooled, place in several small decorative bowls and serve. Or store in an air-tight container until ready for serving.

Yields 2 cups with 2 Tbsp per serving

Per Serving: 49 Calories; 3g Fat; 2g Protein; 5g Carbohydrate; 1g Dietary Fiber

Variations are endless. Simply replace the ginger and the Splenda for any number of spice combinations. Chili powder or Cajun seasoning will become favorites too.

Guacamole

Classic and delicious! Every cookbook needs a guacamole recipe.

2		avocado
1	Tbsp	lemon juice
1/2	tsp	garlic salt
1/4	tsp	chili powder –to taste
2	Tbsps	salsa
1/4	cup	cilantro -- chopped

Weight Loss
4 Servings 6g Net Carbs

I dedicate this recipe to my friend Cynthia who says exactly the same thing every time I serve this dip, "Mmmmm, good guacamole!"

1. Scoop out the avocado and mash well with the lemon juice, garlic salt and chili powder.

2. Let the juices drain off of the salsa before adding to the avocado. Stir in the salsa and cilantro. Serve immediately.

If you are not serving this right away then add 1 Tbsp of sour cream which helps prevent it from turning brown. Also press plastic wrap onto the surface trapping as little air as possible.

I like to eat this with pork rinds but strips of bell peppers or celery are more healthy. I mostly use guacamole as a garnish for Southwestern and Mexican dishes.

Per Serving: 171 Calories; 15g Fat; 2g Protein; 9g Carbohydrate; 3g Dietary Fiber

Roasted Red Pepper Dip

This is a wonderful dip that can also be stuffed into mushrooms
or used on top of veggies or grilled chicken.

14	oz	jar of roasted red peppers
2	cloves	garlic -- minced
1	Tbsp	lemon juice
4	ounces	cream cheese -- room temp
1/2	cup	sour cream
		salt & pepper -- to taste

Weight Loss
4 Servings 7g Net Carbs

1. In a food processor, puree the peppers and garlic with the lemon juice. Add the cream cheese and sour cream. Mix until smooth, scrapping down the side occasionally. Add salt & pepper to taste.

2. Transfer to a serving bowl. Consider a fresh green herb garnish such as cilantro, basil, chives or flat parsley.

Yields ~ 2 cups with 1/2 cup per serving

Per Serving: 191 Calories; 16g Fat; 4g Protein; 9g Carbohydrate; 2g Dietary Fiber

Jicama with Peanut Butter

A great low carb snack especially when you are missing
sliced apples and peanut butter.

1/3 pound jicama
  2 Tbsps peanut butter

<table>
<tr><td>Weight Loss</td></tr>
<tr><td>1 Servings
9g Net Carbs</td></tr>
</table>

I have always loved sliced apples with peanut butter as a snack or light lunch, but the carbs are too high for the weight loss phase (21g net carbs). So I substitute jicama for the apple. The quantity of jicama is about the same volume as 1 whole apple which is generally about 1/4 of a jicama depending on its size.

1. Cut off about 1/4 of the jicama and peel with a knife (or a really sharp vegetable peeler). Slice into sticks.

2. During the summer I just scoop out 2 Tbsps of peanut butter and put it into a custard dish and onto a plate with the sliced jicama. In the winter I sometimes zap the peanut butter in the microwave for a few seconds first.

Per Serving: 244 Calories; 17g Fat; 9g Protein; 18g Carbohydrate; 9g Dietary Fiber

High Fiber Variation: Jicama is high in fiber but I sometimes add a Tbsp of flax seed meal to the peanut butter for even more fiber and an omega-3 boost.
12g net carbs; 300 Calories; 18g Fat ; 15g Protein; 24g Carbohydrate; 12g Dietary Fiber

Onion Dip

You no longer need to buy instant soup mix with preservatives and MSG.

1/2 cup   sour cream
  1 Tbsp onion flakes
  2 tsps Worcestershire sauce
     dash Liquid Barbecue Smoke®
1/8 tsp   garlic powder
1/8 tsp   salt -- more to taste
     dash   pepper

<table>
<tr><td>Weight Loss</td></tr>
<tr><td>2 Servings
6g Net Carbs</td></tr>
</table>

In a small bowl add the onion flakes, Worcestershire sauce and Liquid Smoke. Let it sit for a minute or two. Then add the sour cream, garlic powder, salt and pepper. Serve with celery stalks or pork rinds.

For a party multiply everything by 4 (1 pint sour cream, 2T+2t Worcestershire sauce, etc.) and then finely mince a scallion. Reserve about 1/2 of the green part and mix in the rest. Garnish with the reserve scallion tops.

Per Serving: 137 Calories; 12g Fat; 2g Protein; 6g Carbs; trace Dietary Fiber

Tabouli Stuffed Cucumber Cups

This unusual yet delicious appetizer is made with English seedless cucumbers prepared into cups and then filled with tabouli.

3		English cucumber
1/3	cup	Tabouli - Casbah Brand
1/3	cup	boiling water
1	Tbsp	lemon juice
1/4	tsp	cumin
1	large	tomato -- seeded and chopped
1/4	cup	fresh parsley -- minced
1/4	cup	fresh mint leaves -- minced
1	Tbsp	extra virgin olive oil

Weight Loss

12 Servings
4g Net Carbs

If you do not have the seedless English cucumbers then use the regular ones.

1. First prepare the tabouli. Into a small bowl, add the tabouli mix, the boiling water, lemon juice and cumin. Stir well and cover. Set aside.

2. Remove the stem from the tomato, slice in half and squeeze to remove the seeds (most of them anyway - that's good enough). Dice the tomato. Mince the parsley and mint leaves. Uncover the tabouli and stir. Add the parsley, mint, tomatoes and olive oil. Stir well, cover and refrigerate for 1 hour.

3. Wash the cucumbers to remove the vegetable wax that is usually put on them. I prefer to leave the peels on (test to see if too bitter however), but you can peel them or partial peel them (making attractive stripes). Cut off the ends then cut into 1 inch long slices. It is assume that you can get 8 slices from an English cucumber.

4. Using a rounded teaspoon or a melon baller, scoop out the centers about 2/3 or 3/4 deep. This makes nice cups. Fill each cup with about 1 Tbsp of the tabouli. Refrigerate until ready to serve.

Yields 24 appetizers with 2 cups per serving

Per Serving: 33 Calories; 1g Fat; 1g Protein; 5g Carbohydrate; 1g Dietary Fiber

Mini Raspberry Cheese Cakes

These mini cheese cakes are a sweet and fun addition to a buffet
eaten as an appetizer or as a dessert.

8	ozs	cream cheese -- softened
1/2	cup	sour cream
1/2	cup	Splenda®
1/2	tsp	lemon extract
2		eggs
24		raspberries

Weight Loss

12 Servings
4g Net Carbs

<u>crust</u>

3/4	cup	almond meal
6	Tbsps	Splenda®
1/2	tsp	cinnamon
6	Tbsps	butter -- softened
1	tsp	Just Whites
1	Tbsp	water

Each cheese cake has a whole raspberry in the center. Normally a cheese cake would not like the presence of fruit in the batter. But these mini cakes are not so temperamental. You'll need those mini muffin tins (holds about 2 Tbsp). This recipe makes 2 dozen cheese cakes.

Preheat oven to 325°F

1. Mix together the almond meal, Splenda and cinnamon. Mix in the butter. Using a fork or whisk, mix together the water with the powdered egg whites until all dissolved and frothy. Add to the almonds. Mix well.

2. Spoon out 1 tsp of the crust mixture into each of the muffin mold and press down firmly. Bake at 325°F for 5 minutes. Remove and let cool.

3. Meanwhile, beat together the softened cream cheese and sour cream until smooth with no lumps. This can be done in a food processor, with an electric mixer or by hand. Add the Splenda and lemon extract. If using an electric mixer or food processor then add one egg at a time. If mixing by hand then beat the eggs well, then add to the cream cheese mixture a little at a time and mix until well blended. Repeat 2 or 3 times.

4. Add a single raspberry to each muffin mold. Spoon in 1 scant Tbsp each. Bake at 325°F for 20 minutes or until the mini cakes have risen above the edges and no longer jiggle. Remove from oven and allow to cool for 15 minutes. Cover and refrigerate for 30 minutes (or 24 hours).

5. Using a thin bladed knife or tooth pick, go around the edge of each mini cake to loosen it. Turn over onto paper towels. Arrange on a platter and serve.

Yields 24 cheese cakes with 2 per serving

Per Serving: 191 Calories; 19g Fat; 4g Protein; 5g Carbohydrate; 1g Dietary Fiber

Apples with Almond Butter

A great snack for your low carb maintenance program with plenty of fiber.

1		apple
4	Tbsps	almond butter
1	Tbsp	flax seed meal

Maintenance

2 Servings
15g Net Carbs

1. Slice the apple ultra thin. Leave the skin on, it's loaded with nutrients.

   If you are going to use this as an appetizer then fill a bowl with about 1 cup of water and the juice of 1 lemon. Add the apple slices to the bowl; this will keep them from turning brown (and adds a bit of zesty flavor) refrigerate until ready to use.

2. Mix together the flax seed meal and almond butter. If it does not stir well then zap it in the microwave for just 15 seconds. Spoon out a dollop onto each apple slice.

Per Serving: 266 Calories; 19g Fat; 8g Protein; 20g Carbohydrate; 5g Dietary Fiber

Hummus with Celery

Mashed chickpeas with tahini and lemon is a fantastic snack or appetizer.

2	cups	chickpeas -- canned
3	Tbsps	tahini
2	Tbsps	lemon juice
3	cloves	garlic
1/4	tsp	salt
1/4	tsp	black pepper
	pinch	cumin
1/4	cup	unrefined sesame oil (or olive oil)
1	Tbsp	parsley -- minced
12	stalks	celery

Maintenance

6 Servings
10g Net Carbs

1. Rinse and drain the chickpeas. Crush the cloves of garlic to remove the skin.

2. In a food processor, add the chickpeas, tahini, lemon juice, garlic, salt, pepper and a pinch of cumin. Process until well incorporated. With the machine running drizzle in the oil slowly. Pause and taste test. Adjust seasoning. Add parsley and pulse just a few times.

3. Cut each celery stalk into 3 segments and fill each segment with hummus

Yields 36 appetizers with 6 per serving

Per Serving: 279 Calories; 21g Fat; 9g Protein; 17g Carbohydrate; 7g Dietary Fiber

Polenta Squares with Sun-Dried tomatoes

Bell pepper squares filled with polenta and garnished with sun dried tomatoes.
These have an amazing variety of flavors and textures.
These will generate many compliments.

1	cup	Tomato Polenta Mix – *Fantastic* brand
2 1/4	cups	cold water
1	cup	parmesan cheese -- shredded
6		bell peppers
3	ozs	sun-dried tomatoes, oil-packed

Maintenance
16 Servings
10g Net Carbs

The *Fantastic* brand of polenta mixes are extremely good (they are fantastic, in fact). If you can not find the one which has tomatoes then use the plain one, it is almost as good. Use green, yellow, orange or red bell peppers as you prefer. An assortment looks incredible on a platter.

1. In a deep sauce pan over high heat, add the water and the polenta mix. Bring to a boil then reduce heat and simmer for 5 minutes. Stir occasionally. Remove from heat, stir in the cheese and allow to cool for about 10 minutes.

2. Meanwhile, remove the stems from the peppers and cut into halves. Remove the seeds and membranes. Cut each half into 4 squares. This will yield 48 squares total.

3. Drain the sun-dried tomatoes and slice. You want to end up with 48 slices.

4. Once the polenta has cooled enough to handle, spoon out 1 Tbsp worth per pepper square and garnish with a slice of sun-dried tomato.

Yields 48 squares with 3 squares per serving

Per Serving: 89 Calories; 3g Fat; 4g Protein; 12g Carbohydrate; 2g Dietary Fiber

Spicy Variation: Substitute 24 jalapeno peppers for the bell peppers. Remove stems, cut into halves, remove seeds and membrane. Stuff each half with a Tbsp of polenta and garnish as above.
8g net carbs; 84 Calories; 3g Fat; 4g Protein; 10g Carbohydrate; 2g Dietary Fiber

Reduced Carbs/Spicy Variation: Omit the sun-dried tomato garnish and only have 2 jalapeno pepper halves per serving (so now there are 24 servings instead of just 16).
4g net carbs; 48 Calories; 2g Fat; 2g Protein; 5g Carbohydrate; 1g Dietary Fiber;

SALADS

SALADS

MAINTENANCE RECIPES

~ Regarding Salad Greens ~

Dark Leafy greens are one of the most nutritious things that you can eat regardless of what type of diet you are on. If you are not already in the habit of eating a leafy salad everyday it is something that you might want to strive to achieve.

Try not to get bored with your salads. Mix things up, use different greens, sprouts, sliced veggies, dressings, herbs, etc. One way to approach this is to add only a couple of toppings to each salad (e.g., cucumber & alfalfa sprouts; tomatoes & blue cheese; peppers & pine nuts; and so on) and have something different every day. You don't need to put the same few things onto every salad. I personally like mixed greens over using a single type of green in a salad. I try to vary the greens every couple of days; although I generally include spinach or romaine in every blend. There are various mixes available in those convenient bags of pre-washed greens. Or buy 2 or 3 types of greens at once and mix them in different ratios each day. Experiment with some of the more exotic greens from time to time. If you have access to them try arugula, dandelion greens, frizzee, mache and watercress.

Soaking greens in cold water allows them to plump-up and they become extra crisp when chilled. They only need to soak for a few minutes and then dry them with a salad spinner or toss using paper towels. When storing salad greens it is okay if they are a little damp. Water isn't the problem; it is air. So put them in a bag and seal with as little air in it as possible. If the greens are quite damp then let a little air circulate around them for the first day only.

Spinach and romaine lettuce are the Champions for salad greens. These vegetables have superior nutritional content and many documented studies of remarkable health benefits. From what experts know to date, it is not any single nutrients in the leafy greens that make them so healthy. It seems to be how all the various nutrients are combined and work together. Each of the particular salad greens has their own distinctive set of nutrients that make them special. Spinach is particularly high in vitamins A and K, iron and the coenzyme Q10 (a very powerful antioxidant). Romaine is also a good source of many nutrients including vitamin A, folic acid and potassium. Arugula has properties that aid digestion. And so on. As it is the synergy of the phytonutrients in leafy greens that creates the greatest health benefits, so it is advisable to eat a variety of them frequently whether in salads or as side vegetables (such as Swiss chard, turnips greens, collards, beet greens, kale; all excellent nutrient-dense greens).

Spinach is one of the most nutritious vegetables available and should be eaten as often as possible. It is about as close to a zero carb vegetable that there is and spinach is wonderfully delicious and versatile, adapting itself to a diversity of recipes. Most people can eat as much as they desire without worries (except it is high in vitamin K which can be a problem for people who take blood thinners). But where most people need to pay attention is with the yummy things that we might put on top (excessive butter, high fat dressings, etc.). Most everyone should eat at least 2 cups of salad greens every day, placing an emphasis on spinach and romaine. This philosophy is suitable to every diet not just low carb. You will find in time, that eating two cups of salad greens per day becomes wonderfully addictive. If you have not developed this habit yet then today is a perfectly good day to start.

Leaf Vegetables 1 cup	Carbs grams	Fiber grams	Net Carbs grams
Arugula	0.7	0.2	0.5
Bok Choy	1.5	0.7	0.8
Cabbage	2.8	1.6	1.2
Iceberg lettuce	2.2	0.8	1.4
Radicchio	1.8	0.4	1.4
Red leaf lettuce	2.0	1.0	1.0
Romaine lettuce	1.4	1.0	0.4
Spinach	1.0	0.8	0.2
Watercress	1.1	0.5	0.6

Asparagus & Radicchio Salad

This salad has a beautiful presentation and a wonderful fresh flavor.

1	lb	asparagus
1/4	lb	radicchio

Induction

4 Servings
3g Net Carbs

Dressing

1/4	cup	extra virgin olive oil
2	Tbsps	white wine vinegar
2	tsps	dijon mustard
1	Tbsp	fresh tarragon -- chopped
1	pinch	salt and pepper

1. Cut or snap off tough ends of the asparagus and discard them. Asparagus may then be left whole or cut into bite size pieces. The whole spear has a nicer presentation.

2. Cook asparagus just until tender but still has a crunch to it; do not over cook. If steaming, cook approximately 4 minutes. If boiling, approximately 3 minutes. The spears can also be grilled or broiled.

3. Drain and immediately immerse in cold or iced water to stop the cooking process. When cool, drain.

4. Meanwhile, make the dressing by mixing together the olive oil, vinegar, mustard, tarragon and the salt & pepper. Set aside for at least 15 minutes to allow the flavors to meld. I usually put the dressing ingredients in a jar and shake it to mix.

5. Arrange the radicchio (use either whole leaves or slivered) on a serving platter or on 4 individual salad plates. Top with the asparagus. This can be refrigerated (covered) until 15 minutes before time to serve.

6. Just before serving, mix the dressing again and drizzle over the asparagus.

A sprig of any fresh herb makes a nice garnish. Watercress or bean sprouts also make an attractive garnish.

Per Serving : 143 Calories; 14g Fat; 2g Protein; 5g Carbohydrate; 2g Dietary Fiber

Chicken Caesar Salad

This low carb adaptation of the classic salad is cherished
during the induction phase.

4	cups	cooked chicken -- diced
1	head	romaine lettuce – washed
1		egg
2	tsp	anchovy paste
2	clove	garlic -- crushed
1	tsp	Dijon mustard
1/2	cup	extra virgin olive oil
1	Tbsp	lemon juice (~1/2 lemon)
1/2	tsp	Worcestershire sauce
1/4	tsp	fresh ground black pepper
1/2	cup	Parmesan cheese -- coursely grated

Induction
4 Servings
3g Net Carbs

Whenever I restart with the induction phase, I have this salad nearly every other day. I never get tired of it (but that's just me). The dressing was included in my first cookbook too (*Lauri's Low-Carb Cookbook*), but I had to include it again because it is one of those fundamental salad dressings that should be in every cookbook.

1. Place the egg in boiling water for 1 minute then remove and let cool enough to handle. Separate the egg, discarding the whites and placing the yolk in a small non-metallic mixing bowl. Beat the egg yolk.

   This coddling process is enough to kill any salmonella present– although it is rarely found in eggs any more. If you have pasteurized eggs then you can just use the egg yolk directly without coddling it first (as that it what is meant by pasteurized).

2. Add anchovy paste, oil, mustard, garlic, lemon juice, Worcestershire sauce and pepper. Mix well. Chill dressing for 15 or 20 minutes to allow flavors to meld.

3. Wash and tear lettuce into bite size pieces. Toss in the chicken. Add the dressing and toss. Sprinkle with Parmesan cheese and serve immediately.

Notes:
- Try adding crumbled bacon for no added carbs.
- Herb Cheese Crackers (page 109) are a nice garnish.

Per Serving: 340 Calories; 32g Fat; 10g Protein; 6g Carbohydrate; 3g Dietary Fiber

Dijon Salad with Summer Sausage

Escarole lettuce with a simple Dijon vinaigrette
garnished with slices of summer sausage.

6	oz	summer sausage
1	large	escarole head
2	large	garlic cloves
2	tsps	Dijon mustard
1	Tbsp	red wine vinegar
2	Tbsps	canola oil
1/4	tsp	salt
1/4	tsp	pepper

Induction
4 Servings
3g Net Carbs

1. Thoroughly wash the escarole. Cut or tear into bite size pieces. Dry in a salad spinner.

2. Remove the casing or "skin" from the sausage (and trim the ends, if desired). Cut into 4 equal lengths. Each length will be one serving. Then cut each length into 5 or 6 thin slices.

3. Crush, peel and chop the garlic. Add garlic to a large bowl with the mustard, vinegar, oil and salt & pepper. Whisk thoroughly. Add the escarole and toss until well coated.

4. Divide the escarole onto 4 plates. Arrange the sausage on each plate and serve.

Per Serving: 230 Calories; 20g Fat; 9g Protein; 6g Carbohydrate; 3g Dietary Fiber

Spinach, Egg & Shrimp Salad

This salad is great for brunch, lunch or as a light dinner.
It is topped with my version of Thousand Island dressing.

2	cups	spinach leaves
1	can	shrimp, -- drained
2		eggs -- hardboiled
1		scallion -- chopped

Dressing

1/2	cup	mayonnaise
1	Tbsp	Carb Options™ Ketchup
1	tsp	dill pickle relish
1	tsp	horseradish sauce
1	Tbsp	water
2	drops	lemon extract
		salt and pepper -- to taste

1. For the dressing: put the mayonnaise, ketchup, relish, horseradish, water and lemon extract into a jar and shake well. Taste to see if you prefer some salt or pepper added.

2. On two individual plates place the spinach.

3. Slice the eggs and arrange on the plates. Sprinkle the shrimp evenly over the two plates. Drizzle the dressing over the salad. You probably will not need all of it.

4. Chop or mince the scallion and sprinkle over the salads as a garnish. Serve.

Per Serving: 492 Calories; 53g Fat; 8g Protein; 3g Carbohydrate; 1g Dietary Fiber

Greek Slaw

An herbal vinaigrette dressing along with olives, cucumber and
feta cheese gives this slaw a Greek personality.

1/2	head	cabbage
4	ozs	Greek olives -- pitted
1/2		cucumber
1/4	cup	red onion
3	ozs	feta cheese
1	tsp	dried oregano
1/2	tsp	dried dill weed
1	pinch	dill seed
1/3	cup	white wine vinegar

Induction

**6 Servings
3g Net Carbs**

1. Shredded cabbage finely. Slice Greek olives. Peel cucumber, cut in half, and slice. Cut the onion into slivers.

2. In a medium-size mixing bowl, add the oregano, dill weed, dill seed, and vinegar. Let it sit for about five minutes so that the flavors can meld.

3. Add the cabbage, olives, cucumber, red onion, and feta cheese. Toss together, cover and refrigerate for one hour. Serve

Per Serving: 97 Calories; 8g Fat; 3g Protein; 4g Carbohydrate; 1g Dietary Fiber

Cumin Tuna Salad

This is my favorite way to prepare tuna salad - a touch of cumin
and served on cucumber slices.

1	can	albacore tuna
2	Tbsps	mayonnaise -- or more if needed
1/8	tsp	cumin
1	stalk	celery -- minced
1	Tbsp	cilantro -- minced
1		cucumber

Induction

**2 Servings
3g Net Carbs**

This is a quick and easy low carb lunch.

1. Drain the tuna and put it into a bowl. Add the mayo and cumin and mix well. Then add the minced celery and cilantro and mix.

2. Slice the cucumber and serve on the side.

I usually just have the tuna in a bowl with the cucumber slices along one edge and using a spoon or fork, scoop some tuna onto a slice of cucumber and munch away.

Per Serving: 183 Calories; 13g Fat; 13g Protein; 5g Carbohydrate; 2g Dietary Fiber

Curry Turkey Salad

This salad begs to be eaten for lunch. The crunch, spice and sweetness have a party in your mouth. Add some mangos for extra appeal.

3	cups	cooked turkey breast -- cubed
1	cup	jicama -- diced
3		scallion -- minced
3	stalks	celery -- minced
1/4	cup	walnut -- chopped

Induction
4 Servings
3g Net Carbs

Dressing

2/3	cup	mayonnaise
2	tsps	vinegar
2	tsps	curry powder
1	tsp	Splenda®
		salt and pepper -- to taste

Ask for1/2 inch thick slices of turkey breast from your local deli. This will make nice uniform cubes of meat for this delicious salad.

1. Cube the turkey and dice the jicama. Mince the celery and scallions. In a bowl toss together the turkey, jicama, celery, scallions and chopped walnuts.

2. In a small bowl, whisk together the mayonnaise, vinegar, curry powder, Splenda and slat and pepper to taste. Add enough to the turkey mixture to coat. You may have some dressing left over depending on tastes.

Per Serving: 523 Calories; 37g Fat; 45g Protein; 6g Carbohydrate; 3g Dietary Fiber

Mango Variation: Add 3/4 cup of diced mangos.
8g net carbs; 543 Calories; 37g Fat; 45g Protein; 12g Carbohydrate; 4g Dietary Fiber

Lauri's Egg Salad

Everyone has a favorite way to make egg salad, this is one of mine.

3		eggs -- hardboiled
2	stalks	celery -- chopped
1	Tbsp	bell pepper -- minced
1		scallion -- minced
1½	Tbsps	mayonnaise
1	Tbsp	sour cream
	dash	celery salt
	dash	pepper
	pinch	fresh dill, optional

Induction

2 Servings
2g Net Carbs

1. Dice the hardboil eggs. One way to dice an egg is by using an egg slicer. Slice in one direction and rotate 90 degrees and slice again. This makes match sticks which break into cubes when you mix in the mayo. Trying to turn the egg again to make perfect cubes is more work than it is worth.

2. Stir in the mayo and sour cream. Then add the chopped celery, bell pepper, scallions, celery salt, pepper and fresh dill. Toss and serve.

Per Serving: 198 Calories; 17g Fat; 9g Protein; 3g Carbohydrate; 1g Dietary Fiber

Mock Waldorf Salad

This low carb interpretation of the classic Waldorf is made with jicama instead of apples. It is close enough to the real deal to satisfy that craving.

2	cups	red leaf lettuce
1½	cups	celery -- diced
1	cup	jicama -- diced
1/2	cup	walnuts (or pecans) -- chopped

Induction

4 Servings
3g Net Carbs

Dressing

3	Tbsps	mayonnaise
1	Tbsp	sour cream
1	tsp	lemon juice

1. In a large bowl, combine the mayonnaise, sour cream and lemon juice. Toss in the celery, jicama and walnuts.

2. Line four salad plates with the red leaf lettuce, then spoon the salad mixture in the center or each plate.

Yields enough for two lunch salads or four side salads

Per Serving: 200 Calories; 19g Fat; 5g Protein; 7g Carbohydrate; 4g Dietary Fiber

Arugula & Watercress Salad

The sharp medley of flavors makes this salad truly memorable.

4	cups	arugula
4	cups	watercress
1/4	cup	fresh tarragon -- leaves
1	cup	pitted green olives -- chopped
1	cup	gorgonzola cheese -- crumbled
1/4	cup	sour cream
3	Tbsps	red wine vinegar

Weight Loss
4 Servings
4g Net Carbs

If you don't have fresh tarragon leaves, then add 1 tsp of dried tarragon to the vinegar and let it sit for a few minutes. Tarragon vinegar would be good too.

1. Mix together the sour cream and vinegar. Set aside.

2. Rinse the arugula and watercress. Remove and discard stems. Chop or tear leaves into bite size pieces.

3. Place in a bowl the arugula, watercress, tarragon, and green olives. Pour the dressing over the greens and toss well. Add the cheese and lightly toss again. Serve immediately.

Per Serving : 180 Calories; 15g Fat; 7g Protein; 6g Carbohydrate; 2g Dietary Fiber

Arugula Salad

This simple salad is lovely and delicious.
The dressing can be tailored to compliment your entrée.

2	cups	arugula
1	cup	red leaf lettuce
1/2		orange bell pepper -- sliced
6		cherry tomato -- halved
2	Tbsps	balsamic vinegar
1/4	cup	walnut oil -- unrefined
	pinch	herbs - choose herbs/spices that are being used in your entree. Perhaps cumin & garlic for southwestern, oregano & garlic for Italian, thyme or tarragon for French, etc.

Weight Loss
2 Servings
5g Net Carbs

1. Make the dressing first by adding the vinegar, oil and herbs in a small jar and shake well. It is best if this can be made an hour or so ahead of time.

2. Rip the arugula and lettuce into bite sized pieces and place in a salad bowl. Cut the pepper in half and remove seeds and membrane. Slice the pepper and add to the salad bowl along with the halved tomatoes.

3. When ready to serve, shake the dressing again and drizzle over salad just enough to coat (you may have extra dressing). Toss and serve.

Per Serving: 272 Calories; 28g Fat; 2g Protein; 7g Carbohydrate; 2g Dietary Fiber

Athena Salad

This Greek salad uses baby spinach and romaine and is complimented with roasted bell pepper, olive, feta cheese and Greek vinaigrette.

2	cups	baby spinach leaves
1	cup	romaine lettuce -- shredded
1/3	cup	roasted red pepper -- cut into strips
10		Greek olives
2	oxs	feta cheese

Greek Vinaigrette

1/4	cup	extra virgin olive oil
2	Tbsps	lemon juice
1	Tbsp	water
1/8	tsp	garlic powder
2	tsps	fresh oregano -- 1/2 tsp if dried
	dash	salt and pepper

You can roast your own bell peppers by placing them over an open flame until the skin blisters. Then peel the skin as soon as it is cool enough to handle. But I usually just buy my in a jar (so much easier).

1. In a small jar add the lemon juice, water, garlic, oregano and a dash of salt and pepper each. Shake the jar. Add the olive oil (if you can, set it aside for about 30 minutes to develop deeper flavor).

2. Divide the spinach between two plates, top them with the strips of pepper, 5 olives each and then crumble the feta cheese on top. Shake the vinaigrette jar well and drizzle over the salads. Serve at once.

Per Serving: 395 Calories; 40g Fat; 6g Protein; 7g Carbohydrate; 2g Dietary Fiber

This salad was inspired by the 2004 Summer Olympics in Athens. I named it in honor of Athena, Goddess of wisdom, strategy and invention.

Baby Greens with Walnuts & Blue Cheese

This is one of my favorite salads because it is so simple, but what a great taste! You'll get many compliments and requests to fix it again.

1	bag	mixed baby lettuce leaves (~10 oz)
2/3	cup	walnuts -- roasted and chopped
2/3	cup	blue cheese, crumbled
1/2	cup	walnut oil -- unrefined
1/4	cup	balsamic vinegar
1	pinch	salt and pepper – each

Walnut oil is fundamental to this salad. If you do not have walnut oil then substitute canola oil, but you'll be missing out on an important flavor.

1. Rinse and spin dry the lettuce. Be sure that there is a lot of variety of lettuce and baby greens. Pick out and discard any leaves that don't look perfectly fresh.

2. Place lettuce in a large shallow bowl (such as a pasta bowl). Sprinkle on top the blue cheese and the toasted walnuts.

3. Mix together and blend well the oil, vinegar and salt & pepper. Drizzle dressing over the salad and serve.

This is a great salad to serve with left-over holiday turkey and a dollop of the low-carb Cranberry Sauce (page 356).

Per Serving: 458 Calories; 46g Fat; 11g Protein; 6g Carbohydrate; 2g Dietary Fiber

Induction Variation: Omit the walnuts. Then the walnut oil becomes essential.
2g net carbs; 332 Calories; 34g Fat; 6g Protein; 3g Carbohydrate; 1g Dietary Fiber.

Asian Salad with Tahini Dressing

This salad is colorful and full of flavor.
Consider adding cooked chicken to create a one course meal.

1/2	lb	snow pea pods
2	cups	Chinese cabbage -- shredded
1	cup	red cabbage -- shredded
1/2		orange bell pepper -- sliced
2		scallion -- sliced
2	Tbsps	soy sauce
1	Tbsp	tahini
1	Tbsp	lime juice
1	tsp	Splenda®
1	tsp	fresh ginger -- grated

> **Weight Loss**
>
> **4 Servings**
> **7g Net Carbs**

1. Snip the ends off of the pea pods and cut into halves with a diagonal slice. Also slice the scallions diagonally. Slice the bell pepper into thin slivers. I use a food processor to shred the cabbage but a good knife works just as well and there's less to clean up.

2. In a large bowl, toss the cabbage, snow pea pods, bell peppers and scallions.

3. To make the dressing. Finely grate the fresh ginger root (if using dried ground ginger then use 1/2 tsp). In a small bowl, add the soy sauce and whisk in the tahini until well combined. Add the lime juice, ginger and Splenda. Whisk well.

4. Pour the dressing over the salad and toss well.

Per Serving: 68 Calories; 2g Fat; 4g Protein; 10g Carbohydrate; 3g Dietary Fiber

Cumin Chicken & Goat Cheese Salad

The blend of cumin, cilantro and lime makes this salad a perfect to compliment for cheese enchiladas or other Mexican or Southwestern entrees.

1/4	cup	extra virgin olive oil
2	Tbsps	lime juice
1	tsp	cumin
1/4	cup	red onion -- minced
1		jalapeno pepper -- seeded and minced
1/2	cup	fresh cilantro leaves
1½	lb	chicken breast -- cubed
4	cups	romaine lettuce -- sliced
8	ozs	goat cheese – crumbled

Weight Loss

4 Servings
4g Net Carbs

1. In a large mixing bowl, whisk together the olive oil, lime juice and cumin. Add to it the minced red onion, minced jalapeno pepper and cilantro. Toss.

2. Remove any skin or bones from the cooked chicken. Cut into bite sized pieces and add to the dressing bowl. Toss well.

   This much can be made a day in advance and refrigerated, which will intensify the flavors. Remove from refrigerator 15 minutes before serving.

3. Rinse and dry the romaine lettuce leaves. Slice or rip them into strips.

4. Toss the lettuce with the chicken and dressing until well coated. Add the goat cheese and lightly toss again. Serve.

Yields enough as a lunch salad for 2 or as a side dish for 4.

Per Serving: 627 Calories; 47g Fat; 47g Protein; 5g Carbohydrate; 1g Dietary Fiber

Induction Variation: Omit the onion.
3g net carbs; 623 Calories; 47g Fat; 47g Protein; 4g Carbohydrate; 1g Dietary Fiber.

Festive Romaine Salad

A colorful and nutritious salad which boasts 7 grams of fiber per serving. This salad will give a festive flare to any table.

6	cups	romaine lettuce leaves -- torn
1	cup	cherry tomato -- halved
1/2	cup	orange bell pepper -- diced
1/2	cup	green bell pepper -- diced
1/2	cup	Carb Well Classic Caesar Dressing
4	slices	bacon -- cooked and crumbled
2/3	cup	parmesan cheese -- grated

Weight Loss

4 Servings
6g Net Carbs

1. Cook the bacon in the microwave (on plenty of paper towels) or in a fry pan. Let cool then crumble.

2. In a large salad bowl add the romaine, tomatoes and the bell pepper. Pour on enough of the dressing to coat. Toss. Add the parmesan and bacon and toss again. Serve immediately.

Per Serving: 128 Calories; 5g Fat; 12g Protein; 13g Carbohydrate; 7g Dietary Fiber

Mixed Greens with Salmon & Lemon-Tarragon Vinaigrette

Lemon & tarragon are the perfect compliments to salmon.

6	cups	mixed salad greens
1	lb	salmon -- cooked
1/2	cup	Kalamata olive -- coarsely chopped
1/4	cup	red bell pepper -- chopped
3	Tbsps	extra virgin olive oil
1/4	cup	fresh lemon juice
2	cloves	garlic -- crushed
1/2	tsp	lemon zest
3	Tbsps	fresh tarragon -- finely minced
		salt and pepper -- to taste

Weight Loss

4 Servings
5g Net Carbs

1. The salmon should be broken into large chunks and free of any skin or fat.

2. In a small mixing bowl whisk together the olive oil, lemon juice, garlic, lemon zest and tarragon.

3. In a large bowl, toss the salad greens with just enough of the vinaigrette to lightly coat (about 1/2 more or less).

4. Arrange the greens on individual serving plates. Top each with the salmon, the chopped olives and the chopped bell pepper. Drizzle the remaining vinaigrette over each plate. Serve.

Per Serving: 324 Calories; 22g Fat; 24g Protein; 7g Carbohydrate; 2g Dietary Fiber

Rainbow Salad

This colorful salad is great to serve at parties with grilled meats or other monochromatic entrees. The presentation will get a lot of compliments and looks best on a platter served buffet style. This way people can take just the items that they prefer without fear of being a finicky guest.

6	cups	spinach
18		cherry tomatoes -- cut into halves
1		orange bell pepper -- thinly sliced
1		yellow bell pepper -- thinly sliced
1		avocado -- thinly sliced
1	cup	dill pickle -- small cocktail style
1	cup	blue cheese
1	cup	purple cabbage -- thinly shredded
2	cups	Low Carb Dressings -- Italian, Caesar, Ranch, Blue Cheese or Vinaigrettes

Weight Loss

6 Servings
8g Net Carbs

I dedicate this salad to my Aunt Pat, a fabulous artist in Florida, who incorporates all the rainbow and chakra colors into her paintings. She likes to say, "Eat a rainbow everyday." Not only is this sound nutritional advice, but as a metaphor this is spiritual wisdom too!

So what about blue food? Well, this recipe calls for blue cheese which really isn't very blue. Alternatively you can use blueberries, but they aren't very blue either. Another option is to use edible flowers such as blue pansies. But I just serve this salad on a cobalt blue platter so no one really notices that the blue is minimal in the rainbow. If you are not averse to using food coloring, then you can add one or two drops of blue in a bowl of water and quickly immerse and retrieve the blue cheese to give it a touch of a blue tint (careful not to over-do this). Of course you could also blue tint cauliflower or jicama, although these look particularly weird when blue. Yet that could be fun, depending upon your guests!

1. On a large platter, start arranging the veggies along the edge in an arc, rainbow style. Start with the tomatoes, followed by the orange bell peppers and then the yellow bell peppers. Lay out the avocado slices all aligned so that the yellow edge faces the yellow bell pepper. Then place the cocktail pickles next to the avocados, followed by the blue cheese and ending with the shredded purple cabbage.

    The cocktail dill pickles are optional as you don't really need more green in this salad. But the green coloration of the ones which I purchase from Wild Oats have a bluish hue to them. Besides, I love dill pickles. They can be whole, sliced or quartered.

2. Pile the spinach under the rainbow. Serve the dressings on the side. It's good to offer several different types of dressings.

My blue salad platter is not very big and I prefer that the spinach not hide any portion of the rainbow. So I generally keep half (or more) of the spinach in the kitchen and replenish it after a few people have made their salads. Enjoy; this is a fun salad!

Per Serving: 343 Calories; 32g Fat; 7g Protein; 11g Carbohydrate; 3g Dietary Fiber

Romaine & Basil Salad

Asiago cheese and roasted pines nuts fill out this salad

1	head	romaine lettuce
1/2	cup	pine nuts -- toasted
1/2	cup	Asiago cheese -- crumbled
1/2	cup	basil leaves -- julienne

Weight Loss

4 Servings
5g Net Carbs

Dressing

3	cloves	garlic
1/2	cup	extra virgin olive oil
2	Tbsps	wine vinegar
1	tsp	Dijon mustard
	pinch	salt
	pinch	black pepper

1. Make the dressing first. With the skin still on the garlic cloves, drop them into a small pan of boiling water and cook for 6 minutes. Drain and let cool for a minute. Remove the skins (if they are still on) and smash the garlic in a small bowl, making a paste. Add the mustard, vinegar and a pinch of salt and pepper. Blend well. Whisk in the olive oil. Set aside.

2. To toast the pine nuts, add them to a large non-stick dry skillet over medium heat. Stir occasionally. Transfer to a paper towel as soon as some color starts to form. Carefully watch this process for they can go from doing nothing to being burnt in short order.

3. Tear the lettuce into bite-sized pieces. Cut the basil into strips. In a salad bowl toss together the lettuce, basil, cheese and pine nuts. Whisk the dressing again and drizzle over salad and serve immediately.

Per Serving: 420 Calories; 40g Fat; 11g Protein; 9g Carbohydrate; 4g Dietary Fiber

Salad Nicoise

My low carb interpretation of this classic salad substitutes turnips
for the potato. It's nice served on a huge platter as a bunch dish.

1	head	bibb lettuce
4		romaine lettuce leaves
1		turnip
1/2	lb	green beans -- french style
1	can	albacore tuna
3		eggs, hard-boiled -- sliced
12		cherry tomato -- halved
1	cup	olives -- halved
12	ozs	Carb Well Italian Dressing

> **Weight Loss**
>
> 4 Servings
> 7g Net Carbs

1. Bring a large pot of water to a boil. And prepare a large bowl with iced water.

2. Meanwhile, trim off the stem and root ends of the turnip. Cut the turnip in half then slice in 1/4 inch thick slices.

3. Trim the ends of the green beans. Put the green beans in the boiling water and cook for 2 minutes, uncovered. Using a slotted spoon, remove the green beans and plunge them into the ice water bath. Let them soak for 2 or 3 minutes and transfer to a paper towel.

4. Let the boiling water re-boil and then put the turnips in the boiling water and cook for 5 minutes, uncovered. Using a slotted spoon, remove the turnips and plunge them into the ice water bath, replenish ice if needed. Let them soak for 2 or 3 minutes and transfer to a paper towel.

5. Line a platter or individual plates with the romaine lettuce leaves.

6. Tear up the bibb lettuce into bite-sized pieces and place in a large bowl. Pour a little dressing over the lettuce to lightly coat. Place the lettuce evenly over the romaine. Arrange the sliced eggs along one side of the platter (or plates).

7. In the same bowl used for the lettuce, toss the turnips with a bit of dressing and then arrange the slices on the opposite edge from the eggs. Then toss the green beans with a little bit of dressing and arrange in the center of the platter. Drain the tuna and lightly toss with a touch of the dressing and sprinkle over the green beans.

8. Sprinkle the halved tomatoes and olives over the salad. Serve at once. If you need to store the salad in the refrigerator before serving them do not toss the lettuce and veggies with the dressing before hand. Simply drizzle the dressing over the entire salad just before serving.

Per Serving: 366 Calories; 31g Fat; 13g Protein; 11g Carbs; 4g Dietary Fiber

Salad with Green Beans & Walnut

Freshly minced chives, basil and mint add unexpected flavor to this simple salad.

1/2	lb	green beans -- slender French type
4	cups	romaine lettuce -- thinly sliced
1/2	cup	walnuts -- roasted and chopped
1/4	cup	walnut oil -- unrefined
1/4	cup	sherry vinegar
1	Tbsp	lemon juice
2	Tbsps	fresh chives -- minced
2	Tbsps	fresh basil -- minced
2	Tbsps	fresh mint -- minced
1	pinch	salt and pepper -- each

Weight Loss

6 Servings
4g Net Carbs

1. Whisk together the walnut oil, vinegar, lemon juice, chives, basil, mint and the salt & pepper. Let stand at room temp while you prepare the salad.

2. Rinse green beans and trim the ends. Cut to desired lengths.

3. Steam the green beans until just tender but still a bit crisp (about 2 minutes in the microwave, depending on the green bean variety and amount of crispness desired).

4. Drain off the hot water and plunge beans into an ice water bath to stop the cooking process (and help retain that bright green color). Let sit in bath for at least two minutes. Drain thoroughly.

5. Shred or thinly slice the lettuce.

6. Toss together the green beans, lettuce and walnuts. Re-whisk the dressing then pour it over the salad and toss it again.

Serve immediately. If making the salad in advance, do not add then dressing until just prior to serving.

Per Serving: 163 Calories; 15g Fat; 4g Protein; 6g Carbohydrate; 2g Dietary Fiber

Southwestern Salad with Chicken & Avocado

I love all things southwestern including this spicy salad.

1	head	romaine lettuce
1/2	cup	cilantro leaves
1/2		red onion -- sliced into rings
1	cup	red & green bell peppers -- thinly sliced
1	lb	cooked chicken -- sliced
1		avocado -- sliced into 8 wedges
2	ozs	black olives -- sliced
1/4	cup	canola oil
2	Tbsps	fresh lime juice
1/2	tsp	cumin
1		jalapeno -- seeded and minced

Weight Loss

4 Servings
8g Net Carbs

The chicken for this salad needs to be cooked ahead of time. You can use left over chicken, grill some with your favorite southwest seasonings, or purchase cooked chicken slices (Tyson is a good brand).

1. Mix together the oil, lime juice, cumin and minced jalapeno. I like to put the dressing ingredients in a small jar and then shake it to mix it up.

2. In a large bowl, combine the lettuce, cilantro and onion rings. Toss with a little bit of the dressing, just enough to lightly coat.

3. To neatly slice the avocado, try this method: Cut the avocado in half and remove the pit. With a thin knife, slice through the avocado down the center; all the way through the flesh but not through the skin. Then make a slice on either side; evenly spaced Holding the ends with your thumbs, roll back the skin (turning it inside out) and let the avocado slices fall gently out (you may need to cut the wedges from the skin). Repeat with the other half. This will make 8 slices.

4. Divided the greens onto 4 serving plates. Arrange the chicken, avocado, olives and bell peppers. Drizzle some more dressing over the top and serve.

Per Serving: 463 Calories; 28g Fat; 40g Protein; 14g Carbs; 6g Dietary Fiber

Spicy Shrimp Salad

This salad is great for brunch, lunch or as a light dinner. It can be toned down simply by removing the jalapeno and the red pepper flakes.

1½	lb	shrimp – cooked
4	stalks	celery
1		bell pepper -- seeded
2		scallion -- chopped
4	cups	mixed salad greens
1	Tbsp	red pepper flakes -- as garnish

Weight Loss
4 Servings
5g Net Carbs

Dressing

1	cup	mayonnaise
2	Tbsps	Carb Options™ Ketchup
1	Tbsp	dill pickle relish
1	Tbsp	horseradish sauce
1	Tbsp	lemon juice
1	small	jalapeno -- minced

1. The shrimp should be cooked and have the shells removed. Chill for 1 hour.

2. For the dressing, remove the stem and seeds from the jalapeno pepper and finely mince. Put the mayonnaise, ketchup, relish, horseradish, lemon juice and jalapeno into a jar with a well sealing lid. Shake well. Alternatively, mix dressing ingredients in a food processor.

3. Cut the celery lengthwise then slice on an angle. Slice, chop or mince the bell pepper. Chop or mince the scallions.

4. In a bowl, toss together the shrimp, celery, bell peppers and scallions. Add enough of the dressing to well coat everything (perhaps all of it).

5. On four individual plates, place the mixed greens, then the shrimp mixture. Garnish with the red pepper flakes and serve.

Per Serving: 604 Calories; 50g Fat; 38g Protein; 8g Carbohydrate; 3g Dietary Fiber

Spinach & Prosciutto Salad

This spinach salad is complimented with prosciutto,
pine nuts and Parmesan Cheese

4	cups	baby spinach leaves
6	ozs	prosciutto -- shredded
2/3	cup	pine nuts -- toasted
2/3	cup	parmesan cheese

<table>
<tr><td>Weight Loss</td></tr>
<tr><td>4 Servings
4g Net Carbs</td></tr>
</table>

Dressing

2	Tbsps	red wine vinegar
1	Tbsp	lemon juice
2	cloves	garlic – minced
1	Tbsp	fresh basil – finely minced
1/4	tsp	fresh ground black pepper
1/3	cup	extra virgin olive oil

1. Get the dressing set up first. In a small jar or bowl add the vinegar, lemon juice, garlic, basil and black pepper. Shake or stir. Add the olive oil. Let this sit at room temp while you prepare the rest of the salad.

2. To toast the pine nuts, simply add them to a dry skillet over medium-high heat and casually stir until they start to take on some color. They can burn easily so keep a close watch. Turn them out on a paper towel to cool.

3. If you are using baby spinach, the leaves can be left whole, otherwise tear into bite-sized pieces. Be sure that the spinach is dry. Place in a large salad bowl.

4. Shred the prosciutto into small pieces. I do this with my hands but you can use a knife. Add to the bowl.

5. When ready to serve, shake or whisk the dressing and drizzle some over the spinach and prosciutto and toss well. Use just enough dressing to lightly wet. Add more as needed. Then toss in the pine nuts and parmesan cheese and serve immediately.

Per Serving 443 Calories; 37g Fat; 24g Protein; 6g Carbohydrate; 2g Dietary Fiber

Spinach Salad with Pecans and Maple Vinaigrette

Pecans, onions and peppers dress up spinach and arugula,
but it is the Maple Vinaigrette that pulls it all together.

2	cups	arugula
2	cups	baby spinach leaves
1/2	cup	pecan halves
1/2	cup	orange bell pepper -- slivered
2	Tbsps	red onion -- slivered

<table>
<tr><td>Weight Loss</td></tr>
<tr><td>2 Servings
6g Net Carbs</td></tr>
</table>

Vinaigrette

2	Tbsps	walnut oil -- unrefined
1	Tbsp	balsamic vinegar
1	tsp	maple flavoring
1	tsp	Splenda® -- optional

A simple salad that will truly impress your friends. You can use all spinach or all arugula but the combo it superb.

1. Toss together the spinach and arugula and divide between two plates. Sprinkle on top the slivered onion and peppers. Then add the pecan halves (best to leave them whole). I prefer raw pecan but roasted is good too (as long as they are not too salty).

2. In a small jar, add the walnut oil, vinegar and maple flavoring. Shake well and taste. The sweetness of the vinegar is generally enough to balance the maple flavoring. But some brands are more bitter than others. Add a touch of Splenda if needed. Drizzle dressing over the salad.

Per Serving: 327 Calories; 32g Fat; 4g Protein; 10g Carbohydrate; 4g Dietary Fiber

Spinach Sesame Salad

This is a quick lunch salad for 2 or a side salad for 4.

4	cups	spinach
2		eggs, hard-boiled -- sliced
1		red onion slice
2	Tbsps	toasted sesame seeds

<table>
<tr><td>Weight Loss</td></tr>
<tr><td>2 Servings
5g Net Carbs</td></tr>
</table>

Dressing

1/4	cup	sesame oil -- or canola oil
2	Tbsps	wine vinegar
1	Tbsp	soy sauce
1	Tbsp	tahini -- optional
1/4	tsp	garlic powder
1/4	tsp	Splenda®
1/8	tsp	ginger
1/8	tsp	pepper

1. Prepare the dressing first. In a jar with a tight fitting lid add all the dressing ingredients and shake well. Set aside for about 30 minutes, so the flavors can meld. If you are not using the tahini you can subtract 1g net carb from each of the 2 salads.

2. Be sure that your spinach is dry. Toss the spinach with some of the dressing, just enough to lightly wet it. Divide between 2 plates. Separate the rings of onion and add on top of the spinach. Add the egg slices and sprinkle each with the toasted sesame seeds. Drizzle some more dressing over the eggs and serve immediately.

Per Serving: 433 Calories; 41g Fat; 11g Protein; 9g Carbohydrate; 4g Dietary Fiber

Red Slaw with Raspberries & Walnuts

The color of this slaw helps jazz up the presentation of an ordinary plate but it is the flavor that will get all the attention.

1/2	small	red cabbage
1/4	cup	red wine vinegar
1/2	cup	walnut oil -- unrefined
1	Tbsp	Splenda®
1	cup	fresh raspberries
1/2	cup	walnuts -- coarsely chopped

<table>
<tr><td>Weight Loss</td></tr>
<tr><td>4 Servings
4g Net Carbs</td></tr>
</table>

1. Finely shred the cabbage in a food processor or with a sharp knife.

2. In a large bowl, add 4 or 5 of the raspberries and smash them with the back of a spoon. Add the vinegar and Splenda and mix well. Whisk in the walnut oil, adding it slowly. This step can also be done in a food processor.

3. Toss the cabbage in with the vinaigrette. Cover and refrigerate for at least an hour.

4. Right before serving, toss in the walnuts. Garnish with the remaining raspberries and serve.

Per Serving: 356 Calories; 36g Fat; 4g Protein; 7g Carbohydrate; 3g Dietary Fiber

Jicama Slaw

This colorful slaw is great for a picnic, barbecue or Mexican dinner.

Dressing

2	Tbsps	mayonnaise
1	Tbsp	lime juice
1	tsp	Splenda®
1/4	tsp	cumin
1/4	tsp	garlic powder
1/8	tsp	chili powder -- optional
1/8	tsp	salt

2	cups	jicama -- peeled & grated
1	cup	red cabbage -- grated
1		carrot -- grated
1		red bell pepper -- seeded & julienne
1/2	cup	cilantro -- chopped

Weight Loss
8 Servings
4g Net Carbs

1. Grate the jicama, cabbage and carrots. Julienne the red pepper (cut into thin matchsticks). Toss together.

2. To make the dressing; whisk together the lime juice, mayo, Splenda, cumin, garlic powder, salt and chili powder. You can substitute a dash of Tabasco for the chili powder. Taste test and adjust seasonings to your liking. Let dressing sit for 30 minutes. Whisk again before serving.

3. Pour the dressing over salad and toss well. Garnish with the chopped cilantro just before serving.

Per Serving: 53 Calories; 3g Fat; 1g Protein; 6g Carbohydrate; 2g Dietary Fiber

Chicken Salad Sandwich Wrap

This sandwich is made with a low carb tortilla; I highly recommend the whole wheat tortillas made by *La Tortilla Factory*.

3	ozs	chicken breast -- diced
1	stalk	celery -- diced
1	Tbsp	red bell pepper -- diced
2	Tbsps	mayonnaise
1	dash	cumin -- optional
	dash	fresh ground black pepper -- to taste
1		low-carb whole wheat tortillas

> **Weight Loss**
>
> 1 Serving
> 6g Net Carbs

1. Dice the chicken, celery and bell pepper fairly fine.

2. Stir in the mayo, pepper and cumin.

3. Place the chicken salad at one end of the tortilla. Roll up the tortilla half way tucking in all the chicken salad. Then fold over the ends and roll up the rest of the way. Serve immediately.

Per Serving: 384 Calories; 28g Fat; 28g Protein; 21g Carbs; 15g Dietary Fiber

Induction Variation: Omit the tortilla and wrap the chicken salad in a leaf of red tip lettuce.
1g net carbs, 304 Calories; 25g Fat; 20g Protein; 2g Carbohydrate; 1g Dietary Fiber

Turkey Salad

Left-over turkey gets jazzed up with a tangy mustard dressing

4	cups	cooked turkey -- cubed
1½	cups	celery -- chopped
1/4	cup	red onion -- chopped
1/4	cup	red wine vinegar
1/4	cup	lemon juice
2	Tbsps	canola oil
1/4	cup	Dijon mustard
1	tsp	Splenda®

> **Weight Loss**
>
> 4 Servings
> 5g Net Carbs

1. Whisk together the vinegar, lemon juice, oil, mustard and Splenda. Add the onion and let dressing sit at room temperature for about one hour.

2. In a large bowl, mix turkey and celery. Pour dressing over salad and toss well to coat. Chill for several hours or overnight. Serve on a large salad plate or bowl lined with lettuce leaves.

Per Serving: 341 Calories; 9g Fat; 57g Protein; 6g Carbohydrate; 1g Dietary Fiber

Greek Salad

This salad is more of a classic version than the Athena Salad presented earlier. Here the emphasis is on the vegetables and less on the salad greens.

2	cups	red leaf lettuce
1		cucumber -- cubed
1/2		green bell pepper -- chopped
1/2		red bell pepper -- chopped
2		scallions -- diced
1/2	cup	fresh flat leaf parsley
12		kalamata olives -- pitted
1/4	cup	feta cheese -- crumbled
1/4	cup	extra virgin olive oil
2	Tbsps	wine vinegar
1	tsp	fresh oregano
1/8	tsp	garlic powder

Weight Loss
4 Servings 6g Net Carbs

1. Cut the cucumber into bite-sized cubes. I like to retain the skin and the seeds, but you can remove them if you prefer. Remove the stems and the white membrane from the peppers and slice them into bite-sized pieces. Mince the scallions and rough chop the parsley. Cut the olives in halves. Mix all these together in a bowl.

2. Whisk together the olive oil, vinegar, oregano and garlic powder. Pour 2/3 of the dressing over the vegetables and toss.

3. Line 4 salad plates with the red leaf lettuce. Spoon the vegetables over the lettuce. Crumble 1 tablespoon of feta over each plate then drizzle the remaining dressing over each plate.

Per Serving: 203 Calories; 19g Fat; 3g Protein; 8g Carbohydrate; 2g Dietary Fiber

Marinated Green Bean Salad with Herbs

This is a great side dish for a summer meal of grilled meat, chicken or fish.
You'll want to make the whole batch so you can have left-overs.

1	lb	fresh green beans
1		red bell pepper -- thinly sliced
1/4		red onion -- thinly sliced
4	ozs	capers -- rinsed and drained
2	cloves	garlic -- minced
1	tsp	fresh oregano -- chopped
1	tsp	fresh rosemary leaves -- chopped
1/2	tsp	fresh thyme
1/2	tsp	Splenda®
1/4	tsp	salt
1/4	tsp	cracked black pepper
1/2	cup	extra virgin olive oil
1/2	cup	red wine vinegar

Weight Loss

6 Servings
5g Net Carbs

1. Blanch the green beans by dropping them into boil water for 2 minutes, then strain and put them in an ice water bath to stop the cooking. (If you use frozen beans then blanching is not necessary, just thaw them completely).

2. Put everything into a large re-sealable plastic bag or large Tupperware and shake/toss to get everything coated and mixed together. Refrigerate for at least 4 hours and up to 24 hours. Toss the bag several times while it marinates.

Serve cold or at room temperature.

Per Serving: 198 Calories; 18g Fat; 2g Protein; 8g Carbohydrate; 3g Dietary Fiber

Green Bean & Bell Pepper Salad

A simple and wonderful salad for your garden-fresh, green beans.

8	ozs	green beans
1/2		red bell pepper -- julienne
1/2	cup	red onion slices
1	Tbsp	balsamic vinegar
1/4	cup	Carb Well Italian Dressing

Weight Loss

4 Servings
4g Net Carbs

Fresh green beans are awesome in this salad. But if you only have frozen, you can simply skip the blanching and toss with the onion and peppers. Just be sure they have defrosted by the time you are ready to serve them (about 30 minutes on the counter top or 4 hours in the refrigerator). Canned green beans are not worth a dime in my opinion, and are not recommended for this salad.

1. Remove stem, seeds and membrane from the red bell pepper. Finely julienne. Slice the red onion into thin slivers. In a large Tupperware bowl, toss with the balsamic vinegar.

2. Trim green beans and blanch them by dropping them into boil water for 2 minutes. Drain and toss them in with the onions and peppers. Let the vegetables marinate for 1 hour in the refrigerator. Toss them a couple of times if you remember.

3. When ready to serve, toss in the Carb Well Italian Dressing.

Per Serving: 60 Calories; 4g Fat; 1g Protein; 6g Carbohydrate; 2g Dietary Fiber

Induction Variation: Omit the red onion and add 2 minced scallions (white parts only).
3g net carbs; 57 Calories; 4g Fat; 1g Protein; 5g Carbohydrate; 2g Dietary Fiber.

Broccoli Variation: substitute a head of broccoli for the green beans
5g net carbs, 87 Calories; 5g Fat; 5g Protein; 10g Carbohydrate; 5g Dietary Fiber;

Marinated Zucchini Salad

This salad is best when prepared a day ahead of time

1½	cups	**Carb Well Italian Dressing**	**Weight Loss**
2		**zucchini -- sliced**	
1/4	lb	**fresh mushroom**	**6 Servings**
6	ozs	**black pitted olives -- sliced**	**5g Net Carbs**
8	ozs	**canned artichoke hearts -- sliced**	
2		**scallion -- minced**	

1. Slice or cube the zucchini. Slice or quarter the mushrooms. Add both to a non-metallic mixing bowl.

2. Drain off the liquids from the olives and artichoke hearts (or bottoms). Cut the artichoke into slices. Add the slice olives, artichoke and minced scallions to the bowl. Pour in the dressing and toss. Cover and refrigerate for at least 4 hours - overnight is better.

Per Serving: 200 Calories; 19g Fat; 2g Protein; 7g Carbohydrate; 2g Dietary Fiber

Matchstick Salad with Spicy Citrus Vinaigrette

This salad always reminds me of the Caribbean;
my favorite vacation destination.

1	cup	cucumber -- sliced into matchsticks
1	cup	zucchini -- sliced into matchsticks
1	cup	red bell pepper -- sliced into matchsticks
1	cup	green bell pepper -- sliced into matchsticks
1	cup	jicama -- sliced into matchsticks
1		carrot -- sliced into matchsticks

```
┌─────────────────────┐
│    Weight Loss      │
├─────────────────────┤
│  6 Servings         │
│  5g Net Carbs       │
└─────────────────────┘
```

Vinaigrette

2	Tbsps	balsamic vinegar
1	Tbsp	lemon juice
1	Tbsp	lime juice
1/2	tsp	lemon pepper
1/4	tsp	orange extract
1/4	tsp	cumin
1/4	tsp	chili powder
1/4	tsp	ground allspice
	pinch	salt
1/4	cup	canola oil

This salad is best when the matchsticks are uniform. If you have a vegetable slicer, then this will help a lot. But patient knife work is just as good.

1. In a small non-metallic bowl, add the vinegar, lemon juice, lime juice, lemon pepper, orange extract, cumin, chili powder, allspice and a pinch of salt. Whisk and let sit until after you cut up the veggies.

2. It is nice if your cucumber is seedless and the skin is tasty. If not, then peel and remove the seeds before slicing into match sticks.

3. For the zuke, I usually cut it into quarters lengthwise then cut off and discard the center section before cutting into matchsticks.

4. For the bell peppers, cut off both ends (reserve for some other dish) and then use only the straight sides. Be sure to remove the seeds and membrane.

5. In a large bowl, toss the veggies.

6. Vigorously whisk the vinaigrette while you (or a helper) slowly adds the canola oil. Pour over the veggies and toss. Cover and refrigerate at least 20 minutes or up to several hours.

Per Serving: 115 Calories; 9g Fat; 1g Protein; 8g Carbohydrate; 3g Dietary Fiber

Mock Potato Salad

I really like this salad. Even though, it looks remarkably like potato salad, the taste is rather different. If you don't like turnips then you will not like this salad, no matter how delicious it looks. You can peel the turnips for a milder taste, but I love that "horseradish" flavor of the turnips so I never peel them.

2		turnips
1/4	cup	mayonnaise
1/4	cup	sour cream
1	tsp	mustard
1	tsp	Worcestershire sauce
1	Tbsp	fresh chives -- minced
1	tsp	dill
1/2	tsp	pepper
		salt -- to taste
1	dash	paprika -- for garnish

Weight Loss

4 Servings
4g Net Carbs

1. Cut turnips into bite size cubes. Put into a pot of cold water and bring to a boil. Cook on medium-high heat for 10 minutes or just until a fork pieces through without much resistance. Drain and cool.

2. Mix together the mayonnaise, sour cream, mustard, Worcestershire, chives, dill and pepper. Add salt to taste.

3. Add dressing to cooled turnips and toss. Serve right away or refrigerate for up to two days.

Per Serving: 150 Calories; 15g Fat; 1g Protein; 5g Carbohydrate; 1g Dietary Fiber

Don't confuse rutabagas with turnips. Turnips are white with a purple top. Rutabagas are yellow with a red top. Rutabagas are in the same family but have more sugar and therefore more carbs.

Shrimp & Snow Pea Salad

Shrimp salad is always a big hit at parties. The contrast of the
red and green colors makes this one particularly appealing.

1	lb	shrimp -- cooked
2	cups	snow pea pods
1		red bell pepper -- slivered
2		scallions -- diagonally sliced
1/3	cup	sesame oil
3	Tbsps	vinegar
2	Tbsps	soy sauce
2	tsps	ground ginger
2	tsps	Splenda®
1/2	tsp	Tabasco sauce -- to taste
1	Tbsp	toasted sesame seeds

> **Weight Loss**
>
> 4 Servings
> 7g Net Carbs

1. Shrimp should be fresh cooked and plunged into cold water then shelled and deveined. Or thaw frozen cooked shrimp.

2. Trim off and discard the stem end of the pea pods. If they are large, cut in half with a diagonal cut. Boil 1 or 2 quarts of water. Add the snow peas for 2 minutes (no longer, but 1 minute is okay). Immediately drain and plunge into a bowl of ice water to stop the cooking. Leave in there for a full minute. Drain.

3. Remove and discard the stem, seeds and membrane from the red pepper. Slice into matchsticks. Trim the scallions and slice thinly on the diagonal.

4. In a large non-metallic bowl, whisk together the oil, vinegar, soy sauce, ginger, Splenda and Tabasco sauce. Add to the bowl the shrimp, pea pods, red peppers and scallions. Toss well. Cover and refrigerate for 1 hour. Before serving, toss in the toasted sesame seeds.

Per Serving: 325 Calories; 21g Fat; 26g Protein; 10g Carbs; 3g Dietary Fiber

Smoked Ham & Cauliflower Salad

This is a great lunch salad to make the day after you have baked a ham.

2	cups	ham – cooked & cubed
1/2	head	cauliflower -- thinly sliced
1/2	cup	red bell pepper -- minced
1	cup	celery -- diced
2		scallion -- diced

<table>
<tr><td>Weight Loss</td></tr>
<tr><td>4 Servings
5g Net Carbs</td></tr>
</table>

Dressings

1/4	cup	canola oil
2	Tbsps	vinegar
1	Tbsp	Dijon mustard
1	dash	Liquid Barbecue Smoke® -- optional

I like my cauliflower raw but you can blanch it first if you'd like by dropping the half head into boiling water for about 2 minutes.

1. Thinly slice the cauliflower. Dice the celery and scallions. Mince the red bell pepper. Toss these with the cubed ham.

2. In a small bowl whisk together the canola oil, vinegar, mustard and the Liquid Smoke. Pour over the vegetables and toss. Serve as is or over a bed of lettuce.

Per Serving: 261 Calories; 21g Fat; 13g Protein; 6g Carbohydrate; 1g Dietary Fiber

Avocado & Tomato Salad

A simple salad full of flavor and nutrients.

4	cups	baby lettuce leaves -- mixed greens
1		avocado
2		tomatoes
2	Tbsps	lemon juice
4	Tbsps	extra virgin olive oil
1/2	tsp	salt and pepper -- each

```
┌─────────────────────┐
│ Maintenance         │
├─────────────────────┤
│ 4 Servings          │
│ 11g Net Carbs       │
└─────────────────────┘
```

1. In a large mixing bowl (large enough to hold the mixed salad greens), whisk together the lemon juice, olive oil and salt & pepper. Set aside about 2 Tbsps in a small cup.

2. Toss the salad greens in the large bowl with the dressing and then divide the greens onto four salad plates.

3. Slice the two tomatoes into four thick slices. (The end slices can be discarded or used in another recipe). Place one slice in the center of each of the four plates.

4. Returned the saved dressing to the large bowl. Cut the avocado in half and remove pit. Score the flesh in 1/2 inch squares. Turn the peel inside out and remove the cubes into the large bowl. Gently toss to coat. Then place 1/4 of the avocado onto of each tomato and serve.

Per Serving: 278 Calories; 22g Fat; 7g Protein; 18g Carbohydrate; 7g Dietary Fiber

Mixed Greens with Cucumber and Cashews

The cashews with the Thousand Island Style dressing makes this salad a good compliment for simple grilled steak or chicken.

4	cups	mixed salad greens
1		cucumber -- sliced
1	cup	cashews – dry roasted
1	cup	mayonnaise
2	Tbsps	Carb Options™ Ketchup
1	Tbsp	dill pickle relish
1	tsp	brown mustard
1	Tbsp	water

```
┌─────────────────────┐
│ Maintenance         │
├─────────────────────┤
│ 4 Servings          │
│ 12g Net Carbs       │
└─────────────────────┘
```

1. Peel the cucumber and cut in half lengthwise. Then slice.

2. For the dressing, put the mayonnaise, ketchup, relish, water and mustard in a jar and shake well.

3. On four individual plates, place the mixed greens, then the cucumber, then the cashews. Drizzle the dressing over each salad and serve.

Per Serving: 614 Calories; 63g Fat; 7g Protein; 15g Carbohydrate; 3g Dietary Fiber

Russian Salad

The beets and yellow bell peppers are beautiful together over mixed greens. It is the beets and a sour cream dressing that gives this salad a Russian flare.

3	cups	mixed salad greens
1		beet -- julienne
1/2		yellow bell pepper -- julienne
1/2		cucumber -- sliced

<table>
<tr><td colspan="2">Maintenance</td></tr>
<tr><td colspan="2">2 Servings
10g Net Carbs</td></tr>
</table>

Dressings

1/2	cup	sour cream
1	Tbsp	lemon juice
1		scallion -- finely minced
1	tsp	fresh dill -- 1/4 tsp if dried

I recommend using 1 fresh roasted beet, but substitute about 2/3 cup canned beets if you like.

1. To roast the beet preheat oven to 400°F. Scrub the beet and cut off the root tail. On the stem end leave about 2 inches of stem (this will assist with slicing after it has been roasted). Coat the beet in canola oil and place on a foil lined sheet pan. Roast at 400°F for about 25 minutes or until fork can piece through without too much resistance. Once it has cooled enough to handle, cut slices (hold the stems and start slicing from the root end - handy huh). Then julienne each slice.

2. While the beet is roasting, make the dressing. In a bowl or jar, mix together the sour cream, lemon juice, minced scallions and the fresh dill. Set aside.

3. Julienne the pepper and slice the cucumbers. I like to cut each cucumber slice in half, making half moons.

4. Divide the greens between two plates and top with beets, peppers and cucumbers. Drizzle the dressing over the salad at the last minute and then serve.

Per Serving: 178 Calories; 12g Fat; 5g Protein; 14g Carbohydrate; 4g Dietary Fiber

Mesa Verde Salad

This stacked salad has layers of cucumber, avocado and salsa
which makes an impressive presentation adjacent to a Southwestern grilled
chicken or steak. This may look complicated to make at first glance
but it really is easy once you get the hang of it.

1		cucumber
2	Tbsps	sour cream
1/4	tsp	cumin
1		avocado
1	Tbsp	lemon juice
1/4	tsp	garlic powder
1/4	tsp	chili powder
	dash	salt
1/4	cup	salsa -- chunky style
2		lettuce leaves -- red tip
2	Tbsps	chopped cilantro

Maintenance
2 Servings
11g Net Carbs

This salad can be a little tricky the first time you make it. But once you get the
hang of it you can whip it out rather quickly. Having the right tools is key.
You'll need two cans with both ends cut out. If you have a biscuit cutter, that
works great. I use 6 oz mushroom cans. I like the salad to be as tall (or taller) as
it is wide. You will also need parchment paper or wax paper and then the right
spoon or other devise to help pack down the cucumbers in the first layer. A
vitamin jar (or the like) which just fits inside your can would be ideal. Agile
fingers work okay too.

1. Peel the cucumber, cut in half lengthwise and scoop out and discard the
   seeds. Then dice the cuke fairly fine. Lay them on a stack of paper towels
   and using another towel press them down a little to let them give up a bit of
   their juices. In a small bowl, combine the cukes, sour cream and cumin. Use
   the firmest part of the sour cream up on the edges, not any of the watery part.
   Mix well and set aside.

2. In another small bowl, add the lemon juice, garlic powder, chili power and
   salt. Then add the avocado and smash it with a fork or spoon to mix all
   together. It can be left a bit chunky (my preference) or smashed until
   completely smooth.

3. If you are making this in advance then cut out a square of parchment paper to
   be the foundation so you can move the salad in and out of the refrigerator and
   onto the plates. Otherwise construction the salad directly onto the plate
   where it will be served.

4. Cut two strips of parchment paper that is at least as wide as your cans are tall
   plus 1/2 inch more and make it long enough so it can go around the inside of
   the can at least 1 and 1/2 times. Set the cans where you want the salad to be
   and line them on the inside with the parchment paper.

5. Start with the cucumber and make a layer that is at least 1/2 inch thick and press it down firmly with your fingers or that small jar I mentioned previously. Depending on your cans you may have some cukes left over. That's okay.

6. Then make a layer of the guacamole about as thick as you did the cukes and smooth it out flat.

7. To make the third layer; spoon up some salsa and squeeze out its liquid (back into its container or set aside for some other recipe). Make a layer on top of the guacamole, just enough to cover.

8. If making this part in advance then cover with plastic or more parchment paper and refrigerate.

9. Prepare the lettuce just before you are ready to serve. Roll the lettuce leaves and slice through chiffonade style to make shreds.

10. Now to unveil the salad. While holding the parchment paper still, raise the can up slowly and steadily. Unwrap the parchment paper slowly. Use a butter knife along the inside edge as it unfolds to help the salad keep its shape (this will make sense once you start to do it).

11. Add the shredded lettuce around the base and sprinkle the cilantro on top, careful not to knock the salad over. If you have any left over cukes or guacamole it can be added onto the lettuce in nice little dollops. Serve immediately.

Per Serving: 227 Calories; 19g Fat; 4g Protein; 16g Carbohydrate; 5g Dietary Fiber

---

I love Mesa Verde National Park; it is beautiful any time of year. One Spring visit was particularly lovely. There was a magical pocket of time where I was standing alone, when I was struck with how the sun's rays highlighted the earth tones of a mesa, lushly populated with evergreen trees rising above a crystalline layer of snow on the ground. Oh how I longed for paints, brushes and a canvas. I didn't even have a camera with me (left it in the car - darn it). All I have is the precious memory. This Mesa Verde Salad was created in honor of those wondrous 15 or 20 minutes.

Smokey Salad

Smoked turkey, smoked Gouda and roasted cashews over a bed of greens
and a smoky vinaigrette. This salad is a meal unto itself;
great for lunch or a light dinner.

4	cups	mixed greens
2	ozs	smoked gouda cheese -- cubed
6	ozs	smoked turkey breast -- cubed
		or smoked ham or smoked salmon
1/2	cup	cashews, dry-roasted

<table>
<tr><td>Maintenance</td></tr>
<tr><td>2 Servings
13g Net Carbs</td></tr>
</table>

Dressing

2	Tbsps	balsamic vinegar
1/3	cup	canola oil
1/4	tsp	Worcestershire sauce
	dash	garlic powder
	dash	Liquid Barbecue Smoke®

1. Make the dressing first by putting the ingredients in a jar and shaking well.

2. Toss the greens with a little bit of dressing and divide the greens between two plates.

3. In a bowl, add the cubed turkey, Gouda cheese and cashews. Pour in some of dressing and toss. Divide between the two plates and serve immediately.

Per Serving: 796 Calories; 66g Fat; 38g Protein; 18g Carbs; 5g Dietary Fiber

Induction Variation: Omit the cashews
3g net carbs; 599 Calories; 50g Fat; 33g Protein; 7g Carbohydrate; 4g Dietary Fiber.

Tabouli Salad

This nutritious Middle Eastern salad has too many carbs for your weight loss program but it is wonderful to have occasionally as a small side dish once you get to maintenance.

1/3	cup	**Tabouli - Casbah Brand**
1/3	cup	**boiling water**
1	Tbsp	**lemon juice**
1/4	tsp	**cumin**
1/4	cup	**fresh parsley -- minced**
1/4	cup	**fresh mint leaves -- minced**
1	Tbsp	**extra virgin olive oil**
1		**cucumber**
1	large	**tomato -- seeded and chopped**
2	cups	**spinach -- or lettuce**

Maintenance

3 Servings
11g Net Carbs

I prefer the Casbah brand tabouli mix, but other brands are pretty good too. If you decided to use plain bulgur wheat then increase the cumin, parsley and mint by two or three times.

1. In a mixing bowl, add the tabouli mix, the boiling water, lemon juice and cumin. Stir well and cover. Let sit for 10 minutes while you do the following.

2. Remove the stem from the tomato, slice in half and squeeze to remove the seeds (most of them anyway and that's good enough). Dice the tomato. Peel and dice the cucumber. Mince the parsley and mint leaves.

3. Uncover the tabouli and stir. Add the parsley, mint, tomatoes, cucumber and olive oil. Stir well, cover and refrigerate for 1 hour.

4. On 4 salad plates, make a bed of lettuce and then spoon the chilled tabouli into the centers.

Per Serving: 110 Calories; 5g Fat; 3g Protein; 14g Carbohydrate; 3g Dietary Fiber

Fruit Salad

The way to make a low carb fruit salad is in choosing an appropriate amount and type of fruits. This combo is very satisfying.

1	cup	watermelon -- cubed
1	cup	strawberries -- sliced
1/2	cup	raspberries
1/2	cup	blackberries
4	ozs	Dannon's Carb Control™ Yogurt

> **Maintenance**
>
> 3 Servings
> 10g Net Carbs

1. Remove the seeds from the watermelon (the seedless kind have less flavor) and cut into cubes. Slice the strawberries very thin. Leave the berries whole.

2. In a bowl, toss together the fruit with the yogurt. Serve right away or refrigerate until needed.

Yields 3 cups with 1 cup per serving

Per Serving: 74 Calories; 2g Fat; 3g Protein; 14g Carbohydrate; 4g Dietary Fiber

Reduced Carb Variation: Simply reduce serving size to 3/4 cups and make four servings instead of two.

7g net carbs; 56 Calories; 1g Fat; 2g Protein; 10g Carbohydrate; 3g Dietary Fiber.

Waldorf Salad

This classic salad is a treat for your maintenance program.
See a low carb version on page 134.

4	cups	red leaf lettuce
2	cups	celery -- diced
1		apple -- diced
1	cup	seedless grapes -- cut in halves
1	cup	walnut -- coarsely chopped
2/3	cup	mayonnaise
1/3	cup	sour cream
1	tsp	lemon juice
	dash	salt and pepper

> **Maintenance**
>
> 4 Servings
> 15g Net Carbs

1. In a bowl, combine the mayonnaise, sour cream and lemon juice and some salt and pepper. Toss in the celery, apples, grapes and walnuts.

2. Line four salad plates with the red leaf lettuce, then spoon the salad in the center of each plate.

Per Serving: 558 Calories; 53g Fat; 10g Protein; 20g Carbs; 5g Dietary Fiber

VEGETABLES

VEGETABLES

~ Regarding Vegetables ~

All of the health experts preach the virtues of vegetables no matter what type of diet we are talking about. We all nod our heads in agreement and completely believe that yes we should eat more vegetables. But do we? Are veggies an after thought, something to throw on the plate to make it "pretty", or to keep our steak company, but with little desire to actually eat them? It doesn't matter what kind of eating lifestyle or diet that you have chosen, the foundation really should be vegetables!

During the weight loss phase, there are some vegetable restrictions that come into play, but you can still have at least one leafy green salad and one or two servings of vegetables everyday. Once you've reached your goal weight, then your servings of salads and vegetables can be doubled or tripled or more. Generally the appropriate serving size for a particular individual is the size of your fist for your vegetable and 2 fists for your leafy green salads. For the average American, the volume of a fist is about 1 cup.

Yet not just any vegetable will do when we talk about a low carb weight loss program. But rest assured there are plenty of low carb choices and ways of cooking them to have something different everyday. It is prudent to have several different recipes that you love for every type of vegetable that you typically use. Be advised that there are a number of vegetables that should be avoided with a low carb weight loss program, such as winter squashes, beans, potatoes (including their delightful cousin the sweet potato) as well as corn and peas. However, these can be introduced into your diet in limited portions once you've reached the maintenance phase.

One needs to be cautious about over cooking veggies. To retain the maximum flavor, texture and nutrients, most veggies require a very short cooking time. The fresher the vegetables the better they are (of course) both in texture and nutritional content. But many frozen vegetables are excellent these days as they are usually frozen raw or just lightly blanched. Canned vegetable generally have very few nutrients left in them. So unless you live without a refrigerator for some reason, you are much better served with fresh or frozen veggies. (But it is rather important to have some canned vegetables around for emergencies – particularly if your area is prone to extended periods without electricity). Tomatoes are a notable exception as many brands of tomatoes still have significant nutrients left in them. Pumpkin also does well through the canning process. There are also quite of few other canned goodies like chili peppers, mushrooms, artichoke hearts, sauerkraut, olives, etc. that are very useful in the kitchen.

When preparing fresh vegetables, try to resist peeling them. Many of the vegetable's nutrients are in the peel, especially all those wonderful antioxidants and micronutrients that protects the plant from bacteria, fungus, insects and other unwanted guests. It is logical that nature would design it that way, huh. Those fantastic phytonutrients which protects the plants are also extremely beneficial to us. So unless the cucumber peel is much too bitter or your sauce just won't be right with bits of tomato peel floating around, try to leave the peel on where ever possible.

It is fortunate (or perhaps fate) that just about every low carb vegetable is also nutrient rich (the popular spud can claim neither quality). There are two green vegetables in particular that are very low in carbs and are nutrient powerhouses; broccoli and spinach - our low carb Champions. To read about the exceptional nutritional virtues of spinach see the salad section. But spinach is not just as salad green; it is wonderful cooked as well. It is great lightly braised or steamed with butter and a bit of vinegar. I mostly use cooked spinach in casseroles adding texture as well as taste and nutrients.

Broccoli is one of the vegetable Champions of the low carb diet or any other diet for that matter. This amazing vegetable is rich in vitamins C, A, B_6, B_2, E and vitamin K, as well as a generous supply of calcium, folic acid and fiber. But let's not forget it is also a good source of potassium, iron and polyphenol (that stuff in red wine that makes it a "health food"). Recent research is discovering a multitude of micronutrients in broccoli (including coenzyme Q_{10} an outstanding antioxidant) that all work in concert with each other to provide amazing health benefits. There is an abundance of studies and stories on the internet which document broccoli's tremendous cancer fighting properties. The primary nutrients which reduce the risk of cancer (as well as combating existing tumors) are sulforaphane and the indoles. These beneficial nutrients are also present in broccoli's close cousins, cabbage, cauliflower, Brussels sprouts, and kale. Broccoli is known to boost the immune system, fights off cardiovascular disease as well as reduces the risk for osteoporosis and cataracts.

When you are undecided about what vegetable to have with dinner, go for the broccoli. There are so many delicious, quick and easy ways to prepare it. I have several broccoli recipes in this cookbook, but let your imagination soar with this veggie. Just put a serving of broccoli in a microwave bowl, cover and zap it for 3 minutes if fresh or 2 minutes if frozen. Fresh broccoli may need a teaspoon or two of water, but the frozen will not. And don't throw away the liquids that have accumulated; drink those nutrients that slipped away (or at least offer them to your pets). Now top your broccoli with almost anything; butter and herbs; a low carb salad dressing; olive oil and sun dried tomatoes; simple oil and vinegar; butter and lemon juice; yogurt; tomato sauce; chili peppers; chopped nuts; … the list is endless. Try not to get into a rut; as you might cut back on eating broccoli if you get bored with it. I suggest that after 2 or 3 servings prepared in a particular way, no matter how much you love that method, try something new.

There are many other nutrient-rich, low carb veggies for your culinary pleasures including; asparagus, bok choy, Brussels sprouts, cabbage, cauliflower, green beans, kale, Swiss chard, turnips and all the greens (beet, collards, mustard, turnip, etc.). In the following table, I've provided the carb count for typical vegetables and legumes (beans). As I've mentioned before, not all sources agree on this stuff so don't sweat it if you see slight variations from some other table that you may have. The values shown here are the same as used in the analysis of the recipes in this cookbook.

Vegetables 1 cup Raw unless otherwise noted	Calories	Protein	Carbs	Fiber	Net Carbs
Artichoke hearts: canned	84	6	19	9	10
Asparagus: cooked, chopped	57	6	10	4	6
Beets: cubed	59	2	13	4	9
Beet greens: shredded	7	1	2	1	1
Bell peppers: chopped	40	1	10	3	7
Bok Choy: chopped	9	1	2	1	1
Broccoli: raw, chopped	25	3	5	3	2
Broccoli: cooked, chopped	44	5	8	5	3
Brussels sprouts: quartered	37	3	8	3	5
Butternut squash: cubed	63	1	16	2	14
Cabbage: raw, shredded	22	1	5	2	3
Cabbage: cooked, shredded	33	2	7	3	5
Carrots: raw, chopped	55	1	13	4	9
Carrots: cooked, chopped	69	2	16	5	11
Cauliflower: chopped	25	2	5	3	2
Celery: chopped	19	1	4	2	2
Corn: fresh kernels	133	5	30	4	26
Crookneck squash: chopped	25	1	5	2	3
Cucumber: chopped	13	1	3	1	2
Eggplant: chopped	21	1	5	2	3
Green beans: raw, quartered	34	2	8	4	4
Green beans: cooked, quartered	44	2	10	4	6
Jalapeno peppers: diced	26	1	5	2	3
Jicama: chopped	46	1	11	6	5
Kidney beans: cooked	207	13	38	9	29
Leeks: chopped	54	1	13	2	12
Lentils: cooked	230	18	40	16	24
Lima beans: cooked	216	15	39	13	26
Mushrooms: fresh, chopped	18	1	3	1	2
Mushrooms: canned, sliced	35	3	7	3	4
Okra: sliced	38	2	8	3	5
Onion: chopped	61	2	14	3	11
Parsnips: chopped	100	2	24	7	17
Peas: cooked	134	9	25	9	16

Vegetables 1 cup Raw unless otherwise noted	Calories	Protein	Carbs	Fiber	Net Carbs
Potato: cubed	119	3	27	2	25
Pumpkin: canned	83	3	19	7	12
Radishes: quartered	24	1	4	2	2
Rutabaga: raw, chopped	50	2	11	4	7
Scallion: chopped	31	2	7	2	5
Snow Peas: fresh	41	3	7	3	4
Snow Peas: cooked	67	5	11	4	7
Soy Beans: cooked	254	22	20	8	12
Spaghetti squash: cooked	42	1	10	2	8
Spinach: cooked	41	5	7	4	3
Sweet potato: chopped	139	2	32	4	28
Swiss chard: cooked, shredded	35	3	7	4	3
Tomatillos: chopped	42	1	8	2	6
Tomato: fresh, chopped	38	2	8	2	7
Tomato: canned, chopped	46	2	11	2	9
Turnips: chopped	35	1	8	2	6
Turnip Greens: shredded	15	1	3	2	1
Zucchini: chopped	17	1	4	1	3

Different color vegetables (and fruits) contain different nutrients which create those particular colors. It is a good idea to eat as many different colors as you can, thereby getting as many different nutrients as possible. Choose the vegetables (and fruits) that have the darkest hues. Sometimes you will not see much color variation but other times the colors are dramatically different. I notice this particularly with tomatoes. Do not select pink tomatoes; they simply are not worth the carbs. And look at those apples; a Red Delicious can be pale with yellow areas or it can be such a deep red that it is almost black. The deeper colored fruits and veggies have higher antioxidants and nutrient levels.

Orange foods are a special breed; they contain high levels of carotenoids (including, alpha-carotene, beta-carotene, lycopene, and many more). Red and yellow plants are generally rich in carotenoids too. This class of nutrients has been shown to have superior disease fighting properties, particularly the alpha-carotene and beta-carotene. These are powerful antioxidants that have been demonstrated to protect against cancer and well as improving eye sight and other problems associated with vision. When we think of an orange vegetable most of us will think of carrots first. However, pumpkin is the most potent source of alpha-carotene and is loaded with many of the other beneficial carotenoids as well. It is moderately low in carbs (6g net carbs per ½ cup) and quite high in fiber (over 3g in that same ½ cup). Fresh pumpkins can be quite a lot of work to cook with, but canned pumpkin remarkably retains most of its nutrients and is easy and convenient. I feed a spoonful of pumpkin to my dogs almost everyday and take a spoonful for myself too. It is delicious straight out of the can, but I have some cooked recipes in this cookbook for you too. Carrots are outstanding as well. Those baby carrots are convenient and a wonderful snack; however, their peels have been removed thereby reducing certain nutrient levels. You are better off getting regular carrots and just giving them a good scrubbing. Orange bell peppers are also particularly high in carotenoids as well as vitamin C and are very easy to incorporate into the low carb lifestyle particularly during phases when you need to keep your carbs very low. Other carotenoids rich foods include sweet potatoes, butternut squash, tomatoes and spinach. Yes, I know that spinach is not an orange food but the dark green leafy vegetables are also high in carotenoids, particularly spinach.

Tomatoes require a special note as well. Although they are only moderately low in carbs, they are so high in other nutrients that they should be a staple in your diet. Lycopene is one of the carotenoids which makes food red and tomatoes are loaded with it (also watermelon and red bell peppers, although at somewhat lower concentrations). Lycopene has been attributed with many health benefits including reducing the risk for many types of cancer and improving cardiovascular health. As with most veggies, a good portion of the nutrients are in the skin so don't peel that tomato. The smaller tomatoes have higher concentrations of nutrients than their beefsteak brothers, so go for the plum, cherry and grape tomatoes when convenient.

Legumes (beans) are generally too high in carbs to eat on a regular basis, but they are quite high in certain nutrients (particularly vitamin E, the B vitamins as well as many minerals) and they are very high in fiber. Fortunate for us on a low carb plan, legumes have almost as many nutrients as sprouts as they offer as grown-up adult beans. So eat your bean sprouts. Lentil sprouts are among the best.

Many cooking methods can destroy some of the nutrients in vegetables, especially vitamin C and the essential fatty acids (e.g., omega 3 & 6). However, cooking generally makes the majority of the nutrients more bio-available. So it is a good idea to occasionally eat some portion of your vegetables in their fresh, raw state; particularly broccoli, tomatoes and the orange, red and yellow bell peppers, which are all high in vitamin C. Did you know that steaming a vegetable in the microwave typically destroys fewer nutrients than the conventional steaming methods? Isn't that great!

Lemon Pepper Asparagus

Simple and tasty. The lemon zest curls makes this recipe look elegant.

1/2	lb	**fresh asparagus**
1	Tbsp	**butter**
1/2	tsp	**lemon pepper**
1	tsp	**lemon zest**

Induction
2 Servings
2g Net Carbs

1. Steam asparagus to desired doneness. The amount of time depends on the freshness and thickness of the asparagus and how much crunch that you like. I prefer asparagus that is "pencil size" which I steam for about 2 minutes in the microwave (with 1 Tbsp of water and tightly covered). For conventional steaming, it generally takes 3-4 minutes. Careful not to over-cook.

2. Melt the butter in a small sauce pan or zap it in the microwave. Add the lemon pepper and the lemon zest. Stir. Pour over the asparagus and serve.

The lemon zest can be from a grater type zester that makes tiny little flakes but then use only 1/2 tsp. I use a peeler type zester that makes elegant lemon curls.

Per Serving: 67 Calories; 6g Fat; 1g Protein; 3g Carbohydrate; 1g Dietary Fiber

Variations: Any vegetable. This is particularly good with green beans (4g net carbs) and broccoli (2g net carbs).

Asparagus with Mustard Sauce

Mustard isn't just for hot dogs and ham; it is great on veggies too!

1	lb	**fresh asparagus**
1/2	cup	**water**
1	Tbsp	**Dijon mustard**
2	Tbsps	**extra virgin olive oil (or other unrefined oil)**
1/4	tsp	**black pepper -- freshly ground**
1/4	tsp	**salt**

Induction
4 Servings
2g Net Carbs

1. Cut the asparagus in halves or thirds.

2. Mix together the mustard, oil and salt & pepper.

3. In a covered pot, add the asparagus and the water, cover and place on medium-high heat to bring to a boil. Boil for 3 minutes or until tender and the majority of the water has evaporated. Remove from heat, drain off excess liquid (if any) and place asparagus on serving platter.

4. Drizzle the mustard sauce over the asparagus and serve.

Per Serving: 77 Calories; 7g Fat; 2g Protein; 3g Carbohydrate; 1g Dietary Fiber

Variations: This sauce is good with any vegetable but especially broccoli (2g net carbs), cauliflower (3g net carbs) and Brussels sprouts (5g net carbs).

Baked Italian Asparagus

Although this may look a bit unusual, asparagus is great cooked with tomatoes and Italian herbs. The Parmesan cheese pulls it all together.

3/4	lb	fresh asparagus
1/2	cup	canned, diced tomatoes
1/2	cup	celery -- diced
3		scallions -- minced
1/2	tsp	oregano
1/4	tsp	thyme
1/4	tsp	garlic
1/2	cup	parmesan cheese

Induction
4 Servings 3g Net Carbs

Preheat oven to 350ºF

1. In a bowl, mix together the tomato, onion, celery, oregano, thyme and garlic.

2. Arrange the asparagus in a 9x13 casserole dish. Pour the tomato mixture evenly over the asparagus. Cover, bake at 350ºF for 15 minutes. Uncover and add the parmesan cheese. Bake another 10-12 minutes uncovered.

Per Serving: 69 Calories; 3g Fat; 6g Protein; 5g Carbohydrate; 2g Dietary Fiber

Tarragon Asparagus

Fresh tarragon and shallots give this quick and easy recipe a French flare.

1	lb	asparagus
1	Tbsp	fresh tarragon -- chopped
2	Tbsps	shallots -- chopped
1	Tbsp	butter
1	tsp	olive oil
1/4	cup	white wine

Induction
4 Servings 3g Net Carbs

1. Rinse and trim the asparagus. Chop the fresh tarragon leaves, reserving the tips of a few sprigs to use as a garnish.

2. In a large skillet over medium heat, add the olive oil and butter. Once the butter is melted, add the shallots and sauté for a minute or two, just until soft. (Do not brown). Add the asparagus, tarragon and white wine. Cover (use aluminum foil if your skillet does not have a lid) and let the asparagus steam for three minutes, or until tender.

3. Transfer to a serving platter or individual plates, garnish with the reserve tarragon tips.

The zest of 1/2 of a lemon is also a beautiful and tasty garnish too.

Per Serving: 63 Calories; 4g Fat; 2g Protein; 4g Carbohydrate; 1g Dietary Fiber

Ginger Broccoli

A ginger vinaigrette dresses up ordinary steamed broccoli.

1	head	broccoli -- chopped
2	tsps	fresh ginger
2	tsps	soy sauce
1	tsp	white wine vinegar
1	tsp	sesame oil -- or canola

Induction

4 Servings
3g Net Carbs

1. Peel the ginger root with a sharp knife. Add the peels to the water used to steam the broccoli. Steam the broccoli to your desire of doneness (typically 3-4 minutes). Do not over-cook.

2. Meanwhile, grate the ginger. Whisk together the ginger, oil, soy sauce and vinegar.

3. When the broccoli is done, drizzle the ginger vinaigrette over the broccoli and serve.

Per Serving: 55 Calories; 2g Fat; 5g Protein; 8g Carbohydrate; 5g Dietary Fiber

Creamy Cabbage

Shallots & celery seeds add a nice subtle flavor to this creamy cabbage dish.

1	head	cabbage
2	Tbsps	butter
1		shallot -- minced
1	tsp	celery seeds
1	pinch	garlic powder
1/2	cup	heavy whipping cream
		salt and pepper -- to taste

Induction

6 Servings
2g Net Carbs

1. Remove & discard large outer leaves and core from the cabbage. Slice cabbage (a little thicker than for cole slaw).

2. Bring to a boil a stock pot of lightly salted water. Add cabbage and cook for about 2 minutes. Drain and set aside.

3. In a large skillet, melt the butter over medium heat. Add the celery seeds and the shallots. Stirring frequently, cook for about 2 minutes.

4. Add the heavy cream and bring to a boil. Reduce heat and simmer uncovered for about 3 minutes (or until cream reduces enough to thicken).

5. Add the cabbage, garlic powder, salt and pepper. Heat thoroughly (about 2 minutes). Serve immediately.

Serve this with grilled polish sausage, corned beef or pork chops.

Per Serving: 109 Calories; 11g Fat; 1g Protein; 2g Carbs; trace Dietary Fiber

Pan Fried Cabbage

The beauty of this recipe, besides wonderful flavor, is that it is so quick and easy. For me, this is a mandatory side dish to Sauerbraten (page 230).

1/2	head	cabbage -- shredded
2	Tbsps	butter
1/2	tsp	garlic powder
1	Tbsp	balsamic vinegar

Induction

2 Servings
1g Net Carbs

1. In a heavy skillet, melt the butter over medium-high heat. Add the shredded cabbage and stir fry until the cabbage is nicely browned. You will want to cook this fast so that it gets good color but the cabbage still has a bit of crunch to it.

2. Turn off the heat; add the garlic powder and vinegar. Stir well. Serve.

An optional garnish is 1 Tbsp of sour cream mixed with fresh minced chives.

Per Serving: 111 Calories; 12g Fat; 1g Protein; 2g Carbohydrate; 1g Dietary Fiber

Cauliflower with Straw Mushrooms

This simple side dish is the perfect compliment to Asian main courses such as Teriyaki Chicken (page 273).

1/2	head	cauliflower
2		scallions
1/2	cup	canned straw mushrooms
1	Tbsp	sesame or canola oil
1	Tbsp	soy sauce
1	Tbsp	water
1/4	tsp	ground ginger
1	tsp	Splenda®

Induction

3 Servings
2g Net Carbs

1. Slice the cauliflower into florets.

2. Cut away and discard 1/2 of the scallions' green tops. Cut the remaining portion in half and then julienne.

3. Mix together in a small bowl the soy sauce, water, sweetener and ginger. Set aside.

4. In a large skillet, heat the oil over medium heat. Add the cauliflower and scallions before the oil begins to smoke. Stir fry for about 2 minutes. Add the mushroom and the sauce and cook for another 2 minutes, stirring frequently.

Serve immediately.

Per Serving: 55 Calories; 5g Fat; 1g Protein; 3g Carbohydrate; 1g Dietary Fiber

Creamed Cauliflower

This is a great low-carb substitute for mashed potatoes.
Frozen cauliflower works particularly well here.

2	cups	cauliflower
1	Tbsp	butter
1	Tbsp	heavy whipping cream
1/2	tsp	chives -- minced
		salt and pepper

Induction
2 Servings
2g Net Carbs

Steam or microwave cauliflower until it is very soft. Pour off excess liquids. Put cauliflower, butter and cream in a blender or food processor and puree until smooth. Stir in chives and salt and pepper to taste.

Per Serving: 102 Calories; 9g Fat; 2g Protein; 5g Carbohydrate; 3g Dietary Fiber

Mashed Turnips with Garlic

Similar to mashed potatoes but with a fraction of the carbs and twice as good.

2	large	turnips
1	cup	water
2	Tbsps	butter
1	Tbsp	heavy cream
1/2	tsp	garlic -- crushed and minced
		or 2 tsp of mashed roasted garlic
		salt and Pepper -- to taste

Induction
4 Servings
3g Net Carbs

Feel free to add chives or other herbs

1. Rinse and trim the turnips. If they are from late in the season then you may want to peel them unless you ready love that horseradish taste like I do. Cut the turnips into 1 or 2 inch cubes.

2. In a pan over medium-high heat, bring the water to a boil. Add the turnips, reduce to medium heat, cover, stir occasionally and cook for 6-10 minutes or until they fall apart with the poke of a fork. Pour off most of the water (I pour it into a bowl and see if I need any of this liquid in the next step).

3. Add the butter, cream, garlic and salt & pepper. Mash with a potato masher until creamy (or use a food processor). If more liquid is needed add some of the water they were boiled in (there are some vitamins and flavor in there) for no extra carbs. Or add more cream or butter as you like. Taste test and add salt and pepper, as needed.

Serve right away or cover and put in a warm oven until ready to serve.

Per Serving: 80 Calories; 7g Fat; 1g Protein; 4g Carbohydrate; 1g Dietary Fiber

Mock Rice Pilaf

This low carb look-alike made from cauliflower may become a staple at your home too. Several variations are offered to suit your main coarse.

1/2	head	cauliflower -- grated
1	stalk	celery -- minced
2		scallions -- minced
2	Tbsps	red bell pepper -- minced
1	Tbsp	butter
2	Tbsps	water -- or so
2	Tbsps	Carb Options™ Ketchup
1	tsp	Worcestershire sauce
1/2	tsp	oregano
		salt and pepper -- to taste

> **Induction**
>
> **4 Servings**
> **2g Net Carbs**

1. In a small bowl, mix together the ketchup, Worcestershire sauce and the oregano, set aside.

2. Grate the cauliflower. This is accomplished best by using your grating wheel in your food processor. But you can do this by hand also with a cheese grater. Mince the celery, scallions and peppers quite finely.

3. In a large skillet, melt the butter over medium-high heat. Add the celery, scallions and peppers and sauté for a minute or two. Add the cauliflower and sauté for a minute or so, stirring occasionally until it soaks up all the butter. Do not over-cook. Then splash in the water to let the cauliflower steam a bit (30 seconds or so).

4. Drizzle the ketchup mixture over the veggies (do not dump it all in one spot) and stir well. Taste and add salt or pepper as needed.

Serving Ideas: This goes well with just about any meat, poultry or fish. Adjust the seasoning to compliment your entree.

Per Serving: 38 Calories; 3g Fat; 1g Protein; 3g Carbohydrate; 1g Dietary Fiber

Variations are endless! Here are just a few ideas.

Spanish Rice: Add 2 Tbsps of chopped green olives (stuffed with pimentos) when you add the ketchup.
2g net carbs; 43 Calories; 3g Fat; 1g Protein; 3g Carbohydrate; 1g Dietary Fiber

Italian Rice: Substitute 1 Tbsp *Carb Well Italian Dressing* for the ketcup.
1g net carbs; 53 Calories; 5g Fat; 1g Protein; 2g Carbohydrate; 1g Dietary Fiber;

Mexican Rice: Use jalapeno pepper instead of red bell peppers. Add a 1/4 tsp chili powder with the oregano. Add 2 Tbsps salsa just before you add the ketchup mixture.
2g net carbs; 40 Calories; 3g Fat; 1g Protein; 3g Carbohydrate; 1g Dietary Fiber

French Rice: Use *Carb Option French Dressing* instead of ketchup. Use 1-2 tsp of Herbs Provence instead of the oregano. Use white wine instead of water.
2g net carbs; 65 Calories; 6g Fat; 1g Protein; 3g Carbohydrate; 1g Dietary Fiber;

Caribbean Rice: Substitute 1/4 tsp allspice, 1/4 tsp cumin, 1/4 tsp lemon pepper for the oregano. Omit the Worcestershire sauce. Add to the ketchup, 1 Tbsp lime juice and a couple of drops of orange extract. Add a minced jalapeno with the bell pepper.
2g net carbs; 39 Calories; 3g Fat; 1g Protein; 3g Carbohydrate; 1g Dietary Fiber;

Everyone will find a variation that they love. For an Asian flare, see the nest recipe below.

Mock Fried Rice

This low carb look-alike made from cauliflower is
totally awesome with an Asian stir fry.

1/2	head	cauliflower
2	stalks	celery
2		scallions
1	Tbsp	butter
2	tsps	soy sauce -- or more to taste
1/2	tsp	Splenda®
2	drops	orange extract
1	pinch	ginger
1	pinch	garlic powder

> **Induction**
>
> **3 Servings**
> **2g Net Carbs**

Asian fried rice often will have a bit of cabbage in it. Cauliflower is in the cabbage family and provides this distinctive taste.

1. In a small bowl, mix together the soy sauce, Splenda, orange extract, ginger and garlic powder. Set aside.

2. Grate the cauliflower. This is accomplished best by using your grating wheel on your food processor. But you can do it by hand also with a cheese grater. Mince the celery and scallions quite finely.

3. In a large skillet, melt the butter over medium-high heat. Add the celery and sauté for a minute. Add the cauliflower and scallions and sauté, stirring occasionally until the cauliflower starts to take on a bit of brown color (generally about 3 minutes).

4. Drizzle the soy sauce over the veggies (do not dump it all in one spot) and stir well. Taste and add more soy or pepper as needed.

Serving Ideas: This goes well with the Teriyaki Chicken (page 273).
Per Serving: 48 Calories; 4g Fat; 1g Protein; 3g Carbohydrate; 1g Dietary Fiber

Spaghetti Squash Italiano

A simple and delicious side dish which goes great with grilled meats or chicken.

1		spaghetti squash
1	cup	water
1/2	cup	Carb Well Italian Dressing -- warmed

Induction

4 Servings
2g Net Carbs

Preheat oven to 375°F

1. Slice the squash in half lengthwise. Scoop out and discard the seeds. Place face down in a baking dish, add the water and bake for 30-35 minutes at 375°F. Let cool for 5 minutes or more. (This can also be cooked in the microwave. Zap for 5 minutes, rotate and zap for another 5 minutes. Depending on your microwave in may need another 5 minutes or so.)

2. With a fork, carefully scrape out the insides lengthwise to maintain long strands. They should come out easily, if not it is under-cooked. Place strands in a bowl and add about 1/2 of the dressing (slightly heated, 1 minute in the microwave). Toss. Taste and add more dressing as desired.

Per Serving: 77 Calories; 8g Fat; trace Protein; 2g Carbohydrate; 0g Dietary Fiber

Pasta Sauce Variation: Replace the Italian dressing with heated *Carb Options™ Garden Style* pasta sauce. Add 1/4 cup of shredded parmesan cheese.
3g net carbs; 51 Calories; 3g Fat; 3g Protein; 4g Carbohydrate; 1g Dietary Fiber

Spinach with Mushrooms & Bacon

This is one of my favorite ways to eat cooked spinach.

1	lb	spinach leaves
2	slices	bacon
2	slices	red onion
1/2	lb	mushroom
1/4	tsp	cracked black pepper
1	Tbsp	balsamic vinegar
1	tsp	Dijon mustard

Induction

4 Servings
3g Net Carbs

1. In a small bowl, mix together the vinegar and mustard. Set aside.

2. In a very large skillet over medium-high heat, cook the bacon strips until very crispy. Transfer to paper towel. Crumble when cooled and set aside.

3. Pour off all but 1 Tbsp of the bacon fat. Reduce heat to medium and add the onions, separating them into rings and cook until translucent. Add the mushroom and cracked pepper; cook for 2 minutes, stir occasionally. Add the spinach and cook until just wilted turning the leaves over with tongs as it cooks. Remove from heat and toss in the vinegar mixture. Serve immediately.

Per Serving: 54 Calories; 2g Fat; 5g Protein; 6g Carbohydrate; 3g Dietary Fiber

Swiss Chard Caesar

Simple, delicious and perfect for your low carb induction phase.

6	cups	Swiss chard -- shredded
1	cup	Carb Options™ Caesar Dressing
1/4	cup	Parmesan cheese -- shredded

Induction

2 Servings
2g Net Carbs

1. In a large skillet or pot, over medium-high heat, bring the dressing to a boil. Add the Swiss chard and toss until just wilted.

2. Remove from heat, cover and let steam another minute or two.

Garnish with parmesan cheese (shredded is better than grated).

Per Serving: 342 Calories; 35g Fat; 6g Protein; 4g Carbohydrate; 2g Dietary Fiber

Moroccan Spiced Vegetables

The garlic, lemon and cumin are what give these vegetables that Moroccan flavor.

2		crookneck yellow squash -- cubed
1	cup	broccoli -- chopped
1	cup	cauliflower -- chopped
2	cloves	garlic -- sliced
2	Tbsps	canola oil
1	tsp	cumin
1	Tbsp	lemon juice
1	tsp	Splenda® -- optional
1	Tbsp	lemon zest -- as garnish, optional

Induction

4 Servings
3g Net Carbs

1. Heat oil in a large skillet (or wok) over medium-high heat. Add the squash, broccoli and cauliflower. Stir fry for about 3 minutes.

2. Add the garlic and cumin. Stir and cook for another minute. Remove from heat.

3. Mix the Splenda with the lemon juice. Pour this over the vegetables and stir.

Serve garnished with lemon zest. I like to serve this with a simple grilled meat or fish. This is also good served chilled.

Per Serving: 90 Calories; 7g Fat; 2g Protein; 6g Carbohydrate; 3g Dietary

Almond Broccoli Dijon

This is a delicious combination of flavors. It cooks up quick in the microwave.

2	cups	broccoli -- frozen
2	Tbsps	almond slivers
1	Tbsp	mayonnaise
1	Tbsp	sour cream
1	Tbsp	Dijon mustard

> **Weight Loss**
>
> **2 Servings**
> **5g Net Carbs**

If your almonds are raw then cook as below. But if they are toasted (my preference) then use as a garnish and add them just before serving.

1. In a microwave safe bowl, add the broccoli and zap for 2 minutes to defrost. Add the almonds and zap another 2 minutes to cook (times may vary depending on microwave).

2. Meanwhile; in a small, bowl mix together the mayo, sour cream and mustard.

3. When the broccoli is done, pour off the liquids (the chef gets to drink this!) and toss broccoli with the dressing. Serve immediately.

Per Serving: 164 Calories; 13g Fat; 7g Protein; 10g Carbohydrate; 5g Dietary Fiber

Broccoli Casserole

Broccoli in a creamy sauce with a parmesan crusted top.

1	lb	broccoli -- coarsely chopped
4	ozs	canned mushroom slices
4		scallions -- diced
2/3	cup	mayonnaise
2/3	cup	sour cream
2	tsps	paprika
1/2	tsp	oregano
1/2	tsp	thyme
1/4	tsp	pepper
1/8	tsp	salt
1/2	cup	parmesan cheese -- shredded

> **Weight Loss**
>
> **4 Servings**
> **5g Net Carbs**

1. In a microwave and oven proof casserole dish add the broccoli and 1/2 of the juice from the can of mushrooms (about 1 Tbsp of liquid). Cover and zap in the microwave for 3 minutes for frozen and 4 minutes for fresh broccoli.

2. Meanwhile; in a mixing bow, blend together the mayo, sour cream, paprika, oregano, thyme, salt and pepper. Mix well. When the broccoli is done, stir in the mayo mixture and the mushrooms. Evenly spread out the broccoli.

3. Sprinkle the top with Parmesan cheese and put under a 500°F broiler for about 3-5 minutes or until it begins to bubble.

Per Serving: 426 Calories; 43g Fat; 9g Protein; 9g Carbohydrate; 4g Dietary Fiber

Broccoli & Walnuts with Vinaigrette

This is an elegant way to serve our champion of all vegetables – broccoli!
It is best served hot and still quite crunchy; but left-overs
make a fine lunch salad the next day.

1	head	broccoli -- chopped
2/3	cup	walnuts -- chopped
1	Tbsp	shallot -- minced
1/2	cup	walnut oil
3	Tbsps	balsamic vinegar
	pinch	garlic power
	pinch	salt

Weight Loss

4 Servings
6g Net Carbs

1. Rinse and let dry the broccoli. Cut into bite sized pieces. Mince the shallots and coarsely chop the walnuts.

2. Pour a little bit of the walnut oil (~1 Tbsp) into a large skillet over medium heat. Do not cook with the heat too high. Add the shallots and broccoli. Stir frequently at first to coated everything (add more walnut oil if needed to coat) then stir just occasionally for about 3-5 minutes. You want the broccoli to be heated all the way through but still retaining as much crunch as possible. During the last minute of cooking add the chopped walnuts (if they are raw you can add them earlier).

3. Meanwhile; whisk together the remaining walnut oil, vinegar and garlic powder. If your walnuts were unsalted, then add a pinch or two of salt to the vinaigrette.

4. When the broccoli is cooked to your liking, remove from the heat. Pour the vinaigrette over the broccoli, toss and serve.

Per Serving: 413 Calories; 40g Fat; 10g Protein; 12g Carbs; 6g Dietary Fiber

Brussels Sprouts with Glazed Onions

Onions glazed in balsamic vinegar jazzes up ordinary Brussels sprouts.

12	oz	Brussels sprout
2	Tbsps	butter
1	Tbsp	olive oil
1/4		red onion -- sliced
2	Tbsps	balsamic vinegar
		salt and pepper -- to taste

> **Weight Loss**
>
> 4 Servings
> 5g Net Carbs

1. Rinse Brussels sprouts and trim off outer leaves and bottom stems. Slice in halves.

2. Steam the sprouts over boiling water for 4 minutes. Drain.

3. Meanwhile, have prepared the sliced red onion

4. Heat a skillet over medium high heat, adding 1 Tbsp butter & half the olive oil. Add the Brussels sprouts, toss occasionally and cook until they brown. Transfer sprouts to serving dish, sprinkle with salt and pepper and cover.

5. Add the remaining olive oil and butter to the skillet. Add the onions; stir occasionally until wilted (about 3 minutes).

6. Carefully add the vinegar. Scrape the bottom of the pan with spatula or spoon to loosen the brown bits. Stir and cook only about 30 seconds.

7. Add the onions to the Brussels sprouts, toss and serve immediately.

Per Serving: 119 Calories; 9g Fat; 3g Protein; 8g Carbohydrate; 3g Dietary Fiber

Brussels Sprouts with Buttered Pecans

Brussels sprouts sautéed with pecan always reminds be of cool autumn evenings.

2	cups	Brussels sprout -- trimmed and halved
3	Tbsps	butter
1/2	cup	pecan halves -- chopped
	pinch	Splenda® -- optional

> **Weight Loss**
>
> 2 Servings
> 8g Net Carbs

1. Trim the Brussels sprouts and cut them in half. Steam for about 5 minutes or just until tender (do not over cook). Drain well.

2. Meanwhile, in a skillet over medium heat, melt the butter. Add the chopped pecans and sauté for about 3 minutes. Toss in the Brussels sprouts cook for 1-2 minutes. Sprinkle with Splenda. Serve.

Per Serving: 370 Calories; 36g Fat; 5g Protein; 13g Carbohydrate; 5g Dietary Fiber

Poached Red Cabbage

Red cabbage poached in a flavorful stock and garnished with orange peppers. This makes a beautiful presentation and can transform bratwurst or kielbasa into an impressive dinner.

1/2	head	red cabbage -- shredded
1		scallion -- minced
1/2	cup	chicken stock
1	Tbsp	balsamic vinegar
1	Tbsp	red wine vinegar
1	Tbsp	brown mustard
1/2	tsp	caraway seeds
1/2	tsp	lemon pepper
1/2		orange bell pepper
3	Tbsp	sour cream
1	tsp	fresh dill

Weight Loss
3 Servings
4g Net Carbs

1. In a large skillet over medium-high heat, add the chicken stock, balsamic vinegar, wine vinegar, mustard, minced scallions, caraway seeds and lemon pepper. Bring to a boil while you stir to incorporate the mustard. Add the cabbage, stir and reduce heat. Cover and simmer for 6-8 minutes, stirring occasionally.

2. Meanwhile, remove the seeds and membrane from the orange bell pepper. Slice into the thinnest slivers that you can.

3. When the cabbage is done, use tongs or a slotted spoon to transfer to a serving platter. Toss in the slivers of bell pepper.

4. Serve garnished with the sour cream and a sprinkle of fresh dill.

Per Serving: 54 Calories; 4g Fat; 2g Protein; 5g Carbohydrate; 1g Dietary Fiber

Kielbasa Dinner Variation: Cut one hoop of kielbasa into 6 sections. Drop into boiling water and cook for 3-5 minutes, just until heated through. Drain and add to the serving platter with the cabbage.

7g net carbs; 523 Calories; 45g Fat; 22g Protein; 8g Carbohydrate; 1g Dietary Fiber;

Pepper Jack Cauliflower

Pan fried cauliflower with pepper jack cheese and chili peppers;
a great compliment to grilled chicken or steak.

1/2	head	cauliflower
1	Tbsp	butter
4	ozs	canned chili peppers
2		scallion -- chopped
1/2	tsp	cumin
	dash	salt
2	ozs	pepper jack cheese

Weight Loss

2 Servings
4g Net Carbs

Have everything ready before you start cooking. Slice the cauliflower, chop the scallions and drain the chili peppers. Shred the pepper jack cheese (that's Monterey Jack cheese with jalapeno peppers in it).

1. In a large skillet over medium-high heat, melt the butter and add the cauliflower. Stir occasionally until the cauliflower starts to take on some color (about 5 minutes). Then add the scallions, chili peppers, cumin and a dash of salt. Cook another 2 minutes, stir frequently.

2. Remove from heat, toss in the pepper jack cheese and transfer the cauliflower to a serving dish or individual plates.

Per Serving: 181 Calories; 15g Fat; 8g Protein; 6g Carbohydrate; 2g Dietary Fiber

Chicken Dinner Variation: Make this into a one pot meal by adding 12 oz of diced cooked chicken when you add the scallions and chili peppers (you may need to cook it for a couple of minutes longer to completely heat the chicken).
4g net carbs; 453 Calories; 25g Fat; 49g Protein; 6g Carbohydrate; 2g Dietary Fiber

Pickled Cauliflower

This medley of cauliflower, pickles, onions and bell pepper
makes a nice summer side dish for grilled burgers, bratwurst or the like.
It's pretty served on a leaf of lettuce. It can also be served in smaller portions
as a garnish with any meat dish.

1	head	cauliflower
4	whole	dill pickles
1/2	cup	pickle juice
1/2	cup	apple cider vinegar
2	Tbsps	red onion -- slivered
2	Tbsps	red bell pepper -- slivered
1	clove	garlic -- minced
1	tsp	Splenda®

Weight Loss

6 Servings
5g Net Carbs

1. Separate cauliflower into florets. Steam in the microwave with 1 Tbsp of water for 2-3 minutes. You'll want the cauliflower to retain most of its crispness, so be careful not to over cook it. Drain.

2. Cut the dill pickles into small chunks, about 1/2 the size of the largest florets.

3. Mix all ingredients together in a non-metallic mixing bowl (or a large jar). Cover and refrigerate for at least 8 hours (but 24 hours is better). Drain off liquids before serving.

A sprig of dill makes a nice garnish.

Per Serving: 20 Calories; trace Fat; 1g Protein; 6g Carbohydrate; 1g Dietary Fiber

Grilled Eggplant Parmesan

Grilled eggplant with plenty of cheese smothered in low carb pasta sauce.

1	lb	eggplant
2	Tbsps	olive oil
2	tsps	dried Italian herbs
		oregano, parsley, garlic & rosemary
6	ozs	mozzarella cheese
1/4	cup	parmesan cheese
1	cup	Carb Options™ Garden Style Pasta Sauce
1	Tbsp	parsley -- minced

Weight Loss
6 Servings
5g Net Carbs

Prepare grill

1. Mix olive oil with the herbs; set aside.

2. Slice off both ends of the eggplant, then slice the remainder into 6 round slices (about 3/4 inch thick).

3. Slice mozzarella cheese into 6 round slices.

4. Brush each side of eggplant with the oil mixture and place on a medium-hot grill. Close the lid of the grill. Turn eggplant after 3 minutes. Cook another 3 minutes, then move eggplant away from direct heat on the grill and place 1 slice of mozzarella cheese on each eggplant round.

5. Meanwhile; heat the pasta sauce in the microwave.

6. Place eggplant on serving platter. Pour sauce over the eggplant. Then sprinkle the parmesan cheese and parsley. Serve immediately.

Per Serving: 188 Calories; 14g Fat; 9g Protein; 7g Carbohydrate; 2g Dietary Fiber

French Tarragon Green Beans

This recipe is made quick & easy by using frozen French style green beans and zapping them in the microwave with shallots and tarragon.

2	cups	frozen green beans -- French Cut Style
1	Tbsp	butter
2	tsps	shallot -- minced
1	tsp	fresh tarragon -- chopped
1	Tbsp	tarragon vinegar

Weight Loss

2 Servings
7g Net Carbs

1. In a microwave safe bowl, add the butter, minced shallots and green beans. Cover tightly with plastic wrap and piece with a knife in two places. Zap in the microwave for 2 minutes. Toss or stir and zap for another minute.

2. Remove from microwave, add the tarragon and the tarragon vinegar then toss or stir. Cover again and serve within a couple of minutes.

Per Serving: 95 Calories; 6g Fat; 2g Protein; 10g Carbohydrate; 3g Dietary Fiber

Mediterranean Green Beans

Green beans prepared with sun-dried tomatoes, capers and olive oil transports you to the Mediterranean Sea.

1	lb	green beans -- fresh
1/4	cup	sun-dried tomatoes
2	Tbsps	extra virgin olive oil
1	Tbsp	Dijon mustard
1	Tbsp	lemon juice
2	Tbsps	capers – rinsed and drained

Weight Loss

4 Servings
5g Net Carbs

1. Drain the tomatoes and coarsely chop. Drain and rinse the capers.

2. In a large bowl, mix together the olive oil, mustard and lemon juice. Add the tomatoes and capers; mix well. Set aside.

3. Steam the green beans just until tender (3-5 minutes). The green beans should still have a bit of a crunch to them.

4. Once the green beans are cooked and drained, add them to the mixing bowl and toss with the tomato mixture. Serve immediately.

Per Serving: 110 Calories; 8g Fat ; 2g Protein; 9g Carbohydrate; 4g Dietary Fiber

Garlic Green Beans with Pine Nuts

Green beans sautéed with garlic is topped off with
a splash of wine and toasted pine nuts.

4	cups	green beans
1/4	cup	pine nut
	pinch	salt
1	tsp	olive oil
3	cloves	garlic
1	Tbsp	white wine
1	Tbsp	butter
1	tsp	fresh oregano -- minced

Weight Loss

4 Servings
6g Net Carbs

Fresh green beans are best but frozen will do just fine. Forget about canned green beans.

1. To toast the pine nuts; add to a non-stick skillet over medium heat. Keep the pine nuts moving frequently by stirring or tossing being sure that they are getting turned over. As soon as a bit of color is beginning to show, remove them to a paper towel and sprinkle with a pinch of salt.

2. Trim the green beans and slice the garlic. If it is easier to mince the garlic feel free to do so.

3. Return the skillet to the heat and add the olive oil and garlic. Sauté for 1 minute. Add the green beans and sauté until tender (2-4 minutes). Add the wine and stir. Add the oregano and the butter. Sauté for 1 minute.

4. Transfer to serving platter and garnish with the toasted pine nuts.

Per Serving: 124 Calories; 8g Fat; 4g Protein; 10g Carbohydrate; 4g Dietary Fiber

Stewed Okra

A traditional Southern dish; okra stewed in tomatoes.

3	cups	okra -- sliced 1/2-inch thick
1	Tbsp	canola oil
1	cup	onion -- diced
1	stalk	celery -- diced
1/4	cup	dry white wine
1	cup	canned, diced tomatoes
2	tsp	Creole seasoning

Weight Loss

4 Servings
9g Net Carbs

In a skillet over medium-high heat, heat the oil and add the onions and celery. Sauté until the onions are translucent. Add the wine and deglaze the pan. Add the tomatoes and the seasoning. Bring to a boil and then reduce heat to a simmer. Add the okra, stir, cover and let simmer for 20 minutes.

Per Serving: 99 Calories; 4g Fat; 3g Protein; 13g Carbohydrate; 4g Dietary Fiber

Faux Fries

This low carb adaptation of French fries tastes even better than then real thing. I particularly like the spicy variation provided. Hey McDonald's, do you want to have a French fry cook-off competition!

1/2		**jicama**
1/4	cup	**peanut oil**
1/2	tsp	**salt -- or more if needed**

Weight Loss
3 Servings 6g Net Carbs

Do you ever crave French fries? Well here's your answer. These are so good with a grilled burger and will satisfy that craving completely. The only problem with these fries, is the same problem with all fries: they are fried! High heat frying produces the best flavor results, but the possibility of creating trans fatty acids is a little bit worrisome. The approach is to use fresh refined peanut oil, bring it to temperature without letting it smoke (when it starts to make trans fatty acids), cook quickly and then don't use the oil again. It is leaving oils at high heat over a period of time that is the problem. Some high end restaurants change their fry oil daily; but fast food chains sometimes will go for weeks. Peanut oil is by far your best choice since it can withstand the most heat before starting to breakdown.

1. Peel the jicama. I think a knife works best but a sharp vegetable peeler may work too. The jicama should be sliced just a wee bit bigger than the size of fast food fries.

2. In a fry pan, heat the oil until it quivers but well under the smoke point. Add the fries carefully; using long handled tongs (or wrap your hand in a towel) and cook on each side for about 30-60 seconds or until desired color (the first side will take longer). With tongs or a slotted spoon transfer to paper towels and immediately salt them. They can also be cooked in a deep-fat fryer if you happen to have one.

Serve with low carb Ketchup if desired.

Per Serving: 201 Calories; 18g Fat; 1g Protein; 10g Carbohydrate; 5g Dietary Fiber

Spicy Variation: I like my fries spicy. So before I begin frying I mix together with the 1/2 tsp salt, a scant 1/4 tsp garlic powder and a scant 1/4 tsp of chili powder. Toss this with the fries immediately after cooking.

Confetti Snow Peas

This colorful dish uses finely chopped red, yellow
and orange bell peppers to give it a festive look.

1/2	lb	snow pea pods
1	Tbsp	yellow bell pepper -- diced
1	Tbsp	red bell pepper -- diced
1	Tbsp	orange bell pepper -- diced
1	Tbsp	onion -- diced
1	Tbsp	butter
1	tsp	olive oil
		salt and pepper -- to taste

Weight Loss

3 Servings
5g Net Carbs

1. Chop the peppers and onions into small uniform bits. Remove the ends from the snow peas. If they are larger than bite size then cut them in half at a diagonal.

2. In a skillet or sauce pan over medium-high heat, add the butter and olive oil. Add the onions and sauté for a minute or two. Add the peppers and snow peas and sauté an additional two minutes or just until tender. Do not over-cook. Serve immediately.

Per Serving: 83 Calories; 5g Fat; 2g Protein; 7g Carbohydrate; 2g Dietary Fiber

Patty Pan Squash Stuffed with Pesto

These beautifully scalloped squash are wonderful;
although, they are rarely available at an ordinary grocery store.
Look for them at a farmer's market or a health food store
during the summer months. Use the green, white or yellow type.

2		patty pan squash
2	Tbsps	pesto sauce
1	Tbsp	pine nut -- roasted
1	Tbsp	Parmesan cheese – shredded

Weight Loss

2 Servings
6g Net Carbs

Serving them this way is so attractive on a plate, especially with something that has sauce or gravy running everywhere.

1. Choose squash that stand up well. Cut off the stem end about 1/4 to 1/2 an inch. Using a spoon or knife, cut out a small cavity enough to hold about 1 Tbsp of pesto. Place on a plate or shallow dish and cover. Zap in the microwave for about 4 minutes.

2. Meanwhile mix together the pesto, toasted pine nuts (whole or chopped) and the shredded parmesan cheese. When the squash are done, spoon the pesto into the cavity and re-cover. Let rest for 1 minute covered then serve.

Per Serving: 151 Calories; 10g Fat; 7g Protein; 10g Carbohydrate; 4g Dietary Fiber

Layered Squash Bake

Herbs play the star role in this casserole loaded with zucchini, yellow squash
and pumpkin. Each layer has a different flavor making
this dish a culinary party for your taste buds.

1		zucchini
1		yellow squash
1/2	Tbsp	butter
1	Tbsp	Whey protein powder

Cheese layer

1	cup	cottage cheese, 2% fat
1		egg
1/4	cup	parmesan cheese -- shredded
1	Tbsp	dried onion
1	tsp	fresh oregano – (1/2 tsp if dried)
1/4	tsp	rosemary -- finely minced
1/4	Tbsp	cracked black pepper
pinch	salt	

Pumpkin Layer

1/2	cup	canned pumpkin
1		egg
1	Tbsp	basil (1/2 tsp if dried)
1/4	tsp	cinnamon
1/4	tsp	salt
pinch	pepper	

Topping

1	Tbsp	parmesan cheese
1	tsp	paprika
1	tsp	sage – minced
		(1/4 tsp if dried)
pinch	dill	

This is a great casserole to use up your left over fresh herbs, but you can use
dried herbs also. You can use any herbs that you prefer. It's best to use different
herbs for the different layers for a more exciting eating experience.

Preheat oven to 350°F

1. Butter and dust a standard size loaf pan with whey protein powder. If you
    don't have whey powder, then just skip the dusting. Pyrex or ceramic loaf
    pan work better than metal. Put the loaf pan in the refrigerator while you
    prepare the rest.

2. Slice the zucchini and yellow squash about 1/4 inch thick (or thicker) then
    slicing the rounds into halves, keeping the two squash separate. Set aside.

3. Cheese layer: In a mix bowl, beat the egg well. Add the dried onion,
    oregano, rosemary, pepper and salt. Mix. Fold in the cottage cheese and the
    shredded parmesan cheese. Set aside.

4. Pumpkin layer: In a separate small mixing bowl, beat the other egg and add
    the pumpkin, basil, cinnamon, salt and pepper. (No I didn't forget sweetener,
    this is a savory dish). Mix until well combined.

5. Get the pan from the refrigerator. First form a flat layer on the bottom of the pan with the zucchini, starting at the corners, then along the edge then filling in the middle. You may need to cut a few into smaller pieces to fit into the gaps. You may have a few slices left over (save them for your next salad). Next add 1/2 of the cheese mixture, spreading it evenly over the zucchini and forming a smooth surface using a spatula or large spoon.

6. The next layer is the pumpkin mixture. I find it easiest to place small spoonfuls all over the cheese layer then carefully smooth it out with the spatula. Then place the yellow squash on top of the pumpkin in the same manner as you did the zucchini layer. Then add the remaining cheese mixture.

7. For the topping you can sprinkle each ingredient separately (that's what I do) or blend them together and then sprinkle on top. Place loaf pan in a 350°F oven and cook for 30 minutes. As soon as it comes out, run a knife along the edges. Let cool for about 3 minutes before serving.

Serve warm or at room temperature. Simply spoon out each serving and enjoy the different flavors of each layer.

Although this is categorized as a vegetable, I like it for breakfast too.

Per Serving: 158 Calories; 6g Fat; 17g Protein; 10g Carbohydrate; 3g Dietary Fiber

Summary Squash with Caramelized Onions

Caramelized onions and prosciutto accents a medley of summer squash.

1		zucchini		
1		crookneck squash	**Weight Loss**	
1		patty pan squash		
4	ozs	prosciutto	4 Servings	
1/4	tsp	cracked black pepper	7g Net Carbs	
2	cups	yellow onion slices		
2	Tbsps	butter		
1	tsp	balsamic vinegar		

1. In a sauce pan over medium heat, melt the butter and then add the onion slices. Stir well. Let cook for 10 minutes, stirring occasionally. Add the vinegar and cook another 10 minutes.

2. Meanwhile; slice, cube or julienne the squashes (whichever you prefer). Tear or slice the prosciutto into thin strips.

3. Add the squash to the onions. Stir well. Cook for 3-5 minutes, just until heated through but not mushy. Add the cracker pepper and toss in the prosciutto. Serve right away.

Per Serving: 152 Calories; 8g Fat ; 10g Protein; 10g Carbohydrate; 3g Dietary Fiber

Fried Green Tomatoes

This Southern delight is primarily for the home gardener, since green tomatoes are rarely found in grocery stores. If you have a friend or neighbor growing tomatoes, chances are they have more than they can use and might be willing to give you a few so that you can try this outstanding recipe. It can be used as an appetizer, a vegetable side dish or even as a garnish. Do not try this with ripe tomatoes or you'll end up with mush.

2		green tomatoes
1		egg
1/2	cup	parmesan cheese -- grated
1	tsp	garlic powder
1/4	tsp	cayenne pepper -- or less
		canola oil
		salt -- to taste

Weight Loss

**4 Servings
5g Net Carbs**

The first snow comes reliably to the foothills of Colorado in late September, before all my tomatoes get a chance to ripen on the vine. As soon as snow is in the forecast, I pick 80% of my tomatoes. I cover my plants and hope that they will survive the heavy freeze and let the remaining tomatoes ripen. Green tomatoes that have taken a heavy freeze are not suitable for this recipe but make a fine green tomato salsa.

1. Rinse tomatoes and remove the stem portion. Cut into slices about 1/3 inch thick. You should be able to get 6 slices from each tomato. If your tomatoes are small, add a third tomato to the recipe.

2. In a flat bowl, beat the egg thoroughly. Set aside.

3. On a plate or shallow dish, mix together the parmesan cheese, garlic powder and cayenne pepper.

4. In a frying pan over medium-high heat, add enough canola oil to cover the bottom about a 1/8 inch high.

5. Using your left hand, soak a tomato slice in the egg, then place it on the plate with the cheese. Using your right hand, dredge both sides of the tomato through the cheese. Lightly pat it to encourage the cheese to stick. Set aside or place directly in the fry pan. Using separate hands for the wet and dry portions keeps you from getting to messy. Repeat with each slice.

6. Fry the tomato slices until a medium brown. Turn over carefully and fry the other side. Remove the slices to a paper towel and lightly salt them immediately. Serve immediately; 3 slices per serving.

Try changing the spices to compliment your entree. For example, try an Italian spice mix (generally oregano, parsley, rosemary and garlic) or a southwestern blend (cumin, garlic, chili powder, cilantro and black pepper). A lemon pepper blend is also good. Use your imagination and have fun with it.

Per Serving: 86 Calories; 4g Fat; 7g Protein; 6g Carbohydrate; 1g Dietary Fiber

Buttered Baby Turnips with Wilted Greens

This is a delightful recipe that once was exclusive to the home gardener.
Now that "baby vegetables" are in vogue, you may be able
to find baby turnips with their greens.

1/2	lb	turnips
4	cups	turnip greens
3	Tbsp	herb butter (see page 51) or 2 Tbsps butter with 2 tsps herbs such as oregano, thyme, etc.
1	Tbsp	shallot -- chopped

Weight Loss

2 Servings
6g Net Carbs

The greens on baby turnips are incredibly good. However as the vegetable matures they can become bitter. If you are substituting mature turnips in this recipe then you may want to use some other greens like spinach, Swiss chard or beet greens.

I plant turnips every year. I like to thin them when the turnips are bite-sized and have a nice crop of greens to use for this recipe. If your turnips are bigger, then cut them into bite size.

1. In a large deep skillet, melt 1 Tbsp of the herb butter over medium heat (or 1 Tbsp butter with all the herbs). Add the shallots and the turnips. Stir until well coated, then cover. Cook for about 3 or 4 minutes. Stir occasionally.

2. Meanwhile, rinse the turnip green; be sure to discard any leaves that are turning yellow or are badly bruised. Cut out most of the stem. Leave them wet and coarsely chop. Also melt the remaining butter in a microwave.

3. After the turnips have cooked through, add the greens. Cover for about 30 seconds to allow the water on the leaves to turn to steam. Then stir until evenly wilted. Remove to a serving bowl, pour over the melted butter, toss and serve at once.

Per Serving: 160 Calories; 12g Fat; 3g Protein; 13g Carbohydrate; 5g Dietary Fiber

Beet Variation: Substitute baby beets and beet greens for the turnips and turnip green.
10g net carbs; 168 Calories; 12g Fat; 3g Protein; 15g Carbohydrate; 5g Dietary Fiber

Grilled Turnips with Herb Butter

Turnips are a wonderful vegetable with a mild horseradish after taste.
They are an excellent compliment to any grilled meats or poultry.

4		turnips
1	Tbsp	olive oil
2	cloves	garlic -- crushed
3	Tbsps	butter
2	Tbsps	mixed herbs, fresh -- 1 Tbsp if dried
		salt and pepper

Weight Loss
4 Servings
6g Net Carbs

It's best to prepare the herb butter in advanced. But if you haven't, then place it in the freezer for a few minutes so it can solidify. If it's been refrigerated for awhile be sure to take it out about 20 minutes before serving so it can soften.

Herb Butter:

1. Select a mix of herbs that you like whether fresh or dried or a combination. I like using fresh rosemary, oregano, thyme and flat leaf parsley. Perhaps you might like dill, cilantro and marjoram. Another combination is the ground seeds of cumin, coriander and mustard. Your selection will greatly influence the tenor of the entire dish so look for herbs that compliment your main course. If using fresh herbs, be sure they are dry and minced finely before adding them to the butter.

2. Heat the butter in a small sauce pan or in the microwave just until melted. Remove from heat and stir in the herbs and 1/2 of the garlic (1 clove worth). Let the butter sit at room temperature for at least 10 minute before refrigerating. Stir well just prior to refrigeration.

Turnips:

1. Trim off and discard both the root and leaf ends of the turnips. Slice turnips about 1/4 inch thick (or slightly thicker).

2. In a small bowl or cup, mix the olive oil and 1/2 of the garlic with a dash of salt and pepper.

3. Coat both sides of each turnip slice with the olive oil mixture. You can use a brush or pour the oil on a plate and dredge each slice through it.

4. Place slices on the grill with medium-high heat. Turn once it starts to take on some color (usually about 2-3 minutes) and grill for another 2-3 minutes, just until it starts to turns brown. Alternatively you can pop them under the broiler for about 2 minutes, turn and broil another minute or two.

5. Transfer the turnips to a serving platter and place a dab of the herb butter here and there. Or serve the butter in a decorative cup and place it on the platter so each person can choose the amount of butter they desire (since some people are trying to limit their fat intake).

Per Serving: 141 Calories; 12g Fat; 1g Protein; 8g Carbohydrate; 2g Dietary Fiber

Turnips Au Gratin

This lovely side dish is seasoned with herbs de Provence and goes great
with a roast. Peel the turnips for a mock potato version.

2	large	turnips
1		scallion
1/2	cup	heavy cream
1	Tbsp	brown mustard
1/4	tsp	black pepper
	dash	salt
1	tsp	herbs de Provence
3	Tbsps	parmesan cheese
1	tsp	paprika

Weight Loss

2 Servings
8g Net Carbs

If you are not all that partial to the taste of turnips you can peel them since that is
where the flavors are concentrated.

Preheat oven to 350°F

1. Cut off and discard the root and stem ends. Cut in half, then slice each half
    about 1/4 inch thick, forming half moon shapes. Mince the scallions.

2. Measure out the cream and then add the mustard to the cream and stir in
    well. Add the salt and pepper to the cream.

3. In a small casserole dish, make a layer with half the turnips. Cut pieces to
    help make them fit together like a jig-saw puzzle. Evenly sprinkle 1/2 of the
    herbs de Provence and 1/2 of the scallions over the turnips. Then sprinkle
    about 1/3 of the cheese. Make the next layer the same way. Then pour the
    cream mixture over the casserole and top with the remaining cheese and a
    light dusting of paprika.

4. Cover with foil and bake at 350°F for an hour.

Per Serving: 286 Calories; 25g Fat; 6g Protein; 11g Carbohydrate; 3g Dietary Fiber

Roasted Veggies

I love an assortment of roasted veggies, particularly when I have guests and I don't know what types of veggies that they like. The combinations of veggies and seasonings are endless. Experiment!

1		turnip
1		zucchini
1		crookneck squash
1/2	lb	mushroom caps
1		red bell pepper
1		green bell pepper
1/2		onion
1/2	cup	canola oil
1	Tbsp	red wine vinegar
2	tsps	herbs -- or more if needed

Weight Loss

6 Servings
5g Net Carbs

These can be cooked on a grill or under the broiler; the methods are pretty much the same. I mostly use the broiler because the conditions are more predictable than a grill.

Many of the other low carb veggies are good here too (broccoli, cauliflower, eggplant, asparagus, cabbage wedges, etc.). I love to add sweet potatoes when I can handle a few extra carbs (about 7g net per 1/4 cup), they are awesome when roasted. Cook them for your guests and have just a bite (yum!).

The trick is to try and get everything to cook up at the same rate. This is best accomplished by the placement of each type of veggie with respect to the heat source. But also the size of each piece effects the cooking time too. In general, the squashes cook the fasted and the turnips take the longest. So slice squash thicker than turnips

Your choice of oil, vinegar and herbs should be geared to compliment whatever else you are going to be serving. You can use about 1 cup of low carb Italian salad dressing in a pinch. In fact you don't have to use vinegar or herbs, but a coating of oil is important so that the veggies don't dry out.

I typically use canola and red wine vinegar, but balsamic vinegar comes in at a close second. Also try soy or Worcestershire sauce in addition to or instead of the vinegar. As for the herbs, a mixture is usually best, Herbs de Provence or Mrs. Dash are good choices, as well as Creole, fajita, or steak blends. See below for some ideas for combinations.

1. Cut the veggies as you wish. Here's what I typically do. Cut the turnip in half then slice, forming half moons. Slice the zukes as an angle, forming ovals. Slice the crookneck into rounds. Leave the mushroom caps whole if bite sized. Cut the peppers and onions into squares.

2. In a large bowl add the oil, vinegar and herbs. Mix well. Toss in the cut veggies and let marinate for about 10 minutes. Toss occasionally.

Preheat the broiler.

3. Arrange veggies on a foil lined sheet pan (makes clean up a breeze), keeping in mind the hot spots under your broiler and putting the turnips there and the squash in the "cold" spots or closest to the door.

4. Broil for about 3 minutes then check and see if things need to be rearranged. If anything is about to burn, turn it over and move to a cooler spot. Broil another 3-5 minutes as needed.

5. Toss onto a platter and serve. As an appetizer, provide 1 or 2 dipping sauces.

If you want softer veggies then place in the middle of the oven at 400°F for about 20 minutes.

Per Serving: 199 Calories; 19g Fat; 2g Protein; 8g Carbohydrate; 3g Dietary Fiber

Here are some favorite herb combinations (S&P = salt and pepper):

- Coriander, garlic salt and lemon pepper.
- Paprika, thyme, oregano, and S&P
- Rosemary, parsley, garlic powder and S&P
- Paprika, chili powder and oregano
- Ginger, allspice, cumin and S&P
- Steak blend, Liquid Smoke and Tabasco

Zucchini Creole

This New Orleans style zucchini is a great at the end of the summer when everything is ripe and fresh from the garden.

2	large	zucchini -- about 4 cups
1/2	Tbsp	butter
1	tsp	olive oil
1/2	cup	celery -- chopped
1/4	cup	onion -- chopped
1/4	cup	bell pepper -- chopped
2	cloves	garlic
2/3	cup	Roma tomato -- seeded and chopped
2	tsp	Cajun seasoning
	dash	Tabasco sauce
		salt and pepper -- to taste

Weight Loss

4 Servings
5g Net Carbs

1. Trim the zucchini and cut into cubes. Cube the tomatoes eliminating most of the seeds.

2. In a skillet over medium-high heat, add the butter and olive oil. Add the onion, celery, bell peppers and garlic. Sauté for about 2 minutes. Add the zucchini, tomatoes, Tabasco and herbs. Sauté until zucchini are tender.

3. Taste test and add salt pepper or more Tabasco as desired.

Per Serving: 54 Calories; 3g Fat; 2g Protein; 7g Carbohydrate; 2g Dietary Fiber

Zucchini Strips in Basil Cream Sauce

Julienne zucchini poached in cream accented with garlic, basil and pine nuts.

2		zucchini -- julienne
1	Tbsp	butter
2	cloves	garlic
1	Tbsp	dry sherry
1/4	cup	heavy cream
	pinch	salt and pepper -- each
4	large	fresh basil leaves -- minced
1/4	cup	parmesan cheese -- shredded (not grated)
1/4	cup	pine nuts -- toasted

Weight Loss

2 Servings
7g Net Carbs

If you do not have fresh basil then reduce garlic to 1 clove and then use 1 Tbsp pesto sauce at the end where the basil would have been added.

1. To toast the pine nuts, use a non-stick dry skillet over medium heat. Add the pine nuts and stir occasionally until they just start to get brown. Transfer to a paper towel.

2. In the skillet over medium-high heat, add the butter and the garlic. Sauté for 1 minute (careful not burn). Add the sherry and 30 seconds later add the cream and salt and pepper. Let the cream reduce to about 2 Tbsps. Add the zucchini, toss and reduce heat to medium-low. Cook for 2-3 minutes, until tender. Add the basil, stir and immediately remove from heat. Toss in the cheese and pine nuts and serve.

Per Serving: 337 Calories; 29g Fat; 11g Protein; 10g Carbs; 3g Dietary Fiber

Kale with Toasted Sesame Seeds

This steamed kale is spiced up with a touch of garlic and cayenne pepper and garnished with toasted sesame seeds. This is a wonderful side dish for your simple grilled meats. Kale is extremely high in vitamin A and is a good source of fiber, vitamin C, calcium and other minerals.

1	lb	kale
1	Tbsp	butter
3	cloves	garlic -- minced
1/8	tsp	cayenne pepper
1	Tbsp	sesame seed oil
2	Tbsps	toasted sesame seeds
		salt and pepper -- to taste

Maintenance
4 Servings
10g Net Carbs

1. Rinse the kale well. Cut away the stems and center rib from the leafy greens and discard (or save for making stock). Cut or tear the kale into smaller pieces. If the kale dries off before you are ready to cook it, then dampen it again. The moisture is needed to create steam in the next step.

2. Melt the butter in a small skillet over medium heat. Add the garlic and sauté for about 2 minutes (do not let it burn). Add the cayenne, stir until coated and then add the kale. Toss with tongs and cook until completely wilted.

3. Transfer to serving bowl. Toss in the sesame oil, toasted sesame seeds and salt & pepper. Serve immediately or cover and place in a warm oven until ready.

Per Serving: 108 Calories; 6g Fat; 5g Protein; 13g Carbohydrate; 3g Dietary Fiber

Zacusca - Romanian Vegetables

Roasted eggplant cooked with red bell peppers, onions and tomatoes served on cabbage leaves. This is so good that it may become addictive.

1		eggplant
1		red bell pepper
		or 1/2 cup jarred roasted peppers
2/3	lb	tomatoes -- about 3 medium
2	Tbsps	olive oil
1/3	cup	onions -- chopped
1		bay leaf
1/4	tsp	salt -- to taste
1/4	tsp	ground black pepper -- to taste
4		cabbage leaves

> **Maintenance**
>
> 4 Servings
> 10g Net Carbs

This recipe comes from my sister, Lee, who at the time of this writing is in Romania as a Peace Corps volunteer. She writes to me;

"After the fall harvests in Eastern Europe, much time is spent preserving fruits and vegetables for the upcoming winter months. Cabbages and cucumbers are pickled, fruits are cooked into compotes or jams, and eggplants are roasted, peeled and ground with peppers, onions and tomatoes to make Zacusca (zah-KOO-ska), a wonderful vegetable spread. Although there is no direct translation for Zacusca, it is understood that it originated from Romania's Russian neighbors (although I have heard some of Romania's ethnic Hungarians claim it as well.) The rural women of an extended family generally get together to make this in large quantities and preserve it in sterilized jars. I just make a pot full and snack on it, spread on crackers or on cucumber slices, for a few weeks. I have never seen it listed on a restaurant menu, but I have been served it spooned onto a cabbage leaf as a side dish at peoples homes, and I have been given jars of it as a present from neighbors."

When I tested this recipe, I used roasted red peppers from a jar. But feel free to roast the pepper yourself the traditional way.

1. Roast the eggplant and red bell pepper over an open flame (such as your BBQ grill or if you have a gas stove, directly over the burner) until the skin blackens. (Otherwise roast in the oven as per page 111). Peel immediately. Finely chop the eggplant and peppers and run through a food processor (or through a meat grinder like they do in Romania).

2. Cut the tomatoes in half and squeeze out and discard the seeds and excess liquids. Coarsely chop the tomatoes.

3. In a pot, add the oil and the onions and sauté over medium heat for a few minutes. Then add the tomato and the bay leaf and simmer for about 4 minutes. Add the eggplant and peppers and mix well. Add a pinch of salt

and pepper. Simmer for about 10 minutes. It should be very thick. Discard the bay leaf.

4. Meanwhile, blanch your cabbage leaves. Bring a large pot of water to a boil. Add a pinch of salt. Put the cabbage leaves in the pot and carefully submerse them with a spoon or tongs. As soon as they become flexible (not limp) remove from water and let drain in a colander.

5. Spoon out 1/4 of the Zacusca onto each cabbage leaf and serve immediately.

Yields about 2 cups of Zacusca depending upon the size of your veggies

Per Serving: 123 Calories; 7g Fat; 3g Protein; 15g Carbohydrate; 5g Dietary Fiber

Moroccan Carrots

This is my favorite way to eat carrots. I love the combination of garlic, lemon, cumin and cilantro on just about anything!

2	cups	carrot slices (~3 carrots)
2	cloves	garlic -- sliced
2	Tbsps	canola oil
1	tsp	cumin
2	Tbsps	cilantro -- minced
1	Tbsp	lemon juice
1/4	tsp	salt
1	tsp	Splenda -- optional

Maintenance
2 Servings
12g Net Carbs

1. Heat oil in a large skillet (or wok) over medium-high heat. Add the carrots and stir fry for about 3 minutes.

2. Add the garlic and cumin. Stir and cook for another 2 minutes. Remove from heat. Add the cilantro and stir.

3. Mix the Splenda with the lemon juice. Pour this over the carrots and stir.

I like to serve this with the Moroccan Chicken (page 274)

Consider making a double batch as the left-overs are great served chilled.

Per Serving: 188 Calories; 14g Fat; 2g Protein; 16g Carbohydrate; 4g Dietary Fiber

Some Cooking Terms

Grilling, Broiling and Barbecue

When we think about summer we think about grilling and barbecue. What's the difference, you ask? Well they are very different actually. Grilling is cooking quickly over high heat. Where as barbecue, strictly speaking, is a slow cooking method using low heat. Grilling also requires a grill of some sort, obviously, yet barbecue can be on a grill or in an oven or smoker.

Broiling on the other hand is very similar to grilling, in that it is a fast method using high heat. But with broiling the heat source is above the food. There are a couple of advantages to broiling over grilling. Foremost is that there is less occasion for flare ups as the fats don't fall onto the heat source. This alone makes broiling a preferred method for many chefs. Broiling also tends to have a more uniform heat source than most backyard grills, which provides for better control. Also weather conditions such as wind and ambient temperatures are not a factor when broiling. In most cases, a recipe that calls for grilling can be broiled just as easily. But the reverse isn't always true. There are a couple of broiling techniques that are difficult if not impossible to achieve with grilling (such as browning the top of a casserole or letting the food lay in a bit of liquid or sauce while being broiled).

Yet with all the advantages of broiling over grilling, there is still nothing that can compare to cooking a steak on your backyard grill on a warm summer night. And then there are those exquisite grill marks! What is our love affair with grill marks? Some backyards cooks take so much pride in the appearance of their grill marks that they don't really care if they under cook or over cook a little bit just to get the perfect grill marks.

Boiling refers to cooking a food in boiling water or other liquids such as stock or wine. When the liquid is thick like tomato sauce then this is generally referred to as stewing.

Braising is a moist-heat cooking method that partially submerges the food in a liquid or sauce. Generally the food is first browned in butter or oil and then the braising liquids are added. The braising liquids are usually at a temperature just barely above a simmer maintaining a very gentle boil.

Poaching is similar to braising as it is also a moist-heat cooking method that completely or partially submerges the food in a liquid or sauce. However, when poaching, the liquids are generally brought to a boil and then reduce to a very low simmer before the food item is added and then the temperature is kept well below the boiling point. This technique is often employed with foods that have delicate flavor or texture.

Sautéing is a method of cooking foods quickly in a skillet, pan or wok over relatively high heat; using a small amount of oil, butter or other type of fat.

MEATS

MEATS

MAINTENANCE RECIPES

~ REGARDING BEEF ~

Looking at all the variety of cuts of beef in the grocery store, they all appear surprisingly similar. Often their price tags have a large range than their appearances do. To confuse matters even more, there are inconsistencies in the names for the various cuts. A recipe may call for NY Strip or a Kansas City Steak but your grocer might not carry any steaks with those particular names. This can be frustrating. Well both the NY & KC steaks are basically the same cut of beef. The more generic name is Strip Steak, which is a good quality top sirloin cut. I trust that the information contained in this section will be helpful to you in selecting the best cut of meat for your recipes.

General Cuts of Beef

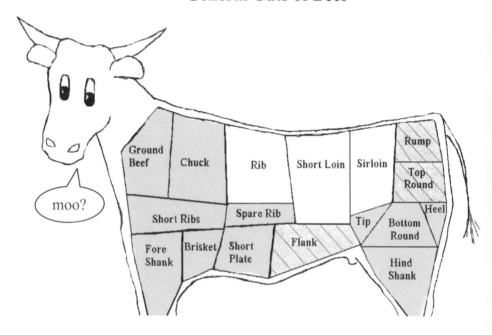

Typical cooking methods depending on USDA Grade

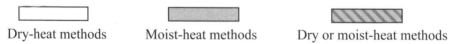

Dry-heat methods   Moist-heat methods   Dry or moist-heat methods

The USDA has established eight grades of meat. Starting with the highest quality, the grades are: Prime, Choice, Select, Standard, Commercial, Utility, Cutter and Canner. You will rarely find USDA Prime at a grocery store as this grade is typically made available only to the finest restaurants. Neither will you see the last three grades at your fresh meat counter as they are used primarily for processed meat like sausages and canned meats products. Most frozen dinner packages use USDA Commercial, unless stated otherwise. The average home cook is mostly interested in the Choice and Select grades. The quality of the meat is just as important to our selection of cooking method as is the cut of meat.

The most tender cuts are from the back of the animal, primarily from the rib, short loin and sirloin sections. Beef cuts from these sections are suitable for cooking with dry-heat methods such as, grilling, broiling, sautéing and pan-frying. Tenderness depends on the type and age of the animal (younger is more tender but older is more flavorful), the amount of fat in the muscle and the lack of connective tissues. The higher grade meats are more tender.

The tougher cuts of meat tend to have more flavor and are generally more economical. These cuts can be made tender by cooking them with a moist-heat methods (braising, stewing, pot roast, etc.), grinding the meat, or tenderizing by pounding or using marinades or enzymes.

Ground Beef (aka Hamburger)
Any cut of meat can be ground to make hamburger. The highest quality (and most expensive) usually comes from the round or sirloin and typically has less than 10% fat. This type of ground beef can easily become dry when cooked, so it is most suitable for recipes that have a sauce rather than for hamburger patties or meatloaf. The next grade of ground beef is the ground chuck which typically has 15 – 20% fat. This is perfect for the all-American hamburger since it has enough fat to provide great flavor and keep it juicy. Regular ground beef comes from trimmings of other cuts, as well as the Short plate, Shanks, Heel and from the ground beef cut near the neck. Although regular ground beef is the least expensive, it can have as much as 30% fat and will have the most shrinkage when cooked.

Chuck
The chuck section is typically used for ground beef, stew meat and roasts. Unless this cut is ground, it is best cooked using moist-heat methods. This is where we get the boneless chuck roast. One of the best cuts for a pot roast is the blade roast. When shopping for this roast, look for the cut that has the longest blade bone. This will be the most tender and the most flavorful.

- Ground beef
- Stew meat
- Chuck roast
- Blade roast
- 7-bone roast
- Cross rib roast
- Cross rib steak

Short Ribs
This entire cut requires long, slow moist-heat cooking methods. In addition to the actual short ribs which are the smaller ends of the ribs, this section also gives us the arm roast and the shoulder roast.

Rib
The rib section of beef is between the Chuck and the Short Loin and is very tender and characterized by good marbling of fat through the muscles. Steaks

from this cut lend themselves well to dry-heat methods of cooking yet moist-heat methods will make them even more tender. Most Prime Rib served at fine restaurants is a USDA Prime grade, standing rib roast and is considered by some to be one of the best cuts of beef you can get, having a nice balance between flavor and tenderness. Some popular names of cuts from the rib section include:

- Rib roast (boneless & rolled)
- Standing rib roast (w/rib bone)
- 7-Bone roast

- Rib Eye steak
- Spencer steak
- Delmonico

Short Loin

This is the most tender and most expensive of all the cuts. The most tender muscle is the appropriately named tenderloin which runs the length of this cut and into the sirloin cut. The short loin is most often cut into steaks with the exception of the tenderloin roast or chateaubriand. All of our favorite cuts come from the short loin. Common names include:

- Tenderloin roast
- Chateaubriand
- Tournedos
- Fillet mignon
- Porterhouse steak

- T-Bone steak
- Strip steak (NY or KC)
- Shell steak
- Club steak
- Minute steak

Sirloin

This cut is found between the short loin and the flavorful yet tough rump section. The sirloin can be cut into roasts or steaks with or without bone. The tenderloin and top sirloin are the most tender, then the bottom sirloin (sometimes referred to simply as sirloin) and then the sirloin tip. The boneless steaks typically carry these same names. All of the sirloin cuts are suitable for dry-heat cooking methods except for the tip which requires a moist-heat method. The common names for the bone-in steaks are as follows:

- Pin bone
- Flat bone

- Round bone
- Wedge bone

Rump: This section of beef is one of the most flavorful although it can be a little tough. The rump is mostly used for roasts and cooked with moist-heat, however a rump steak is very flavorful and if tenderized can be cooked with dry-heat methods.

Top Round: Of all the cuts from the rear of the cow, the top round is regarded as the most tender. This section of meat is generally cut into steaks; top round steak, butterball steak and London broil (also see Flank) but you can find top round roasts as well. The top round can also be cooked with either dry or moist-heat, although you should prefer USDA Choice grade for your dry-heat recipes.

Bottom Round: The bottom round is generally a tough cut that is a little more tender at the top but becomes progressively more tough the closer to the shank. This section is where we get cube steaks, the eye of the round and bottom round roasts all of which require slow, moist-heat methods of cooking.

Short Plate
This cut includes some short ribs but its primary cut is the skirt steak. There was a time when the skirt steak was the most economical cut of beef, but with the rise in popularity with southwestern cuisine and fajitas, the price of this cut has risen dramatically. This is a long flat cut of meat which is rather tough but quite flavorful. It can be marinated, quickly grilled and cut into strips (as with fajitas) or it can be stuffed, rolled and then braised.

Flank
The meat in the flank is general tough and requires tenderizing. The primary cut from the flank is the London broil which is generally cut thick (1" or more), marinated, grilled and sliced thinly across the grain. Yes, the Top Round also has a cut called London Broil which is superior to the flank cut, in my opinion. But generally the Flank is cut thin and prepared and cooked exactly as a skirt steak for fajitas.

Veal and Baby Beef
Veal is prized for its firm, delicately textured, creamy white colored meat. Veal refers to a young calf that is typically 1 to 3 months old but can be as much as 6 months (lower grade veal). Baby Beef is from calves between 6 and 12 months old and has a darker color, more course yet more flavorful meat. Veal is considered to be an inappropriate choice of meat in some circles, because the calf is slaughtered at such a young age. But I don't really follow this objection. Perhaps some people are thinking of the animal's age in human terms, but regular cuts of beef typically come from animals that were only 1 to 2 years old. So I personally don't see a huge difference in philosophy here. I don't use much veal, but it is the price that drives me away, not some moral issue.

Liver, Kidneys and Such
I personally have never cared for liver, kidneys, tongue, tripe etc. Therefore, I have not provided any recipes for them. If you like such things watch out for the carbs; 6 oz of liver has over 10g net carbs!

When Will That Steak be Done?
Cooking the perfect steak to the perfect level of doneness is an art that requires practice. An experienced cook can gage the doneness of a steak by its firmness when touched with a finger. Generally rare is the same firmness as the heel of your thumb when that hand is at rest. For medium-rare, touch the index finger to the thumb and then feel the firmness of the heel of the thumb, and so on (see table below). If you eat a lot of steaks (particularly grilled) then this technique is a great thing to learn and to practice. I've just never gotten the hang of this, so I use an instant read thermometer (which isn't actually instant, mine takes about

20-30 seconds to stabilize on a temperature).
It is best for them to be inserted into the side
of the steak so that it can penetrate past the
center, which improves accuracy. You can
also estimate how done your steak is by
timing how long it takes to cook a certain

thickness of steak to your liking. However, this is generally different for each
grill and broiler and is best determined by the trial and error method until you
find the proper correlation for your equipment (however you'll also need to
factor in such matters as ambient temperature, humidity and wind).

When we are talking about steaks, "well-done" is considered an oxymoron to
most chefs! At a high-end steak house, the wait-staff may raise a disapproving
eyebrow if you request your steak to be cook more than medium. Do you enjoy
receiving silly looks from wait-staff (it can be fun)? If so, try ordering your next
steak by specifying the internal temperature? "Yes, I prefer my steak cooked to
140°F; thank you!"

Checking Your Steak for Doneness

Temperature	Doneness	Touch Technique
120-130°F	Rare	Relaxed thumb
130-140°F	Medium-rare	Touch index-finger to the thumb
140-150°F	Medium	Touch middle-finger to the thumb
150-160°F	Medium-well	Lightly push ring-finger onto thumb
160-170°F	Well done	Push baby-finger onto tip of thumb
170-180°F	Overdone	
>180°F	Dog Food! Tee, hee! Great for a stock base.	

When I accidentally overcook a steak, I usually set it aside to make stock or
sometimes I just feed it to my dogs (yep, they are completely spoiled and very
well fed!). I generally add a few extra steaks to the grill anyway because I love
left-over sliced steak. But most good cuts of steak don't have a lot of flavor left
once they have been over-cooked on a grill, consequently they are not great as
stew meat. So unless I want to make some beef stock soon, then I'd rather just
give it to my boys.

My preferred method for cooking a steak is to grill it on each side for about 4-5
minutes (depending upon thickness) then to move it to an area on that grill that is
not over direct heat and close the lid. Depending on weather conditions it is
generally ready about 10 minutes later. I can control cooking time somewhat
by the proximity to the direct heat. This method allows for me to get in to take
temperatures after about 5 minute to gage how things are progressing and
make adjustments as needed. If your grill space is full then you can finish off
the steaks in a 300°F oven.

Remove steaks from the grill (or oven) about 5°F under your desired end temperature, as the steak will continue to cook while it rests. Yes, the steak is tired after all that cooking and wants to rest for about 5 minutes before it is sliced. This allows the juices to be reabsorbed and not run all over the plate as soon as it is sliced.

When cooking a roast (beef, pork, chicken or otherwise), it is a good idea to remove it from the oven about 5-10°F sooner than your desired temperature since the heat retained in the roast will continue the cooking process for a few minutes.

~ REGARDING PORK ~

Pork generally refers to swine that are less than one year old and typically are between 6 and 9 months old. Older animals have more flavorful meat but can be much tougher and generally are not sold in a typical grocery store. The names of the large cuts of pork are similar to that for beef, but there are a few differences. One obvious exception is the term **ham** which is unique to pork and is the hip and hind shank portions of the pig. Another deviation is the pork butt which is actually a shoulder roast and not the corresponding cut to a beef rump roast. My grocery store uses the term shoulder roast but you can still find it labeled butt roast. Pork steaks typically have the generic name of "pork chop" regardless of which cut it came from. But you can find more specific names for the better cuts such as pork loin chop, pork sirloin chop, etc.

Most pork consumed in the United States is cured pork such as bacon and ham. But the consumption of fresh pork is on the rise as some people are turning away from beef, both for health and economic reasons. Today's pork is significantly leaner than it was just a dozen years ago. The lower fat content appeals to the fat conscious crowds, but this comes at a price in the taste department. As pork becomes more and more lean, cooking methods need to be slightly modified. Older cookbooks may call for pork to be cooked to an internal temperature of 170°F to 185°F degrees. Today's pork will be overcooked at those temperatures. Most experts today recommend cooking pork to an internal temperature of 150°F for the leanest cuts like the tenderloin and up to 165°F for cuts with more fat like a shoulder roast.

Although trichinosis was once a prevalent concern, it is now very rarely an issue. Even so, experts still tell us to cook pork to a minimum internal temperature of 137°F which will assure the immediate death of any trichinae present. But most people stretch that further to a minimum of 150°F to factor in any inconsistencies that may be present in a meat thermometer. One should also observe normal precautions and hygiene standards when handling pork as you would for any raw meat.

Basic Meat Loaf with Gravy

This is my basic meatloaf recipe. I vary the herbs depending upon what I have available, often replacing the sage with rosemary. There's many ways to flavor meat loaf so I have provided a couple of variations.

1	lb	ground beef
1	lb	ground pork
2		eggs
2		scallions -- minced
2	tsps	Worcestershire sauce
1	tsp	thyme
1	tsp	sage
1	tsp	oregano
1/2	tsp	salt
1/4	tsp	pepper
1/4	tsp	Liquid Barbecue Smoke®
2/3	cup	water

Induction
4 Servings **3g Net Carbs**

Gravy

1	Tbsp	butter
1	Tbsp	flour
1½	cups	chicken broth
1	tsp	Kitchen Bouquet
		pan drippings

Preheat oven to 350°F

1. In a large bowl, beat the eggs. Add the minced scallions, Worcestershire sauce, thyme, sage, oregano, salt, pepper and Liquid Smoke. Beat the eggs well. Add the pork and the beef and squish it all together with your hands until well blended.

2. Shape meat into a loaf while slapping the outside sharply, compacting the meat and eliminating air bubbles. Place in a casserole dish so that the sides of the loaf do not touch the sides of the dish. This will allow the sides to brown. Pour the water around the loaf.

3. Place in a 350°F oven and cook uncovered for 40 minutes. Transfer loaf to a platter. Let cool for 5 minutes before slicing and serving.

For the Gravy:

4. Using a wooden spoon and some of the chicken broth for the gravy, scrape up all the brown bits on the bottom and sides of the casserole dish. Pour the pan dripping thru a strainer into a cup. Let sit a minute and spoon off excess fat.

5. In a sauce pan over medium heat, melt the butter and add the flour stirring continuously for 2 minutes. Add the pan drippings and whisk vigorously. Add the remaining chicken broth and the Kitchen Bouquet and continue to whisk until it comes to a boil.

Slice the meat loaf and serve the gravy on the side.

Per Serving: 741 Calories; 60g Fat; 43g Protein; 4g Carbohydrate; 1g Dietary Fiber

All of the following meat loaf variations start off with 1 lb of ground beef, 1 lb of ground pork and 2 eggs. All are prepared and cooked in the same manner as the Basic Meat Loaf (except no gravy has been included). All listed ingredients are mixed in with the eggs prior to adding the meat.

Spanish Meat Loaf Variation

1/2	cup	Spanish olives -- chopped	1	tsp	oregano
1/2	cup	Spanish onion -- minced	1/2	tsp	salt
2	Tbsps	dry sherry	1/4	tsp	pepper
1	tsp	paprika			

3g net carbs; 722 Calories; 58g Fat; 41g Protein; 4g Carbohydrate; 1g Dietary Fiber

Barbeque Meat Loaf

1/4	cup	Carb Option BBQ Sauce	1/2	cup	onions -- minced
2	tsp	Steak & Chop seasoning	1/2	tsp	salt

3g net carbs; 695 Calories; 56g Fat; 41g Protein; 3g Carbohydrate; trace Dietary

Cajun Meat Loaf

1	Tbsp	Cajun seasoning	3		scallions -- minced
2	clove	garlic -- minced	1		jalapeno -- minced

3g net carbs; 697 Calories; 57g Fat; 41g Protein; 3g Carbohydrate; 1g Dietary Fiber

French Meat Loaf

1	Tbsp	Herbs de Provence	2		scallions -- minced
1	Tbsp	Worcestershire sauce	1	stalk	celery – minced
1	Tbsp	Dijon mustard	1	tsp	salt

2g net carbs; 693 Calories; 57g Fat; 41g Protein; 2g Carbohydrate; trace Dietary Fiber

Meat Balls: It is easy to make meat balls from any of the meat loaf recipes. Add another egg and shape into balls; place them on a sheet pan and baking for 20-25 minutes (depending on the size of the meat balls). Alternatively, they can be fried in a skillet (no oil necessary) cooked in several batches, turning the meatballs to brown all sides (about 10-15 minutes per batch).

London Broil

This classic grilled, top round, steak is perfect for the low carb induction phase. This has lots of flavor with minimal carbs.

2	lbs	London broil
1/2	cup	Carb Options™ Asian Teriyaki Marinade
1/2	cup	Carb Options™ Barbeque Sauce
1/2	cup	water
2	tsp	Steak & Chop seasoning

Induction

4 Servings
3g Net Carbs

The hickory flavored barbeque sauce is better than the original flavor for this particular recipe. Although, I prefer the original flavor for most other recipes.

1. With a knife or fork pierce both sides of the steak.

2. Place meat in a zip-lock baggie along with the marinade, barbeque sauce, seasonings and water. Seal and squish around to blend and distribute. Refrigerate for 2-3 hours (or overnight).

3. Discard marinade and grill over medium heat or broil about 5 inches from the element. This is best cooked rare to medium rare 130°F to 140°F. For a 1/2 inch thick steak, ~3 minutes per side; 1 inch thick, ~6 minutes per side; and a 1½ inch thick steak, ~10 minutes per side.

4. Allow to rest for 5 minutes before slicing at an angle against the grain.

Per Serving: 667 Calories; 54g Fat; 41g Protein; 3g Carbohydrate; 0g Dietary Fiber

Tuscan Rump Roast

This pot roast is cooked quickly and served rare to medium-rare. A simple au-jus gravy is served with the meat, but a traditional gravy made with a French roux is also described.

2	lbs	beef rump roast – USDA Choice
1	Tbsp	fresh rosemary -- minced
1	slice	lemon zest -- minced
1/4	cup	extra virgin olive oil
1	tsp	fresh ground black pepper
1	tsp	salt
1/3	cup	red wine
1	cup	chicken stock
2	tsps	Dijon mustard
1	tsp	kitchen Bouquet

Induction

4 Servings
3g Net Carbs

If using a less tender cut of meat then after browning, braise it slowly in the traditional pot roast manner.

1. Season the meat with salt and pepper and let it rest while mincing the lemon zest and rosemary.

2. In a large heavy pot, heat the olive oil on medium-high heat. Brown the roast on all sides; about 3 minutes per side.

3. Meanwhile; mix together the wine, stock, mustard, zest, rosemary and any left over salt and pepper. Add this mixture to the pot. Bring to a boil and cover (use aluminum foil if pot does not have its own lid). Cook for 20 minutes turning the roast frequently so that all sides have a turn in the liquid.

4. Place roast on a carving board or platter. Let rest for 7 minutes.

5. For the gravy: The easiest thing to do is simply strain the liquids and serve it in an au-jus manner (add more salt & pepper if desired).

6. Slice the roast at the table or just prior to serving. Serve with the gravy.

Per Serving: 460 Calories; 25g Fat; 50g Protein; 2g Carbohydrate; trace Dietary

Traditional Gravy Variation: After removing the roast, turn up the heat to high and reduce liquids to ~1 or 1½ cups. Meanwhile, in a sauce pan, make a roux by heating 1 Tbsp butter in a sauce pan over medium-high heat and add 1 Tbsp of white flour once the butter begins to bubble. Stir well until flour is completely dissolved. Stir in about 1/3 of the juices stirring quickly (a whisk makes this job easier). Once thicken, reduce heat to low and add the remaining juices, stir well (add more salt & pepper if desired).

4g net carbs; 493 Calories; 28g Fat; 51g Protein; 4g Carbohydrate; trace Dietary Fiber;

Roast Beef Sandwich Wrap

Instead of using bread or a tortilla to make your sandwiches, try using a large lettuce leaf. I like the large red tip lettuce. Not only is it easy to make into the wraps, it is also colorful. Experiment with different meats and cheeses.

1	large	lettuce leaf
4	slices	deli roast beef
1	slice	Gruyere cheese
1	Tbsp	mayonnaise
1		tomato slice
		fresh ground black pepper

Induction
1 Serving
2g Net Carbs

1. Rinse a large lettuce leaf and pat dry with a paper towel. The stem end may need to be trimmed off if it is large and stiff.

2. Lay the lettuce flat and layer the roast beef slices across the lettuce. Then apply the mayonnaise and pepper. Then layer on the cheese, followed by the tomato placed in the middle.

3. To roll up, start at one edge and roll so that the stem end is tightly wrapped and the leafy tip is more loosely wrapped forming a cone. With just a little bit of practice this will become very fast and simple.

Per Serving: 251 Calories; 22g Fat; 14g Protein; 2g Carbs; trace Dietary Fiber

Barbecue Pork Roast

This is a simple roast to make and will make your house smell delicious.

4	lb	Pork butt roast
2	tsps	canola oil
1	cups	water
3/4	cup	Carb Options™ Barbeque Sauce
1	Tbsp	Worcestershire sauce
1	Tbsp	Steak & Chop seasoning
1	tsp	chili powder
1/2	tsp	Liquid Barbecue Smoke®

Induction
6 Servings
3g Net Carbs

1. Randomly pierce the surface of the roast with a sharp knife. In a heavy skillet over medium-high heat, add the oil and brown the roast on all sides.

2. In a mixing bowl, combine the water, barbeque sauce, Worcestershire sauce, seasoning, chili powder and Liquid Smoke. Mix well. Pour sauce over roast and bring to boil. Reduce heat, cover and simmer 2 hours or until pork is fork-tender. Baste roast with sauce during cooking time. Remove pork from pan, cool slightly and slice or chop to serve.

Per Serving: 700 Calories; 49g Fat; 59g Protein; 3g Carbs; trace Dietary Fiber;

Caribbean Pork Shoulder Roast

The blend of cumin and citrus flavors gives an unusual flair
to this pork shoulder roast.

3	lb	pork shoulder roast
4	cloves	garlic -- crushed
1	Tbsp	ground cumin
1	tsp	dried oregano
1	tsp	salt
1/4	tsp	ground black pepper
3	Tbsps	dry sherry
1	Tbsp	balsamic vinegar
2	Tbsps	lemon juice
1	Tbsp	lime juice
1/2	cup	water
2	Tbsps	canola oil
1/2	tsp	orange extract
few	dashes	Tabasco sauce – optional

Induction
6 Servings
2g Net Carbs

1. To make the marinade, mix together in a bowl all ingredients except the pork.

2. Place roast in a gallon size zip-lock baggie. Pour the marinade over the roast and close the baggie trapping as little air as possible. Refrigerate at least 8

hours and up to 2 days. Be sure to turn the roast every time you open the refrigerator so that all sides are in the down position for at least 2-4 hours.

Preheat oven to 325°F

3. Place pork in a roasting pan along with the marinade. Cover with a pan lid or foil. Roast for 2 hours, then remove the cover and continue roasting for at least another 30 minutes. The roast should be cooked until the center reaches at least 150°F (slightly pink) or up to 165°F (well done).

4. Remove from oven and loosely cover with foil for at least 10 minutes before carving.

5. Scrape the bottom and sides of the roasting pan with a wooden spoon to loosen up and dissolve any dark bits. Strain the liquids into a sauce pan and bring to a slow boil to reduce slightly. Taste and adjust seasoning accordingly. Add a drop or two of extracts (orange, lemon and/or lime) to intensify the citrus flavors, but be careful not to over power the cumin (which should be the predominate flavor).

6. Carve the roast into thick slices and place them on a platter. Add the juices from carving into the sauce and stir well. Drizzle the sauce over the pork.

If you desire a darker color for the sauce add a tsp of kitchen bouquet. You can also thicken the sauce with 1/2 tsp of guar gum whisked into the sauce. You could also make gravy with the traditional roux method. But remember thickening the sauce a roux will add a few carbs.

Per Serving: 461 Calories; 35g Fat; 30g Protein; 2g Carbs; trace Dietary Fiber

Beer-Braised Pork Chops

Low carb beer is used as the braising liquid for pork chops and mushrooms.

4		boneless pork chops -- 1½ inches thick	
1	Tbsp	butter	**Induction**
4	ozs	mushrooms -- sliced	
1/2	tsp	thyme	**4 Servings**
8	ozs	Aspen Edge low carb beer	**2g Net Carbs**

1. Melt butter in heavy skillet over medium-high heat and quickly brown pork chops on both sides. Remove.

2. Add mushrooms and thyme to pan and sauté about 2 minutes allowing the mushrooms to soak up the butter. Return chops to skillet, add beer; bring to a boil. Cover and reduce heat to lowest setting and simmer 15 minutes.

3. Spoon out the mushrooms (with a bit of liquid) to serve over the chops.

Per Serving: 176 Calories; 8g Fat; 20g Protein; 2g Carbs; trace Dietary Fiber

Roasted Pork Tenderloin with Herbs

Fresh herbs and bacon add incredible flavor to this pork tenderloin.
The two tenderloins are tied together to provide more even cooking.

2	pound	pork tenderloin (2 tenderloin, 1 lb each)
2	cloves	garlic -- diced fine
1	Tbsp	olive oil
1	Tbsp	butter
1	sprig	fresh sage
2	sprigs	fresh thyme
2	sprig	fresh rosemary
6	slices	bacon

> **Induction**
>
> **4 Servings**
> **1g Net Carbs**

This tenderloin is cooked to an internal temperature of 150°F. This is considered medium-well and should have just the slightest touch of pink. Since the tenderloin cut is very low in fat, it will become very dry if it is overcooked. It is best to use a meat thermometer.

Preheat oven to 400°F. Rinse and pat dry the tenderloins.

1. Finely dice the garlic (smashed roasted garlic can be used for a milder taste). Remove herb leaves from stems, discarding the stems (or save them for making soup stock). Coarsely chop through the herbs to slightly bruise them. You should have about 3 tablespoons of herbs. Add a few drops of the oil to the herbs and garlic to form a paste.

2. Rub the herb paste onto the tenderloins. Place one tenderloin on top of the other in opposite direction so that the large end of one mates with the smaller end of the other, making a uniform thickness. Any herbs that have fallen off should be stuffed between the two tenderloins.

3. Carefully wrap the bacon around the tenderloin. Be careful not to lose any of the herbs. Use kitchen butcher's twine to secure the bacon and tie the two tenderloins together. First tie the twine around the two ends (and in the middle, if the tenderloin is fairly long). Then tie the twine lengthwise wrapping it snuggly around the previously tied twine, as illustrated.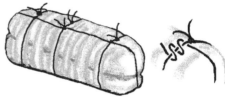

4. In a heavy skillet over medium-high heat, add the remaining olive oil and the butter. Sear the roast on all sides until nicely browned (about 10 minutes).

5. Place the tenderloin in an uncovered roasting pan and place in 400°F oven. Roast for about 20 minutes or until a meat thermometer reads 150°F. Remove from oven immediately and let rest for 10 minutes (loosely covered before removing the twine and carving. Strain pan juices and skim off excess fat. Serve juices with the pork roast.

Per Serving: 386 Calories; 19g Fat; 51g Protein; 1g Carbs; trace Dietary Fiber

Pork Chops in Mustard Cream Sauce

This outstanding sauce derives its flavor from shallots, sherry, herbs and Dijon mustard. Also try this recipe with turkey cutlets, chicken or steaks.

10	oz	pork chops (2 chops)
1	tsp	olive oil
1/2	Tbsp	butter
1	Tbsp	shallot -- chopped
1/2	cup	heavy cream
2	Tbsps	Dijon mustard
1	Tbsp	dry sherry
1/2	tsp	dried thyme
1/2	tsp	dried oregano
		salt and pepper -- to taste

Induction
2 Servings
3g Net Carbs

1. Heat the oil in a large skillet over medium-high heat. Add the pork chops and cook until well browned, about 4 minutes per side. Remove chops and cover them to keep warm.

2. Add the butter and the shallots and sauté for about 1 minute.

3. Remove the skillet from the heat and slowly add the sherry. Pour from the tablespoon and not directly from the bottle.

4. Return the skillet to the heat and add the cream, mustard, thyme, oregano and some salt & pepper. If using fresh herbs then wait and add them in the last two minutes of cooking.

5. Bring sauce to a boil stirring frequently. Reduce heat to low and add the pork chops to the skillet (with any juices that may have accumulated). Simmer uncovered for 3 minutes then turn the chops over and simmer for an additional 2 minutes.

Serve immediately.

Per Serving: 516 Calories; 43g Fat; 25g Protein; 4g Carbohydrate; 1g Dietary Fiber

Broiled Lamb Chops with Mint & Rosemary

Mint & rosemary are natural companions to lamb.

2	8 oz	lamb chops
2	Tbsps	butter
1	tsp	fresh rosemary leaves
1	tsp	fresh mint leaves
	pinch	salt & pepper -- each

> **Induction**
>
> 2 Servings
> 0g Net Carbs

1. Mince the mint and rosemary leaves. In a small microwave proof bowl, add the butter, mint and rosemary. Zap for about 30 seconds. Let sit a couple of minutes and zap for 30 seconds again.

2. Drizzle about 1/4 of the butter over the chops and brush to spread it around. Season with a pinch of salt and pepper. Turn the chops over and repeat. This will leave about 1/2 of the butter mixture to drizzle over the chops after they have cooked.

3. Place a broiler pan so that it is about 6 inches below the broiler. Let the pan heat up for a minute or two. Carefully add the lamb chops. Broil for about 10 minute per inch of thickness for medium-well done. Turn the chops after half the cooking time. Remove from oven and drizzle the remaining butter over the chops. Let rest 5 minutes before serving, lightly covered with aluminum foil.

Try the Mint Pesto (page 364) as a garnish, or stuffed into large broiled mushrooms as a side dish (you can add the mushroom to the broiling pan when you turn the chops and then stuff them while the chops rest).

Per Serving: 658 Calories; 59g Fat; 29g Protein; trace Carbs; trace Dietary Fiber

Beef Bourguignon

Bourguignon wine is the primary braising liquid for this flavorful roast.

2	lb	beef top round
2	cups	button mushrooms -- sliced
2	cups	dry red wine -- (Bourguignon)
2	Tbsps	butter
2	cloves	garlic -- finely minced
1	cup	pickled onions – cocktail type
1	Tbsp	tomato paste
1	Tbsp	Worcestershire sauce
		salt & pepper -- to taste
1		bouquet garni

> **Weight Loss**
>
> 4 Servings
> 7g Net Carbs

Bouquet Garni: This is made by placing herbs and aromatic vegetables in a pouch made with cheese cloth and tied off with butchers twine. For this recipe I suggest the following for your bouquet garni:

- 1/4 cup of celery tops
- 1 bay leaf
- 1 sprig of fresh rosemary
- 1 sprig of fresh oregano
- 1 Tbsp fresh parsley

1. Cut the beef into bite-sized cubes. Trim away any extra fat.

2. In a large pan over medium-high heat, add the butter and brown the beef.

3. Add the garlic, stir and cook another minute of so (don't burn the garlic).

4. Add the wine and the bouquet garni. Reduce the heat to a simmer, cover and cook for 2 hours.

5. If the mushrooms are very small they can be left whole, otherwise quarter them. Add the mushrooms, onions, tomato paste, Worcestershire sauce and salt & pepper. Stir and cook on simmer for another 30 minutes.

6. Remove and discard the bouquet garni before serving.

Per Serving: 564 Calories; 27g Fat; 50g Protein; 8g Carbohydrate; 1g Dietary Fiber

Beef Teriyaki with Bok Choy

This quick and easy low carb version is a hit every time.

1	lb	sirloin steak -- boneless
1	cup	Carb Options™ Asian Teriyaki Marinade
2	tsps	canola oil
2	cups	bok choy -- shredded
1		scallion -- julienne
1/4		red bell pepper -- julienne
1	stalk	celery -- julienne
2	Tbsps	Carb Options™ Asian Teriyaki Marinade

Weight Loss

2 Servings
4g Net Carbs

1. Slice steak into strips. Put them into a large re-sealable plastic bag with the 1 cup of marinade. Squish around to be sure that all pieces are coated well. Refrigerate for at least 30 minutes but 2 hours is better.

2. Julienne the scallions, bell pepper and celery. Shred the bok choy (about the size used in cole slaw)

3. In a wok or a large skillet, heat the oil over medium high heat. To protect yourself from splatter, use a kitchen mitt or cover your hand loosely with a kitchen towel or dampened paper towel. Using tongs, remove the pieces of steak from the bag and carefully place in the wok. Discard marinade. Stir fry for about 2 minutes. Add the scallions, bell pepper, celery and bok choy and stir fry for another 3-4 minutes. Add 2 Tbsps of fresh marinade sauce. Stir and serve immediately.

Per Serving: 533 Calories; 37g Fat; 43g Protein; 6g Carbohydrate; 2g Dietary Fiber

Braised Steak with Blackberry Sauce

This recipe calls for your choice of beef steaks but it is also a great way to cook venison, buffalo or elk steaks.

4	8 oz	beef sirloin steaks
1	Tbsp	butter
2	Tbsps	shallot -- minced
2	Tbsps	bell pepper -- minced
1	stalk	celery -- minced
1	cup	water -- or stock
1	tsp	dried thyme
1/2	cup	dry sherry
1/4	cup	balsamic vinegar
1/2	pint	blackberries
	dash	salt & pepper -- to taste

```
┌──────────────────────┐
│     Weight Loss      │
├──────────────────────┤
│   4 Servings         │
│   6g Net Carbs       │
└──────────────────────┘
```

1. Mince the shallots, celery and bell peppers.

2. In a very large skillet, melt the butter over medium high heat and sauté the shallots, celery and bell peppers for 3 or 4 minutes. Remove from skillet and reserve.

3. Add the steaks and seer them for 3 minutes per side. Do not crowd the steaks, so if they are too large for your skillet, then do this in two batches. If too much juice accumulates in the pan, thereby inhibiting browning, then pour off the liquids into the bowl with the shallots.

4. Return the steaks to the skillet; add the shallots mixture, thyme and the stock (or water). Reduce heat to medium low and simmer for 10 minutes per inch of thickness. Lightly cover with aluminum foil. Turn the steaks after 5 minutes.

5. In a separate sauce pan over medium heat, add the sherry and vinegar and bring to a boil. Add the blackberries; stir frequently smashing the fruit against the side of the pan. Once the berries have completely disintegrated, remove from heat. If you find the seed objectionable then simply pour the sauce through a strainer, forcing the pulp through with the back of a spoon.

6. Once the steaks are cooked, remove them to a plate and cover with the foil. Add the blackberry sauce to the liquids in the skillet and bring to a slow boil. Taste test and add salt and pepper as desired. Pour 1/2 of the sauce onto 4 plates, add the steaks and then drizzle the remaining sauce over the steaks.

This is great served with a simple steamed vegetable (such as broccoli, green beans or zucchini) or a mix of vegetables.

Per Serving: 591 Calories; 35g Fat; 52g Protein; 8g Carbohydrate; 2g Dietary Fiber

Flank Steak in Red Wine Sauce

This flank steak is cooked in red wine for an hour which tenderizes
it and provides great flavor.

2	lb	flank steak
1	Tbsp	butter
2	cloves	garlic -- minced
1/2	cup	Carb Option Ketchup
1	cup	red wine
		fresh ground black pepper
1	tsp	fresh rosemary leaves -- 1/2 tsp if dry
1	tsp	fresh oregano -- 1/4 tsp if dry
1	Tbsp	fresh parsley -- 1 tsp if dry
1/4	lb	button mushroom -- sliced
		salt and pepper -- to taste

> **Weight Loss**
>
> 4 Servings
> 4g Net Carbs

1. Slice the flank steak across the grain into 1/4 inch thick slices.

2. Coarsely chop the fresh herbs; set aside.

3. In a deep skillet, melt the butter over medium-high heat and add steak strips to sear them for 1 minute. Add the garlic, tomato sauce, wine and some black pepper. Reduce heat and simmer for 45 minutes, covered.

4. Add the mushroom and fresh herbs, stir well and simmer another 15 minutes. If you are using any dried herbs, add them in step 3 when you add the wine.

Taste test and add salt and pepper as desired.

Try serving this with creamed cauliflower or grilled turnips for a hearty winter dinner.

Per Serving: 487 Calories; 27g Fat; 45g Protein; 4g Carbs; trace Dietary Fiber

German Meatballs

Flavorful meat balls swimming in a delicious mushroom cream sauce.

1	lb	ground beef
2	eggs	
1	Tbsp	Worcestershire sauce
1	tsp	paprika
1	tsp	oregano
1/2	tsp	garlic powder
1/4	tsp	liquid Barbecue Smoke®
4	ozs	canned mushrooms
1	tsp	Kitchen Bouquet
1	cup	sour cream

> **Weight Loss**
>
> **3 Servings**
> **7g Net Carbs**

You can use all beef or use a combination of ground meats (pork, veal, turkey or buffalo). Let the meats reach room temperature before preparation.

1. In a large mixing bowl, add the eggs, Worcestershire, mustard, paprika, oregano, garlic powder, and liquid smoke. Mix well with a fork or whisk.

2. Add the ground beef and blend well using your well washed hands. Form meatballs by rolling a small portion in the palm of your hands (rubbing a little oil on your hands will help keep the meat from sticking). Place meatballs on a tray or platter until ready to cook.

3. In a large skillet over medium-high heat, add one batch of meatballs at a time and brown well on all sides and cook through (about 8 minutes per batch). Gently transfer to a bowl and cover (to retain the heat). Repeat until all the meatballs have been cooked.

4. Pour off any grease (but leave the bits of meat in the skillet).

5. Add the canned mushrooms with the liquid. Reduce heat to medium. Add the Kitchen bouquet and the sour cream. Stir until well mixed.

6. Gently add the meatballs back to the skillet and spoon the sauce over the meatballs to cover. Cook until heated through (but <u>do not boil</u>). This should only take a minute or two. Transfer to serving platter and serve immediately.

Fresh chopped chives or parsley make a nice garnish.

Per Serving: 637 Calories; 52g Fat; 32g Protein; 8g Carbohydrate; 1g Dietary Fiber

Kansas City Strip Steak with C&C Sauce

This awesome sauce is in honor of my folks, Cliff & Carolyn, (hence the name) who always served steaks with peppers & onions in a vermouth butter sauce.

2		top sirloin steaks -- Kansas City Strip
1	Tbsp	Steak & Chops Seasoning
		salt -- to taste
1/4		yellow onion -- slivered
1/2		bell pepper -- slivered
3	Tbsps	butter
1/4	cup	dry vermouth
1	Tbsp	Worcestershire sauce
1	Tbsp	balsamic vinegar
1	tsp	Kitchen Bouquet

Weight Loss

2 Servings
7g Net Carbs

This recipe is an adaptation of my parents' steak sauce. It is my favorite way to serve steaks whether grilled, broiled or pan fried. I change the sauce from time to time by adding mushrooms or various herbs. But the vermouth butter sauce base is really the key. For years, I thought that my folks' sauce was the only decent way to serve a grilled steak. It is so good that all other steaks paled in comparison (even steaks served at the best steak house restaurants). Thanks Mom and Dad for spoiling me this way and providing me with this splendid culinary pleasure. I love you deeply; more than words can ever express.

1. Sliver the onions and peppers as you would for fajitas. Gather your ingredients and have them ready before starting the steak. It takes about the same time to make the sauce as it does to cook the steaks.

2. Dust the steaks with the steak seasoning and salt on both sides. The steaks can be grilled, broiled or pan fried. In any case, sear the steaks on both sides for several minutes and then let them finish in a 300°F oven or with indirect heat on the grill.

3. Meanwhile; in a sauté pan over medium-high heat, melt 1 Tbsp of the butter and add the onions and peppers. Sauté for 2 or 3 minutes. Add the vermouth and let the alcohol boil off for a minute. Then add the remaining butter, Worcestershire sauce, balsamic vinegar and Kitchen Bouquet. If you did not pan fry then also add a pinch of salt and a pinch of the steak seasoning mix. Reduce heat to a simmer until the steaks are ready.

Serve the steaks whole or sliced. Smother steaks with the sauce!

Per Serving: 343 Calories; 22g Fat; 22g Protein; 8g Carbohydrate; 1g Dietary Fiber

Reduced Carb Variation: Use only half of the onion and bell pepper.
5g net carbs; 330 Calories; 22g Fat; 22g Protein; 5g Carbohydrate; trace Dietary Fiber.

Mushroom Variation: Add 4 oz of mushrooms with the onions and peppers.
7g net carbs; 350 Calories; 22g Fat; 23g Protein; 9g Carbohydrate; 2g Dietary Fiber

Rueben Casserole

This quick and easy dish can be made with the traditional corned beef or with kielbasa or other mild sausage.

2	lbs	corned beef brisket -- cooked, sliced 1/4" thick
24	oz	canned sauerkraut -- unsweetened
2	tsps	Splenda® -- optional
1	Tbsp	mustard
2	Tbsps	mayonnaise
1	tsp	caraway seeds -- crushed
4	ozs	Swiss cheese -- sliced or grated

Weight Loss

4 Servings
4g Net Carbs

Although I prefer the corned beef, any type of sliced sausage is good in this recipe. You can use a combination if you'd like. The meats should be fully cooked. Baking this dish is actually just heating it up.

Get the unsweetened sauerkraut if you can find it and then use the Splenda if you'd like.

Preheat oven to 350°F

1. Toss the sauerkraut with the mustard, mayonnaise, and caraway seeds (and the Splenda if you are using it). Sprinkle 1/2 of the mixture on the bottom of a casserole dish (8x8 would be about right).

2. Slice the corned beef (and/or sausages) into bite size pieces. Distribute the meat evenly over the sauerkraut. Then add the remaining sauerkraut. Then top it off with the Swiss cheese.

3. Bake at 350°F for 20 minutes. You can serve this right away or let it sit in the oven on the lowest setting until ready to serve.

Serve with a green salad or green vegetable.

Per Serving: 632 Calories; 48g Fat; 43g Protein; 8g Carbohydrate; 4g Dietary Fiber

Rueben Wrap

This sandwich utilizes a low carb tortilla instead of rye bread toast.

3	ozs	corned beef brisket -- thinly sliced
1	oz	Swiss cheese slice
1	oz	sauerkraut
1	dash	caraway seed
1	tsp	brown mustard – to taste
1		Low-carb whole wheat tortillas

Weight Loss

1 Serving
7g Net Carbs

1. On a microwave safe plate, stack the corned beef then the caraway seeds, then the sauerkraut and then topped with the cheese. Microwave just until the cheese melts (about 1 minute or so).

2. Spread the mustard in the middle of the low carb tortilla. Then place the heated corned beef, sauerkraut and cheese to one edge of the tortilla.

3. Roll up the tortilla half way, tucking in all the goodies. Then fold over the two ends and finish rolling it up.

This sandwich can get soggy quickly so serve it immediately.

Per Serving: 364 Calories; 24g Fat; 29g Protein; 22g Carbs; 15g Dietary Fiber

Russian Round Steak

Round steak slowly cooked in a delicious sauce enhanced with sour cream.

2	lbs	round steak
4		scallions
1/2	Tbsp	butter
1	Tbsp	canola oil
1/2	cup	dry sherry
8	ozs	canned mushroom -- with juice
4	ozs	tomato paste
1	Tbsp	Worcestershire sauce
1	tsp	thyme
1/2	tsp	paprika
1/4	tsp	cracked black pepper
1/4	tsp	salt
1	cup	sour cream

Weight Loss
6 Servings
7g Net Carbs

1. Mince the scallions and reserve about 1/2 of the green portion for a garnish at the end.

2. Cut the steak into strips against the grain (or in cubes if you prefer). Heat the butter and oil in a deep skillet over medium-high heat. Brown the meat. You might want to do this in several batches. If the meat is over crowded then it will not brown sufficiently.

3. Add the scallions (less the reserved green portion) at the end of the last batch. Add the wine and return all the meat to the skillet. Add the mushrooms with their liquid, tomato paste, Worcestershire sauce, thyme, paprika, salt and pepper. Blend all together and reduce heat to a simmer. Cover and cook at your lowest heat for 1 hour or more. Check on it with a stir occasionally and to be sure it is not boiling.

4. Five minutes before serving, add the sour cream and stir to incorporate. Taste test and add salt or pepper as needed.

Suggest serving with some type of turnips, Brussels sprouts or cabbage. If you are on the maintenance program then by all means serve with beets.

Per Serving: 453 Calories; 30g Fat; 32g Protein; 9g Carbohydrate; 2g Dietary Fiber

Sauerbraten

Ginger and vinegar give this beef pot roast the classic sour flavor.

2	lb	beef pot roast -- with bones
1	Tbsp	butter -- or oil
1/2	cup	red wine vinegar
1	cup	water
1	Tbsp	Worcestershire sauce
1		bay leaf
1	tsp	ground ginger
2	tsps	onion salt
1/2	tsp	pepper
1	tsp	Splenda®
1/4	cup	sour cream
1/4	cup	fresh parsley -- chopped

Weight Loss

4 Servings
4g Net Carbs

The best cut of beef pot roast for this recipe is one that has some bones and is about 1½ inches thick. The bones add lots of flavor. But you can also use an inexpensive chuck or shoulder roast. Also try this recipe with stew meat.

Preheat oven to 300°F

1. Heat butter (or cooking oil) in skillet over medium-high heat. Brown meat on both sides (about 3 minutes per side).

2. Remove meat to a deep casserole dish (preferably one with a lid). The meat should just fit inside without a lot of extra room. And the dish should be at least 1/2 inch deeper than the meat is thick.

3. With the heat turned off, deglaze the skillet by adding the water and scraping up all the brown bits off the bottom of the skillet using a wooden spoon or a spatula.

4. Add the vinegar, Worcestershire sauce, bay leaf, onion powder, ginger, sweetener, salt and pepper. Stir and then pour over the pot roast.

5. Cover securely with a lid or aluminum foil. Cook at 300°F for 3 hours. If convenient, half way through the cooking time, turn the meat over (especially if the liquids do not cover the meat).

6. Remove liquids from casserole dish. Discard the bay leaf. Boil the liquids until reduced by about half.

7. Let the roast rest for about 10 minutes. Cut meat away from the bone and place on serving platter.

8. Pour some of the juices over the meat. Garnish with sour cream and parsley. (Serve extra juices on the side).

Cabbage is the natural compliment to this recipe; try the Pan Fried Cabbage (page 176)

Per Serving: 540 Calories; 41g Fat; 37g Protein; 4g Carbs; trace Dietary Fiber

Seared Steak with Garlic Mushrooms

Mushrooms, garlic and white wine are great flavor compliments to pan seared steaks. This recipe calls for porterhouse steaks, but any cut of steak is fine.

20	oz	**porterhouse steaks (2 steaks)**
1	Tbsp	**butter**
1	tsp	**olive oil**
3	cloves	**garlic -- chopped**
6	ozs	**fresh mushrooms -- quartered**
2	Tbsps	**fresh parsley -- chopped**
2	Tbsps	**dry white wine**

Weight Loss

2 Servings
5g Net Carbs

1. In a heavy skillet over medium-high heat, melt the butter and add the olive oil. Add the steaks and sear them without moving them for 2 minute. Check for dark brown color (they may need more time if they were quite crowded in the skillet). Turn and repeat. Remove steaks from skillet and cover with foil to keep them warm (or put them in a 200°F oven).

2. Add to the skillet the garlic and sauté for about 30 seconds. Add the mushrooms and continue to sauté for another minute or two, until the mushrooms have softened and given up some of their liquid.

3. Add the wine and scrape up any bits stuck to the pan. Add the parsley and stir well. Cook until the majority of the liquid has evaporated (but do not cook dry).

4. Return the steaks to the skillet and add any juices that may have accumulate on the platter. Cook for 1 full minute.

Serve at once.

Per Serving: 399 Calories; 22g Fat; 41g Protein; 6g Carbohydrate; 1g Dietary Fiber

Pot Roast De La France

This basic pot roast is flavored with red wine, shallots and herbs.

3	lbs	7-bone beef chuck roast -- 1" thick
1	Tbsp	butter
1/2	cup	red wine
1	cup	chicken stock
2	Tbsp	shallots -- minced
1	stalk	celery -- minced
1	Tbsp	Worcestershire sauce
2	tsp	Kitchen Bouquet
2	tsp	Dijon mustard
2	sprigs	rosemary
4	sprigs	oregano
8	sprigs	thyme
1		bay leaf

Weight Loss
4 Servings
4g Net Carbs

roux -- optional
1	Tbsp	butter
1	Tbsp	flour

Preheat oven to 325°F

1. In a large skillet over medium-high heat, melt the butter and sear the meat on both sides. Remove meat to a roasting pan or larger casserole dish. Add the shallots and the celery to the skillet and sauté for about 1- 2 minutes. Add the red wine to deglaze, scraping up any brown bits. Add the stock, Worcestershire sauce, Kitchen Bouquet and mustard. Stir until everything is well blended and heated through. Pour over the pot roast.

2. Tuck the sprigs of herbs along the edges of the pan submerging them with a spoon. Cover the pan tightly with a lid or aluminum foil. Roast for 20 minutes at 325°F. Reduce heat to 250°F and cook for 2 hours.

3. Transfer roast to a platter and let rest 15 minutes before serving.

4. Strain the cooking liquids into a gravy boat and serve on the side. Discarding herbs.

Per Serving: 777 Calories; 56g Fat; 54g Protein; 4g Carbs; trace Dietary Fiber

For a thicker gravy: In a sauce pan over medium heat, melt 1 Tbsp butter. Add 1 Tbsp flour and stir constantly for about 1 minute. Pour in about 1/4 cup of the strained cooking liquids and whisk vigorously until thick. Add another 1/4 cup of liquids, whisk vigorously. Add remaining liquids and whisk. Serve gravy on the side.

6g net carbs; 810 Calories; 59g Fat; 55g Protein; 6g Carbs; trace Dietary Fiber

T-Bone Steak with Rosemary, Onions and Gorgonzola

Caramelized onions with rosemary are perfect for a grilled steak.
The gorgonzola cheese tops it off perfectly.

2	8-oz	t-bone steaks, trimmed
		salt and pepper
1	cup	yellow onion slices
2	Tbsps	butter
1	tsp	balsamic vinegar
1/2	tsp	rosemary
2	Tbsps	gorgonzola cheese

Weight Loss

2 Servings
5g Net Carbs

1. In a sauce pan over medium heat, melt the butter and then add the onion slices. Stir well. Let cook for about 10 minutes, stirring occasionally. Add the vinegar and rosemary and cook another 10 minutes.

2. Meanwhile, prepare your grill (or broiler). Season the steaks generously with salt and pepper. Grill to your liking.

3. Serve with caramelized onions piled on top of each steak and sprinkled each with gorgonzola cheese.

Per Serving: 409 Calories; 27g Fat; 35g Protein; 6g Carbohydrate; 1g Dietary Fiber

Lemon-Garlic Pork Chops

Grilled or broiled these flavorful chops are quick & easy.

2½	lb	boneless pork top loin chops (4 chops)
1/3	cup	lemon juice
1/4	cup	olive oil
2	Tbsps	garlic -- crushed
1	Tbsp	dried tarragon -- crushed
		Paprika

Weight Loss

4 Servings
4g Net Carbs

1. For the marinade; in a small bowl combine the lemon juice, olive oil, garlic and tarragon. Place pork chops in plastic bag; pour marinade over chops; seal bag. Marinate in the refrigerator for 6-8 hours or overnight. Drain chops, discarding marinade. Place chops on rack in broiler pan so the chops are 4-5 inches from heat.

2. Sprinkle the chops with a little paprika. Broil for 5-6 minutes or until brown. Turn chops and sprinkle with paprika. Broil for 5-6 minutes more or until chops are just done to your liking (I suggest internal temperature of 150°F for the slightest hint of pink, but no more than 160°F of it will become too dry).

Per Serving: 462 Calories; 26g Fat; 51g Protein; 4g Carbs; trace Dietary Fiber

Pork Cubana

Citrus flavors and Caribbean spices bring new life to pork chops.

1	lb	pork loin chops
1	tsp	canola oil
1	tsp	cumin
1	tsp	chili powder
1/2	tsp	oregano
1/2	tsp	ground allspice
1/2	tsp	lemon pepper
1/4	tsp	salt
1	tsp	butter
2		scallions
1/4		red bell pepper
1		jalapeno – seeded and minced
1	clove	garlic

Weight Loss

2 Servings
6g Net Carbs

Cubana Sauce

1/3	cup	water
2	Tbsps	balsamic vinegar
1	Tbsp	lemon juice
1	Tbsp	lime juice
1	Tbsp	rum -- or dry sherry
1/4	tsp	orange extract
1/2	tsp	guar gum

The chops in this recipe are pan fried but they could just as easily be grilled or broiled.

1. To make the sauce: In a small bowl, add the water, vinegar, lemon juice, lime, juice, rum (if using) and orange extract. Mix well. While whisking vigorously add the guar gum. Continue whisking awhile after it has dissolved to be sure that it does not lump. If it does lump, strain and try again. Set aside.

2. Cut the top green section off of the scallions, mince them and set aside for the garnish. Coarsely chop the bottom white sections. Slice 1/4 of a red bell pepper. The jalapeno should be finely minced. Omit the seeds for they'll create a bitter taste. Crush the garlic clove under a heavy knife or cleaver, remove the skin and mince. Set aside.

3. On a plate, mix together the cumin, oregano, chili powder, allspice, lemon pepper, and salt. Dredge the pork chops into this mixture. Heat the oil in a fry pan over medium-high heat, add the chops and cook for about 3 minutes per side, until it is starting to brown. Remove chops to a plate and cover with foil.

4. Reduce heat to medium; add the butter to the pan and the scallions, bell peppers, jalapeno and garlic. Sauté for about 1 minute stirring frequently. Add the Cubana sauce, stir and scrape up any brown bits from the bottom and sides of the pan. Once it comes to a boil, reduce heat to a low simmer. Return chops to the pan to heat through about 5 minutes. Light cover, turn the chops every minute or so. Do not let the sauce boil again.

Serve chops with the sauce drizzled over and garnished with the scallion tops.

Per Serving: 315 Calories; 17g Fat; 29g Protein; 8g Carbohydrate; 2g Dietary Fiber

Pork Roast Mazatlan

Pork loin roast with a splendid south-of-the-border sauce.

2	lbs	pork loin roast
1/4	cup	water
1	Tbsp	canola oil
1/2	cup	yellow onion -- chopped
2	Tbsps	lime juice
2	cloves	garlic -- chopped
1		jalapeno -- seeded
1	tsp	chili powder
1/4	tsp	salt
1/8	tsp	black pepper
1	cup	chicken broth
1	tsp	Kitchen Bouquet -- optional
2	tsps	Splenda®
2	Tbsps	cilantro -- minced

> **Weight Loss**
>
> 4 Servings
> 4g Net Carbs

1. For the marinade, in a blender combine water, onion, oil, lime juice, garlic, jalapeño pepper, chili powder, salt and pepper. Place the pork loin in a re-sealable plastic baggie and pour the marinade over the pork. Try to eliminate most the air when you seal the bag. Refrigerate 4 hours or overnight. Turn it a few times so that all sides get well marinated.

Preheat oven to 350ºF

2. Transfer the pork to a roasting pan, reserving the marinade. Roast uncovered for about 45 minutes or until an internal temp of about 155ºF. Transfer to a platter and cover with foil to rest while you make the sauce.

3. Deglaze roasting pan with the chicken broth, scraping up all those yummy brown bits. Pour this into a saucepan over medium high heat and add the reserved marinade, Kitchen bouquet and Splenda. Bring to a boil then cook for about 5 minutes. Remove from heat and stir in the cilantro.

4. Slice the roast and serve with the sauce drizzled over the pork or on the side.

Per Serving: 358 Calories; 26g Fat; 25g Protein; 5g Carbohydrate; 1g Dietary Fiber

Pulled Pork

Simple recipe for slow roasted barbeque pork roast.

5	lbs	pork shoulder roast (butt roast)

Dry Rub

4	Tbsps	paprika
3	Tbsps	kosher salt
2	Tbsps	Splenda®
1	Tbsp	chili powder
1	Tbsp	garlic powder
1	Tbsp	dry mustard

1/2	cup	water
13	oz	Carb Options BBQ Sauce

```
Weight Loss

8 Servings
6g Net Carbs
```

1. In a small bowl, mix together the dry rub ingredients. Place the roast in a large bowl and sprinkle the mixed spices over the entire roast, then rub it in. If you wear those thin latex gloves then the rub will stick to the roast better. Cover and refrigerate for several hours but overnight is best so then you can start the roast in the morning.

2. Preheat oven to 275°F. Remove roast from the refrigerator. Pat the meat to be sure that the rub is still sticking. Place in a roasting pan and cook at 275°F for about 8 hours or when the meat easily falls apart. Transfer the roast to a platter and let it rest for 10-15 minutes.

3. Meanwhile, put the roasting pan over medium-high heat and add the water to the roasting pan to deglaze, being sure that you scrape up all those yummy brown bits. A wooden spoon is good for this step. Then add the barbecue sauce, stir and heat through. Then reduce heat to lowest setting.

4. After the roast has rested, it is time to pull it. Stabilize the roast with a fork that has long tongs. Then with another fork start pulling the meat apart and place the meat in a shallow bowl. Pour in a little bit of the barbecue sauce at a time; just until the meat is very lightly coated (don't drown it). Serve with the extra sauce on the side

Per Serving: 536 Calories; 39g Fat; 38g Protein; 8g Carbohydrate; 1g Dietary Fiber

Ham & Spinach Soufflé

Breakfast, lunch or dinner; this soufflé is good any time of the day.

10	ozs	spinach
4	ozs	ham -- diced
1	cup	parmesan cheese -- fresh grated
1	tsp	unsalted butter
5		eggs
1½	cups	cream
1/4	tsp	salt and pepper -- each

Weight Loss
4 Servings
6g Net Carbs

Preheat oven to 375°F

1. If using fresh spinach, remove stems and chop coarsely. Rinse well and while still wet place in a large skillet on high heat. Stir occasionally for about 2 minutes or until wilted. Once it cools, drain off liquids and set spinach aside.

2. If using frozen spinach, defrost according to directions on the package. Drain off any excess liquid and set aside.

3. Butter the bottom and sides of a gratin dish or soufflé dish. Using ~1/3 cup of the Parmesan cheese, dust the pan so that the sides and bottom of the pan is coated with cheese.

4. Separate the eggs. Set the whites aside. Beat the yolks with a whisk until very well beaten. Add the cream, salt & pepper and whisk again. Add the spinach, ham and 1/3 cup of the cheese. Stir.

5. Beat the egg whites until firm yet still a little soft (not dry peaks). Gently fold (not stir) eggs whites into spinach mixture and slowly pour into baking dish. Sprinkle the remaining 1/3 cup of cheese on top.

6. Bake at 375°F, uncovered, for about 35 minute until the soufflé is set and the top is brown and puffy. Turn off oven, open the door, but leave soufflé in the oven for about 10-15 minutes.

7. Serve immediately by spooning directly from the baking dish onto individuals plates.

Per Serving: 467 Calories; 38g Fat; 24g Protein; 8g Carbohydrate; 2g Dietary Fiber

Spicy Pork Chops with Cumin Raita

These mild curry pork chops are tempered with cool, cucumber cumin raita.

2	lb	pork sirloin chops (4 chops)
1	Tbsp	canola oil
2	tsps	ground coriander
1	tsp	ground turmeric
1/2	tsp	salt
1/2	tsp	ground black pepper
1/8	tsp	dry mustard
1	dash	cayenne

Raita

1		cucumber
8	oz	plain yogurt
3	Tbsps	chopped fresh cilantro
1/4	tsp	ground cumin
1/2	tsp	ground coriander

> **Weight Loss**
>
> 4 Servings
> 7g Net Carbs

1. Rub the chops with canola oil. Mix together the coriander, turmeric, salt, pepper, cayenne and dry mustard and rub this seasoning mixture evenly over chops. Cover and refrigerate overnight.

2. For the Raita: Peel the cucumber and remove the ends. Grate the cucumber and mix together with the yogurt, cilantro, cumin, and coriander. Refrigerate overnight.

3. The pork chops can be grilled or broiled. Cook for 5 minutes per side per inch thickness.

Serve with Cumin Raita.

Per Serving: 410 Calories; 26g Fat; 35g Protein; 8g Carbohydrate; 1g Dietary Fiber

Veal Oscar

Braised veal cutlets with asparagus and crab smothered in a Béarnaise sauce!
Outstanding! This is one of my favorite special occasion meals.
You can substitute pork or chicken for the veal.

1/2	cup	Béarnaise sauce (page 354)
1/2	lb	Alaskan king crab legs
12		asparagus spears
12	ozs	veal cutlets
		salt and pepper
1	Tbsp	butter
1/2	cup	veal stock -- or chicken stock
1	Tbsp	dry sherry
1	tsp	paprika -- as garnish
2	tsps	fresh chives – minced, as garnish

> **Weight Loss**
>
> 2 Servings
> 6g Net Carbs

You'll want the timing on this meal to come out perfectly, so get familiar with the instructions well before time to cook. I recommend having the table set and ready to go. If you plan to have a salad as well, prepare that first.

Set oven to 150°F

1. Prepare the béarnaise sauce (page 354) and keep in a 150°F oven. That recipe will make more than you'll need here but make the full batch anyway. You just may want a little extra.

2. Remove the meat from the crab legs and carefully cut or tear into bite-sized pieces. Place in a bowl, cover with aluminum foil and place in the warm oven.

3. Arrange asparagus spears on a microwave safe plate with 1 Tbsp water. Tightly cover with plastic wrap pierced with a knife (one small hole is fine). Zap for 3 minutes then transfer to the oven.

4. Depending on the veal cutlets, they may be two thick steaks or 4 thinner ones. Either way is fine. This recipe assumes the thick cutlets. If using the thin ones, reduce the braising time to 3 minutes.

5. Season the veal cutlets on both sides with salt and pepper.

6. In a skillet over medium-high heat, melt the butter. Add the cutlets and sear both sides (2-3 minutes per side). Transfer to a plate. Add the sherry and cook ~30 seconds then add the stock. Bring to a boil as you scrape up any brown bits. Reduce heat to a simmer. Add the cutlets, loosely covered with lid or foil and braise for 5 minutes. Remove from heat and uncover.

7. Recommended plating: Arrange the asparagus spears just off center of the plate with 3 spears pointing one way and 3 pointing the opposite direction. It is great if you can get them to stack. Then lean the veal cutlet(s) against the asparagus. Sprinkle the crab meat over the veal and asparagus. Drizzle the béarnaise sauce over the veal and asparagus in a zigzag fashion perpendicular to the direction of the asparagus. Sprinkle the paprika and chives around the edge of the plate. Serve at once.

Per Serving: 442 Calories; 19g Fat; 57g Protein; 8g Carbohydrate; 2g Dietary Fiber

Variations

For pork: use good quality top loin chops (no bones) and cook exactly the same way as above.

For chicken: use boneless, skinless chicken breasts. Pound thin and braise for 15 minutes (or flatten and braise for 25 minutes). When using chicken, you may have time to start it first, then prepare the béarnaise sauce, asparagus and crab while it cooks (especially if you have a helper in the kitchen).

Enjoy your special occasion, whatever it is!

Texas Barbecue Beef Brisket

Although this takes all day to cook it is worth it if you love barbecue.
The sauce is sweet and spicy, just the way I like it.

| 5 | lbs | beef brisket -- whole |

Dry Rub

5	Tbsps	paprika
2	Tbsps	kosher salt
2	Tbsps	Splenda®
1	Tbsp	ground black pepper
1	Tbsp	chili powder
1	Tbsp	garlic powder
1	Tbsp	onion salt
1	Tbsp	cumin

Basting & Serving Sauce

2	cups	Carb Options™ Barbeque Sauce
1/2	cup	apple cider vinegar
2	Tbsp	Blackstrap molasses
1	Tbsp	dry rub
2	Tbsps	canola oil
2		jalapeno -- seeded and minced
1/2	cup	water

The basting sauce is called a mop in the professional barbecue circles. They use a basting utensil that indeed looks like an old fashioned mop. A regular basting brush will work just as well.

1. Mix together the dry rub ingredients. Set aside 1 Tbsp of the dry rub for the basting sauce.

2. Sprinkle 1/2 of the dry rub on the brisket and literally rub it in. If you wear thin latex gloves the rub seems to stick to the meat better. Turn the brisket over and rub in the remaining dry rub. Wrap in plastic and refrigerate overnight.

Preheat oven to 250ºF

3. Basting Sauce. In a sauce pan over medium heat, add the canola oil and the minced jalapeno peppers. Cook for 1 minute then add the barbecue sauce, vinegar, molasses and the reserved tablespoon of the dry rub. Cook for about 3 minutes, stirring frequently. Pour 1/2 the sauce into a bowl to be used when serving the brisket (refrigerate it until ready to serve). Add the 1/2 cup of water to the remaining sauce to be used as the mop for basting.

4. Place brisket in a large roasting pan. Baste both sides with some of the basting sauce. Turn brisket so that the fat side is up. Roast for 4-6 hours until tender, basting with more sauce every 30-45 minutes. When done,

remove brisket to a serving platter and let it rest for 15 minutes before slicing thinly across the grain.

5. Warm the reserved serving sauce and serve on the side.

Optional: Combine the pan juices with the reserved serving sauce and any left over basting sauce. Bring to a boil and slow boil for 3 minutes. Serve sauce on the side.

Per Serving: 596 Calories; 31g Fat; 63g Protein; 15g Carbohydrate; 2g Fiber

Beef Enchiladas

Quick and easy, low carb enchiladas smothered in green chili sauce.

1	lb	ground beef
1	tsp	cumin
1/2	tsp	salt and white pepper -- each
1/2	cup	505 Green Chile Sauce
1/2	cup	Monterey jack cheese
4		Low Carb Green Onion Tortilla

Maintenance
4 Servings
10g Net Carbs

Topping

1	cup	505 Green Chile Sauce
1/2	cup	cheddar cheese, shredded

Use any low carb tortilla that you have available. What is called for here are the smaller ones (~6 inch diameter) that have the green onion flavor; from La Tortilla Factory (they are the best in my opinion).

Preheat oven to 350°F

1. In a non-stick skillet over medium-high heat, add the ground beef and cook it through stirring frequently (about 8 minutes). Drain off the fat. Add the cumin, salt and pepper and stir. Add the 1/2 cup of the green chile sauce and heat through, stirring occasionally. Remove from heat, add 1/2 cup of Monterey jack cheese, and stir.

2. Lay out the 4 tortillas on a flat surface. Divide the beef mixture evenly among them placing it on the lower 1/3 portion of each tortilla. Roll up each tortilla and place seam side down in an 8x8 casserole dish. Allow a little bit of separation between the enchiladas.

3. Cover with the remaining cup of the green chile sauce and sprinkle the top with the remaining cheese. Bake in a 350°F oven (uncovered) for 15 or 20 minute, until the cheese is completely melted and starting to bubble.

Serve with the Avocado & Tomato Salad (page 158) or try the Southwestern Salad (with or without the chicken included).

Per Serving: 488 Calories; 34g Fat; 32g Protein; 19g Carbs; 9g Dietary Fiber

Stir-Fried Beef Strips

Beef strips with a thick and spicy sauce. This recipe is quick and easy.

3	lbs	beef top round -- cut into strips
1	tsp	chili powder
1/2	tsp	ground ginger
1/2	tsp	garlic salt
1/4	tsp	pepper

1	cup	salsa
1/2	cup	peanut butter
2	Tbsps	soy sauce
2	Tbsps	balsamic vinegar
1	Tbsp	Splenda®
1	Tbsp	water

1	Tbsp	canola oil
2	Tbsps	scallions -- sliced diagonally, as a garnish

> **Maintenance**
>
> **4 Servings**
> **10g Net Carbs**

1. In a bowl, combine chili powder, ginger, garlic salt and pepper. Add beef strips and toss to coat. Set aside.

2. Meanwhile, in a medium saucepan combine salsa, peanut butter, soy sauce, vinegar, molasses, Splenda and water. Bring to boiling, stirring often. Remove from heat. Set aside.

3. In a large skillet or wok, heat oil over medium-high heat. Add beef and stir fry for 2-3 minutes, until cooked through. Add the sauce and stir thoroughly.

Serve garnished with scallions. Goes great with the Mock Fried Rice (page 179).

Per Serving: 825 Calories; 49g Fat; 85g Protein; 13g Carbohydrate; 3g Fiber

Sweet & Sour Pork

This classic dish is converted to low carb just by substituting guar gum for the cornstarch.

2	lbs	boneless pork top loin -- cut into strips
1	Tbsp	sesame oil
3	cloves	garlic -- minced
3		scallions -- minced
1	Tbsp	fresh ginger root -- grated
1		red bell pepper -- sliced
2		carrots -- sliced
1/4	lb	snow peas
1	cup	water
4	Tbsps	rice vinegar
4	Tbsps	soy sauce
3	Tbsps	Splenda®
1	Tbsp	lemon juice
1	tsp	orange extract
1/2	tsp	guar gum

Maintenance

4 Servings
11g Net Carbs

1. Prepare all your ingredients first. Mince the scallions and reserve 1/2 or more of the green portion to use as a garnish. The pork can be cubed or cut into strips. Slice and mince the veggies.

2. In a bowl, whisk together the water, vinegar, soy sauce, Splenda, lemon juice and orange extract. Add guar gum and whisk until dissolved. Set aside.

3. In wok or large non-stick skillet, heat the sesame oil over medium-high heat. Stir-fry the ginger, garlic, scallions, peppers and carrots for about 3 minutes. Add pork and stir-fry for 3 more minutes. Add the snow peas and toss. Add the sauce, stir and cook 1 more minute.

Serve garnished with scallion greens.

Per Serving: 343 Calories; 13g Fat; 42g Protein; 14g Carbohydrate; 3g Fiber

Weight Loss Variation: Omit the carrots.
8g net carbs; 328 Calories; 13g Fat; 42g Protein; 10g Carbohydrate; 2g Dietary Fiber

Lamb & Eggplant Stacks

The spices with the lamb and the eggplant give this dish a Mediterranean flare. This could also be made with ground beef if preferred.

1		eggplant
12	ozs	ground lamb
1	Tbsp	olive oil
2	Tbsps	yellow onion -- diced
1/2	tsp	ground cumin
1/2	tsp	dried oregano
1/2	tsp	cinnamon
1	dash	cayenne pepper
1/3	cup	Carb Options™ Garden Style Pasta Sauce
1	Tbsp	fresh flat-leaf parsley -- chopped
1/4	cup	parmesan cheese
		salt and pepper -- to taste

> **Maintenance**
>
> **2 Servings**
> **12g Net Carbs**

Preheat oven to 375°F

1. Trim off and discard the ends of the eggplant. Slice it into six rounds. Salt both sides of each round and place in a colander with a weighted bowl placed on top. Or place on thick, folded dish towels and put a weighted casserole dish on top. Let the eggplant drain for about 20 minute. Rinse and pat dry.

2. In a large skillet, heat oil over medium heat. Add onion and sauté for about 5 minutes, stirring occasionally. Add the cumin, oregano, cinnamon and cayenne pepper and cook one full minute more.

3. Add the lamb and a pinch of salt and pepper. Cook for about 5 minutes or until nicely browned. Be sure to stir frequently. Remove from heat. Drain out most of the fat. Stir in the pasta sauce.

4. In a baking dish, place two eggplant rounds. Spoon on top 1/3 of the lamb. Sprinkle on top of that a little bit of the cheese. Then create two more layers of eggplant, lamb and cheese the same way. Sprinkle on top any remaining cheese.

5. Cover with foil and bake for 45 minutes at 375 F. Remove the foil and bake another 15 minutes. Serve immediately with a garnish of chopped parsley.

Per Serving: 554 Calories; 38g Fat; 36g Protein; 19g Carbohydrate; 7g Fiber

POULTRY

POULTRY

~ Regarding Poultry ~

Poultry is my preferred source of protein. I mostly use chicken, turkey and Cornish game hens as these are the most economical sources of animal protein and are widely available. Occasionally I enjoy cooking duck, goose, squab or pheasant but mostly I wait to have these at the high-end restaurants which specialize in the more exotic birds. Ostrich is rather tasty too.

Poultry can be cooked by any method and this versatility adds to their appeal. Although this may sound boring to some people, I mostly enjoy poultry that has been slowly roasted, whole and without stuffing. It is the simplest way for me, the most economical and in my opinion, the most flavorful. The only drawback is that it takes longer to cook. But there is nothing better than home-made stock and the most convenient way to make it is with whole poultry right after the meat has been cut away. See page 322 for stock recipe. However, it is hard to beat the convenience of chicken that has already been cut-up into easily manageable parts, especially if you have a strong preference for either white or dark meat. The majority of my recipes are for cut-up chicken, but generally you can substitute your preferred cuts.

At any given time you will find my freezer well stocked with poultry. I typically roast 25-35 chickens per year, as well as a dozen or more Cornish game hens and 3 or 4 turkeys. I look for bargains and then stock up. In mid-November, the local grocery stores sell turkeys for $4 or $5 each: that translates to about 20-25¢ per pound! So I get as many as my freeze will hold. Unlike beef, most poultry freezes well, retaining both good texture and good flavor.

Cooking Temperatures and Techniques

When roasting poultry, it is best when you can preheat the oven to 400-450°F and then reduce the heat to 325-350°F after the bird is in and the oven door is closed. The roasting temperature for chicken and small fowl is best at about 350°F but any poultry over 10 pounds is better when cooked at 325°F.

Poultry needs to be cooked thoroughly until the juices run clear. This is due to salmonella which is much too prevalent in commercial poultry operations. Salmonella starts to die off at 150°F but for safety reasons (and measurement inaccuracies) it is best to reach temperatures in excess of 165°F. The internal temperature of poultry is generally tested with a meat thermometer inserted into the thigh and should reach 180°F for chicken and 175°F for turkey before removing them from the oven (they will continue to cook and temperatures will generally rise another 5°F). You can over-cook roasted chicken and turkey only about 5°F before they start to dry out and get tough. Other types of fowl, especially wild game, are more tolerant of being slightly over-cooked as their high fat content helps keep the meat moist.

After removing roasted poultry from the oven, cover them loosely with foil and let them rest before carving, so that the juices can be drawn back into the core of the meat, helping to keep it moist and flavorful. The resting period is approximately 10-15 minutes for whole chicken and 15-20 minutes for whole turkey. Smaller birds and cuts of chicken generally only need about 5 minutes of resting time.

Do not rely on those plastic pop-up thermometers which sometimes are already inserted in the bird when purchased. They are unreliable and they are set for too high of a temperature (typically 190°F). If you do not have a meat thermometer then you'll need to cook by timing it. Roasting temperatures and times for unstuffed poultry are as follows:

Game hen (<2 lbs) @ 350°F	30-35 minutes per pound
Chicken (3-6 lbs) @ 350°F	20-25 minutes per pound
Small Turkey (<16 lbs) @ 325°F	15-20 minutes per pound
Larger Turkey (>16lbs) @ 325°F	13-15 minutes per pound

Another method for testing doneness is by twisting the leg. If the bone gives way from the socket then it is actually over cooked and if there is no flexibility at all then it has not yet finished cooking. You will be looking for something in between. This method takes practice but once mastered it is quite reliable. I generally cook my game hens this way as they are too small for my meat thermometer. Since they have more tolerance to being over-cooked I'll let them cook until the leg just barely gives way in the socket.

Stuffing Poultry

I do not stuff chicken or turkey; there are too many things that can go wrong and it takes much longer to cook. Small birds such as Cornish game hens and squab are wonderful to stuff as they cook relatively quickly anyway and the amount of stuffing in quite small.

When stuffing poultry, fill the cavity only 3/4 full and do not pack it down. The stuffing should be loose and able to expand. The stuffing can be made in advance; however, do not place it in the poultry until the very last minute (to minimize the growth of bacteria) before roasting. The stuffing must reach an internal temperature of 165°F in order to be absolutely sure that it is safe to eat. Unfortunately, once the stuff has reached this temperature, the meat is typically over-cooked. That is the primary reason why I don't stuff chicken or turkey.

Basting

Most cookbooks recommend basting poultry while it roasts in order to keep the meat moist. I've had no luck at all with this method. I find that it dries out the meat even more and increases the required cooking time by as much as double. Every time you open the oven door to baste, all of the heat escapes from the oven. The outside portion of the meat begins to cool, slowing the rate of heat transfer into the core of the bird. Then these outer portions have to reheat and this dries them out. So I generally say no to basting roasted poultry. Grilled poultry is another matter altogether, and it is recommended to baste frequently.

The best way I have found to keep the meat moist is to cook with the skin left on. Right before putting it into the oven, I coat the skin with butter and herbs. The skin and butter helps seal in both the moisture but also the heat. I do not usually cover game hens or chickens up to 4 pounds. With larger poultry such as turkey, I make a tent out of foil and lay it loosely over the bird for the first two hours, then I remove the foil (but reserve it for the resting period after it is cooked). The loose foil tent will allow some moisture to accumulate and then fall back down onto the meat, thereby self-basting without having to open the oven every 30 minutes (as some cookbooks recommend).

Have you seen those roasting bags? They work great for turkeys, particularly if you don't have a thermometer. When using these you are actually steaming or poaching the turkey rather than roasting it, but it will still brown a little bit on top. These bags are ideal for the novice cook or when cooking poultry with the skin removed. Simply follow the direction on the package.

Skinless & Boneless
Even if you do not want to eat the skin, it is generally best to leave it on when cooking with dry heat methods (roasting, grilling, broiling, pan frying) as it will provide better heat distribution and will help retain the moisture in the meat. If you are braising or poaching then it is generally best to remove the skin so that the meat can absorb the flavors of the cooking liquids and removing the skin will also reduce the fat content of the recipe.

Bones are flavorful and give off their flavor to both the meat and the cooking liquids (or pan drippings). So for most recipes I generally encourage using chicken that is still on the bone. Boneless chicken not only has less flavor, but it cooks faster and so can become over-cooked much more easily. But there is no denying the convenience of having the bones removed. I have only a few recipes where I recommend boneless chicken. Yet for the other recipes, I generally advise on how to reduce the cooking time if you decide to use boneless chicken anyway. Turkey cutlets are becoming more and more popular. Since turkey is very low in fat, these boneless cuts tend to be the most susceptible to drying out. Moist heat methods are generally the easiest way to cook boneless poultry.

Another reason for choosing poultry on the bone, is that it takes more work to eat it. Cutting around the bones naturally slows down the eating process and reduces the chances of over-eating. This is especially important to me when I have purposefully made extra portions so I can have left-overs for future meals. If I eat too fast, then I don't realize that I am full already and I start eyeing those extra portions.

Herb Roasted Poultry with Gravy

Whole roasted chicken, turkey or Cornish game hens is a standard fare in my home. It's simple and delicious. And oh how wonderful the house smells!

1	whole	roasting chicken
1	cup	water (or chicken stock)
3	sprigs	fresh rosemary
3	sprigs	fresh oregano
3	sprigs	fresh sage
3	sprigs	fresh thyme
3	Tbsps	butter
1	tsp	garlic powder
1/2	tsp	pepper
3	stalks	celery
1/4	med	onion
1	tsp	Kitchen Bouquet -- optional
1/4	tsp	guar gum

Induction

4 Servings
1g Net Carbs

Why not roast two chickens at once, it is not any more work and the left-over chicken can be used in many of the recipes in this cookbook. This recipe can also be made with dried herbs (a pinch of each in step 3 and ~1/2 tsp each in step 4) or any left-over herb butter that you might have in the fridge. I roast whole chickens frequently. It's the most economical way to prepare chicken, and I also want those bones for home-made chicken stock (see page322).

For a turkey; double the recipe. If using Cornish games hens; you'll need 3 or 4 of them and use only 1/2 sprig of each herb in the cavity in step 3.

Preheat oven to 400°F

1. Thoroughly rinse the chicken and place in your roasting pan. Add 1 cup of water or stock to the bottom of the pan.

2. Cut the celery stalks in half. Place three pieces in the bottom of the roasting pan and the remainder in the cavity of the chicken along with the onion.

3. Put 1 sprig of each of the herbs into the cavity of the chicken. With the remaining herbs, remove the leaves from the stems. Mince the herb leaves. Throw the stems in the bottom of the roasting pan.

4. Place the minced herbs in a small bowl with the butter, garlic powder and pepper. Melt the butter in the microwave.

5. Brush the chicken with the melted butter and herbs. Be sure to coat thoroughly.

6. Place a meat thermometer into the thigh; be sure not to touch a bone. (For a turkey; make a loose fitting tent out of aluminum foil for the first 2 hours of roasting.

7. Place in the oven and reduce heat to 350°F (or 325°F for a turkey). Roast until the thermometer reaches 180°F degrees (170°F for turkey) and remove from oven promptly.

   This will take approximately 1 hour and 15 minutes depending on the size or your chicken (if cooking two chickens at a time then expect it to take 20 minutes more). For Cornish game hens; it will take 30-45 minutes. For a 20lb turkey this will take 4-5 hours.

8. Transfer to a carving platter, loosely cover with foil and let it rest 10-15 minutes. (For a turkey; rest 15-20 minutes. For Cornish game hens ~5 minutes). Before carving, remove the herbs, celery and onion from inside the chicken; save these if you are going to make stock (highly recommended; see page 322).

9. Strain the pan dripping into a gravy separator. Save the herbs and celery for your stock. If you don't have a gravy separator then strain into a wide mouth jar. Let the liquids settle then pour off most of the fat (leaving a little helps add flavor).

10. Pour 1/2 of the separated pan drippings back into the roasting pan over medium heat. Be sure to scrape up the brown bits from the sides or bottom. Boil for 2-3 minutes letting the liquids reduce in volume, concentrating the flavors.

11. In the other half of the liquids, add 1/4 tsp of guar gum per cup of pan drippings; stir well. Add this thicken stock to the roasting pan and whisk vigorously. Add the Kitchen Bouquet to enhance flavor and color. Taste and add salt or pepper if needed. Strain again if needed.

Variation: Use a turkey breast with or without the skin.

Per Serving: 804 Calories; 62g Fat; 57g Protein; 1g Carbs; trace Dietary Fiber

Traditional Gravy Variation: Eliminate the guar gum. Add all of the separated pan drippings to the roasting pan in step 10. Boil to reduce and scrape up all those delicious brown bits. Estimate the amount of liquids (generally about 1 cup for chicken). In a sauce pan, melt 1 Tbsp of butter for every cup of liquid. Then add 2-3 tsp of flour for every cup of liquid and stir well for 1-2 minutes. Add the reduced pan dripping and stir vigorously while it comes to a boil. Once thickened, reduce heat and add the Kitchen Bouquet. Taste and add salt and pepper as needed.

3g net carbs; 836 Calories; 64g Fat; 58g Protein; 3g Carbohydrate; trace Dietary Fiber

Aspen Chicken

Chicken braised in Coors' Aspen Edge low carb beer
jazzed-up with some Southwestern flavors.

3	lbs	cut-up chicken, no skin
1	Tbsp	butter
1		Anaheim chili pepper -- sliced
1/2	cup	yellow onion -- sliced
12	ozs	Aspen Edge Beer
	dash	cumin
	dash	Liquid Barbecue Smoke®
1/4	tsp	salt
1/4	tsp	black pepper
3	Tbsps	salsa
1	Tbsp	fresh cilantro leaves -- minced

> **Induction**
>
> **4 Servings**
> **3g Net Carbs**

Use any cut of chicken that you prefer, but please remove the skin. As usual I prefer the chicken on the bone but boneless works fine in this recipe too, just reduce the simmer time to 20 minutes.

Anaheim peppers are quite mild, I recommend using the seeds and membrane. If you don't want this dish to be spicy then substitute 1/2 of a green bell pepper for the Anaheim pepper and substitute canned dice tomatoes for the salsa.

1. In a large skillet or soup pot, melt the butter over medium-high heat and sauté the onion and chili peppers until the onions are translucent. Add the beer, cumin and Liquid Smoke. Go easy on both of these, no more than a scant 1/4 tsp of cumin and even less Liquid Smoke (you can always add more at the end if needed). Bring to a boil. Add the chicken, bring back to the boil. Turn the chicken and then reduce heat, cover and simmer for 35 minutes (30 minutes if just breast meat).

2. Transfer chicken to a platter and cover. Boil the cooking liquids until they reduce down to less than 1 cup. Add the salsa and cook for 1 minute. Stir occasionally. Reduce heat to medium-low, return the chicken (and any juices) to the skillet and continue to cook another minute, turn the chicken and cook another minute. Stir occasionally. Taste and adjust seasoning as needed.

3. Transfer the chicken back to the platter (or to individual plates) spoon the sauce over the chicken and garnish with the minced cilantro.

Per Serving: 255 Calories; 8g Fat; 41g Protein; 4g Carbohydrate; 1g Dietary Fiber

Cheesy Chicken with Artichoke

This is a great low carb comfort food that is gooey and fun to eat;
therefore it's probably not very suitable to serve to company.

3	lbs	cut-up chicken -- no skin, no bones
1	can	artichoke bottoms -- chopped
3		scallions -- chopped
1	Tbsp	butter
2	stalks	celery -- diced
1	tsp	thyme
1/4	cup	white wine
1/4	cup	heavy cream
1/4	cup	cheddar cheese -- grated
1/4	cup	Monterey jack cheese -- grated
1/4	cup	mozzarella cheese -- grated
	dash	Tabasco sauce -- optional
1/4	cup	parmesan cheese

Induction
4 Servings
3g Net Carbs

Preheat oven to 350°F

1. Cut the boneless, skinless chicken parts into bite sized pieces. In a non stick frying pan, brown the chicken in batches and transfer to a lightly greased casserole dish (you don't need to cook the chicken completely through at this step). Arrange the chicken into an even layer. (You can minimize this step by using precooked or left-over chicken but then remember to reduce the cooking time to 20 minutes).

2. Sprinkle over the chicken the chopped artichoke bottoms and scallions.

3. In a sauce pan over medium-high heat, melt the butter and sauté the celery for a minute or so. Add the white wine and let it boil for a full minute. Reduce heat to medium heat. Add the cream, cheddar, jack and mozzarella cheeses and the thyme. If you want it spicy then add the Tabasco sauce at this time too. Stir constantly until the cheeses melt.

4. Pour cheese sauce over chicken, top with the parmesan cheese and bake for 35 minutes, uncovered.

Per Serving: 604 Calories; 25g Fat; 84g Protein; 4g Carbohydrate; 1g Dietary Fiber

Chicken Marsala

This is the classic recipe. By eliminating the flour, it becomes low carb.

4		chicken breast halves -- no skin, no bone
	dash	salt and pepper -- each
1	Tbsp	butter
1	tsp	olive oil
1	Tbsp	shallots -- minced
1	clove	garlic -- minced
1	cup	mushroom -- sliced
1/2	cup	Marsala wine
1/2	cup	chicken stock
1	Tbsp	fresh Italian parsley -- chopped

Induction
4 Servings
2g Net Carbs

This is best when chicken breasts are lightly pounded flat to a uniform thickness. To accomplish this, unfold a chicken breast and cover with thick plastic wrap (or two layers of regular plastic wrap). Lightly pound the chicken with the smooth side of a meat mallet (or a small yet sturdy frying pan) until a uniform thickness but not too thin. Season lightly with salt and pepper.

1. In a large skillet over medium-high heat, add the butter and oil. Brown the chicken on both sides, remove and set aside (~5 minutes per side). This should be done in two batches so as not to crowd the chicken slowing the browning process (unless your skillet is big enough). Set chicken aside.

2. Reduce the heat to medium; add to the skillet the shallots, garlic and mushrooms and cook until the mushrooms are tender. Add the Marsala wine and cook for a full minute scraping up any of the delicious brown bits still clinging to the pan.

3. Add the chicken stock, bring to a boil. Add the chicken and parsley. Reduce heat to low, cover and simmer for 10-15 minutes. Serve immediately.

If you'd like for the sauce to be thick, you can dissolve 1/2 tsp of guar gum in the chicken stock (be sure it is cold) before adding it to the pan. Or you can make this the classic way and dust the chicken with flour before browning it; but be sure to add 2g carbs per serving for every Tbsp of flour.

Per Serving: 196 Calories; 6g Fat; 28g Protein; 2g Carbs; trace Dietary Fiber

Chicken with Mushroom Cream Sauce

Generous portions of chicken drenched in a creamy, flavorful, mushroom sauce. This is just the ticket for a delicious low carb evening meal.

2	lb	chicken breast halves -- no skin, no bones
1/2	Tbsp	butter
1	tsp	olive oil
3		scallions
4	ozs	fresh button mushrooms -- quartered
1/2	cup	dry white wine
1	tsp	dried thyme
	dash	nutmeg
1		bay leaf
1/4	cup	heavy cream
1/4	cup	sour cream
		salt and pepper -- to taste

Induction

4 Servings
3g Net Carbs

Fresh mushrooms are the key to this recipe. But feel free to substitute portabella, crimmi, shitake or other mushrooms as you prefer.

1. Cut chicken into bite sized pieces. Mince the scallions and separate the white portion from the green portion which will be used as a garnish.

2. In a heavy skillet over medium heat, add the butter and olive oil. Add the chicken pieces and sauté until the chicken for about 2 minutes.

3. Add the white portions of the scallions to the skillet and cook for about 1 minute. Then add the mushrooms and cook for about 2 minutes. Reduce heat to low.

4. Add the wine, thyme, nutmeg and bay leaf. Cover and simmer for about 15 minutes, stir occasionally.

5. Add the heavy cream and sour cream. Taste test and add salt or pepper as desired.

6. Remove bay leaf. Serve garnished with minced green scallion tops.

Per Serving: 404 Calories; 17g Fat; 54g Protein; 4g Carbohydrate; 1g Dietary Fiber

Grilled Cornish Game Hens

This simple recipe is always a favorite with my guests.
Fresh herbs make the basting sauce earthy and aromatic.

2		Cornish game hens
1	cup	Carb Well Italian Dressing
3	Tbsps	butter
1	tsp	fresh oregano – finely minced
1	tsp	fresh thyme
2	sprigs	fresh rosemary

Induction
2 Servings
1g Net Carbs

This recipe assumes 1 hen per serving. But if you are serving a salad and vegetable then this is enough for 4 people.

1. Rinse well the hens. Using good kitchen shears remove the backbone by cutting along each side of it (a sharp knife works well too). Also break the wishbone so that the hens can lie flat. Place hens in a large re-sealable plastic bag with the Italian dressing. Try to remove as much air as possible while sealing the bag closed. Refrigerate for at least 2 hours or overnight.

2. Remove hens from the refrigerator about 10-15 minutes before grill time. Discard marinade.

3. Pull off the top leaves of the rosemary sprigs and mince. You should have about 1 tsp worth. Reserve the remaining rosemary for step 5.

4. In a small bowl, place the butter, oregano, thyme and rosemary. Zap in the microwave for about 30 seconds, just enough to melt the butter. Set aside.

5. Prepare your grill so that you have a heat source on only one side of the grill. Under the grate on the cool side, place the rosemary sprigs reasonably close to the heat but not touching it. Oil the grate and place the hens on the cool side, breasts side up. Cover and cook undisturbed for 15 minutes. (Feel free to start grilling vegetables and/or meats on the hot side after the 15 minutes.)

6. With a basting brush, start basting the hens with the herb butter mixture every 5 minutes or so for another 15 to 25 minutes keeping the grill covered as much as possible. Check for doneness with an instant read thermometer reading 180°F in the center of the breast; or by twisting the leg bone to see if it can move easily in the joint; or by cutting into the thigh joint where it meets the breast and checking for clear liquid.

Serve with grilled or roasted vegetables (see page 198)

Per Serving: 825 Calories; 64g Fat; 58g Protein; trace Carbs; trace Dietary Fiber

Grilled Spicy Citrus Chicken

Grilled chicken basted with spicy citrus vinaigrette

1	lb	chicken breasts -- no skin
2	Tbsps	balsamic vinegar
1	Tbsp	lemon juice
1	Tbsp	lime juice
1/2	tsp	lemon pepper
1/4	tsp	orange extract
1/4	tsp	cumin
1/4	tsp	chili powder
1/4	tsp	ground allspice
	pinch	salt
1/4	cup	canola oil
2	Tbsps	water
1	tsp	Dijon mustard
1/2	tsp	Splenda®

Induction
2 Servings
3g Net Carbs

I prefer my chicken on the bone, but if you use boneless then reduce cooking time by 5 or 10 minutes (internal temperature of 180°F).

1. In a small non-metallic bowl, add the vinegar, lemon juice, lime juice, lemon pepper, orange extract, cumin, chili powder, allspice and a pinch of salt. Vigorously whisk the vinaigrette while you (or a helper) slowly add the canola oil. (This can also be done in a food processor).

2. Rinse chicken and pierce deeply several times with a fork or knife. In a baggie pour 1/2 of the vinaigrette (reserve the remainder) and add the skinless chicken pieces. Squish it around to get the pieces coated. Do this every 5 minutes for 15 or 20 minutes. Discard marinade.

3. With the reserved vinaigrette add 2 Tbsp of water, mustard and Splenda. This will be used as the basting sauce.

4. Meanwhile prepare your grill; just fire up one side of the grill. Over a medium-high heat, sear the chicken pieces on both sides. About 2 minutes per side with the lid up. Then move the chicken to the non-heated side of the grill, close the lid and cook for about 30 minutes. With a spoon or basting brush start basting chicken after about 10 minutes and then continue every 5 minutes or so until done.

Per Serving: 395 Calories; 30g Fat; 27g Protein; 3g Carbs; trace Dietary Fiber

Grilled Chicken with Spinach Sauce

This spinach sauce is rich and creamy. It is a delectable way to dress-up ordinary grilled chicken. Also try it on fish or pork chops.

3	lbs	cut-up chicken
10	ozs	frozen spinach -- chopped
2	Tbsps	fresh parsley -- chopped
2	tsps	fresh thyme -- chopped
1	tsp	mustard
2/3	cup	mayonnaise

Induction

4 Servings
1g Net Carbs

Any chicken parts can be used for this recipe with or without skin or bones. I personally prefer the thighs; grilled with the skins on then removing the skins just before adding the spinach sauce.

1. Season chicken with salt and pepper. Grill (or broil) to your liking.

2. In a microwave safe bowl, add the chopped frozen spinach and zap it until it is completely thawed and thoroughly heated. This usually requires it to be stirred one or two times before completely heated through. Drain and squeezed out excess liquid. (*See note.)

3. Add to the spinach the parsley, thyme, mustard and mayonnaise. Mix well.

4. Spoon the sauce over the cooked chicken and serve immediately.

Per Serving: 573 Calories; 43g Fat; 47g Protein; 3g Carbohydrate; 2g Dietary Fiber

*Note: This liquid has significant nutrients as well as flavor. So consider drinking it (the chef's bonus), reserve it for stock or offer it to your pets. My dogs love extra cooking liquids; but the cat, not so much.

Mustard Crusted Chicken Thighs

Chicken thighs slathered in mustard and herbs.

8		chicken thighs -- no skin
1/2	cup	brown mustard
1	Tbsp	Mrs. Dash
1/4	tsp	salt

Induction

4 Servings
2g Net Carbs

This baked chicken dish has a lovely crust formed by the mustard. It you love chicken skin, then leave it on for an extra crunch. Cook only enough for a single meal as left-overs are disappointing. Using a roasting rack inside a roast pan will allow the entire piece of chicken to form a mustard crust. Feel free to substitute breasts. If you do not have Mrs. Dash, then blend together any dried herbs that you have available to make up one Tbsp (thyme, marjoram, oregano, sage, paprika, rosemary, etc.).

Preheat oven to 350°F. Prepare a roasting rack with cooking spray or an oiled paper towel.

1. Remove the skin from the thigh. Rinse and pat dry with a paper towel.

2. Mix together the mustard, Mrs. Dash and the salt in a shallow bowl. There are a couple of approaches to coat the chicken pieces. You can roll them in the mustard mixture, you can spoon it on or you can brush it on. I personally prefer using a spoon.

3. Place the chicken pieces on the oiled rack set inside a pan (I like to line my pan with aluminum foil for an easier clean up). Bake for 35 minutes. Serve at once.

Consider serving with pan fried or steamed cabbage.

Per Serving: 154 Calories; 9g Fat; 18g Protein; 2g Carbs; trace Dietary Fiber

Parmesan Crusted Chicken

This is a simple and crispy oven baked chicken

3	lbs	chicken breasts
1	bottle	Lawry's Herb and Garlic Marinade
1½	cups	Parmesan cheese -- grated
1/2	tsp	garlic powder
1	tsp	paprika
1	tsp	dried oregano

> **Induction**
>
> **4 Servings**
> **2g Net Carbs**

1. Thoroughly rinse chicken and pat dry with a paper towel. You can remove the skin if you like.

2. Deeply pierce each piece of chicken 5 or 6 times with a knife or fork. In a large re-sealable plastic bag, combine chicken parts and the Marinade. Try to eliminate most of the air as you seal the bag. Gently shake to make sure all pieces are coated. Marinate in refrigerator for at least 30 minutes (or overnight).

Preheat oven to 350°F. Prepare a baking rack; oil or use a vegetable spray.

3. Pour the Parmesan cheese onto a plate. Mix in the garlic powder, paprika and oregano.

4. Remove chicken from marinade, discarding used marinade. Shake off excess liquid. Roll chicken onto the cheese to coat. Arrange the chicken on rack in a roasting pan. Bake in preheated 350°F oven until meat is no longer pink and juices run clear. This will be about 40 to 45 minutes (approx. 180°F).

Per Serving: 435 Calories; 21g Fat; 57g Protein; 2g Carbs; trace Dietary Fiber

Madeira Chicken

Chicken poached in Madeira wine and topped with a delicious mixture of olives, capers and shallots.

4 lbs   chicken breasts -- no skin

Marinade

1	cup	Madeira
1	Tbsp	shallots -- minced
1	clove	garlic -- minced
2	Tbsps	fresh rosemary leaves -- 1 Tbsp if dried
2	Tbsps	fresh oregano – 2 tsp if dried
	dash	salt and pepper -- each

Topping

1/3	cup	black olives -- pitted
1/3	cup	green olives -- pitted
2	Tbsps	capers -- rinsed and drained
2	Tbsps	shallots -- minced
2	Tbsps	bell pepper -- minced
2	Tbsps	fresh Italian parsley -- chopped
1	Tbsp	extra virgin olive oil
		fresh ground pepper -- to taste

The chicken parts can have the bones, or not; but the skin should be removed. (If using boneless chicken reduce amount to 3 lbs).

1. Rinse the chicken and pierce deeply with a fork or knife. Place chicken in a large plastic baggie with the marinade ingredients. Marinade for at least 1 hour or overnight. Turn the bag occasionally to be sure that the chicken gets well coated.

2. The topping can be made while the chicken is cooking or at the same time as the marinade and then refrigerated until ready to use. However, the topping is best at room temperature when served. Chop the olives, capers and parsley. Mince the shallots and bell peppers and toss with the olives. Add fresh cracked black pepper and olive oil, toss well.

Preheat oven to 375°F

3. Put the chicken and marinade in a deep casserole dish (you want a snug fit). Add water (or chicken stock) to almost cover the chicken, if needed. Bake at 375°F for 10 minutes then reduce heat to 300°F and poach for 50 minutes.

4. To serve, transfer the chicken to a serving platter discarding most of the cooking liquids. Top with the olive mixture. Cover with aluminum foil and let rest for 5-7 minutes before serving. It can be kept in a warm oven (180°F or less) for up to 15 minutes, if desired.

Per Serving: 346 Calories; 12g Fat; 54g Protein; 3g Carbohydrate; 1g Dietary Fiber

Rosemary & Garlic Chicken

Chicken braised in a robust rosemary and garlic sauce.

1		cut-up chicken -- no skin
2	tsps	fresh rosemary leaves
4	cloves	garlic -- minced
1	tsp	olive oil
1/2	Tbsp	butter
1/2	cup	white wine
1/2	cup	chicken stock
	dash	salt and pepper
1/4	tsp	guar gum
1/2	tsp	Kitchen Bouquet

Induction

4 Servings
2g Net Carbs

This recipe calls for 1 cut up chicken fryer with the skin removed. However feel free to substitutes just breast meat or just thighs, if preferred. I personally prefer the thighs in this recipe. Just be sure to remove the skin or it will have too much fat. The bones add flavor but boneless cuts will work equally as well.

1. In a large nonstick skillet over medium-heat, add the butter and olive oil. When the butter melts add the rosemary and garlic. Stir constantly for about 30 seconds. Do not let the garlic burn. Add the chicken pieces and cook for 1 full minute per side.

2. Carefully add the wine; let it boil for about 1 minute. Then add the chicken stock. Reduce the heat to low, cover and simmer for 30 minutes. (If your skillet does not have a cover, then make one out of aluminum foil). Transfer chicken to a plate and cover.

3. Add the kitchen bouquet and the guar gum to the juices. Mix well. Increase the heat to medium-high and let boil until the sauce thickens and reduces to about 1 cup.

4. Add the chicken back into the skillet (along with any juices). Coat each piece with the sauce. Serve immediately.

Per Serving: 257 Calories; 10g Fat; 32g Protein; 2g Carbs; trace Dietary Fiber

Spinach & Feta Stuffed Chicken Breasts

Crispy chicken skin adds incredible flavor to this dish. If you are trying to minimize saturated fats then skip this recipe and try something else.

4		**chicken breast halves**
1/2	cup	**frozen spinach -- thawed and drained**
1		**egg**
3	Tbsps	**feta cheese**
2	Tbsps	**flax seed meal -- optional**
1/2	tsp	**oregano -- 1 tsp if fresh**
1/4	tsp	**garlic powder**
	pinch	**nutmeg**
2	Tbsps	**butter -- melted**
1	tsp	**oregano -- 2 tsp if fresh**
1/2	tsp	**paprika**

Induction

4 Servings
2g Net Carbs

The flax seed meal adds omega 3 oil which helps counteract some of the ill effects of the saturated fat.

Preheat oven to 350°F. Lightly grease a baking pan.

1. In a small bowl, mix together the butter, 1 tsp oregano and the paprika. Set aside.

2. Thaw the spinach in the microwave and squeeze off the excess liquids. (*See note). Alternatively you can steam fresh spinach

3. In a mixing bowl, beat the egg. Add the spinach, feta cheese, flax seed, 1/2 tsp oregano, garlic powder and a pinch of nutmeg. Blend well.

4. Rinse and pat dry the chicken breasts. Slide your finger under the skin creating a pocket but be carefully not to tear any holes in the skin. Stuff the spinach mixture under the skin of each breast. Place in the greased baking pan. Using a basting brush, coat the skin with the butter paprika mixture.

5. Bake at 350°F, uncovered for 40 minutes or until juices run clear or internal temperature of 180°F. If the skin is not crispy then put the pan under the broiler for the last 3 to 5 minutes.

Per Serving: 371 Calories; 23g Fat; 36g Protein; 5g Carbohydrate; 3g Dietary Fiber

*Note: This liquid has significant nutrients, as well as flavor. So consider drinking it (the chef's bonus), reserve it for stock or offer it to your pets. My dogs love extra cooking liquids; but the cat, not so much.

Tarragon Chicken

Chicken breasts baked in a creamy tarragon sauce makes for an elegant main dish that is quick & easy to prepare.

3	lb	**chicken breasts -- no skin, no bone**
1/2	cup	**sour cream**
2	Tbsps	**dry sherry**
2	Tbsps	**Dijon mustard**
2	tsps	**dried tarragon**
1	pinch	**ground pepper**
1	pinch	**salt**

Induction

4 Servings
2g Net Carbs

Preheat oven to 350°F.

1. Rinse and pat dry the chicken.

2. If you prefer to use fresh tarragon, the leaves can be simply stripped off the stems and left whole, but bruise them slightly to encourage their flavor. Cutting fresh tarragon makes them turn black and can give an off color to the dish. Use about 1 Tbsp worth.

3. In a 9x9 backing dish, mix together the sour cream, sherry, mustard tarragon, salt and pepper.

4. Add the chicken and turn them to coat well. Adjust the chicken so it forms just 1 layer. Cover and bake for 35 minutes.

Serve immediately.

Per Serving: 480 Calories; 15g Fat; 77g Protein; 2g Carbs; trace Dietary Fiber

Baja Chicken

The spices in this recipe give the sauce a nice kick
which is tempered by the sour cream.

1		**cut-up chicken**
1	Tbsp	**canola oil**
2	tsps	**chili powder**
2	tsps	**cumin**
1/2	tsp	**garlic powder**
1/2	tsp	**salt**
4	oz	**green chilies -- canned, diced**
1/4	cup	**onion -- finely diced**
3/4	cup	**chicken broth**
1/4	cup	**cilantro leaves**
2/3	cup	**sour cream**

Weight Loss
4 Servings
5g Net Carbs

Use a whole cut-up chicken or your preferred cuts. This is best when the chicken is still on the bone. I prefer to remove the skin, but you choose.

1. Rinse and pat dry the chicken pieces.

2. Mix together on a plate, the chili powder, cumin, garlic powder and salt.

3. Roll the chicken into the spices.

4. In a deep skillet, heat the oil on medium-high heat. Add the chicken and brown on each side. About two minutes per side.

5. Add to the skillet the chilies, onion, garlic and chicken broth. Stir. Once the broth comes to a boil, reduce the heat to a simmer and cover. If the skillet doesn't have its own cover then use aluminum foil. Simmer for 40 minutes (25 minutes for boneless).

6. Remove the chicken to a deep serving dish (a casserole dish works nicely). Cover.

7. Skim off any excess fat from the sauce. This step is not necessary if you used skinless chicken.

8. Turn up heat and reduce the liquids to about 1/2 cup, scraping up any yummy browned bits and scraping down the sides.

9. Turn off the heat and add the cilantro. Stir. Then add the sour cream. Mix well.

10. Pour the sauce over the chicken. Serve immediately.

Consider serving this with the Jicama Papaya Salsa (page 363) or the Avocado Tomato Salad (page 158) or perhaps a variation of the Southwestern Salad (page 144).

Per Serving: 346 Calories; 20g Fat; 35g Protein; 6g Carbohydrate; 1g Dietary Fiber

Chicken in Coconut Sauce

This mild coconut sauce is awesome and gives chicken a Hawaiian flare.
You can find unsweetened shredded coconut in most health food stores.

3	lb	chicken breasts - no skin
1/4	cup	unsweetened coconut meat -- shredded
1/2	tsp	Splenda® -- optional
3		scallions
2	tsps	unrefined coconut oil -- (or canola oil)
1	Tbsp	ground coriander
1	tsp	ground cumin
14	oz	canned coconut milk -- unsweetened
1	tsp	lemon pepper
1/4	tsp	salt

Weight Loss

4 Servings
5g Net Carbs

You can use a whole cut-up chicken or just the cuts that your prefer, with or without the bones. But be sure to remove the skin and cut off as much fat as possible. Wash hands thoroughly.

1. Chop the scallions and keep the white and green parts separate. Set aside the green portion for the garnish.

2. Heat a large non-stick skillet over medium heat. Add the shredded coconut and toast until a light golden brown. Stir frequently and don't get too far from it because once it starts to brown it can burn quickly. Remove to a saucer, bowl or paper towel. Toss with the Splenda (optional).

3. In the same skillet over medium heat, add the coconut oil, coriander and cumin. Blend. Add the chicken pieces and increase the heat one notch to medium-high. Cook on each side about 2 or 3 minutes.

4. Add the coconut milk, lemon pepper, salt and the white parts of the scallions. Stir and spoon the sauce over the chicken pieces until it comes to a boil. Then reduce heat to a simmer, lightly cover with a piece of foil and cook for 40 minutes, turning over the chicken after 20 minutes. (Reduce the time in half if you are using boneless chicken).

5. Remove chicken to a platter and cover with the aluminum foil. Increase heat to medium-high and boil to reduce the sauce by about one half, stirring occasionally (10 to 20 minutes depending how humid the day is and how hot your stove is). Taste test and add more salt if needed.

6. Place the chicken back into the skillet just to warm it up again. Garnish with the green portion of the scallions and the toasted coconut.

Consider serving with the Hawaiian Salsa (page363) and a simple arugula salad (page 135) for an elegant dinner.

Per Serving: 443 Calories; 31g Fat; 38g Protein; 6g Carbohydrate; 1g Dietary Fiber

Chicken & Veggies in Pesto Cream Sauce

This one pot meal is perfect for your busy schedule.

2	cups	cooked chicken -- diced
1	cup	broccoli -- chopped
1	cup	zucchini -- chopped
1/4	tsp	garlic powder
1/2	cup	water
2	ozs	canned mushroom slices
3/4	cup	heavy cream
3	Tbsps	pesto sauce
2	Tbsps	Parmesan cheese -- grated

Weight Loss

2 Servings
7g Net Carbs

You can use left-over chicken or pre-packaged cooked chicken (such as Tyson's). Your broccoli can be fresh or frozen. Zucchini is best fresh. Substitute fresh or frozen cauliflower for the zucchini if you prefer.

1. Cut up the chicken and veggies into bite sized pieces.

2. In a large skillet over medium-high heat, add the water and garlic powder and bring to a boil. Add the broccoli, zucchini and mushrooms. Cover and cook for 3 minutes. Add the chicken and the cream. Cook uncovered about 5 minutes, stir occasionally. The cream will reduce (boil down) and become a thick sauce. Remove from heat.

3. Stir in the pesto sauce. Serve garnished with the Parmesan cheese.

Per Serving: 713 Calories; 52g Fat; 53g Protein; 10g Carbs; 3g Dietary Fiber

Chicken Quesadilla

La Tortilla Factory's Low-Carb Whole Wheat Tortillas is what makes this a hit. This is a quick and easy lunch.

1		Low-carb whole wheat tortillas
1/2	cup	chicken pieces -- cooked and diced
1/4	cup	cheese -- shredded
1	Tbsp	salsa

Weight Loss

1 Servings
6g Net Carbs

Use any type of cheese that you like. Try a blend. I generally use cheddar with Monterey Jack. If you use a pepper Jack cheese then you can skip the salsa which makes this recipe even easier. It's great with left-over turkey too.

1. You need to have a large non-stick skillet that can hold a tortilla easily. Heat the skillet to medium (or half way to medium high). Add the tortilla and let it get warm (about 1 minute) then flip it over.

2. Place the chicken over 1/2 of the tortilla up to about 1/2 inch from the edge. Sprinkle the cheese over the chicken and then the salsa over the cheese. I

like to press out a bit of the liquid from the salsa, especially if the quesadillas might sit for a little bit or might get reheated.

3. Fold over the tortilla and flatten with a spatula. Once it starts to brown it is time to flip it. Slip a spatula under the curved, open edge and turn over the quesadilla. Let brown on that side too. Then slide it onto a plate.

4. Using a sharp knife or pizza cutter, cut into 3 or 4 wedges.

It is best to serve them right away. But if you are going to make extra batches, they can sit in a warm oven for a few minutes. If you plan to do this, consider using pepper jack cheese and eliminate the salsa or serve it on the side.

Extra salsa, guacamole and sour cream are nice on the side (be sure to add the extra carbs!).

Per Serving: 258 Calories; 15g Fat; 23g Protein; 20g Carbs; 14g Dietary Fiber

Chicken Verde

This simple recipe is something that even your teenagers will enjoy.
It uses that wonderful 505 Green Chile Sauce as the base.

3	lbs	**chicken breast -- no skin, no bone**
8	ozs	**505 Green Chile Sauce**
12	ozs	**frozen broccoli -- chopped**
1	cup	**cheddar cheese -- shredded**

Weight Loss

4 Servings
6g Net Carbs

Preheat oven to 350°F

1. Cut the boneless, skinless chicken parts into bite sized pieces. In a non-stick frying pan, brown the chicken in batches and transfer to a lightly greased casserole dish (you don't need to cook the chicken completely through at this step). Arrange the chicken and frozen chopped broccoli into an even layer. (You can minimize this step by using pre-cooked or left-over chicken but then remember to reduce the cooking time to 20 minutes).

2. Spread the green chile sauce evenly over the chicken. Top with shredded cheddar cheese and bake for 35 minutes uncovered.

Per Serving: 563 Calories; 18g Fat; 86g Protein; 9g Carbohydrate; 3g Dietary Fiber

Chicken Jambalaya

This low carb adaptation uses cauliflower instead of rice.
It is close enough to the real thing to serve to non low carb guests.

2	lbs	chicken breast -- no skin, no bone
1	lb	chorizo sausage
4		scallions -- minced
2	stalks	celery -- minced
2	cloves	garlic -- minced
1/2		green bell pepper -- seeded and diced
1/2		red bell pepper -- seeded and diced
1	head	cauliflower -- grated
1/4	cup	chicken broth
1	Tbsp	Cajun seasoning
1/4	cup	Carb Options™ Ketchup

> **Weight Loss**
>
> 4 Servings
> 8g Net Carbs

1. Grate the cauliflower. This is accomplished best by using your grating wheel on your food processor. But you can also do it by hand with a cheese grater. Set aside.

2. Cut off the top 1/3 of the green part, mince and set aside for a garnish. Mince the rest of the scallions and the garlic. Dice the celery and the bell peppers.

3. Remove casing from chorizo and cut into bite-sized pieces. Cut chicken into bite sized pieces.

4. In a large heavy pot over medium heat, cook the chorizo until it renders it's fat and starts to turn brown (about 5 minutes) transfer to a bowl. Add the chicken to the pot and stir fry until cooked through (about 5 minutes depending on size of pieces), transfer to the bowl.

5. Pour off the fat, except for about 1 Tbsp worth. Add the celery, the white part of the scallions, the garlic and the bell peppers. Sauté for about 2 minutes. Add the cauliflower and cook another 2 minutes stirring frequently. Add the chicken stock and Cajun seasoning and cook for about 1 minute letting the stock boil. Add the ketchup, stir to incorporate. Add the chorizo and chicken and heat through.

Garnish with the reserve scallion tops and serve. This is a one pot meal for 4 or a side dish for 8.

Per Serving: 731 Calories; 17g Fat; 80g Protein; 10g Carbs; 2g Dietary Fiber

Chicken Paprika

This classic chicken dish is perfect for the carb conscious life style.
This is one of my favorite ways to cook cut-up chicken.

3	lb	**cut-up chicken -- no skin**
1/2	cup	**onion -- diced**
1	Tbsp	**paprika**
1/2	Tbsp	**butter**
3/4	cup	**chicken broth**
1	cup	**sour cream**
	dash	**salt and pepper**
1	Tbsp	**fresh parsley -- minced**

Weight Loss
4 Servings
4g Net Carbs

Be sure that your paprika is fresh (not older than about 6 months) because it is such a predominate flavor. I prefer the sweet Hungarian variety. Use any cut of chicken that you prefer, but be sure to remove the skin. This recipe is best with meat still on the bone. If using boneless chicken reduce cooking time by 10 minutes.

1. Remove the skin from the chicken. Rinse well and set aside. Wash hands thoroughly.

2. In a large skillet over medium-heat, melt the butter and add the onion. Sauté until almost translucent (about 1 or 2 minutes) stirring frequently. Add the chicken and cook for about 2 minutes on each side.

3. Turn the pieces so that the bone side is down and the fleshy side is up (so that the meat does not over-cook and the bones can add some extra flavor). Then carefully add the chicken stock and then the paprika. Add a tiny pinch of salt and pepper (however, if you are using canned chicken stock, DO NOT add salt at this time - wait until after the sour cream and see if it is needed then). Stir lightly between chicken pieces to blend, until the liquids come to a boil. Reduce heat to medium-low, cover and simmer for 40 minutes. Use aluminum foil if you do not have a cover. Turn the chicken over during the last 10 minutes of cooking.

4. Remove chicken to serving platter, cover to keep warm (placing in a 180°F oven is even better). Increase heat to boil and reduce the liquids to about 1/2 of a cup (~5-8 minutes). Stir frequently and be sure to scrape up any brown bits stuck to the bottom of the skillet. When liquids are reduced, turn down the heat to low, add the sour cream and stir or whisk until it is well incorporated. Taste test to see if more salt is needed.

5. Pour sauce over the chicken and garnish with the parsley. Chopped cilantro or chives are nice alternative garnishes. (If you do not have a fresh herb for a garnish then you can add a dried green herb before the reduction of the liquids.)

Per Serving: 368 Calories; 19g Fat; 43g Protein; 5g Carbohydrate; 1g Dietary Fiber

Chicken with Apricot Mustard Sauce

The mustard in this sauce is a nice compliment to the sweetness of the apricots. Although this recipe requires a little extra work, its flavor is worth it!

1		cut-up chicken -- no skin
		salt and pepper
8		dried apricot halves -- diced
1½	cups	water
3	Tbsps	Splenda®
2	cloves	garlic -- minced
	drop	canola oil
2	Tbsps	brown mustard
2	Tbsps	water
3/4	cup	water
1/4	tsp	guar gum
1/4	tsp	salt
	dash	pepper

Weight Loss

4 Servings
6g Net Carbs

You can use a whole chicken, a cut-up chicken, or just the cuts that you prefer. The skin can be left on if you chose, but I make the exception for this roasted chicken. This sauce is also good on turkey breast or pork chops.

Be sure that your dried apricots are unsweetened. You can also use 4 fresh apricots if they happen to be in season.

Preheat oven to 350ºF

1. Rinse well the chicken and arrange in a baking dish or roasting pan, generously season with salt and pepper.

2. In a sauce pan, add the diced apricots, the 1½ cups water and the 3 Tbsp of Splenda. Bring to a boil, and then reduce heat to a simmer. Stir frequently until reduced to about 1/2 to 2/3 cup. Pour into a blender or food processor and process until fairly smooth. (Leave in the bowl for now).

3. In the same sauce pan (don't wash it out yet), add a drop of oil and sauté the garlic just until the point you start to see some color. Immediately add 2 Tbsp of mustard and 2 Tbsp of water and turn off the heat. Stir well. Add this mixture to the apricots and pulse several times.

4. Remove about 6 Tbsps of the apricot mixture to a small bowl to use for basting the chicken. Start off by drizzling about 1/2 of this (~3 Tbsp) over the chicken and coat evenly using a basting brush. Place chicken in 350ºF oven and roast for 20 minutes. Then baste with the remaining 3 Tbsp and continue cooking until an internal temperature of 180ºF (about 40 minutes longer for a whole chicken and only 15 minutes for skinless breast meat).

5. Meanwhile, pour the remaining contents of the food processor bowl back into the sauce pan. Use 3/4 cup of water to rinse out the processor bowl and

add this to the sauce pan. Also add the guar gum, 1/4 tsp salt and a dash of pepper. Stir well while bringing to the boil. Set aside until the chicken is ready. Reheat once ready to serve with the chicken. I generally serve the sauce on the side, but you could also drizzle it over the chicken just before serving.

Per Serving: 231 Calories; 8g Fat; 33g Protein; 7g Carbohydrate; 1g Dietary Fiber

Curry Chicken in Spinach

I could live off of this stuff. I love making this when I have a super busy schedule and need left-overs that can merely be heated and eaten.

2	lbs	chicken thighs -- no skin, no bone
10	ozs	frozen spinach -- thawed
1	Tbsp	butter
2	Tbsps	curry powder
2		scallion -- minced
14	ozs	coconut milk
1/2	tsp	guar gum
		salt -- to taste

Weight Loss

4 Servings
5g Net Carbs

I typically use chicken thighs but you can use breast meat or a combination.

I prefer to use frozen spinach just because it is easier, but if you want to use fresh (just steam it in a covered skillet with a tiny bit of water). In either case; save the liquids that are formed to add to the recipe.

1. Cut the chicken into bite sized pieces and place in a bowl; set aside. (Wash up well before preceding).

2. In a large skillet or a soup pot, melt the butter over medium-high heat. I suggest searing the chicken in two batches. Add just 1/2 Tbsp of the curry powder and 1/2 of the chicken. Stir-fry until all sides of the chicken pieces have been seared. Transfer to a bowl and then add another 1/2 Tbsp of the curry powder and the remaining chicken. Sear and then transfer to the bowl.

3. If there is no fat remaining in the skillet add a bit more butter (or oil). Add the remaining curry powder and the scallions. Sauté for about 1 minute.

4. Add the coconut milk and the guar gum and stir well as it comes to a boil. Reduce heat; add the chicken and spinach (with it's liquids). Simmer for 30 minutes, with cover slightly ajar. Stir occasionally. Add the salt at the end to taste.

I usually just eat this by itself. But if I have guests, then I usually broil an assortment of veggies that I tossed with canola oil and some coriander, garlic powder and lemon pepper (see page 198).

Per Serving: 551 Calories; 33g Fat; 55g Protein; 11g Carbs; 6g Dietary Fiber

Coq Au Vin

This interpretation of the classic French dish is incredibly tasty
and reasonably low in carbs.

4	lbs	cut-up chicken
4	slices	bacon
1/2	cup	onion -- finely chopped
2	Tbsps	shallot -- finely chopped
2	cloves	garlic -- finely chopped
1/2	lb	fresh button mushroom -- quartered
1	cup	dry red wine
1	cup	chicken stock
4	sprigs	fresh thyme -- 1 tsp dried
1		bay leaf
1	Tbsp	tomato paste
		salt and pepper -- to taste
2	Tbsps	fresh parsley -- chopped

Weight Loss

4 Servings
8g Net Carbs

Preheat oven to 350°F

1. In a large skillet over high heat fry the bacon until crispy. Transfer to bacon to paper towel. Crumble bacon when it cools.

2. Cook the chicken parts in the bacon fat until brown all over. Work in batches. Transfer chicken to a deep casserole dish that has a lid (aluminum foil can be used as a lid).

3. Pour off most of the bacon fat, leaving about 1 Tbsp. Over medium-high heat, sauté the onions, shallots and garlic for about 2 minutes. Add the mushrooms and cook for another 2 minutes; stirring frequently. Add the red wine and the chicken stock and bring to a boil.

4. Remove from heat and pour the wine & mushrooms over the chicken. Add the thyme, bay leaf and half the bacon. Cover and cook in a 350°F oven for about 1 hour.

5. Carefully pour or ladle out the majority of the liquids into a sauce pan. Remove and discard the bay leaf. Return the chicken to the oven, covered. Reduce heat to 200°F.

6. Add the tomato paste to the liquids and bring to a boil. Cook sauce, stirring frequently until the sauce thickens enough to coat the back of a spoon (approx 15 minutes). Taste test and add salt and pepper as desired.

7. Place the chicken on to a serving platter (add any liquids to the sauce). Pour the sauce over the chicken and garnish with the remaining bacon and the parsley.

Per Serving: 730 Calories; 44g Fat; 61g Protein; 9g Carbohydrate; 1g Dietary Fiber

Teriyaki Chicken

This low carb version is made quick and easy by using *Carb Options™ Asian Teriyaki Marinade*. This marinade is quite salty so don't add more salt.

1	lb	chicken breast -- no skin, no bone
1	cup	Carb Options™ Asian Teriyaki Marinade
2	tsps	canola oil
2		scallions -- julienne
1/4		red bell pepper -- julienne
1	stalk	celery -- julienne
1	Tbsp	Carb Options™ Asian Teriyaki Marinade

Weight Loss

2 Servings
4g Net Carbs

1. Cut chicken into strips or bite-sized cubes. Put in a large re-sealable plastic bag with 1 cup of the marinade. Squish it around to be sure that all pieces are coated well. Refrigerate for at least 30 minutes but 2 hours is better.

2. Julienne the vegetables.

3. In a wok or a large skillet, heat the oil over medium-high heat. To protect yourself from splatter, use a kitchen mitt or cover your hand loosely with a kitchen towel or dampened paper towel. Using tongs, remove the chicken pieces from the bag and carefully place in the wok. Discard the marinade. Stir fry for about 2-3 minutes.

4. Add the vegetables and stir fry for another 2-3 minutes. Add a Tbsp of fresh marinade sauce. Stir and serve immediately.

Per Serving: 332 Calories; 12g Fat; 51g Protein; 5g Carbohydrate; 1g Dietary Fiber

Moroccan Chicken

This adaptation of a traditional Moroccan dish is rich with flavor.

2		chicken breasts -- no skin
1/8	cup	fresh cilantro -- minced
1/8	cup	fresh flat leaf parsley -- minced
1	clove	garlic -- minced
1/2		lemon – zested and juiced
2	tsps	ground cumin
1	tsp	turmeric
1/2	tsp	cinnamon
1/2	tsp	salt
1/2	cup	water
1	Tbsp	olive oil
1/4	tsp	guar gum

Weight Loss

2 Servings
4g Net Carbs

Use chicken that is still on the bone for this recipe. This adds a lot more flavor to the dish. Fresh cilantro and parsley are key for this recipe. If you only have dried herbs right now, then I advise that you choose a different recipe until fresh cilantro and parsley are available.

1. Remove the skin and rinse off the chicken. Set aside.

2. Mince the garlic, parsley and cilantro very finely. Add to a large zip lock baggie (or a bowl). Setting the baggie in a large bowl helps keep it upright and makes filling it easier.

3. Wash the lemon with soap and warm water to remove any wax. Zest 1/2 of a lemon with a zester or a grater. Be sure not to get any of the bitter white part. Squeeze the lemon, strain out the seeds. This should yield 3 to 4 Tbsps. Add only half of the juice to the marinade (save the rest for another recipe). Add the cumin, turmeric, cinnamon, salt, water and oil to the marinade.

4. Add the chicken and squeeze out most of the air and seal the baggie.

5. Marinate for at least 30 minutes at room temperature, or up to several hours in the refrigerator.

6. Place the chicken and the marinade into a large deep skillet over medium-high heat. (If desired, use another 1/3 cup of water to rinse out the marinade baggie and add to the skillet). Arrange the chicken so that the boney side is down and the fleshy side is up.

7. Cover (if your skillet doesn't have a cover then use aluminum foil). As soon as it comes to a boil, reduce the heat to low and simmer. Simmer for 30 minutes, turn the chicken over and simmer another 20 minutes.

8. Remove chicken from the skillet to rest (covered).

9. Stir in the guar gum. Turn up the heat and bring the liquids to a boil for a couple of minutes and reduce it to about 1/2 cups of liquid.

10. Drizzle the sauce over the chicken just before serving.

Per Serving: 214 Calories; 9g Fat; 28g Protein; 5g Carbohydrate; 1g Dietary Fiber

Roman Chicken

Chicken braised in a robust tomato sauce.

1		cut-up chicken – no skin
2	cloves	garlic -- finely chopped
1/4	cup	olive oil
1/4	cup	dry white wine
12	ozs	canned, diced tomatoes
1/2		green bell pepper
1/2		red bell pepper
1	Tbsp	fresh oregano
2	tsps	fresh rosemary
1	tsp	fresh thyme
		salt and pepper -- to taste

Weight Loss

4 Servings
4g Net Carbs

As usual, I recommend chicken cuts which are still on the bone, but it is best to remove the skin. If you are using boneless chicken, reduce cooking time in step 4 to 20 minutes.

1. Seed the bell peppers and cut into strips.

2. In a large fry pan, heat the oil over medium heat. Add the chicken; cook for about 3-4 minutes per side.

3. Add the wine and garlic and cook for 5 minutes.

4. Add the canned tomatoes with the juices. Stir to distribute. Reduce the heat to a simmer and cook for 30 minutes, loosely covered.

5. Add the peppers, oregano, rosemary, thyme, salt and pepper. Turn over the chicken and cook for another 10 minutes or until the chicken is thoroughly cooked.

Per Serving: 362 Calories; 21g Fat; 33g Protein; 6g Carbohydrate; 2g Dietary Fiber

Roasted Balsamic Game Hens

Balsamic vinegar, garlic and rosemary add incredible flavor to
Cornish games hens. Roasting the head of garlic transforms
it from pungent to sweetness.

2		**Cornish game hens**
2/3	**cup**	**balsamic vinegar**
1/3	**cup**	**water**
1	**Tbsp**	**olive oil**
1	**head**	**garlic**
1	**Tbsp**	**dehydrated onion flakes**
2	**sprigs**	**rosemary**
	pinch	**salt and pepper**

This is great with any type of poultry; chicken, duck, squab or quail, etc.

1. Thoroughly rinse the game hens. They can be left whole or you can remove the back bone and lay them out flat. Place them is a large re-sealable plastic bag. Add the vinegar, water, oil, onion flakes, rosemary sprigs and the salt and pepper.

2. Remove the outer loose skin off the garlic head. With a sharp knife cut off the top 1/4 of the head, exposing just the tips of the raw garlic. The head can be left whole or broken in halves. Don't worry if a clove or two breaks off; just toss them into the bag too. Add the garlic to the plastic bag and seal, removing as much air as possible. Refrigerate for at least 2 hours or over night.

Preheat oven to 400°F

3. Place the hens, garlic and rosemary into a roasting pan breast side up. Add 1/2 cup of water and roast tightly covered for 15 minutes. Uncover, reduce heat to 350°F and continue roasting another 20 minutes or until juices run clear (or internal temp of 180°F).

4. Remove hens to a platter and let rest 5-10 minutes before serving. Serve as is with the roasted garlic on the side, or use the garlic to flavor Creamed Cauliflower or Mashed Turnips (page177), as a side dish.

Smashing each garlic clove with the back of a spoon renders its soft, sweet flesh.

Per Serving: 746 Calories; 54g Fat; 58g Protein; 6g Carbs; trace Dietary Fiber

Roasted Cornish Hens with Vegetables

Low Carb Italian dressing adds flavor to these Cornish game hens
roasted with zucchini and bell peppers.

2		**Cornish game hen**
1	cup	**Carb Well Italian Dressing**
1	tsp	**oregano**
1	tsp	**rosemary**
2	large	**zucchini**
1		**green bell pepper**
1		**red bell pepper**
1/2		**yellow onion**

> **Weight Loss**
>
> **3 Servings**
> **7g Net Carbs**

You can substitute chicken breasts or pork chops for this recipe too. This is a great meal for 2 to 4 people depending on appetite.

Preheat oven to 400°F

1. In a bowl, add the Italian dressing and the oregano and rosemary. Stir with a fork or whisk.

2. Remove the stem from the bell peppers. Wash out the seeds. Cut into 1 inch square pieces. Cut away the white membranes if you like. Slice the zucchini into 1/2 inch thick rounds. Cut the onion into 1 inch square pieces. Put the vegetables into a roasting pan or large casserole dish. Pour about 1/3 of the dressing over the veggies and toss to coat.

3. Rinse the hens well. With kitchen shears, cut out the back bone by cutting along each side. Open up the hens so that they lay flat, breaking the wishbone helps. Dredge the hens in the dressing mixture then place on top of the vegetables. Pour the excess dressing over the hens and vegetables.

4. Place roasting pan in the oven and reduce heat to 350°F. Roast for 35-45 minutes or until you can easily twist a drumstick bone out of the socket.

5. Let rest for 5-10 minutes. Cut each hen in half. Serve ½ hen per person with the vegetables evenly divided. The extra portion of hen is for those with a further appetite.

Per Serving: 681 Calories; 53g Fat; 41g Protein; 11g Carbs; 4g Dietary Fiber

Roasted Turkey Breast with Cranberry Gravy

Turkey is not just for the holidays, it's great all year. By using just the breast cut, the hassle factor is reduced and it cooks up much more quickly.

3	lbs	turkey breast – no skin
1	Tbsp	butter
1	tsp	paprika
1/2	tsp	thyme
1/4	tsp	black pepper
1	stalk	celery
1		shallot -- minced
1		bay leaf
1	cup	chicken stock
1	cup	cranberries
1	Tbsp	balsamic vinegar
1	tsp	kitchen Bouquet
1	tsp	Splenda®
1/2	tsp	guar gum

Weight Loss
4 Servings
4g Net Carbs

I prefer using the turkey breasts with the bone and skin intact, because it is less expensive and has more flavor. But to reduce fats, use a skinless turkey breast. The cranberries can be fresh, frozen or dried (be sure they are unsweetened).

Preheat oven to 400°F

1. Rinse the turkey and place in roasting pan.

2. In a small bowl, add the butter, paprika, thyme and black pepper. Zap in microwave for a few seconds to melt the butter. Using a basting brush, coat the top of the turkey with the butter and herbs.

3. Cut the stalk of celery in half (just so it fits in the pan better) and place on each side of the turkey. To the pan, add the shallots, bay leaf and chicken stock.

4. Cover the pan with aluminum foil in a tent fashion, not contacting the turkey too much (you can omit this step if cooking a turkey with the skin still on).

5. Place in oven, reduce heat to 350°F, and roast for 30 minutes. Remove foil (save the foil for later), add cranberries and roast another 30 minutes or until turkey has an internal temperature of 175°F.

6. When turkey is done, remove from oven and transfer to a platter and cover with foil to rest for 10 minutes while you make the gravy.

7. Remove and discard the celery and bay leaf. Pour juices into a gravy separator or otherwise skim off the fat. In a blender, add the vinegar, Kitchen Bouquet and Splenda. Pulse to blend. Add the guar gum and pulse again. Add about 1/2 cup of the pan juices and blend. Add the rest of the juices and cranberries and puree. Taste and adjust seasoning as needed. It

will probably need salt if you used home-made stock. Use more Splenda if your cranberries were extra tart.

8.   Slice the turkey and serve with the gravy on the side or drizzled over the turkey slices.

Per Serving: 308 Calories; 5g Fat; 57g Protein; 6g Carbohydrate; 2g Dietary Fiber

Key West Turkey Cutlets

Generous portions of grilled turkey with a tangy, key lime marinade.

3	lbs	turkey breast cutlets
3/4	cup	Nellie & Joe's Key Lime Juice
1/2	cup	water
2	Tbsps	canola oil
1	Tbsp	Splenda®
1	tsp	ground ginger
1	tsp	salt
1	tsp	lemon pepper
1	tsp	thyme

Weight Loss

4 Servings
5g Net Carbs

1.   Place all ingredients in a zip-lock baggie and marinate for at least 1 hour (or over night).

2.   Prepare grill. Remove turkey from marinade.

3.   Boil marinade in a sauce pan for 5 minutes. Place turkey on grill over medium heat for about 5 or 6 minutes per side. Baste with the boiled marinade. Do not over-cook.

I like to serve this with the green bean variation of the Lemon Pepper Asparagus (page 173). Left-overs are great the next day when sliced and tossed with a fresh green salad.

Per Serving: 417 Calories; 11g Fat; 73g Protein; 5g Carbs; trace Dietary Fiber

Sage Turkey with Zucchini

This quick & easy dish is great for using up left-over holiday turkey or turkey cutlets. You can also get turkey breast sliced fresh from the deli.

2	lb	cooked turkey breast meat -- cubed
2		zucchini -- sliced
12	leaves	fresh sage -- chopped
1	clove	garlic -- minced
1	Tbsp	olive oil
2	Tbsps	dry vermouth
1	Tbsp	lemon juice
	dash	salt
	dash	lemon pepper
4	Tbsps	parmesan cheese
4	Tbsps	pine nut -- toasted

Weight Loss

4 Servings
4g Net Carbs

If you are getting your cooked turkey from the deli, have them slice it ~1/2 inch thick so you can cut it into nice sized cubes.

1. Sauté the zucchini, sage and garlic in the olive oil over medium heat. Cook for about 3 minutes. Add the turkey, vermouth, lemon juice, salt and lemon pepper. Stir well. Loosely cover and cook for 2 or 3 minutes, stirring occasionally.

2. Put turkey in a serving dish and garnish with the parmesan cheese and toasted pine nuts.

Per Serving: 357 Calories; 12g Fat; 54g Protein; 6g Carbohydrate; 2g Dietary Fiber

Chicken Enchiladas

This quick & easy low-carb version makes dinner a simple task.

2	cups	chicken pieces -- cooked and shredded
1/2	cup	505 Green Chile Sauce
1/2	cup	cheddar cheese, shredded
4		Low Carb Green Onion Tortillas

Topping

| 1 | cup | 505 Green Chile Sauce |
| 1/2 | cup | cheddar cheese, shredded |

Maintenance

4 Servings
10g Net Carbs

This recipe requires cooked chicken. So you can use left-overs, Tyson chicken strips or canned chicken. This is just as good with left-over turkey or pork. If you do not have 505 Green Chile Sauce, then substitute which ever brand of green chile sauce that you have available (look for a brand with <6g net carbs per 1/4 cup serving). *La Tortilla Factory* makes an awesome green onion low carb tortilla (~6" diameter) which is recommended for this recipe. But use any low carb tortilla that you have available.

Preheat oven to 350°F

1. Shred or dice the chicken. In a sauce pan over medium heat, add the 1/2 cup of the green chile sauce and the chicken. Stir occasionally until it is heated all through. Remove from heat, add 1/2 cup of cheddar cheese, stir.

2. Lay out the 4 tortillas on a flat surface. Divide the chicken mixture evenly amongst them, placing it on the lower 1/3 portion of each tortilla. Roll up each tortilla and place seam side down in an 8x8 casserole dish. Allow a little bit of separation between each enchilada.

3. Cover the enchiladas with the remaining cup of the green chile sauce and sprinkle the top with the remaining cheese. Bake in a 350°F oven (uncovered) for 15 or 20 minute, until the cheese is completely melted and starting to bubble. Do not over-cook; low carb tortillas get soggy quite fast.

Serve with the Avocado & Tomato Salad (page 158) or try the Southwestern Salad (with or without the chicken included).

Per Serving: 375 Calories; 23g Fat; 28g Protein; 19g Carbs; 9g Dietary Fiber

Turkey Wrap

Turkey and bacon are complimented by avocado, pepper jack cheese and radish spouts then wrapped in a low carb tortilla.

1		**Low-carb whole wheat tortillas**
1	Tbsp	**mayonnaise -- or chipotle dressing**
2	slices	**cooked bacon**
4	ozs	**turkey slices, fat free**
1	slice	**jalapeno cheese**
2	slices	**avocado**
1/4	cup	**radish sprouts**

Maintenance
1 Serving
15g Net Carbs

Use any low carb tortilla that you have available. I recommend the ones made by *La Tortilla Factory* (they are the best in my opinion). This is a very satisfy lunch that will hold you through the entire afternoon.

This sandwich wrap is especially good with the Chipotle Dressing (page 354), but using mayonnaise is more convenient, unless you have Chipotle Dressing made up already.

1. On a microwave safe plate, place the turkey with the cooked bacon on top and the cheese on top of that. Zap for about 30 seconds or just until the cheese melts.

2. Slather the mayo onto 1/2 of the tortilla. Place the turkey, bacon and cheese in the middle of the mayo. Add the avocado slices and the sprouts and then wrap-up.

Per Serving: 538 Calories; 37g Fat; 41g Protein; 30g Carbs; 15g Dietary Fiber

Stir Fried Chicken with Mango Sauce

Strips of chicken breasts stir fried with bok choy in an Asian style mango sauce.

2/3	cup	mango -- cubed
1	lb	chicken breast strips
1/4	tsp	garlic powder
1/4	Tbsp	lemon pepper
1/4	tsp	salt
1	Tbsp	butter
4	large	bok choy leaves
2		scallion -- minced
1	cup	water
1	Tbsp	soy sauce
1	Tbsp	balsamic vinegar
1/2	tsp	fresh ginger root -- grated
1/2	tsp	guar gum

> **Maintenance**
>
> 2 Servings
> 13g Net Carbs

One mango will typically yield about 1 1/3 cups when diced, so this recipe needs about 1/2 of a mango. In some locations, you can also buy mango strips in a jar or frozen cubed mangos.

1. Slice mango on either side of its large seed. Cut into strips. Then with a thin knife, slice off the skin by having each strip skin side down on a cutting board and running the knife horizontally as close to the skin as you can. Be sure to cut off the flesh around the edge of the seed too. Dice into cubes about the size of a grape. Set aside 2/3 cups (save the rest for some other recipe).

2. In a bowl, mix together the salt, lemon pepper and garlic power. Toss in the chicken breast strips. Set aside. Wash your hands, knife and work surface.

3. Cut the rib out of the bok choy leaves and dice it. Shred or chop the leaves. Mince the scallions.

4. In a wok or large skillet over medium-high heat, melt the butter and add the chicken and stir fry for about 3 minutes. Add the diced bok choy ribs and cook for 1 minute. Add the scallions and the bok choy leaves, toss, and cook for about 2-3 minutes.

5. Meanwhile, in a small bowl mix together the water, soy sauce, vinegar, and grated ginger. Mix well. Add guar gum, stir enough to dissolve and immediately add to the wok. Stir well.

6. Reduce heat to a simmer, add the mangos. Let simmer for 3 -5 minutes.

Per Serving: 387 Calories; 12g Fat; 54g Protein; 16g Carbs; 3g Dietary Fiber

Weight Loss Variation: Substitute papaya for the mango.
8g net carbs; 370 Calories; 12g Fat; 54g Protein; 11g Carbohydrate; 3g Dietary Fiber;

Peppers Stuffed with Turkey & Wild Rice

This recipe calls for ground turkey but you could just as easily
use ground beef, pork or buffalo (or a mixture of ground meats).

1	cup	water
1/3	cup	wild rice
1/2		bay leaf
1/2	tsp	thyme
1/4	tsp	salt and pepper -- each

Maintenance
3 Servings
15g Net Carbs

1	lb	ground turkey
3	stalks	celery-- finely minced
3		scallions -- finely minced
2/3	cup	Carb Options™ French Dressing
3		red bell peppers

You can use any color bell pepper that you prefer. I like the red or orange best for this dish. Choose bell peppers that are able to stand upright. If you can't find any then you can cut them into halves and serve two halves per person.

1. In a small sauce pan with a well fitting lid, bring the water to a boil and add the rice, bay leaf, thyme and the salt and pepper. Stir, bring back to the boil, cover and reduce heat to a simmer. Cook for 40 minutes. Drain, lightly rinse and remove the bay leaf. (This part can be made a day in advance, if you wish).

2. Meanwhile, mince the celery very finely and mince or chop the scallion.

3. In a skillet over medium-high heat, add the ground turkey and cook until it has lost all of its pinkness. Turn off heat and add the minced celery and scallions. Toss or stir. Pour in the French dressing and add salt and pepper to taste. Stir well. (This part can also be made a day in advanced).

Preheat oven to 350ºF

4. Cut off the tops of the bell peppers, rinse out the seeds and with a knife carefully cut off any white membrane. Toss together the turkey and the wild rice.

5. Place the peppers on a cookie sheet and stuff them (loosely) with the turkey mixture. Be sure the peppers are not touching each other. Loosely place a sheet of aluminum foil on top off them (to help reduce evaporation). Bake for 20 minutes. (Bake for 25 minutes if the turkey and rice were made in advanced and were cold when added to the peppers).

Per Serving: 487 Calories; 32g Fat; 30g Protein; 20g Carbs; 5g Dietary Fiber

FISH & SHELLFISH

FISH & SHELLFISH

~ REGARDING FISH & SHELLFISH ~

When I think of fish, I first think of salmon, mahi-mahi, and tuna because these are my favorites. But there are uncountable varieties of fish and shellfish and there are many ways to prepare them. I can not possibly list all the types and combinations but there are a few things to which I would like to give some special attention.

Nutritional experts recommend that we get 2-4 servings of fish per week. For some people, this is their lifestyle anyway. For others, this may be a challenge. If you do not enjoy eating that much fish then I recommend that you consider taking fish oil supplements in order to assure that you get adequate Omega 3 fatty acids (see pages 37 & 40).

Farmed versus Wild: This is a controversial topic in some circles. For me there is no debate, I think wild is better. I believe that the risks associated with mercury content (zinc and selenium helps block the absorption of mercury) is less than the risks associated with the antibiotics and other drugs given to farm fish. But on the other hand, the availability of wild fish is quite limited in some areas of the country. Living in Colorado, I end up eating a fair amount of farmed fish, particularly salmon. If you are fortunate enough to live near the coast, I suggest that you do a bit of research and find out which kinds of fish in your area typically has the lower mercury levels. We are generally best off using the types of fish that are the most popular in our own area, as this will assure a fast turn-over of inventory which generally means that the fish is reasonable fresh. I generally like to cook fresh fish the same day that I purchased it; otherwise I go for frozen fish.

Wild Salmon is by far my most favorite fish on the planet. I prefer northern Pacific types particularly the Alaskan salmon. However the price tag of wild salmon can scare me away sometimes. Finding fresh wild salmon is a rare occasion in my part of Colorado, except when ordering at the high end restaurants. Fortunately, wild Alaskan salmon can also be found frozen and canned. Nothing can compare to wild salmon when we look at nutrients; it is loaded with omega 3 fatty acids.

Salmon lends itself to a huge range of recipes and preparation methods; grilled, broiled, poached, baked, smoked, etc. I've included several salmon recipes in this cookbook from appetizers, breakfast, salads and entrees. I mostly use salmon fillets because all the bones have already been removed, which makes life easier. But steaks are often a bit cheaper and sometimes I just prefer that shape. In my recipes, you can generally substitute one for the other.

Tuna is one of the most popular fish in America, especially canned tuna, and it is a good source of omega 3 fatty acids. There are many varieties throughout the world, but in the US we mostly see albacore and yellowfin tuna (although bluefin, bonito and skipjack are gaining some popularity). Albacore has firm white meat with a mild flavor and is the most expensive of the canned tunas.

Yellowfin tuna is also known as *ahi* and has pink meat (turning grey when cooked) and a stronger flavor than albacore (but still mild). Yellowfin is typically what is used in canned "light" tuna and is a favorite in restaurants as it is suitable to a variety of cooking techniques as well as raw (sushi).

I have found a lot of contradictory information regarding tuna. Some sources say that canned tuna has more mercury and less omega-3 than fresh tuna; other sources claim exactly the opposite. I've also read that albacore is the safest with respect to mercury content but I have found a few sources which state it is the worst offender. Then there is the whole "dolphin friendly" issue which is being challenged too. It is hard to determine the truth. I personally think that the mercury content has nothing to do with the canning process and is merely a function of the actual fish that is being canned. As for omega-3, it seems logically that fresh fish would have more than processed canned fish. My preference is to use albacore for canned tuna and yellowfin for fresh tuna. But experiment with whatever types are most prevalent in your area.

Mahi-Mahi is also known as *dolphinfish* and *dorado* and is found in warm water all over the planet. I prefer the Hawaiian name mahi-mahi so that it is not confused with its mammal cousin; the dolphin. This fish has firm flesh and a wonderful mild flavor. You can find them in all sorts of sizes ranging from about 5 pounds to as big as 40 pounds. Do not try to get too fancy with this fish; its mild flavor can easily be over powered by marinades and heavy sauces. It is best when grilled or broiled with just a bit of oil/butter and simple seasonings or a light marinade. But it also pairs well with simple sauces and salsas that are added after cooking.

Trout is my favorite fresh water fish. They are basically fresh water salmon and as such they are also very high in omega-3 fatty acids. Most trout that you will find in grocery stores are from farms and generally have a milder flavor than the wild trout which are more difficult to find. But here in Colorado, fresh wild trout is sometimes available, especially if you have a friend or family member who is an avid fisherman. I love it when I get asked for new trout recipes. I generally say, "Well, I'd be happy to show you; perhaps you could bring some over and I'll supply the side dishes!" Oh how yum to have friends that fish! The simplest way to prepare trout is to generously slather Lemon-Sage Butter (page 52) on the inside and grilled them over medium heat for about 10-15 minutes (depending on the size). Or if you don't have a grill, a broiler works just as well. Or you can wrap them in foil and bake at 350°F for about 20 minutes.

SHELLFISH

There are two basic categories of shellfish, crustaceans (e.g., shrimp, lobster and crabs) and mollusks (e.g., scallops, mussels and oysters). For the low carb dieter, we need to be mindful that shellfish are not zero carbs, although many are generally still quite low. The lowest per serving is crab and one of the highest is bay scallops. Shellfish contain no fiber.

GRAMS OF CARBS FOR SHELLFISH

Serving: 6 ounces	CARBS grams	Serving: 6 mollusk	CARBS grams
Bay scallops, uncooked	4.0	Clams	2.3
Crab meat, uncooked	0.1	Mussels	3.4
Lobster meat, uncooked	0.8	Oysters	2.0
Shrimp, raw, shelled	1.5	Sea Scallops	1.5

Shrimp are probably the most popular shellfish in the American diet. Most of the shrimp sold in the US comes from our own coastal waters. There are many species, colors and classifications of shrimp available around the world. In the US, shrimp are generally sold by size rather than type. Markets use to employ vague terms such as Jumbo or Cocktail when describing shrimp. But more and more we are seeing them sold by the weight count; which is the number of shrimp tails per pound. A high number count, say 80-100, are the miniature shrimp where as the jumbo class typically has 12-15 tails per pound.

Unless you live near the coast, it is best to buy shrimp frozen (cooked or raw). The enzymes in shrimp breakdown the proteins quickly as soon as they leave the water which starts turning the meat to mush. For the best flavor and texture of frozen shrimp, buy them raw (also known as green) with their shells still on. Defrost them slowly such as simply moving them to the refrigerator for 24 hours. For the best flavor and texture, cooking shrimp in their shells is generally best no matter what cooking methods that you employ. However, I typically get raw, shelled, deveined, 20 count frozen shrimp. For me, I find these to be the best balance of flavor, convenience and price.

Scallops, mussels, oysters and clams are all part of the mollusk family. Mollusks are best served very, very fresh; consequently I rarely use mollusk at home. However, scallops are okay when frozen and are easily available in most markets. There are two types; the bay scallop and the sea scallop. Bay scallops are the tiny ones (typically 100 per pound) predominately from our Atlantic coast, although not abundantly available. They are very sweet and incredibly succulent as well as being rather expensive. They cook up very fast (generally within 1-2 minutes) so be careful not to over-cook them thereby eliminating their delicate texture. Sea scallops are more plentiful and therefore less expensive. They are much larger (typically 30 per pound) and although they are not as tender as the bay scallop, they still have quite a sweet and delicious flavor.

Salmon Mexicana

This quick and easy recipe is wonderfully delicious. Since the salmon is baked in an aluminum foil tent the clean up is a snap.

2	6-oz	salmon fillets
1/2	cup	Mexican-style stewed tomatoes
1/4	cup	black olives
1	Tbsp	lime juice
2	Tbsps	fresh cilantro -- chopped

> **Induction**
>
> 2 Servings
> 3g Net Carbs

Preheat oven to 375°F

1. In a bowl, toss together the tomatoes, olive slices, lime juice and cilantro.

2. Use heavy duty foil or a double thickness of regular foil. Cut off about 2 feet or more and place on a baking pan. Shape up the edges a bit. Place the salmon fillets in the center of the foil. Pour the tomato mixture over the salmon. Fold up the edges of the foil and crimp to keep all the juices in. Bake at 375°F oven for 20 minutes.

3. Remove from oven and carefully open the top of foil to allow the steam to escape. Place salmon fillets on plate or serving platter and pour the tomatoes on top. Serve right away.

Per Serving: 237 Calories; 8g Fat; 35g Protein; 5g Carbohydrate; 2g Dietary Fiber

Lemon Curry Salmon

Curry adds compelling flavor to the salmon dish.

2	6-oz	salmon steaks -- or fillets
1	tsp	curry powder
1/2	tsp	lemon pepper
1/4	tsp	garlic powder
1	pinch	salt
2	slices	lemon

> **Induction**
>
> 2 Servings
> 1g Net Carbs

Preheat oven to 375°F

1. In a small bowl mix together the curry, lemon pepper, garlic powder and a pinch of salt).

2. Place the salmon in the center of a large sheet of aluminum foil. Cover the steaks with the curry mixture. Place a slice of lemon on top of the steaks.

3. Form a tent with the aluminum foil, firmly crimping the top and ends, leaving a big pocket of air over the steaks. Bake at 375°F for 12 minutes per inch thickness.

Per Serving: 203 Calories; 6g Fat; 34g Protein; 1g Carbs; trace Dietary Fiber

Flounder in a Mushroom Cream Sauce

Delicate flounder poached in a cream sauce with mushrooms.

2	lb	flounder fillets
2	Tbsps	heavy cream
1/2	cup	water
1	Tbsp	lemon juice
1/2	cup	fresh mushrooms -- sliced thin
1/4	tsp	nutmeg
1/4	tsp	paprika
	dash	salt and pepper

Induction

3 Servings
1g Net Carbs

Flounder is also known as Dover Sole. It has a mild flavored that goes well with other delicate flavors such as in this mushroom cream sauce. Fresh mushrooms (try portabella, cremini or shitake) are essential to this recipe. Save your canned mushrooms for something else. Serve with a colorful salad or a medley of summer squashes.

1. Rinse fillets in cold water and pat dry with paper towels.

2. Mix together the cream, water and lemon juice. Pour this into a large skillet and bring to a slow boil over medium-high heat, stirring frequently.

3. Add fillets to skillet. They should be completely covered by the liquid. Poach for 3 minutes then transfer to a platter and cover.

4. Add the mushrooms, nutmeg, paprika and salt to the poaching liquids in the skillet and cook for about 2 minutes, stirring frequently.

5. Reduce heat to low and return the fillets to the skillet. Cook for another 2 minutes, then serve.

Per Serving: 315 Calories; 7g Fat; 58g Protein; 2g Carbohydrate; 1g Dietary Fiber

Mahi Mahi with Cumin, Lime & Cilantro

Simple spices add just enough character to this sautéed mahi mahi.

14	ozs	Mahi Mahi (2 fillets)
1/2	tsp	paprika
1/4	tsp	cumin
1/4	tsp	garlic salt
1	Tbsp	lime juice
2	Tbsps	butter
1/4	cup	cilantro leaves -- chopped

> **Induction**
>
> 2 Servings
> 2g Net Carbs

1. Rinse fish and pat dry.

2. Mix the cumin, garlic salt and paprika. Sprinkle herbs over both sides of fillets. Lightly pat to be sure herbs stick to the fish.

3. In a large nonstick skillet, melt 1/2 of the butter over medium-high heat.

4. Add fillets and sauté for 1-2 minutes, then turn over. Fish should be cook for a total of about 4 minutes per 1/2 inch thickness (at the thickest part).

5. Transfer fish to a platter and cover. Add remaining butter, lime juice and cilantro to the skillet. Heat until butter melts.

6. Pour sauce over fish and serve.

Other mild white fish are also suitable for this recipe; such as sole, sea bass, halibut, monkfish, etc.

Per Serving: 289 Calories; 14g Fat; 38g Protein; 2g Carbs; trace Dietary Fiber

Seabass with Tarragon Cream Sauce

Rich and creamy tarragon sauce provides complexity
and elegance to sautéed seabass.

14	ozs	sea bass fillets
1/2	tsp	paprika
1/4	tsp	pepper -- ground
1/4	tsp	onion salt
2	Tbsps	butter
1	Tbsp	shallot -- minced
1	Tbsp	fresh tarragon -- minced
1	Tbsp	tarragon vinegar
1/4	cup	whipping cream

> **Induction**
>
> 2 Servings
> 3g Net Carbs

1. Rinse fish and pat dry.

2. Mix the pepper, onion salt and paprika. Sprinkle herbs over both sides of fillets. Lightly pat to be sure herbs stick to the fish.

3. In a large nonstick skillet, melt 1/2 of the butter over medium-high heat.

4. Add fillets and sauté for 1-2 minutes then turn over. Fish should be cook for a total of about 4 minutes per 1/2 inch thickness (at the thickest part).

5. Transfer fish to a platter and cover.

6. Pour off any liquids from the skillet. Add remaining butter and shallots. Heat until shallots are starting to soften (about 1 minute). Add vinegar to deglaze pan. Add fresh tarragon, stir. Add cream and heat through.

7. Return fish to skillet for just a minute. Then transfer back to the platter and pour the sauce over the fish.

Other mild white fish works well too, such as sole, halibut, monkfish, etc.

Per Serving: 405 Calories; 27g Fat; 38g Protein; 3g Carbs; trace Dietary Fiber

Caribbean Yellowtail Snapper

Grilled snapper marinated in a spicy citrus sauce.

2	lbs	yellowtail snapper fillets

Induction
4 Servings
3g Net Carbs

Marinade

1	cup	water
2	Tbsp	lime juice
1	Tbsp	lemon juice
2	tsps	lemon zest
1/4	tsp	orange extract
2		jalapeno peppers – finely minced
1		shallot -- minced
1	Tbsp	fresh thyme
2	tsps	ground allspice
1	tsp	cinnamon
1	Tbsp	soy sauce
		salt and pepper -- to taste

1. In a large shallow dish, add all of the marinade ingredients. Mix well.

2. Add the snapper and turn to coat. Cover and refrigerate for 30 minutes to an hour.

3. Grilled or broiled fish over very high heat for about 5 minutes. Carefully turned and cook another 2-3 minutes, until desired doneness.

Per Serving: 346 Calories; 12g Fat; 53g Protein; 4g Carbohydrate; 1g Dietary Fiber

Shrimp Scampi

This traditional shrimp scampi is cooked in white wine and flavored with lemon.
It can be served as main course or an appetizer.
Try it over a bed of fresh baby spinach.

2/3	lb	shrimp -- peeled and deveined
2		scallion -- chopped
2	cloves	garlic -- minced
1/2	Tbsp	butter
1	tsp	olive oil
1/2	cup	dry white wine
1	Tbsp	lemon juice
1	Tbsp	fresh parsley -- chopped
1	tsp	lemon zest

> **Induction**
>
> **2 Servings**
> **3g Net Carbs**

1. In a skillet over medium-high heat, add the oil, butter, scallions and garlic. Sauté for about 1 minute.

2. Add the white wine and shrimp. Sauté until the shrimp turn pick (about 2 or 3 minutes). Remove from heat and add the lemon juice, parsley and toss.

Garnish with lemon zest.

Per Serving: 258 Calories; 8g Fat; 31g Protein; 4g Carbohydrate; 1g Dietary Fiber

Halibut with Creamy Dijon Sauce

Baked halibut smothered in a rich and creamy mustard sauce.

2		halibut steaks (6 oz)
1/2	cup	sour cream
3	Tbsps	mayonnaise
2	Tbsps	Dijon mustard
1/2	tsp	paprika
1/4	tsp	garlic powder
1/4	tsp	lemon extract
	dash	salt
	dash	lemon pepper

> **Induction**
>
> **2 Servings**
> **3g Net Carbs**

Preheat oven to 400°F

1. In a small mixing bowl, mix together the sour cream, mayo, mustard, paprika, garlic, lemon extract, lemon pepper and salt. Blending well.

2. Place halibut in lightly greased baking dish. Pour sauce on top of the halibut. Cover and bake for 20 minutes (or a bit longer if steaks are thicker than 1 inch).

Per Serving: 473 Calories; 34g Fat; 38g Protein; 4g Carbohydrate; 1g Dietary Fiber

Halibut in Chardonnay Cream Sauce

Poached halibut with a simple white wine cream sauce.

4		halibut fillets (8 oz each)
1/3	cup	onion -- chopped
1	cup	Chardonnay
1/4	tsp	salt
1/2	tsp	pepper
1/4	cup	sour cream
2	Tbsps	chives -- snipped

Induction
4 Servings
3g Net Carbs

1. In a large sauce pan, add the onions, salt & pepper and the wine. Place on medium-high heat until it boils. Reduce heat to low, add the fish, cover and leave for 5 minutes.

2. Carefully remove the fish from the pan onto a serving platter and cover with aluminum foil. The fish will continue to cook a bit more.

3. Bring the cooking liquids to a boil, stirring occasionally until reduced to about ½ cup. Turn off heat and add the sour cream, stir until well blended.

4. Pour the sauce over the fish and garnish with the chives. Serve immediately.

Per Serving: 327 Calories; 8g Fat; 48g Protein; 2g Carbs; trace Dietary Fiber

Broiled Colorado Trout

Trout fillets seasoned with a southwestern dressing and broiled.

2	rainbow trout (or 4 fillets)
1 Tbsp	lime juice
1 Tbsp	fresh parsley -- finely minced
1 tsp	cumin
1 tsp	paprika
1/2 tsp	garlic powder
1/4 tsp	chili powder
1/4 tsp	salt
1/4 tsp	black pepper
1/4 cup	olive oil

Induction

2 Servings
2g Net Carbs

1. Cut off and discard the head and tail. Gut and fillet open the trout and remove the bones. Leave the skin on, it helps with serving. Line a shallow broiling pan with aluminum foil and lightly oil it. Lay the trout open on the pan with the skin side down.

2. Place a rack 6-8 inches from the broiler. Preheat boiler.

3. In a bowl add the lime juice, minced parsley, cumin, paprika, garlic powder, chili powder, salt and pepper. Mix well. Add a Tbsp of olive oil and whisk well. Repeat until all the oil is incorporated.

4. Brush the dressing onto the trout. Place the pan under the broiler and cook for 5 to 6 minutes, with the oven door cracked open.

Per Serving: 489 Calories; 34g Fat; 42g Protein; 3g Carbohydrate; 1g Dietary Fiber

Grilled Trout with Lemon Sage Butter

Rainbow trout slathered with lemon sage butter and then grilled.

| 2 | rainbow trout |
| 2 | lemon wedges |

Induction

2 Servings
1g Net Carbs

Lemon/Sage Butter

1 tsp	canola oil
1 Tbsp	fresh sage -- minced
4 Tbsps	butter -- sliced and cubed
1/8 tsp	lemon extract

1. To make the lemon sage butter, be sure that sage leaves have been rinsed and are completely dry. Finely mince the sage.

   Heat 1 tsp of canola oil over medium heat in a small sauce pan. Add the sage and cook for about 2 minutes. Remove from heat and add the cubed butter and the lemon extract. Stir until well blended.

2. Pour about 1/2 of the butter in a small bowl to use for the trout. (Set aside the remainder for some other recipe; perhaps a veggie side dish of grilled zucchini or turnips).

3. Generously brush the inside of each trout with the butter. Then brush the out side of the trout. Grill over medium heat for a total of 10-15 minutes depending on the size. Turn the trout over after about 5 minutes.

Serve with the lemon wedges.

Per Serving: 522 Calories; 39g Fat; 41g Protein; 1g Carbs; trace Dietary Fiber

Ginger Salmon

This poached salmon dish cooks up in less than 15 minutes.

2		salmon steaks
1	cup	chicken broth -- or water
2	cloves	garlic -- minced
2	tsps	fresh ginger -- grated
	pinch	black pepper
2	Tbsps	dry white wine
1/2	cup	heavy cream
2		scallions -- chopped
2	Tbsps	red bell pepper -- minced

Weight Loss

**2 Servings
4g Net Carbs**

Have everything prepared before starting the cooking.

1. In a heavy skillet over high heat, bring to a boil the chicken broth, garlic, ginger and a pinch of black pepper.

2. Add the salmon steaks, reduce heat to low, cover and simmer for 3 minutes. (If using fillets with the skin, start with the skin side up). Gently turn over the steaks and simmer another 4 minutes (covered). Remove the salmon to a platter. Cover and keep in a warm oven (150°F max).

3. Add the wine to the poaching liquids. Turn up the heat to medium-high and reduce the liquids to about 1/2 a cup, stirring frequently. Add the cream and reduce the heat to medium-low, whisking constantly until the sauce thickens (about 1-2 minutes).

4. Add the chopped scallions and minced red bell pepper, stir. Taste test and add salt and pepper as desired. Return the salmon steaks to the skillet spoon the sauce over the steaks; reheating the salmon for 1-2 minutes. Serve.

Per Serving: 445 Calories; 29g Fat; 38g Protein; 5g Carbohydrate; 1g Dietary Fiber

Pecan Crusted Salmon

Ground pecans are a great low carb substitute for breading fish.

1	lb	salmon fillets
1	cup	pecan
1/2	cup	butter
1/4	tsp	thyme – 1 tsp if fresh

> **Weight Loss**
>
> 2 Servings
> 6g Net Carbs

Use any type of firm fish that you have available in your area. Be sure it has no bones or skin. Also try other fish for this recipe (halibut, mahi mahi, ono, ahi)

Preheat oven to 400ºF.

1. Light grease a baking dish large enough for the fillets without them being crowded.

2. Coarsely grind the pecans in a food processor. Pour onto a plate.

3. Melt the butter with the thyme in the microwave for a few seconds. Generously brush the fillets with the butter on both sides. Press each fillet onto the ground nuts on both sides. Place in the baking dish and bake for 10 minutes per inch of thickness. The nuts should be a golden brown but do not let them burn. Serve immediately.

Per Serving: 1031 Calories; 90g Fat; 50g Protein; 10g Carbohydrate; 4g Fiber

Poached Salmon with Leek Sauce

The pureed leek sauce is beautiful and delicious with the salmon.

2		salmon steaks
1	cup	chicken broth -- or water
1	Tbsp	shallot
1	Tbsp	butter
1		leek

> **Weight Loss**
>
> 2 Servings
> 7g Net Carbs

1. Cut off and discard the top 1/2 to 2/3 of the green portion of the leek. Slice the leek length wise and rinse thoroughly under the tap to remove the sand and grit. Then rough chop the leeks

2. Remove the skin from the shallots, rough chop. Since the size varies a lot, have enough that if they were minced they would fill a Tbsp.

3. In a heavy skillet over high heat, bring to a boil the chicken broth, shallots and leeks. Reduce heat and cook at a very gentle boil until the leeks are very soft (about 5 to 8 minutes generally). With a slotted spoon remove the leeks and shallots to a blender or food processor. Add the butter to the leeks and about 1 Tbsp of the cooking liquid. Puree until smooth, adding more cooking liquids if it is too thick.

4. Add the salmon steaks to the cooking liquids; reduce heat to low, cover and simmer for 3 minutes. If using fillets with the skin, start with the skin side up. Gently turn over the steaks and simmer another 3-4 minutes (covered).

To serve, you can spoon the pureed leeks onto the individual serving plates and then put the salmon on top or you can drizzle the puree over the salmon.

Per Serving: 298 Calories; 12g Fat; 37g Protein; 8g Carbohydrate; 1g Dietary Fiber

Salmon & Broccoli with Lemon Beurre Blanc Sauce

Beurre blanc is a classic white butter sauce. This one is jazzed up with lemon.

4		salmon steaks
1	head	broccoli
1/2	cup	Carb Well Italian Dressing

Lemon Beurre Blanc

1/2	cup	white wine
1/2	cup	white wine vinegar
1	Tbsp	shallot – finely minced
2	Tbsps	heavy cream
1	cup	butter
3	Tbsps	lemon juice
1	Tbsp	lemon zest

> **Weight Loss**
>
> 4 Servings
> 7g Net Carbs

You will need ~1 lemon, but it's good to have an extra on standby. Zest ~1 Tbsp worth and set aside as a garnish. Juice the lemon. You should get about 3 Tbsps worth. If not then squeeze the second one.

1. To make the sauce: In a sauce pan over medium-high heat, boil the wine, vinegar and shallots until it reduces to about 1/4 cup (15 or 20 minutes). Stir occasionally.

2. While the sauce base is reducing, prepare the salmon & broccoli. Preheat broiler with a rack about 8 inches away. Cut the broccoli into spears, put in a bowl and pour about 1/2 of the dressing over them and toss. Use the rest of the dressing to brush onto the salmon steaks. On a foil lined sheet pan (to make clean-up easier) place the salmon steaks and broccoli spears. Broil for 5 minutes, turn the steaks and broccoli and broil another 5 minutes. Turn off the heat, but leave in the oven until the sauce is ready.

3. Once the sauce has reduced, set heat to lowest setting and whisk in the cream. Then add the butter, about 3 Tbsps at a time, whisking thoroughly (do not let it boil). Whisk in the lemon juice. Pour over the salmon and broccoli and serve immediately.

Serve garnished with the lemon zest.

Per Serving: 771 Calories; 63g Fat; 39g Protein; 12g Carbohydrate; 5g Fiber

Salmon Paella

This low carb adaptation is made from cauliflower instead of rice and then broiled salmon is served on top. This is a great dish for a dinner party.

4		salmon fillets
2	Tbsps	canola oil
1	tsp	lemon pepper
8		lemon slices

<table>
<tr><td colspan="3">Weight Loss</td></tr>
<tr><td colspan="3">4 Servings
4g Net Carbs</td></tr>
</table>

1	head	cauliflower -- grated
1	stalk	celery -- minced
2		scallion -- minced
1/2	cup	red and green bell pepper -- minced
1	Tbsp	butter
1/4	cup	dry white wine
4	Tbsps	Carb Options™ Ketchup
2	Tbsps	lemon juice
1	Tbsp	Worcestershire sauce
1	tsp	oregano

Seafood paella typically has an assortment of fish. Feel free to swap out _ the salmon for another type of fish. Just be sure that it has the same thickness so that it cooks in the same amount of time.

The salmon will be broiled and then finished off in the oven. So you will need to place a rack just under the broiler and another in the middle of the oven.

First, prepare everything for making the paella. Then you'll want to start the salmon, then cook the paella, then assemble.

1. In a small bowl, mix together the ketchup, lemon juice, Worcestershire sauce and the oregano, set aside.

2. Grate the cauliflower. This is accomplished best by using your grating wheel on your food processor. But you can do it by hand also with a cheese grater. Mince the celery, scallions and peppers quite finely. Set aside.

3. Rub each salmon fillet with canola oil and place on a foil lined sheet pan, skin side down. Sprinkle each with the lemon pepper. Place under the broiler for 5 minutes. Turn off broiler and set oven to 300ºF. Place two lemon slices on each fillet and cook until the "rice" is ready.

4. In a large skillet, melt the butter over medium-high heat. Add the celery, scallions and peppers and sauté for a minute or two. Add the cauliflower and sauté for a minute or so, stirring occasionally until it soaks up all the butter. Then splash in the water to let the cauliflower steam a bit (30 seconds or more).

5. Drizzle the ketchup mixture over the veggies (do not dump it all in one spot) and stir well. Taste and add salt or pepper as needed.

6. To assemble: Heap the paella in the center of a platter and lean each salmon fillet along the sides.

Serve with a green salad and or green vegetable.

Per Serving: 320 Calories; 16g Fat; 35g Protein; 6g Carbohydrate; 2g Dietary Fiber

Shrimp Addition: To stretch this recipe to serve 6 people, add 1 lb of shrimp (still in the shell). Place the shrimp on the pan with the salmon when you move it from the broiler to the oven in step 3. Prior to assembling in step 6; cut the salmon fillets into halves or thirds.
4g Net Carbs; 272 Calories; 11g Fat; 36g Protein; 5g Carbohydrate; 1g Dietary Fiber;

Macadamia Nut Crusted Ahi

Macadamia nut and ginger are natural flavors to compliment
ahi tuna (also known as yellowfin tuna).

1	lb	yellowfin tuna (2 fillets)
1	cup	macadamia nut
1/2	cup	unsalted butter
2	Tbsps	grated gingerroot

> **Weight Loss**
>
> 2 Servings
> 4g Net Carbs

Use any type of firm fish that you have available in your area. Be sure it is fresh or freshly thawed with no bones or skin.

Preheat oven to 400°F.

1. Lightly grease a baking dish large enough for the fillets without them being crowded.

2. Finely chop the macadamia nuts in a food processor. Pour onto a plate.

3. Melt the butter with the ginger in the microwave for a few seconds. Generously brush the fillets with the ginger butter on both sides. Press each fillet onto the chopped nuts on both sides. Place in the baking dish and bake for 10 minutes per inch of thickness. The nuts should be a golden brown but do not let it burn.

Serve immediately.

If you can handle some extra carb serve with the Hawaiian salsa (page 363) or the Savory Mango Sauce page 358, for an outstanding dinner.

Per Serving: 1126 Calories; 98g Fat; 59g Protein; 10g Carbohydrate; 6g Fiber

Crawfish Creole

Bring a touch of New Orleans into your kitchen with this crawfish casserole.

1½	lbs	crawfish tail, whole – peeled
1	Tbsp	butter
1/3	cup	onion -- chopped
1/4	cup	green bell pepper -- chopped
1/4	cup	celery -- chopped
1	clove	garlic -- minced fine
2	Tbsps	Creole seasoning
1	pinch	salt
1/2	cup	mayonnaise
1/2	cup	sour cream
2	Tbsps	brown mustard
1	dash	Tabasco sauce -- to taste
1		scallion -- minced
1	Tbsp	parsley

Weight Loss
4 Servings
7g Net Carbs

Preheat oven to 400°F

1. In a large skillet over medium heat, add the butter, onions, celery and bell pepper. Cook for 3 about minutes.

2. Add the crawfish tails, garlic and Creole seasoning. Stirring frequently cook for about 5 minutes. Add salt, stir and remove from heat. Let cool.

3. Meanwhile; In a mixing bowl, blend together the mayonnaise, sour cream, mustard, scallions, parsley and dash of Tabasco sauce.

4. Mix 1/2 of the mayonnaise mixture with the crawfish. Spoon into a casserole dish. Spread the remaining mayonnaise mixture over the top.

5. Bake at 400°F for about 15 minutes.

Per Serving: 439 Calories; 35g Fat; 28g Protein; 8g Carbohydrate; 1g Dietary Fiber

Baby Lobster Tails with Lemon Butter Sauce

Lobster tails swimming in a lemon butter sauce served over
asparagus and fresh spinach leaves.

4	baby	lobster tails
2/3	lb	asparagus spears -- or broccoli
1	Tbsp	shallot -- minced
1		lemon
4	Tbsps	butter
3	cups	fresh spinach -- baby

Weight Loss
2 Servings
4g Net Carbs

I find these small lobster tails frozen at Safeway. The shells have already been cracked. If yours are not, then after they have thawed, strike it sharply with a cleaver lengthwise.

1. Zest the lemon enough to get about 2 tsp of zest. Juice the lemon into a small bowl and remove all the seeds, but leave the pulp.

2. Steam the lobster tails for 6 minutes. You can use plain water or you can add white wine or crab boil herbs (such as Old Bay seasoning or see page 53) to the water. When cool enough, crack open shell and carefully remove the meat. Cut each lengthwise and set aside until ready to add it to the next step. Don't worry if the meat is not yet cooked through.

3. In a large skillet over medium heat, melt 1 Tbsp of the butter with the shallots. Add the asparagus (or broccoli) spears and cook for 3 - 5 minutes or until heated through but still crunchy (you don't want to cook away all the vitamins), stir occasionally. Add the remaining butter, lemon juice and lemon zest. Cook until butter is melted and then add the lobster meat. Coat the lobster tails with the butter. If the meat was cooked through when you cut it in half then cook for only 30 seconds to one minute just to warm it. If the flesh was still translucent then cook for about 3 minutes while you pull out the vegetables, to arrange on the plates.

4. Divide the spinach between two plates and arrange the asparagus so they all align. Lean the lobsters against the asparagus at an angle for a pretty presentation. Drizzle the remaining butter sauce over each plate. Serve immediately.

Per Serving: 490 Calories; 26g Fat; 57g Protein; 7g Carbohydrate; 3g Dietary Fiber

Lobster Scampi with Steamed Spinach

Lobster cooked with butter, wine and garlic served over steamed spinach. Yum!
Shrimp, crawfish or monkfish are nice alternatives
if lobster is too much of a stretch for your budget.

1	lb	lobster tails
1/2	stick	butter
6	cloves	garlic -- minced
1/4	cup	white wine
1	Tbsp	Worcestershire sauce
1	Tbsp	Dijon mustard
1	tsp	paprika -- Hungarian
	dash	salt and pepper -- optional
1	Tbsp	lemon juice
8	ozs	spinach leaves

Weight Loss

2 Servings
7g Net Carbs

For the best flavor, the cooking of the lobster and the spinach needs to be timed perfectly and served immediately. So be sure that the table is completely set and everything else is ready to go (e.g. salad is prepared and on the table, water glasses are already filled, etc.)

1. Lobster should be at room temperature prior to cooking. Remove meat from shell. The easiest way to do this is by striking the tails lengthwise with a sharp cleaver and then breaking the tail apart. Cut the lobster meat into bite sized pieces.

2. In a sauce pan, melt butter over medium-low heat. Add the minced garlic and cook for a minute.

3. Add the white wine, Worcestershire sauce, mustard, and paprika. Whisk together until well blended. Add a dash of salt & pepper and simmer for about 5 minutes.

4. Meanwhile, rinse well the spinach leaves. If leaves are large, cut them into smaller pieces. Bring your steamer to a boil but do not add the spinach until you are ready to cook the lobster. The spinach should be added to the steamer 1 minute after the lobster is added to the sauce pan

5. Add lobster to the sauce pan and simmer for 3 minutes, stir occasionally. Do not over cook. Turn off the heat and stir in the lemon juice.

6. Drain the spinach well. Divide between two plates. Spoon the lobster over the spinach with plenty of the juices. Serve immediately.

Per Serving: 476 Calories; 26g Fat; 46g Protein; 10g Carbohydrate; 3g Fiber

Red Snapper with Bell Pepper Salsa

Grilled or broiled red snapper served with a colorful salsa is perfect for any season. The mild flavors should appeal to almost anyone.

2	lb	red snapper -- fillets
1	Tbsp	canola oil
4	Tbsps	lime juice
1	cup	red and yellow bell pepper -- minced
2		scallions -- minced
1/2	cup	cilantro -- minced

Weight Loss
4 Servings
5g Net Carbs

Salsa:

1. In a non-metallic bowl mix together the bell peppers, minced cilantro and the minced scallions (both white and green portions). Add 2 Tbsp of lime juice (not all 4 Tbsps) and toss. Cover and chill while you prepare the fish.

2. You can kick up the flavor by adding a few dashes of Tabasco or a 1/2 tsp of chili powder. A minced jalapeno pepper is also an option.

Grilled Snapper:

1. Rinse and pat dry the fish. I prefer to leave the skin on to make turning the fillets easier.

2. Mix together the oil and 2 Tbsps of the lime juice.

3. Baste both sides of the fish with the oil/lime mixture. A pinch of salt and pepper is optional.

4. To grill, place the snapper fillets skin side up on a hot oiled grill. Grill for about 4 minutes. Carefully turn over with a large spatula. Generously baste with the oil/lime mixture. Turn heat down to medium and grill for another 5-6 minutes, just until it flakes easily and most (if not all) of the translucence is gone from the center. Remove from heat immediately.

Serve on a platter or individual plates with a generous spoonful of salsa on top or to the side.

This can also be cooked under a broiler. It's best to broil it with the skin side down and don't turn it over. But be sure to baste it frequently.

Per Serving: 284 Calories; 7g Fat; 48g Protein; 6g Carbohydrate; 1g Dietary Fiber

Scallops Over Asparagus

Garlic and lemon add a depth of flavor to the sherry cream sauce.
This dish is quick and easy yet elegant enough for any special occasion.

3/4	lb	sea scallops, whole
1	clove	garlic -- minced
1		scallion -- minced
1	tsp	canola oil
1/4	cup	sherry
1/4	cup	heavy whipping cream
1/4	tsp	lemon extract
	dash	salt and pepper -- each
1/2	lb	asparagus spears
1	tsp	lemon zest – as a garnish
few	sprigs	chives -- as a garnish

> **Weight Loss**
>
> 2 Servings
> 9g Net Carbs

Have everything ready before you start cooking. Trim the asparagus, mince the garlic and scallions, prepare garnish and have all ingredients out and handy.

1. Steam asparagus for about 3 minutes. Remove from heat but leave covered until the scallops are done.

2. Meanwhile, in a non-stick frying pan over medium-high heat, add the oil and quick fry the scallops about 30-60 seconds per side. Transfer to a plate.

3. Add the garlic and scallions and sauté for about 1 minute. Add the sherry and stir, let the alcohol cook off (about 30 seconds) then add the cream, lemon extract and salt and pepper and cook for about 2-3 minutes, stirring occasionally. Reduce the heat, add the scallops and cook for another 2-3 minutes.

4. Place the asparagus on individual plates. Spoon the scallops over the asparagus with plenty of the sauce.

Serve at once garnished with lemon zest curls and chives.

Per Serving: 333 Calories; 15g Fat; 31g Protein; 11g Carbohydrate; 2g Dietary Fiber

Tijuana Shrimp

Marinated shrimp which is broiled or grilled and served
with a spicy tomato sauce.

32		jumbo shrimp -- peeled and deveined

Marinade

1	Tbsp	canola oil
2	Tbsps	lime juice
1	Tbsp	lemon pepper
1	tsp	paprika
	dash	salt

Sauce

8	ozs	canned tomatoes with green chilies
1		serrano pepper -- seeded and chopped
1	Tbsp	onion -- minced
1	clove	garlic -- chopped
		salt and pepper -- to taste

Weight Loss

4 Servings
4g Net Carbs

1. Combine the marinade ingredients in a bowl. Add the peeled and deveined shrimp and marinate for at least 10 minutes (while you make the sauce).

2. In a food processor, add the canned tomatoes including the juice, the pepper, onion and garlic and process until smooth. Pour the tomato mixture into a sauce pan and bring to a boil. Reduce heat to low and simmer for about 5 minutes. Taste and add salt and pepper as needed.

3. Remove shrimp from marinade (discard marinade and arrange the shrimp in on a baking sheet so that they all lay flat. Broil for about 2 minutes per side. Alternatively shrimp can be skewered and grilled.

4. Pour about 1/2 to 2/3 of the tomato sauce onto a serving platter. Arrange the shrimp on top of the sauce and drizzle the remaining sauce over the shrimp.

Serve immediately.

Per Serving: 107 Calories; 5g Fat; 12g Protein; 4g Carbs; trace Dietary Fiber

Shrimp Imperial

Sautéed shrimp smothered in a rich and creamy sauce and then baked.

1	lb	shrimp -- peeled and deveined
1/4	cup	onion -- minced
1/4	cup	red bell pepper -- minced
1/4	cup	celery -- minced
2	cloves	garlic -- minced
1	Tbsp	butter
1	pinch	salt

> **Weight Loss**
>
> 4 Servings
> 4g Net Carbs

Sauce

1/2	cup	mayonnaise
1/2	cup	sour cream
1	Tbsp	mustard
1	tsp	Worcestershire sauce
1/4	tsp	fresh ground pepper
2	Tbsps	fresh Italian parsley -- minced
1	tsp	fresh thyme
1/2	tsp	paprika
1/4	tsp	lemon extract

Preheat oven to 400°F

1. In a large skillet over medium-high heat, add the butter. Once melted, add the celery, bell pepper and onions. Cook for 2-3 minutes.

2. Add the shrimp and garlic. Cook for 3-4 minutes or until shrimp just turn pink (do not over cook). Stir frequently. Remove from heat and add a pinch of salt. Toss. Let cool.

3. In a small bowl, mix together the mayonnaise, sour cream, mustard, Worcestershire sauce, pepper, parsley, thyme and lemon extract.

4. To assemble, divide shrimp into 4 ramekin (or gratin dishes or large scallop shells). Spoon the mayonnaise mixture over each dish and sprinkle with a dash of paprika.

5. Place ramekins on cookie sheet and bake in 400°F oven for about 15 minutes or until bubbling and starting to brown.

The shrimp and sauce can be made a few hours in advance and refrigerated until ready to bake.

You can substitute the shrimp with crab, lobster or scallops. A mix of these shell fish would also be nice.

Per Serving: 420 Calories; 34g Fat; 25g Protein; 5g Carbohydrate; 1g Dietary Fiber

Sedona Shrimp

Shrimp marinated in a southwestern blend and then grilled, broiled or stir fried.

2	lbs	shrimp -- fresh
1/3	cup	olive oil
2	Tbsps	lime juice
1/4	cup	white wine -- optional
3	cloves	garlic -- crushed
1	tsp	tabasco sauce
2	tsps	chili pepper flakes
1	Tbsp	cumin
1	tsp	salt

Weight Loss
4 Servings
5g Net Carbs

Garnishes
1/4	cup	cilantro -- fresh & chopped
1/4	cup	red bell pepper -- diced

1. In a large re-sealable baggie, pour in the olive oil, lime juice, wine, tabasco, garlic, chili flakes, cumin, and salt. Mix about and then add the shrimp. Remove as much air as possible before sealing the bag. Refrigerate at least 30 minutes but 1 or 2 hours in preferable.

2. Choice one of the three cooking methods:

    Broil: Place shrimp in a single layer (skewers can be used) in a shallow baking dish. Broil as close to heat as possible for 2 minutes on each side. Shrimp should turn a bright pink/orange, curl up and started to sizzle along the edges.

    Grill: Place skewered shrimp on preheated grill. Cook 2 minutes per side. Shrimp should turn a bright pink/orange, curl up and started to sizzle along the edges.

    Stir Fry: In a large skillet (or a wok) over high heat. Cook shrimp, stirring frequently, for 4 minutes. Shrimp should turn a bright pink/orange, curl up and started to sizzle along the edges.

3. Place shrimp on platter and sprinkle with the fresh cilantro and diced bell peppers. Serve immediately.

This makes quick and easy entrée for 4 or an appetizer for a crowd.

Per Serving: 429 Calories; 22g Fat; 47g Protein; 6g Carbohydrate; 1g Dietary Fiber

As an Appetizer: Put 2 or 3 shrimp on a cocktail skewer and serve on a platter. Or leave the tip of the shell on the tail and serve on a platter or in a bowl. They can be served hot or chilled.

Shrimp & Asparagus Stir Fry

Low carb teriyaki sauce helps make the meal quick and easy.

1	lb	shrimp -- peeled and deveined
2	lbs	asparagus spears
1	Tbsp	peanut oil
4	cloves	garlic
2	Tbsps	Carb Options™ Asian Teriyaki Marinade
1	Tbsp	wine vinegar
1	Tbsp	lemon juice

Weight Loss

4 Servings
5g Net Carbs

1. In a mixing bowl, blend together the teriyaki marinade, vinegar and lemon juice. Add the shrimp, toss well to coat and set aside.

2. Cut the asparagus into bite-sized lengths (about an inch). Mince the garlic.

3. In a wok (or skillet) over medium-high heat, add the oil, garlic and asparagus and stir fry for about 2 minutes. Then carefully add the shrimp and sauce. Stir fry for 1-2 minutes, just until the shrimp turns pink, then turn off heat and cover for about 2 minutes.

Serve immediately.

Per Serving: 186 Calories; 6g Fat; 26g Protein; 8g Carbohydrate; 3g Dietary Fiber

Swordfish with Tomatillo Sauce

This spicy tomatillo sauce adds a Mexican flare to grilled swordfish.
This sauce is great on other fish steaks such as halibut, shark, mahi mahi, etc.

2	8 oz	swordfish steaks
2	tsps	lemon pepper
1/4	cup	yellow onion -- chopped fine
1	clove	garlic -- minced
2	tsps	canola oil
4		tomatillos
1	small	jalapeno pepper -- seeded
1/4	cup	fresh cilantro
1/4	cup	chicken stock – or water
1	Tbsp	lemon juice
		salt and pepper -- to taste
2	sprigs	fresh cilantro -- as a garnish

Weight Loss

2 Servings
7g Net Carbs

1. In a food processor bowl, add the tomatillos, jalapeno, cilantro, chicken stock and lemon juice. Process until smooth.

2. In a skillet over medium-high heat, add the canola oil, onions and garlic. Sauté for 1 or 2 minutes until the onions start to become translucent. Add the

tomatillo mixture and cook just until it comes to a boil. Reduce heat and simmer for 10 minutes. Taste test. Add salt and pepper as needed.

3. Meanwhile, season the swordfish with a dash of salt and the lemon pepper on each side. Grill or broil the swordfish steaks for about 4 minutes per side. Fish should be firm to the touch.

4. Serve immediately with the tomatillo sauce poured over the swordfish.

Per Serving: 360 Calories; 15g Fat; 46g Protein; 9g Carbohydrate; 2g Dietary Fiber

Baked Tilapia

Baked tilapia with Asian vegetables and a teriyaki sauce.

2		tilapia fillet
1½	cups	Napa cabbage -- shredded
1/2	cup	mushroom -- sliced
8		snow pea pods -- halved
2		scallions -- chopped
2	Tbsps	red bell pepper, minced
3	Tbsps	Carb Options™ Asian Teriyaki Marinade
1	Tbsp	lemon juice
1	tsp	fresh ginger root -- grated
1/4	tsp	lemon pepper
2	Tbsps	cilantro -- chopped

Weight Loss

2 Servings
7g Net Carbs

Tilapia is a mildly flavored fish with good texture. It is becoming more and more popular as it is generally quite economical.

Preheat oven to 375°F

1. In a large bowl, whisk together the Teriyaki marinade, lemon juice, ginger and lemon pepper. Add the shredded cabbage, mushrooms, pea pods, scallions, and red pepper. Toss to coat everything.

2. Lightly oil a baking pan, place the tilapia in the pan. Pour the vegetables and sauce over the fish and tightly cover the pan with foil. Bake at 375°F for 20 minutes.

Per Serving: 238 Calories; 3g Fat; 44g Protein; 10g Carbohydrate; 3g Dietary Fiber

Rainbow Trout with Tahini Sauce

2		rainbow trout
1/2	cup	parsley -- chopped
2	Tbsp	lemon juice
3	cloves	garlic -- minced or pressed
1	tsp	cumin
1	tsp	olive oil
1/3	cup	tahini
1/4	cup	water
4	slices	lemon – cut into halves

Weight Loss

2 Servings
8g Net Carbs

Preheat oven to 375°F

1. Add to a food processor the parsley, lemon juice, garlic, cumin and the olive oil. Process until well blended. Add 2 Tbsp of the tahini and blend again.

2. Place each trout on a separate sheet of heavy duty foil (or double sheets of regular foil). Place 1 heaping Tbsp of the parsley mixture inside each trout and spread it evenly. Place two half slices of the lemon inside each trout and place two half slices on top. Wrap securely and bake for 20 -25 minutes at 375°F.

3. Meanwhile, in a small sauce pan over low heat, warm up the remaining mixture from the food processor and add the remaining tahini and the water. Do not boil just warm it. Stir occasionally.

4. Remove trout from oven and carefully cut open the foil using a fork or knife. After all the steam has escaped, carefully transfer trout to individual plates.

Serve with the sauce on the side.

Per Serving: 379 Calories; 27g Fat; 25g Protein; 13g Carbohydrate; 5g Fiber

Seafood Platter with Lemon Herb Butter

Crab legs, shrimp and scallops with broccoli & asparagus served with lemon herb butter. This is best eaten with your fingers for a deliciously tactile experience.

1	lb	shrimp
2	lbs	Alaskan king crab legs
1/2	lb	sea scallops
1	lb	asparagus spears
1	head	broccoli
1	Tbsp	Old Bay Seafood seasoning
1		lemon
2	sticks	butter
1/4	tsp	each of garlic powder, oregano, thyme

Weight Loss

4 Servings
9g Net Carbs

Although this recipe calls for crab legs, shrimp and scallops, feel free to add or substitute clams, mussels or lobster. However see page 289 for the carb count.

If you use frozen seafood be sure they are completely thawed before cooking (this is best done with a slow thaw over night in the refrigerator. Try not to force a thaw in the microwave or under running water.

You'll need a roasting pan that has a rack and a cover. The cover can be fashioned out of aluminum foil. If you do not have the rack, then improvise with a cookie cooking rack, steaming baskets or the like.

Preheat oven to 350°F

1. Cut the lemon in half and juice into a small bowl. Remove seeds. Reserve juice and rind.

2. Cut the broccoli into spears. Trim off the ends of the asparagus.

3. In a large roasting pan with a rack, pour in as much boiling water as you can without submerging the rack. Add the Old Bay seasoning and the lemon rinds into the water. Place in the rack and stack on the crab legs, broccoli and asparagus. Then strategically place the shrimp and scallops on top of things such that they won't fall thru the rack into the liquid. Cover and place in a 350°F oven and steam for about 12 minutes.

4. Meanwhile melt the butter with the herbs. Keep warm until ready to serve. Add the lemon juice just before serving.

5. Using tongs transfer to a serving platter. A platter that has a lid is wonderful but everything in this meal is still fine when they cool off to room temperature.

I recommend serving the lemon butter in individual ramekins on each plate. It's nice if everyone has their own shell fish cracker and seafood forks. Nut crackers and fondue forks work great.

Per Serving: 795 Calories; 49g Fat; 76g Protein; 15g Carbohydrate; 6g Fiber

Tuna Casserole

This low carb version of the classic is great for a casual dinner. Feel free to substitute left over chicken or turkey for the tuna with no additional carbs.

1	cup	low carb pasta
1	Tbsp	butter
1/4	cup	onion -- finely chopped
1/4	cup	celery -- finely chopped
4	ozs	mushroom -- canned
2	cups	broccoli -- chopped
1	Tbsp	fresh parsley -- chopped
12	ozs	sour cream
1	can	tuna -- drained
1	cup	sharp cheddar cheese -- grated

Weight Loss

4 Servings
9g Net Carbs

I think that low carb pasta is mediocre at best. I use Carb Fit Rotini type for this casserole (which has 9g net carbs per 1 cup uncooked). Hopefully better brands will emerge on the market as time goes by.

Preheat oven to 350°F

1. Cook the pasta in boiling water according to the directions on the package except reduce time by 1 minute. Try to be precise. If the package specifies a range such as 8 to 9 minutes, then cook 7 minutes for this recipe.

2. Meanwhile; melt the butter in a large skillet over medium-high heat. Add the onions and celery and cook for about a minute. Add the mushrooms, broccoli and parsley and cook for another 3 minute or so.

3. Add the tuna and sour cream and heat through.

4. Drain the pasta and add to the skillet just to mix it together. Add about 1/3 of the cheese and stir again.

5. Pour the mixture into a casserole dish and top it with the remaining cheddar cheese. Place in a 350°F oven for about 15 minutes or until the cheese melts. Alternatively you can place the casserole under the broiler for about 3-5 minutes to brown the cheese with crispy bubbles.

Also try this with left-over chicken or turkey.

Per Serving: 455 Calories; 33g Fat; 28g Protein; 13g Carbohydrate; 4g Fiber

Salmon Casserole

This simple dish is made with low carb pasta, ranch dressing and canned salmon.

1	cup	**low carb pasta**
8	ozs	**canned salmon**
1	cup	**ranch salad dressing**
1/4	tsp	**dill**
4	ozs	**canned mushroom slices**
2		**scallions -- chopped**
4	ozs	**parmesan cheese**

Maintenance
3 Servings
12g Net Carbs

I use Carb Fit Rotini type for this casserole (which has 9g net carbs per 1 cup uncooked).

Preheat oven to 350°F

1. Cook the low carb pasta in boil water according to the directions on the package except reduce the time by 2 or 3 minutes. Drain well.

2. Meanwhile, drain and flake the salmon; set aside.

3. In a large bowl, mix together the ranch dressing, mushrooms, dill and scallions.

4. When pasta is cooked and drained, add it to the ranch dressing mixture. Mix well. Add the flaked salmon and gently toss until well distributed. Spoon into a butter casserole dish. Top with the parmesan cheese and bake at 350°F for about 20 minutes.

Per Serving: 768 Calories; 60g Fat; 44g Protein; 16g Carbohydrate; 4g Fiber

Seafood Crepes

This low carb adaptation is perfect for that special occasion.
It is a lot of work but you can make the crepes ahead of time.

Crepes

2		egg
1/4	cup	Carb Countdown™ Milk, 2%
1/4	tsp	salt
1/4	tsp	lemon pepper
1/2	cup	Whey protein powder
1	Tbsp	butter

> **Maintenance**
>
> 2 Servings
> 10g Net Carbs

Sauce

3	Tbsps	butter
1	cup	heavy cream
3		egg yolks
1	Tbsp	sherry
1	Tbsp	lemon juice
1/2	tsp	paprika

Filling

1/2	lb	shrimp
1/2	lb	sea scallops
2		scallion
1	Tbsp	butter

Crepes: This takes a little bit of practice, if you are not already familiar with the technique. You are going to want 4 crepes total. (There should be enough to do a mini crepe as the first one to get the hang of it, using about 2 T of the batter. But the instructions below are written as if you are already somewhat familiar with making crepes).

1. In a small bowl, beat the eggs. Add the milk and spices and beat again. Then beat in the whey powder, mix well. It may be a little lumpy but that's okay.

2. Heat a crepe pan or a small non-stick skillet over medium-high heat. Once it is hot, melt a tiny bit of butter and spread it around. Ladle in about 4 Tbsp of the egg mixture and immediately tilt the pan around so that the batter evenly covers the bottom of the pan. Set it back onto the heat and let it cook for about 20 or 30 seconds. Carefully lift up an edge to see if it has begun to brown. When it is a nice golden brown, carefully flip it over and cook another 30 seconds. Remove to a paper towel or parchment paper. Repeat with a tiny bit of butter and another ladle of batter until you have 4 crepes.

3. If you are not using the crepes right away layer parchment paper between them and slip into a large baggie or place on a plate and cover with plastic. Refrigerate up to two days.

4. For the sauce: In a sauce pan over medium-low heat, melt butter and add the sherry and lemon juice. Beat together the egg yolks, cream and paprika. Slowly pour the egg mixture into butter mixture, stirring constantly until thicken. Set aside. (But near the stove so it stays warm).

5. For the filling: Cut the shrimp and scallops into 3 or 4 pieces each. Mince the scallions keeping about 1/2 of the green tops set aside for a garnish. In a skillet, melt the butter and add the white portion of the scallions. Sauté for one minute. Add the shrimp and scallops and sauté until the shrimp are completely pink (about 2 or 3 minutes). Reduce heat to low. Add about 1/2 cup of the sauce and mix well. Turn off the heat.

6. To assemble: Place a crepe on a flat surface and scoop out 1/4 of the filling and place it across the lower third of the crepe and then carefully roll up. Transfer to a plate with the seam side down. Repeat for the other crepes with 2 crepes per plate. Pour the remaining sauce over the crepes and garnished with the reserved scallion tops. You may need to lightly reheat sauce but do not boil it.

Per Serving: 1310 Calories; 92g Fat; 102g Protein; 11g Carbohydrate; 1g Fiber

Teriyaki Salmon with Mango Yogurt Sauce

This grill salmon is a delightful dish for a summer evening.

2		**salmon fillets**
1/2	**cup**	**Carb Options™ Asian Teriyaki Marinade**
1	**Tbsp**	**mint -- minced**

Maintenance
2 Servings
12g Net Carbs

Yogurt Mango Sauce

2		**Dannon's Carb Control™ Yogurt -- peach**
2/3	**cup**	**mango -- diced**
2	**tsps**	**Carb Options™ Asian Teriyaki Marinade**

1. Place salmon fillets in a zip-lock baggie and add the teriyaki sauce. Turn to cover. Marinate for 15 minutes. Pour off marinade and discard.

Prepare your grill and preheat the oven to 200°F. Have an oven-proof platter ready.

2. Over a hot grill, cook the salmon for 3 minutes on each side (start with the skin side up). Transfer the fish to a platter, cover and place in the oven and cook for 15 minutes.

3. Meanwhile, make the mango sauce. Slice mango on either side of it's large seed. Cut into strips. Then with a thin knife, slice off the skin by having each strip skin side down on a cutting board and running the knife horizontally as close to the skin as you can. Be sure to cut off as much of the flesh around the edge of the seed too. Dice into cubes about the size of a grape. Set aside about 2/3 cups (save the rest for some other recipe).

4. Mix the yogurt with the 2 tsp of Teriyaki sauce and stir in the diced mangos.

Serve with the sauce poured over the fish and garnish with the minced mint.

Per Serving: 255 Calories; 8g Fat; 34g Protein; 13g Carbohydrate; 1g Dietary Fiber

SOUPS & STEWS

SOUPS & STEWS

Important Note: All of the soups that call for chicken stock were developed using home-made chicken stock. Sorry, but I did not test many of the recipes using commercial chicken stock products.

Why food manufacturers can not come up with a decent chicken stock is beyond my imagination. If you prefer the convenience of pre-packaged stock, then choose the low-sodium kind that comes in a box type container rather than the cans. For some reason these seem to taste a little better. Stock can be frozen.

Broth is different from stock. Broth is typically made with just water, meat and salt (plus occasionally preservatives and coloring). Stock is more flavorful as it is made with the addition of the bones as well as aromatic vegetables and herbs.

Chicken Soup Cold Remedy

This chicken soup is a must for a cold or flu, but I like to make it even
when I feel fine. The garlic, ginger, rosemary and parsley all have
medicinal properties to help boost the immune system.
But there is just something about chicken soup that soothes the soul.

1		roasted chicken -- de-boned
8	cups	chicken stock
1	Tbsp	butter
1/4	med	yellow onion -- sliced
2	Tbsps	fresh ginger root -- grated
5	cloves	garlic -- minced
1	sprig	fresh rosemary
12	sprigs	fresh Italian parsley
		salt and pepper -- to taste

Induction
6 Servings
2g Net Carbs

1. Pull all the meat off the chicken bones. (Save the skin and the bones for making homemade stock when you feel better). Cut meat into bite sized pieces. Set aside.

2. Pull most of the leaves off of the parsley & rosemary. Keep them separate and coarsely chop each.

3. In a large soup pot, melt the butter over medium heat. Add the onions as soon as the butter is melted and sauté until translucent. About 3 minutes.

4. Add the garlic and ginger, stirring frequently for about 1 full minute.

5. Add the chicken stock and the rosemary leaves. Raise heat to bring to a boil for about 5 minutes. Then reduce heat to a simmer.

6. Add chicken pieces and simmer for 5 minutes. Taste test and add salt and pepper to your liking.

7. Add the parsley leaves for the last minute of cooking. Serve immediately.

Refrigerate left-overs; it keeps for several days.

Per Serving: 190 Calories; 7g Fat; 23g Protein; 2g Carbs; trace Dietary Fiber

Chicken or Turkey Stock

Homemade stock is far superior to anything you can purchase in a store.

1	bunch	chicken bones & skin
		(2 chickens or 1 small turkey)
3	stalks	celery
1/4	med	onion
10	stalks	fresh assorted herbs
		rosemary, sage, thyme, oregano
		or about 2 Tbsps of assorted dried herbs
4	quarts	cold water (same a 1 gallon or 16 cups)
		salt and pepper -- to taste

Induction

3 Servings
0g Net Carbs

This is best made fresh after roasting a chicken or turkey. But you can also purchase whole roasted chickens from most grocery stores and then use this after you have removed most of the meat. You can also save bones and skin in a baggie or Tupperware in the freezer until you have enough to made stock (at least 1 whole chicken worth).

I usually make stock immediately after dinner when having roasted chicken (or turkey). I de-bone the rest of the roasted chicken (or turkey) and use the herbs, celery and onion from the roasting pan and cavity. In that case, I don't need to add anything else but water. I recommend using the whole wings for the stock and not bothering to try to get that meat off for eating. In fact, you don't have to get too picky about pulling the meat off the bones in general. The extra meat creates extra deep flavor.

1. Start with cold water (straight from the tap is generally cold enough); this helps pull the juices out more efficiently as it is slowly heated. Place everything in a large stock pot over medium heat. Put the cover on but slightly to the side so that some steam can escape.

2. Once it comes to a boil, reduce the heat to a very gentle boil for 3 hours or more (I try to get about 4 or 5 hours when I can). Stir occasionally breaking up the bones as you go. Add more water if the bones are not covered with liquid (unless it is just the last 15 minutes or so of cooking).

3. Pour the liquids through a strainer into a large bowl. If you have more than 4 cups of liquids, it did not boil down enough. Taste to see if it needs salt or pepper.

4. Ladle the stock into glass jars with tight fitting lids (I use mason jars, but old pickle or peanut butter jars work just as well). Do not use plastic containers. Be sure that there is at least 1/2 inch of fat on top of the liquid in each jar. The fat will keep the stock fresh for about 3-4 weeks in the refrigerator (or about 4 months if frozen).

Unlike commercial stock, this one will be gelatinous. When ready to use, spoon off the fat first and discard it. If only using a portion of the jar of stock, then spoon the fat into a small bowl. Remove as much stock as needed. Put the fat back into the jar and zap it in the microwave until liquefied. Let cool, then cover and refrigerate again.

Yields about 3 cups of stock in addition to a layer of fat

Per Serving: 22 Calories; trace Fat; 1g Protein; 0g Carbohydrate; 0g Dietary Fiber;

After straining the stock from the bones, I generally rinse the bones with 2 or 3 cups of cool water and strain this off and give the liquids to my dogs. They love it! In fact, after about 2 hours or so into the process of making stock, they generally start to get excited in anticipate of this delicious treat.

Hot & Sour Soup

This classic is converted to a low carb soup by substituting guar gum for the cornstarch and a touch of Splenda for the sugar.

4	cups	**chicken stock**
1	cup	**chicken breast -- cut in 1" strips**
2		**scallions -- minced**
1/2	cup	**bamboo shoots, canned -- julienne**
1/2	cup	**straw mushrooms -- halved**
1/2	tsp	**crushed red pepper -- hot or mild**
1	tsp	**Splenda®**
1	Tbsp	**soy sauce**
3	Tbsps	**vinegar**
1	tsp	**guar gum**
2		**eggs -- beaten**

> **Induction**
>
> **4 Servings**
> **3g Net Carbs**

1. Mince the scallions keeping the white and green parts separate (the greens will be used for a garnish).

2. In a soup pot, add the chicken stock, chicken, white portion of scallions, bamboo shoots, halved mushrooms, hot peppers, Splenda, soy sauce, vinegar and guar gum. Stir well. Bring to a slow boil for about 10 minutes. Reduce to a simmer. When ready to serve, remove from heat and very slowly swirl in the egg.

Serve garnished with the minced scallion tops.

Per Serving: 137 Calories; 4g Fat; 18g Protein; 4g Carbohydrate; 1g Dietary Fiber

Tofu Variation: Add 6 oz of diced tofu at the simmer
4g Net Carbs; 170 Calories; 6g Fat; 21g Protein; 5g Carbohydrate; 1g Dietary Fiber

Lime & Ginger Chicken Soup

This quick and easy soup explodes with flavor.

1		roasted chicken
1	Tbsp	butter --
1	Tbsp	ginger root -- grated
1	Tbsp	coriander -- ground
1/8	tsp	cayenne pepper
5	cups	chicken stock
		salt -- as needed
2	Tbsps	Nellie & Joe's Famous Key West Lime Juice
1/4	cup	cilantro -- fresh & chopped

Induction

4 Servings
2g Net Carbs

1. De-bone the roasted chicken and cut meat into small bite size pieces. (Reserve the bones and skin to make stock; see page 322).

2. In a soup pan, melt butter on medium heat. Add the garlic, coriander and cayenne and sauté for 1 minute. Add ginger and sauté 1 minute (careful not to burn). Add chicken stock, bring to a boil and add the chicken, then reduce heat and simmer for at least 10 minutes. Taste test and add salt if needed.

3. Just before serving, stir in the lime juice and cilantro.

Yields about 8 cups with 2 cups per serving

Per Serving: 261 Calories; 11g Fat; 33g Protein; 2g Carbs; trace Dietary Fiber

Broccoli & Turkey Soup

Broccoli & turkey are enhanced with fresh thyme and oregano.

1	lb	broccoli -- chopped
1	lb	cooked turkey -- diced
1/2		yellow onion -- minced
2	Tbsps	olive oil
4	cups	chicken stock -- or turkey stock
1	tsp	thyme -- 1/2 tsp if dried
1	tsp	oregano -- 1/2 tsp if dried
1/4	tsp	pepper
		salt -- as needed

Induction

4 Servings
3g Net Carbs

This is great for leftover roasted turkey, especially if you make your own stock first. But you can have your local deli cut turkey breast into 1/2 thick slices that you can then dice up for this soup. Fresh herbs are recommended.

1. In a large soup pot, heat the oil over medium-high heat and add the onions. Sauté for a minute or two until they start to become translucent. Add the broccoli and sauté for about 2 minutes more.

2. Add the stock and bring to a slow boil. If your herbs are dried, add them now. Cook for about 10 minutes

3. Add the turkey. If your herbs are fresh, then add them now. Cook for another 5 minutes. Serve.

Per Serving: 239 Calories; 9g Fat; 30g Protein; 6g Carbohydrate; 3g Dietary

Cream of Leek & Turnip Soup

This pureed soup is nothing short of awesome! It is so simple that it is elegant.

1	large	turnip -- or 2 small ones
1	large	leek -- or 2 small ones
2	Tbsps	butter
2	cups	water
1/2	cup	cream
1/2	tsp	salt
1/4	tsp	pepper

Induction
4 Servings
3g Net Carbs

I dedicate this soup to my friend Connie who simply loves turnips. I can't prepare them without thinking about her.

The biggest challenge for me with this soup is to keep my herb Goddess personae under control; for this soup is best made with pure water (not stock) and seasoned only with salt and pepper. The soup is very rich and filling so even though it yields only 3 cups, it can easily serve four people if used as a starter. It's great with a grilled steak and a simple green salad.

1. Cut off and discard the dark green portion of the leek and the root end. Slice the leek lengthwise and thoroughly rinse out all the sand and grit. Rough chop.

2. Trim off and discard the turnip stem and root end. Do not peel. Cut into cubes.

3. In a soup pot over medium-high heat, melt the butter, add the leeks, turnips, water and salt and pepper. Bring to a full boil. Then reduce heat to a simmer or gentle boil for about 25 minutes, until the turnips are fork tender. Stir occasionally.

   This soup is not finicky, slow it down, speed it up, whatever you like. If you want to cook super fast then cut the leeks and turnips into smaller pieces.

4. This soup is best pureed; so pass it through a blender or food processor in batches or use a hand held wand blender immersed right into the soup pot. Pour in the cream and stir. Taste test and add ONLY salt and pepper as needed. Trust me on this.

If you'd like to garnish it, I recommend just a tiny bit of fresh snipped chives or finely minced scallion greens.

Per Serving: 145 Calories; 13g Fat; 1g Protein; 4g Carbohydrate; 1g Dietary Fiber

Mint & Lemon Chicken Soup

Fresh mint adds an unusual twist to this zesty lemon chicken soup.

2	lbs	chicken breast, no skin, no bone
1	Tbsp	butter
1	stalk	celery
1/2	cup	onion
2	cloves	garlic -- smashed
6	cups	chicken stock
2	Tbsps	fresh parsley -- chopped
2	Tbsps	fresh mint leaves -- chopped
2	tsps	lemon zest
2	Tbsps	lemon juice
		salt and pepper -- to taste

Induction

4 Servings
3g Net Carbs

If you don't have fresh mint and parsley then don't bother making this soup. Dried herbs are not a good compromise here.

1. Cut the chicken into small bite sized pieces. Wash hands thoroughly.

2. Chop the celery and onion. You'll need about 4 sprigs each of mint and parsley. Remove the mint and parsley leaves from their stems. Chop the leaves and set aside. Optional: cut up the stems and put them in a tea ball or in cheese cloth as a bouquet garni.

3. Zest the lemon until you get about 2 tsp (or about ½ lemon worth). Juice the lemon to get about 2 Tbsp; remove seeds.

4. In a soup kettle over medium-high heat, add the butter, celery and onions. Sauté for about 2 minutes, then add the garlic stir for a few seconds then add the chicken pieces and cook for about 2 minutes stirring frequently. Add the chicken stock and lemon zest (and bouquet garni if using). Bring to a boil then reduce heat to a simmer and cook, covered for about 15 minutes.

5. Add the lemon juice, mint and parsley and cook for another 5 minutes uncovered (don't let it boil). Remove the bouquet garni (if using) before serving. Taste to see if it needs salt or pepper.

Per Serving: 342 Calories; 9g Fat; 52g Protein; 4g Carbohydrate; 1g Dietary Fiber

Southwestern Chicken Soup

This delicious soup can be prepared in under 30 minutes.
Adjust the spiciness with the type and amount of peppers chosen as described.

4		chicken breasts, no skin, no bones
1/2	Tbsp	butter
1/2	cup	onion -- diced
1	clove	garlic -- minced
1		zucchini -- cubed
5	cups	chicken stock
2	Tbsps	chipotle chile canned in adobo
1/4	cup	black olives -- canned
1/2	tsp	cumin
1/2	tsp	thyme
1/4	cup	cilantro leaves, whole
1	Tbsp	lime juice

Induction
4 Servings
3g Net Carbs

1. Remove the skin and bones from the chicken. Cut into bite sized pieces.

2. Rinse the chipotle peppers (unless you want your soup super hot). Alternatively, you can use mild green chili peppers or even a green bell pepper for no spicy heat at all. Dice the peppers.

3. In a large soup kettle over medium-high heat, add the butter and onions. Stir frequently. When the onions just begin to become translucent (about 2 minutes) add the minced garlic and the cubed zucchini. Stir frequently for about 1 minute.

4. Add the chicken stock, chicken pieces, chipotle peppers, black olives, cumin and thyme. Bring to a boil. Reduce heat to a simmer, cover and cook for 15 minutes.

5. Just before serving, add the cilantro leaves and the lime juice.

Consider any of the following garnishes, grated cheese (Monterey Jack, cheddar or pepper jack), grated jicama, diced avocado or minced scallions.

Per Serving: 208 Calories; 6g Fat; 29g Protein; 5g Carbohydrate; 2g Dietary Fiber

Pumpkin Coconut Soup

Pumpkin is not just for Thanksgiving. This unusual soup gives pumpkin
a twist with the lime and cilantro added.

15	ozs	canned pumpkin -- unsweetened
2	14 oz	canned coconut milk -- unsweetened
2	cups	chicken broth
1	Tbsp	shallot -- minced
1		lime -- zested and juiced
	pinch	salt
1	tsp	black pepper -- coarsely ground
1	cup	cilantro leaves, whole
2		scallions -- julienne

Weight Loss

8 Servings
7g Net Carbs

1. Zest the lime and then juice it into a soup kettle. Remove any seeds. Add the chicken broth and shallots and bring to a boil. Add the pumpkin and coconut milk and bring to a very slow boil. Taste test and add salt and pepper as desired. Cook for about 15 or 20 minutes at a slow boil or simmer.

2. The cilantro leaves can be left whole or given a course chop. The scallions should be thinly julienne. I like to first cut off the root end and any green tips that are a bit "off". Then I cut in half which basically give you a green end and a white end. The white end is easy to julienne cutting lengthwise 5 or 6 times. With the green end I like to cut thinly on a bias (about 15%).

3. When ready to serve, add the cilantro and cook another minute. Ladle into individual bowls and garnish with a bit of the julienne scallions.

Consider toasted coconut flakes as an alternative garnish.

Per Serving: 229 Calories; 22g Fat; 4g Protein; 9g Carbohydrate; 2g Dietary Fiber

Creamy Broccoli & Leek Soup

This delicious soup can be served chunky or pureed.

1	lb	broccoli -- chopped
2	cups	leeks, white portion only -- sliced
3	cups	chicken stock
1	tsp	dried oregano
1	oz	vermouth
1	cup	heavy cream
4	ozs	Swiss cheese -- grated
		salt and pepper -- to taste

Weight Loss

4 Servings
7g Net Carbs

1. Thoroughly rinse the leeks. Cut off the majority of the green tops. Slice leek lengthwise and rinse again to be sure all the sand is rinsed out from between the leaves. Slice thinly. Generally 1-2 leeks will yield the 2 cups.

2. Chop the broccoli fairly small if the soup is to be served chunky style.

3. In a soup pot over high heat, bring the chicken stock to a boil. Add the broccoli, leeks, oregano and vermouth. Once it returns to the boil for a full minute, reduce heat to a simmer and cook for 10 minutes.

4. Transfer about 1/2 of the vegetables to a food processor or blender and puree. (Or puree all of it). Return puree to the pot.

5. Add cream and stir in thoroughly. Taste and add salt and pepper as desired.

6. Ladle into individual soup bowls and garnish with an ounce of grated Swiss cheese on top of each. Serve at once.

Per Serving: 385 Calories; 30g Fat; 13g Protein; 10g Carbohydrate; 3g Fiber

Roasted Eggplant Soup

A thick and creamy soup bursting with robust flavors.

1	large	eggplant
2	Tbsps	olive oil
3		scallions
4	cloves	garlic -- minced
4	cups	chicken stock
1	Tbsp	dry sherry
1/2	tsp	each of thyme, oregano & rosemary
1/8	tsp	cayenne pepper
2/3	cup	heavy cream
1/2	cup	Romano cheese -- grated

Weight Loss
4 Servings
8g Net Carbs

Preheat oven to 375°F

1. Piece the skin of the eggplant in 6 to 10 places with a knife. This will prevent the eggplant from exploding. Place on a roasting pan. Place in a 375°F oven and roast for 30 minutes. Allow to cool. Once the eggplant is cool enough to handle, peel off and discard the skin. Chop the flesh and set aside.

2. Mince the scallions, keeping the white and green parts separate (the green part will be used as a garnish). Heat the oil in a soup pot over medium-high heat; add the onion and garlic. Cook for 1 minute. Add the chicken stock, sherry, thyme, oregano, rosemary and cayenne pepper. Bring to a boil for 15 minutes. Remove from heat.

3. Add the eggplant. Puree the soup by using a food processor or blender (in batches) or use a hand held blender. Reheat to just under a boil, add the cream and stir well. Taste test and add salt & pepper as desired.

Serve in individual bowls garnished with Romano cheese and the green mince onion tops.

Per Serving: 316 Calories; 26g Fat; 8g Protein; 11g Carbohydrate; 3g Dietary Fiber

Curried Zucchini Soup

This marvelous soup can be served hot or cold, smooth or chunky.
The curry flavor is very mild but add a bit more cream if you
would like it toned down even more.

4	cups	zucchini
1	Tbsp	canola oil
4		scallion -- minced
1	tsp	garlic -- minced
2	tsps	curry powder
3	cups	chicken stock
1/4	tsp	lemon extract (or 2 Tbsp of lemon juice)
1/2	cup	heavy cream
		salt and pepper -- to taste

Weight Loss

4 Servings
5g Net Carbs

You'll need to decide whether you want the soup to be pureed or chunky before you add the cream. I prefer to puree about 1/3 to 1/2 of the soup.

Small to "normal" sized zucchini are best in this soup. But if you have some over grown zukes in your garden, then they can be used also with a little bit of extra work. Just peel off some of the skin with a vegetable peeler. Remove the seeds. Slice or cube. If they are slightly bitter, then add 1 or 2 tsp of Splenda with the chicken stock. It is best to completely puree the soup when using the extra large zukes.

1. Cut off and discard the stem and blossom ends of the zucchini. The zukes can be cubed or sliced depending on how you'd like the final soup to look. If it will be completely pureed, then this does not matter of course.

2. Heat the oil in your soup pot over medium-high heat. Add the scallions, garlic and curry powder. Cook for about 1 minute, stir occasionally. Add the zucchini and stir to coat. Cook for 2 or 3 minutes, stir occasionally. Then add the chicken stock and the lemon extract. Bring to a boil then cover and reduce to a simmer. Cook for 15 - 20 minutes.

3. To puree, either use a hand held blender or use a food processor or regular blender. (The last two will need to be done in batches). I prefer to use a hand held blender directly in the soup pot for just a bit leaving plenty of chunks. However, if I plan to serve this cold then I completely puree all of the soup.

4. Add the cream to the soup and cook for about 3 minutes over medium heat. Taste test and add salt and pepper to your liking (it will probably need a bit of both).

Per Serving: 176 Calories; 15g Fat; 3g Protein; 7g Carbohydrate; 2g Dietary Fiber

Tomato Soup with Basil & Mint

Basil and mint add a new appeal to tomato soup. This soup is fine made
with canned tomatoes and dried herbs, but it is outstanding
when fresh plum tomatoes and fresh herbs are available!

2	lbs	plum tomatoes
1	cup	chicken stock
2	tsps	olive oil
1/2	cup	onion -- chopped
1	clove	garlic -- crushed
1	Tbsp	fresh basil -- chopped
1	Tbsp	fresh mint leaves -- chopped
1/2	cup	heavy whipping cream
		salt and pepper -- to taste
		bouquet garni (5 peppercorns, bay leaf and 2 whole cloves)

Weight Loss
6 Servings
6g Net Carbs

Make a bouquet garni by folding several layers of cheese cloth around your herbs
and tying it off with a string. Use peppercorns, bay leaf and whole cloves.

1. The tomatoes would traditionally be peeled and seeded. Feel free to do that.
   I prefer to leave the peel on (for the extra nutrients). Remove the stems and
   cut into halves. Squeeze each half over a bowl and most of the seeds will
   come out. Discard the seeds. Chop the tomatoes.

2. In a soup pot over high heat, add the chicken stock, tomatoes and bouquet
   garni. Bring to a boil and then reduce heat to a simmer. Cover and cook for
   20 minutes.

3. Meanwhile; sauté the onion and garlic in olive oil until tender. Add to the
   soup pot.

4. After the soup has cooked for 20 minutes, remove the bouquet garni and
   puree the soup with a hand mixer or by putting it through a food processor or
   blender. Return the soup to the soup pot.

5. Add the cream, mint and basil. Simmer for at least 5 minutes or up to 15
   minutes more.

Taste test and add salt and pepper as needed.

Per Serving: 121 Calories; 9g Fat; 2g Protein; 8g Carbohydrate; 2g Dietary Fiber

Slap Me Silly Chili

Wow!! A spicy low carb chili that is good enough to write home about.

1	lb	extra lean ground beef
6	ozs	chorizo
		(or other sausage meat)
1/2	cup	bell pepper -- diced
1/3	cup	yellow onion -- chopped
3	ozs	chipotle chile canned in adobo -- minced
2	Tbsps	chili powder
1	Tbsp	mustard
2	tsps	cumin
1	tsp	garlic powder
1	tsp	dried oregano
1/2	tsp	cinnamon
1/4	tsp	salt
1/4	tsp	cracked black pepper
1	cup	canned, diced tomatoes -- with juices
2/3	cup	Carb Options™ Barbeque Sauce

Weight Loss

6 Servings
6g Net Carbs

The heat in this chili is provided mostly by the chipotle chile peppers and their adobo sauce. About 1/2 can is all that I can handle in this recipe. This chili is at the limit of my heat tolerance; however I lean towards the whimpy side in these matters. If you want more kick after the chili is made, then simply add more of the chipotle. If you are heat sensitive perhaps add less. Also see milder variation below.

To cut the fat content in half, use ground buffalo meat instead of the beef. Using ground turkey will accomplish the same task but the flavor is just mediocre to me (so add 1 or 2 tsps of extra chili powder).

1. Chop chorizo sausage into small pieces. (If the chorizo has a casing, be sure to remove that first).

2. In a large heavy pot over medium-high heat, add the chorizo and ground beef, stir frequently to break-up the beef. Cook until the beef starts to brown (8-10 minutes) and gives off its fat. Pour off excess fat. (If you use the extra lean beef as recommended then you should not have much).

1. Add the onions, bell peppers and cook 2 minutes, stirring frequently.

2. Stir in the remaining ingredients (chipotle with its sauce, chili powder, mustard, garlic, cumin, oregano, cinnamon, salt, pepper, canned tomatoes with all of its juices and the barbecue sauce). Stir occasionally until it boils, then immediately reduce the heat, cover and simmer for 45 minutes. Check on it every 5-10 minutes with a thorough stir to redistribute heat and to make sure that it is not boiling.

3. If it gets too thick then add 1/2 cup of water or stock.

4. Serve at your convenience with any or all of the following garnishes (but careful: these carbs are not included in the analysis):

Cheddar cheese	fresh cilantro
Monterey Jack cheese	chopped scallions
sour cream	diced bell peppers
guacamole	salsa

Suggest serving with a simple salad with cool cucumbers.

Per Serving: 367 Calories; 27g Fat; 22g Protein; 9g Carbohydrate; 3g Dietary Fiber

Milder Variation: Omit the chipotle peppers and substitute 2 jalapeno peppers with the seeds removed. Remember that the larger the jalapeno the more mild the heat. For extra mild remove the membrane from the jalapeno as well. Mince the jalapeno and add with the onions and bell peppers.

Beef Stew with Herbs de Provence

A hearty stew, perfect for a cold winter day.

2	lbs	rump roast, trimmed
2	Tbsps	olive oil
1	cup	celery -- chopped
1/2	cup	yellow onion -- chopped
2	cloves	garlic -- minced
3/4	cup	dry red wine
3	cups	beef broth -- low salt
2	Tbsps	Carb Options™ Ketchup
1	Tbsp	herbs de Provence
2	tsps	Worcestershire sauce
1/4	tsp	ground pepper

Weight Loss

4 Servings
5g Net Carbs

If you do not have herbs de Provence then see page 53 and improvise with the herbs listed there.

1. Trim and cut beef into bite sized pieces.

2. Heat the oil in a pot over medium-high heat. Brown the beef cubes in batches making sure they are not crowded. Using tongs or a slotted spoon, remove each batch to a bowl.

3. Add to the pot, the celery and onions. Sauté for 1 minute stirring frequently. Add the garlic and cook another 30 seconds or so. Add the red wine, broth, ketchup, herbs, Worcestershire and pepper. Bring to a boil and scrape up any brown bits that might be stuck to the pot. Boil for about 2-3 minutes, reducing the liquids. Stir occasionally.

4. Add the meat and reduce heat to simmer. Cover and simmer for 30 minutes.

Per Serving: 462 Calories; 18g Fat; 59g Protein; 6g Carbohydrate; 1g Dietary Fiber

Hungarian Goulash

This is not the traditional goulash which is a stew meat that has been cooked for hours. This one can be on the table in about 30 minutes because it calls for a good quality cut of beef.

3	lbs	beef top sirloin
6	oz	mushroom -- thinly sliced
1/4	small	onion -- thinly sliced
1/2		red bell pepper -- chopped
2	Tbsps	paprika -- Hungarian
1/2	cup	beef stock -- low salt
1	cup	sour cream
		salt & pepper -- to taste
2	Tbsps	parsley -- chopped

Weight Loss

6 Servings
4g Net Carbs

This stew has very little broth. It is thick enough to eat with a fork and can easily be served as the main entrée. Add more beef stock if you prefer.

1. Steaks should be about 1 inch think. Cut into strips about 1/4 inch thick, by cutting across the grain.

2. Place a non-stick skillet on medium-high heat. (If not non-stick then add a dab of butter). When hot, add the meat and stir fry until browned. Don't crowd the meat, so you will probably need to do a few batches. Each will take about 3 minutes. Transfer beef to a bowl, leaving the fat in the skillet.

3. Add the mushrooms to the skillet and stir fry until browned (about 3 more minutes). Transfer mushrooms to the bowl with the beef.

4. Add the onions to the skillet and stir fry until lightly brown (about 2 minutes). Add red bell peppers and stir.

5. Reduce heat to medium, add the paprika to the onions & peppers and stir.

6. Add the stock and bring to a boil, then reduce to a simmer and return the beef and mushrooms to the skillet, plus any accumulated juices. Stir occasionally cooking for 10 minutes.

7. Add the sour cream, stir until well mixed and then remove from heat.

8. Transfer to a serving bowl (or individual soup bowls) and garnish with the chopped parsley. Serve.

Per Serving: 570 Calories; 41g Fat; 44g Protein; 5g Carbohydrate; 1g Dietary Fiber

Tex-Mex Beef Stew

Barbeque sauce and cumin pair up in this hearty stew
to create that southwestern Texas flavor.

1	lb	beef top sirloin steaks -- boneless
1	Tbsp	canola oil
2	cups	beef broth – low salt
1/2	cup	salsa
3	Tbsp	Carb Options™ Barbeque Sauce
2		zucchini -- cubed
1		red bell pepper -- sliced
1	tsp	ground cumin
1/2	tsp	chili powder
1	tsp	guar gum
4	Tbsps	sour cream
4	Tbsps	fresh cilantro -- chopped

```
+----------------------+
|     Weight Loss      |
+----------------------+
| 4 Servings           |
| 7g Net Carbs         |
+----------------------+
```

1. Trim off any excess fat from the steaks. Slice into 1/2" thick strips. In a skillet, heat oil over medium-high heat, and add about half the beef and stir fry for 2 minutes. Remove from pan; set aside. Repeat with the other half of the beef.

2. In the same skillet, add the broth, salsa, zucchini, bell pepper, cumin and chili powder. Bring to a boil; reduce heat to medium-low and simmer for about 3 minutes.

3. Remove about ½ cup of liquids from the skillet and mix with the guar gum. Stir vigorously until completely dissolved and then add to the skillet. Stirring well to be sure that it does not form lumps.

4. Return beef to pan for about 1 minute to reheat. Then serve immediately.

Serve immediately topped with sour cream and chopped cilantro.

Per Serving: 356 Calories; 23g Fat; 29g Protein; 10g Carbs; 3g Dietary Fiber

Vietnamese Soup

Intensely flavorful, clear broth soup with beef, cabbage and bean sprouts.

3	lbs	beef shank -- with bone
1	lb	beef bones -- optional
6	quarts	water
1	whole	shallot
1	piece	ginger -- about 3 inches
3	pieces	star anise
1		cinnamon stick
1	can	bean sprouts – drained and rinsed
1	cup	Chinese cabbage -- finely shredded
2		scallions -- minced
1	cup	cilantro leaves, whole -- coarsely chopped
1	whole	lime -- cut into 6 wedges

Weight Loss

6 Servings
5g Net Carbs

1. Add beef shanks and beef bones to cold water in a large stock pot then put it on high heat. Bring to a boil. Skim off and discard any froth that may rise to the surface. Continue boiling (and skimming as needed) for about 20 minutes.

2. Meanwhile; peel and thinly slice the shallots and the ginger.

3. Reduce heat to a very slow boil. Add ginger, shallots, anise and the cinnamon stick. Cover pot and boil very gently for about 2 hours or until meat is easily removed from the bones.

4. Removes the bones and meat from the pot and set aside to cool for a few minutes. Remove and discard the cinnamon and star anise.

5. Once the beef is cool enough to handle, pick the meat from the bones and shred into small pieces. Discard the bones. Return the meat to the stock. Reduce heat to a simmer until ready to serve.

6. Just before serving, add the bean sprouts, cabbage, and scallions. Stir and heat until cabbage just wilts (about 1 or 2 minutes). Immediately remove from heat.

7. Ladled the soup into 6 bowls. Sprinkle the cilantro on top and serve with a wedge of lime.

Per Serving: 299 Calories; 16g Fat; 32g Protein; 7g Carbohydrate; 2g Dietary Fiber

Moroccan Stew

This Moroccan lamb stew is good any time of year, but is particularly hearty for a cold winter night. If you don't care for lamb then try using beef. It's just as good but a different flavor.

3	lbs	lamb shoulder -- stew meat
1		lemon
1	Tbsp	apple cider vinegar
4	cloves	garlic -- minced
1½	tsps	cumin
1	tsp	salt
1/2	tsp	cinnamon
1/2	tsp	ginger
1/2	tsp	turmeric
1/2	cup	cilantro leaves -- minced
2	Tbsps	mint leaves -- minced
1	cup	chicken stock -- or water
12	ozs	canned, diced tomatoes
1		yellow onion -- chopped

> **Weight Loss**
>
> 6 Servings
> 6g Net Carbs

1. Cut the lamb into bite sized cubes. Trim away any gristle from the meat.

2. Zest the lemon and then squeeze all the juice out into a large re-sealable bag. Remove any seeds. Add the zest, vinegar, minced garlic, cumin, salt, cinnamon, ginger and turmeric. Shake to blend. Add the minced cilantro and mint leaves and the lamb. Seal and toss/shake until everything is well coated. Squeeze out the excess air, reseal and refrigerate over night.

3. In a heavy soup kettle over high heat, add the chicken stock (or water), canned tomatoes with their juice and the chopped onions. Bring to a boil. Add the lamb and all the marinade that you can scrape out of the bag. Return to the boil then reduce heat to a simmer. Cover and simmer for about 1½ hours until the meat is very tender. Stir occasionally.

Serve hot.

Per Serving: 505 Calories; 39g Fat; 31g Protein; 7g Carbohydrate; 1g Dietary Fiber

Barbados Stew

Stewed chicken in a lemon, curry, coconut broth.

3	lbs	cut–up chicken -- no skin
2	Tbsps	butter
2	cups	cabbage -- finely shredded
3		scallions -- minced
2	Tbsps	curry powder
1	tsp	lemon pepper
14	ozs	coconut milk
3	cups	chicken stock
1	tsp	guar gum
3	Tbsps	lemon juice
2	tsps	lemon zest
2	Tbsps	lime juice
1	tsp	lime zest
4	slices	lime -- as a garnish
		salt and pepper -- to taste

Weight Loss
4 Servings
9g Net Carbs

Use any cut of chicken that you prefer, just remove the skin. This is best with the chicken left on the bone but these are pretty big pieces for a stew. I once asked the butcher to remove the back bone and then cut a whole chicken into a dozen pieces for me. He looked at me weird, but he did it. It was prefect for this recipe. If you use boneless chicken, reduce the simmer time in step 2 to about 20 minutes.

1. Give the cabbage a fine shred and mince the scallions.

2. In a soup pot, melt the butter over medium heat. Add the cabbage and sauté until it starts to turn a little bit brown (3-5 minutes). Add the scallions, curry powder, and lemon pepper. Mix well sautéing for another minute. Add the coconut milk and the chicken stock. Bring to a boil. Add the chicken and bring to a boil again. Then reduce heat, cover and simmer for 45 minutes to an hour. Check on it occasionally with a good stir and make sure it is not boiling.

    I like to stir enough towards the end to knock the meat off the bones (a fork helps) and then fish out the bones before serving (but that's just me). You can also serve it with the bones and provide a fork, soup spoon and a pile of damp towels, so you and your guests can get your fingers into it as you lick the juices off the bone (so much fun). Provide an extra bowl to dispose of the chicken bones.

3. Meanwhile, prepare the lemon & limes. You'll need 1 lemon and 2 limes for this recipe. Zest the lemon and just one of the limes and put the zest in a small bowl and set it aside to garnish at the end. Juice the zested lemon and lime into a small bowl and set aside. From the second lime, cut off 4 slices and set aside, as garnish.

4. Once the stew has finished cooking it is time to thicken it. Ladle 1 cup of the soup stock into a bowl, add the guar gum whisking vigorously. Then pour this back into the soup pot. This stew can sit at a simmer until you are ready to serve.

5. Just before serving, stir in the lemon/lime juice. Ladle the stew into individual bowls and garnish with a slice of lime and a sprinkle of zest.

Per Serving: 498 Calories; 37g Fat; 31g Protein; 14g Carbs; 5g Dietary Fiber

I love the Caribbean! It is my favorite vacation destination! I often dream about the warm turquoise waters, the incredible coral reefs, the fantastically joyful people and the diversity of culinary delights. The food in the Caribbean is amazingly eclectic with influences from Africa, Portugal, Spain, France, Holland, South America and India. There is something in the Caribbean for everyone – if you just know where to look!

While in Barbados one year; I stayed at a resort where every night they served a stew similar to this one. It typically had some type of white fish, occasionally it had chicken and one night it was made with lobster! I couldn't get enough of it. My journal talks about that stew more than the beach! This is my best shot at recreating it in a low carb fashion.

Theirs was probably made with lemon grass and with the citrus fruit which they call lemon – however it looks and tastes much more like key limes. They probably also used regular onions instead of the scallions and no doubt some type of flour or corn starch as a thickener.

Yucatan Chicken Soup

Diced avocado is the crown jewel for this scrumptious Mexican soup.

4		chicken breasts, no skin, no bone
2	Tbsps	canola oil
1	tsp	cumin
1	tsp	paprika
1/2	tsp	oregano
1/4	tsp	cinnamon
1/4	tsp	salt
1/4	tsp	black pepper
1		jalapeno chile pepper -- seeded and minced
1/2	cup	onion -- chopped
2	cloves	garlic -- minced
1/2	cup	tomato -- seeded and chopped
4	cups	chicken stock
3	Tbsps	lime juice
1/4	cup	cilantro leaves, whole -- chopped
1		avocado – diced, as the garnish

Weight Loss

4 Servings
8g Net Carbs

1. In a bowl, add the cumin, paprika, oregano, cinnamon, salt and pepper.

2. Rinse the chicken and pat dry. Cut into cubes. Add to the spices and toss. Set aside. Wash hands thoroughly.

3. Remove and discard seeds from the jalapeno (unless you prefer things super hot) and mince the pepper. Chop the onion.

4. Crush and mince the garlic. Cut the tomato in half and squeeze to release and discard seeds. Chop the tomato.

5. In a soup kettle over medium high heat, add the oil. Once hot add the onions and jalapeno peppers. Stir and cook for about 1 minute. Add the chicken. Stir and cook for about 2 minutes. Add the garlic and tomato. Stir and cook for about 1 minute. Add the stock and 2 Tbsps of the lime juice reserving 1 tablespoon for below). After it comes to a boil, reduce to a simmer and cook for 15 minutes.

6. Meanwhile, chop the cilantro. To dice the avocado, cut in half and remove the seed. With a knife score the avocado down to the peel, both lengthwise and crosswise. Turn the peel inside out and cut off the flesh into a small bowl with the remaining lime juice.

7. When the soup is done, remove it from the heat and stir in the cilantro while the soup is still very hot. Ladle the soup into 4 bowls and spoon 1/4 of the avocado into each bowl. Serve immediately.

Per Serving: 326 Calories; 18g Fat; 29g Protein; 10g Carbs; 2g Dietary Fiber

Crab Soup

This crab soup has an interesting blend of flavors highlighted by the low carb beer, diced turnips and Old Bay seasoning. A great yet unusual combo.

3/4	lb	lump crabmeat
1	Tbsp	butter
1		turnip -- diced
2	stalks	celery -- chopped
3		scallion -- minced
1		Aspen Edge low carb beer
2	cups	water
1	cup	tomatoes, canned -- diced
1	tsp	Old Bay Seafood seasoning
1/4	tsp	lemon pepper
1/4	tsp	salt

Weight Loss
4 Servings
5g Net Carbs

1. In a soup pot over medium-high heat, melt the butter and add the turnips. Sauté for about 2 minutes, then add the celery and sauté for 1 minute and add the scallions and sauté for another minute.

2. Then add the beer, water, tomatoes (with their juices), Old Bay, lemon pepper and salt. Bring to a boil and then reduce heat and simmer for 15 minutes. Stir well.

3. Just before serving, add the crabmeat and simmer another 2 minutes. Stir gently; you don't want to break up the crabmeat too much.

Per Serving: 150 Calories; 4g Fat; 17g Protein; 7g Carbohydrate; 2g Dietary Fiber

Induction Variation: Omit the turnip and reduce tomatoes to 1/2 cup. Add 1-2 tsp horseradish, before adding the crabmeat.
3g Net Carbs; 138 Calories; 4g Fat; 16g Protein; 4g Carbohydrate; 1g Dietary Fiber

Lobster Bisque

Pureed lobster bisque beautifully served with
a slice of lemon and fresh snipped chives.

1/2	lb	cooked lobster meat -- diced
1	Tbsp	butter
1		shallot -- minced
1	stalk	celery -- minced
2	cups	chicken stock
1	cup	canned, diced tomatoes
2	Tbsps	dry sherry
1/4	tsp	thyme
1/4	tsp	paprika
1	cup	heavy cream
4		egg yolk
4		lemon slices
1	Tbsp	fresh chives -- snipped

Weight Loss
4 Servings
6g Net Carbs

1. In a soup pot over medium heat, sauté the shallots and celery in the butter for about 2 minutes stirring frequently (do not brown them). And the chicken stock, tomato with its juices, sherry, thyme and paprika. Add 1/3 lb of the lobster (reserving the remainder for a garnish). Bring to a slow boil and cook for 5 minutes.

2. Puree the soup in batches using a blender, food processor or hand blender until completely smooth. Return to soup pot.

3. Beat together the egg yolks and then add the cream and beat again. Add about 1/2 cup of the puree to the egg and cream and mix well. Slowly add this mixture to the pot, stirring constantly until it thickens. Taste test and add salt or pepper as desired.

4. Pour into individual bowls, garnish with a thin slice of lemon floating in the center. Mince the remaining lobster and sprinkle it and the chives around the lemon slice. Serve at once.

Per Serving: 382 Calories; 31g Fat; 17g Protein; 7g Carbohydrate; 1g Dietary Fiber

Borscht

This Russian beet soup is excellent completely pureed.
But for a bit more rustic effect leave it a bit chunky.

3	cups	chicken stock
1/4	cup	apple cider vinegar
1	Tbsp	Worcestershire sauce
2	lbs	beets -- scrubbed and cubed
2	Tbsps	olive oil
1/2	cup	yellow onion -- sliced thin
1	stalk	celery -- chopped
1	cup	cabbage -- shredded
1	tsp	thyme
1/2	tsp	salt
1/4	tsp	pepper
1/4	cup	sour cream -- as garnish
1	Tbsp	fresh chives -- snipped

Maintenance

4 Servings
16g Net Carbs

You can peel the beets if you desire, but you'll be throwing out some nutrients. I just scrub them well and then cut into cubes (about the size of a grape). The juice may stain your cutting board so use that small spare one that you take on camping trips. I suppose you could make this with canned beets (although I've never tried it that way. I'd think you would want to add them with the stock and not sauté them with the other veggies.) Save the beets greens to serve as a side dish.

1. In a soup pot over medium-high heat, add the olive oil, beets, sliced onion, and the chopped celery. Sauté for 3 minutes. Add the cabbage and sauté another 3 minutes. (Yes, everything is supposed to turn that color. Isn't it lovely!)

2. Add the stock, vinegar, thyme and salt and pepper. Bring to a boil and then reduce heat, cover and simmer for 20 minutes. Stir occasionally.

3. Your can puree all of the stew if you like but I generally only do about 1/2 of it, especially if this is the main course. You can use a food processor, blender or a hand held blender wand. Taste test and add salt or pepper as needed.

Serve garnished with a dollop over sour cream and snipped fresh chives.

Per Serving: 194 Calories; 10g Fat; 4g Protein; 21g Carbohydrate; 5g Dietary Fiber

One day I was making this for a small dinner party when one of my friends arrived with 2 unexpected guests. I had some left over grilled steak in the refrigerator which I diced and added at the end just to heat through. It was a big hit! So feel free to add some left over beef, if you are so inclined.

Carrot Basil Soup

Beautiful, flavorful and nutritious! This soup always grabs people's attention.

6	large	carrots -- chopped
1	cup	onion slices -- chopped
2	cloves	garlic -- minced
4	cups	chicken broth
1/4	tsp	lemon pepper
1/2	cup	heavy cream
3	Tbsps	fresh basil leaves -- minced
		salt and pepper -- to taste

Maintenance
4 Servings
14g Net Carbs

Garnishes

4	Tbsps	sour cream -- optional
4	Tbsps	pine nuts -- toasted
1	Tbsp	fresh basil leaves -- julienne

1. To julienne basil leaves; stack them on top of each other and roll the up lengthwise. Slice finely. Set aside.

2. In a soup pot, melt the butter over medium heat and sauté the onions for 3 minutes. Add the garlic and sauté another minute.

3. Add the broth, carrots and lemon pepper. Bring to a boil and then reduce heat and simmer for about 30 minutes, until carrots are very tender.

4. Puree the soup in batches using a food processor or blender. Or use a hand held wand blender immersed directly into the soup.

5. Return the soup to the pot, add the cream and 3 Tbsps of minced basil. Cook for 5 minutes. Taste test and add salt and pepper as needed.

6. Ladle soup into 4 bowls. Garnish each with 1 Tbsp of sour cream, 1 Tbsp of toasted pine nuts and a pinch of julienne basil.

Per Serving: 281 Calories; 20g Fat; 10g Protein; 18g Carbohydrate; 4g Fiber

Beef & Barley Stew

This hearty stew is a welcomed addition to have occasionally on the low carb maintenance plan.

2	lbs	beef round -- or shoulder
		salt and pepper
1	Tbsp	butter
6	cups	beef broth
2	Tbsps	Worcestershire sauce
1/2		yellow onion -- diced
1/3	cup	barley
2	stalks	celery -- diced
1		turnip -- diced
1/2	lb	mushroom -- diced
1	tsp	thyme
1	tsp	rosemary
1		bay leaf
1/4	tsp	celery seed

Maintenance
4 Servings
24g Net Carbs

1. Cut the beef into bite sized cubes. Season with salt and pepper.

2. In a large soup pot, melt the butter over medium-high heat. In batches sear the beef on all sides until browned (about 5 minutes per batch). Remove each batch to another bowl while cooking the other batches. After the last batch add the onion and cook until it starts to brown.

3. Then add the stock, Worcestershire sauce and the beef (with any juices that may have gathered in the bottom of the bowl). Bring to a boil. Reduce heat to a low simmer and cook for 1 hour with the lid balanced to the side. Stir occasionally and be sure it is not boiling again.

4. Meanwhile; dice the celery, turnips, and mushrooms.

5. After 1 hour, add the barley, celery, turnips, mushroom and the herbs. Stir well and cook 35-45 minutes, until the barley is tender. Remove bay leaf. Taste and adjust seasoning as desired. Add more stock if needed.

Serve at your leisure.

Per Serving: 552 Calories; 20g Fat; 62g Protein; 31g Carbohydrate; 7g Fiber

I generally serve this as a main course all by itself. But if served with a salad then reduce portions to make 6 servings.

16g Net Carbs; 368 Calories; 13g Fat; 41g Protein; 21g Carbohydrate; 5g Dietary Fiber;

Ham & Lentil Soup

This hearty soup adds occasional variety to your low carb maintenance lifestyle. It is an outstanding source of fiber with 16 grams per serving (that's 1/2 of the daily recommended amount)!

1	cup	lentils
4	cups	water -- or stock
2	cloves	garlic -- smashed
1	tsp	dried oregano
1/4	tsp	cumin
1		bay leaf
2	Tbsps	butter
2	cups	celery -- chopped
1/2	cup	onion -- minced
2	cups	ham, fully cooked -- diced
		salt and pepper -- to taste

```
+------------------------+
|     Maintenance        |
+------------------------+
| 4 Servings             |
| 17g Net Carbs          |
+------------------------+
```

1. In a soup pot, add the lentils, water (or stock), garlic, oregano, cumin and bay leaf. Bring to a boil and then cover and reduce to a simmer for 1 hour. Remove bay leaf.

2. Meanwhile; in a fry pan, melt the butter over medium heat. Add the onions and celery and sauté for about 5 minutes. Add to the lentils (within the first 15 minutes of their cooking time).

3. Add the ham to the lentils. Cover and simmer for about 15-20 minutes until heated through. Stir occasionally in a gentle manner. Taste and add salt and pepper as desired.

Per Serving: 445 Calories; 19g Fat; 35g Protein; 33g Carbohydrate; 16g Fiber

DRESSINGS, JAMS
SAUCES & SUCH

DRESSINGS, JAMS, SAUCES & SUCH

Note: Since condiments typically accompany other dishes and are not generally served on their, I could not reasonably classify them as Induction, Weight Loss or Maintenance. So instead they have been organized by type of condiment.

Note: EVOO = extra virgin olive oil

Balsamic Vinaigrette

This simple dressing made with balsamic vinegar
can be tailored to match your entree.

1/4	cup	unrefined walnut oil – or EVOO
2	Tbsps	balsamic vinegar
1/4	tsp	herbs

**2 Servings
1g Net Carbs**

Choose herbs/spices that are being used in your entree. Perhaps cumin & garlic for southwestern; oregano & garlic for Italian; thyme or tarragon for French; etc.

As a generic dressing I use about 1/8 tsp of garlic powder and a pinch each of salt and fresh ground pepper.

- Add the vinegar, oil and herbs in a small jar and shake well. It is best if this can be made an hour or so ahead of time.

I much prefer the taste of walnut oil (unrefined if you can find it) over extra virgin olive oil. I also enjoy knowing that I am getting a significant amount of omega 3 essential fatty acid. But substitute extra virgin olive oil if you prefer the taste (or the price).

Yields 1/3 cup; enough for 2 large salads

Per Serving: 243 Calories; 27g Fat; 0g Protein; 1g Carbohydrate; 0g Dietary Fiber

Dijon Garlic Vinaigrette

Blanching the garlic first makes a much smoother flavor.

1/2	cup	extra virgin olive oil
2	Tbsps	white wine vinegar
3	cloves	garlic
2	tsps	Dijon mustard
	pinch	salt
	pinch	black pepper

**5 Servings
1g Net Carbs**

1. With the skin still on the garlic cloves, drop them into a small pan of boiling water and cook for 5-6 minutes. Drain and let cool for a minute.

2. Remove the skins (if they are still on) and smash the garlic in a small bowl making a paste.

3. Add the mustard, vinegar and a pinch of salt and pepper. Blend well. Whisk in the olive oil.

Yields about 2/3 cup with 2 Tbsps per serving

Per Serving: 196 Calories; 22g Fat; trace Protein; 1g Carbs; trace Dietary Fiber

Greek Vinaigrette

A classic salad dressing from the Greek Isles.

3	Tbsp	lemon juice -- about 1 lemon worth
1	Tbsp	water
3	Tbsps	feta cheese
1	Tbsp	fresh oregano -- 1/2 t if dried
1/4	tsp	garlic powder
	dash	salt and pepper
1/2	cup	extra virgin olive oil

> **4 Servings**
> **1g Net Carbs**

In food processor, add the lemon juice, water, feta cheese, garlic, oregano and a dash of salt and pepper each. Pulse a few times; scrape down the sides. With the motor running, slowly add the olive oil.

Makes about 1 cup each serving is a generous 1/4 cup (4 Tbsps).

Per Serving: 262 Calories; 29g Fat; 1g Protein; 1g Carbs; trace Dietary Fiber

Raspberry Vinaigrette

Fresh raspberries contribute tremendous flavor to this salad dressing.

1/3	cup	raspberries
1/3	cup	red wine vinegar
1	Tbsp	balsamic vinegar
1/4	tsp	thyme
	pinch	salt and pepper
2/3	cup	unrefined walnut oil -- or EVOO
1	clove	garlic -- cut in half

> **5 Servings**
> **1g Net Carbs**

1. In a bowl, smear the garlic halves on the bottom and side of the bowl to release just a touch of its oil and flavor. Discard the garlic (or reserve it for some other recipe).

2. Add the raspberries and the vinegars to the bowl. Smash together. You can strain the seed out if you desire.

3. Add the thyme, salt and peppers. While whisking vigorously, add a little of the walnut oil at a time.

You can use extra virgin olive oil (EVOO) if you prefer.

Makes about 1¼ cups with 4 Tbsps per serving

Per Serving: 264 Calories; 29g Fat; trace Protein; 2g Carbs; 1g Dietary Fiber

Tarragon Vinaigrette

This is a classic yet simple French salad dressing

1/4	cup	extra virgin olive oil
2	Tbsps	tarragon vinegar
2	tsps	fresh tarragon -- chopped
1	tsp	Dijon mustard
1	pinch	salt and pepper

2 Servings
1g Net Carbs

Mix together the olive oil, vinegar, mustard, tarragon and the salt & pepper. Set aside for at least 15 minutes to allow the flavors to meld. I usually put the dressing ingredients in a jar and shake it to mix.

Makes just under 1/2 cup; enough for 2 large salads

Per Serving: 243 Calories; 27g Fat; trace Protein; 1g Carbohydrate; trace Dietary Fiber

Spicy Citrus Vinaigrette

This is great over a salad but it is also outstanding as a marinade or basting sauce for grilled chicken or fish.

2	Tbsps	balsamic vinegar
1	Tbsp	lemon juice
1	Tbsp	lime juice
1/2	tsp	lemon pepper
1/4	tsp	orange extract
1/4	tsp	cumin
1/4	tsp	chili powder
1/4	tsp	ground allspice
	pinch	salt
1/4	cup	canola oil

4 Servings
2g Net Carbs

1. In a small non-metallic bowl, add the vinegar, lemon juice, lime juice, lemon pepper, orange extract, cumin, chili powder, allspice and a pinch of salt. Let sit for about 5 or 10 minutes.

2. Vigorously whisk the vinaigrette while you (or a helper) slowly add the canola oil.

Makes slightly over 1/2 cup with 2 Tbsps per serving

Per Serving: 126 Calories; 14g Fat; trace Protein; 2g Carbohydrate; trace Dietary

Sesame Dressing

Sesame oil and tahini are the stars of this salad dressing

1/4	cup	sesame oil
2	Tbsps	white wine vinegar
1	Tbsp	tahini
1	Tbsp	soy sauce
1/2	tsp	Splenda®
1/4	tsp	garlic powder
1/8	tsp	ground ginger
1/8	tsp	pepper

2 Servings
3g Net Carbs

Tahini is sesame seed butter. Look for products that do not include sugar.

- In a jar with a tight fitting lid, add all the dressing ingredients and shake well. Set aside for about 30 minutes, so the flavors can meld.

Makes about 1/2 cup with 4 Tbsps per serving

Per Serving: 294 Calories; 31g Fat; 2g Protein; 4g Carbs; 1g Dietary Fiber

Thousand Island Dressing

Low Carb Thousand Island style dressing; serve it over salads or vegetables.

1	cup	mayonnaise
4	Tbsps	Carb Options™ Ketchup
2	Tbsps	dill pickles -- relish
2	tsps	brown mustard
1	tsp	Worcestershire sauce
1	Tbsp	water

6 Servings
1g Net Carbs

Put the mayonnaise, ketchup, relish, mustard, Worcestershire and water in a jar with a well sealing lid. Shake well.

Makes 1½ cups with 4 Tbsp per serving

Per Serving: 269 Calories; 31g Fat; 1g Protein; 1g Carbs; trace Dietary Fiber

Tahini Dressing or Sauce

Lime juice and fresh ginger make this perfect as a dressing for your Asian salads and it is a great sauce poured over veggies, fish or chicken.

2	Tbsp	tahini
1	Tbsps	soy sauce
1	Tbsp	lime juice
1	Tbsp	water
1	tsp	Splenda®
1	tsp	fresh ginger -- grated

2 Servings
3g Net Carbs

- Finely grate the fresh ginger root (if using dried ground ginger then use 1/4 tsp). In a small bowl add the soy sauce and whisk in the tahini until well combined. Add the lime juice, ginger and Splenda. Whisk well.

Makes 1/4 cup with 2 Tablespoons per serving

Per Serving: 97 Calories; 8g Fat; 3g Protein; 5g Carbohydrate; 2g Dietary Fiber

As a Dipping Sauce: This makes a great dipping sauce for fresh cut veggies. Make a double batch and eliminate the water.
7g Net Carbs; 194 Calories; 16g Fat; 6g Protein; 10g Carbohydrate; 3g Dietary Fiber

Creamy Avocado Dipping Sauce or Dressing

This is not guacamole but it is an equally good dipping sauce, stretching an avocado a little bit further. It can also be made into an outstanding southwestern salad dressing.

1		avocado
1/2	cup	sour cream
1	tsp	lemon juice
1/4	tsp	chili powder
1/4	tsp	garlic powder
		salt and pepper -- to taste

4 Servings
4g Net Carbs

- Thoroughly mash the avocado with the lemon juice. Then add the sour cream, chili powder and garlic powder. Taste and adjust seasoning as desired.

This is a good consistency for a dipping sauce (pork rinds are great with this, as are sliced veggies).

Yields about 1 cup with a generous 1/4 cup per serving

Per Serving: 144 Calories; 14g Fat; 2g Protein; 5g Carbohydrate; 1g Dietary Fiber

For a Salad Dressing: Add 2 Tbsp Carb Countdown™ milk (2%)
4g Net Carbs; 147 Calories; 14g Fat; 2g Protein; 5g Carbohydrate; 1g Dietary Fiber

Chipolte Dipping Sauce

Great for a party dip or put it on chicken or steaks

1/2	cup	mayonnaise
1/2	cup	sour cream
3		chipotle chile canned in adobo
	pinch	salt

4 Servings
1g Net Carbs

- To make the chipotle sauce you can either; mince the chilies (with a bit of the sauce from the can) and stir it into the mayo and sour cream; or you can put all 3 ingredients in a food processor or blender.

- Taste before you add the salt for it might not need it depending on your brand of Chipotle.

If it is too spicy (wait for the heat, it is slow to arrive) then simply add more mayo or sour cream. If the heat is right but the sauce is too thick then add a bit of water. Of course if you want more heat then add more chipotle (only 0.5g net carbs per Tbsp).

Makes about 1 cup with 4 Tbsps per serving

Per Serving: 260 Calories; 29g Fat; 2g Protein; 1g Carbs; 1g Fiber

Bearnaise Sauce

This blender version is much easier than the old fashion double boiler method. Two versions: one if you have tarragon vinegar and the second if you do not.

1/4	cup	tarragon vinegar
1	tsp	fresh tarragon – 1/2 tsp if dried
1/2	tsp	lemon pepper
	pinch	paprika
3		egg yolks
1	tsp	shallots -- minced
1	tsp	Dijon mustard
3/4	cup	butter -- melted
		salt -- if needed

4 Servings
2g Net Carbs

1. In a sauce pan, add the tarragon vinegar, tarragon, lemon pepper and the pinch of paprika. Boil it down until it reduces to about 2 Tbsps. Set aside and let cool to room temp. Then strain into a cup.

2. In a microwave safe bowl, add the butter and zap until completely melted.

3. In the blender, put the egg yolks, minced shallots, mustard and pulse a few times. Scrape down the sides. With the blender on lowest speed, very slowly pour in the melted butter. Continue to blend for about 30 seconds to 1 minute allowing the butter to cook the egg yolk. Then pour in the vinegar mixture. Taste and add salt if needed.

4. Place in a ceramic container in a warm oven until ready to use.

If you do not have tarragon vinegar, then you can use white wine vinegar (or apple cider vinegar or if you must, distilled vinegar). Triple the amount of tarragon and add a whole clove (or a dash of ground cloves). Then follow the above directions.

Makes about 1 cup with 1/4 cup (4 Tbsps) per serving

Per Serving: 354 Calories; 38g Fat; 3g Protein; 2g Carbs; trace Dietary Fiber

Lemon Beurre Blanc

A classic French butter sauce has been jazzed up
with a bit more lemon. It is great on fish, poultry or veggies.

1/2	cup	white wine
1/2	cup	white wine vinegar
1	Tbsp	shallot
2	Tbsps	heavy cream
1	cup	butter
3	Tbsps	lemon juice

5 Servings
3g Net Carbs

1. In a sauce pan over medium-high heat, boil the wine, vinegar and shallots until it reduce to about 2-3 Tbsps (15 or 20 minutes).

2. Set heat to lowest setting and whisk in the cream. Then add about 3 Tbsps of the butter at a time, whisking thoroughly (do not let it boil). Whisk in the lemon juice and serve immediately.

Makes 1¼ cup of sauce with 1/4 cup per serving (4 tbsp)

Per Serving: 369 Calories; 39g Fat; 1g Protein; 3g Carbs; trace Dietary Fiber

Walnut Butter Sauce

This sauce is great over any steamed vegetable or on a grilled steak or chicken.

1/2	cup	walnuts -- roasted
1/2	cup	unsalted butter (1 stick)
1	tsp	walnut oil
1	clove	garlic -- minced
1	tsp	shallot -- minced

6 Servings
1g Net Carbs

In a sauce pan over medium heat, add the walnut oil. Add the garlic and shallots and sauté for 1 minute. Turn heat to the lowest setting, add the walnuts and stir. Add the butter and stir. Pour into a small bowl, cover and refrigerate for an hour.

Yields about 3/4 cup with 2 Tbsps per serving

Per Serving: 207 Calories; 22g Fat; 3g Protein; 2g Carbohydrate; 1g Dietary Fiber

Tartar Sauce

A great sauce for grilled, broiled or poached fish. But it is also good on veggies such as broccoli, asparagus, cauliflower and Brussels sprouts.

1/2	cup	mayonnaise
1/2	cup	sour cream
3	Tbsps	dill pickle -- relish
1		scallion -- minced
1	Tbsp	lemon juice
1	Tbsp	capers -- rinsed and smashed
1	tsp	horseradish -- optional
1/4	tsp	lemon pepper

> **5 Servings**
> **2g Net Carbs**

1. Rinse and smash the capers. Finely mince the scallions (use just a tiny bit of the green portion).

2. In a jar or bowl, mix everything together. Cover and refrigerator for 15 minutes or more.

Makes about 1¼ cups; each serving is 4 Tbsps

Per Serving: 210 Calories; 24g Fat; 1g Protein; 2g Carbs; trace Dietary Fiber

Cranberry Sauce

This low carb adaptation is so simple to make
and it is a must with a turkey dinner.

3	cups	cranberries -- (12 oz)
1/2	cup	water
1/2	cup	Splenda® -- to taste
1/8	tsp	ground clove
1/8	tsp	ground allspice

> **8 Servings**
> **4g Net Carbs**

You can use fresh or frozen cranberries. If using dried, unsweetened cranberries then use only 1 cup and increase the water to 3/4 cups. This is rather sweet so you may want to reduce Splenda a little bit until after it is cooked and then see if you want it sweeter.

- Place everything in a sauce pan and bring to a boil. Reduce heat, cover and simmer for 8 minutes. Stir occasionally.

Makes just a bit more than 1 cup with 2 Tbsp per serving.

Per Serving: 18 Calories; trace Fat; trace Protein; 6g Carbohydrate; 2g Fiber

Cranberry Chutney

This sweet and spicy cranberry sauce is great served on the side as a relish or can be used as a base for a sauce for grilled turkey cutlets.

12	ozs	cranberries -- fresh or frozen (~3 cups)
2		apricots -- finely diced
1/2	cup	water
1	Tbsp	balsamic vinegar
1/4	cup	onion -- minced
1/4	cup	celery -- minced (~1 stalk)
2		jalapeno chile pepper -- seeded and minced
2	tsps	fresh ginger root -- grated
1	tsp	cinnamon
1/4	tsp	cloves
1/4	tsp	allspice
1/8	tsp	chili powder
1/3	cup	Splenda®

8 Servings
7g Net Carbs

This sauce is more flavorful than it is hot, but there is a tiny bit of heat that develops slowly. The heat is in the membrane of the jalapeno. You can remove that for a milder version. If you really want a kick then add another jalapeno.

You can use fresh or frozen cranberries. If you use dried unsweetened cranberries reduce amount to 1 cup and increase the water to 3/4 cups. You can use fresh or dried apricots, but if dried be sure they have not been sweetened.

- Put everything into a pot over medium heat and let it come to a gentle boil for about 3-5 minutes. Stir frequently. Then reduce heat and simmer for about 10 minutes. Stir occasionally. The cranberries should pop open and the sauce will thicken. Serve warm or chilled.

Makes about 1½ cups with 3 Tbsp per serving

Per Serving: 30 Calories; trace Fat; trace Protein; 9g Carbs; 2g Dietary Fiber

If you omit the apricots then subtract 1g net carbs per serving.

Mango Sauce

This savory sauce is excellent over fish or chicken. You can also jazz up veggies such as steamed broccoli.

2/3	cup	mango
1/2	Tbsp	butter
2		scallion -- minced
1	cup	water
1	Tbsp	soy sauce
1	Tbsp	balsamic vinegar
1/2	tsp	fresh ginger root -- grated
1/4	tsp	lemon pepper
1/2	tsp	guar gum

4 Servings
5g Net Carbs

One mango will typically yield about 1 1/3 cups when diced, so this recipe needs about 1/2 of a mango. You can also buy mango strips in a jar or frozen, cubes.

1. Slice mango on either side of its large seed. Cut into strips. Then with a thin knife, slice off the skin by placing each strip skin side down on a cutting board and running the knife horizontally as close to the skin as you can. Be sure to cut off as much of the flesh around the edge of the seed too. Dice into cubes about the size of a grape. Set aside 2/3 cups (save the rest for some other recipe).

2. Sauté scallions in butter for 1-2 minutes.

3. Meanwhile; in a bowl, mix together the water, soy, vinegar, grated ginger and lemon pepper. Mix well. Add guar gum, stir enough to dissolve and immediately add to the scallions and bring to a boil.

4. Reduce heat to a simmer, add the mangos. Let simmer for 3-5 minutes.

Makes about 1½ cups with ~1/3 cup per serving

Per Serving: 37 Calories; 2g Fat; 1g Protein; 6g Carbohydrate; 1g Dietary Fiber

Papaya Variation: Substitute papaya for the mango.
3g Net Carbs; 28 Calories; 1g Fat; 1g Protein; 4g Carbohydrate; 1g Dietary Fiber

Raspberry Sauce - Sweet

This recipe is a simple sweet raspberry sauce which can be used over ice cream, cheese cake or the like. But also try it over brie cheese as an appetizer or as a garnish for winter squash (pumpkin or butternut squash) or topping off steamed bitter greens (kale or Swiss chard).

2	cups	raspberries
1	cup	water
1	Tbsp	Splenda® -- to taste
1/4	tsp	guar gum -- or less

6 Servings
2g Net Carbs

Depending on the sweetness of your berries, you may need more or perhaps less of the Splenda.

1. In a sauce pan over medium heat, add the water and the berries. Cook for about 10 minutes until the berries have broken up and formed a sauce. Taste to see if you desire any Splenda. If you intend to strain the sauce to remove the seeds then this is when to do it. Simply pour through a strainer and push the pulp through using the back of a spoon.

2. To thicken the sauce add a pinch of guar gum (up to 1/4 tsp) and stir vigorously. It takes a bit of time for the guar gum to thicken fully (about 3 minutes). It does not have to be on the heat to thicken. If you accidentally get it too thick then just add more water.

Yields about 1½ cups with 1/4 cup (4 Tbsp) per serving

Per Serving: 21 Calories; trace Fat; trace Protein; 5g Carbohydrate; 3g Fiber

Raspberry Sauce - Savory

This savory raspberry sauce can be used on vegetables (spinach is great) but it is best poured over poultry, fish or wild game.

2	cups	raspberries
1	cup	water
1	clove	garlic -- finely minced
1	Tbsp	balsamic vinegar -- to taste
	pinch	rosemary
	pinch	oregano
	dash	salt and pepper
1/4	tsp	guar gum -- or less

6 Servings
2g Net Carbs

1. In a sauce pan over medium heat, add the water, berries, vinegar, garlic, rosemary, oregano, salt and pepper. Cook for about 10 minutes until the berries have broken up and formed a sauce. If you intend to strain the sauce to remove the seeds, garlic bits and herb leaves this is when to do it. Simply pour through a strainer and push the pulp through using the back of a spoon.

2. Taste and adjust seasoning. Careful, it will be hot.

3. To thicken the sauce, add a pinch of guar gum (up to 1/4 tsp) and stir vigorously. It takes a bit of time for the guar gum to thicken fully (about 3 minutes). It does not have to be on the heat to thicken. If you accidentally get it too thick then just add more water.

Yields about 1½ cups with 1/4 cup (4 Tbsp) per serving

Per Serving: 22 Calories; trace Fat; trace Protein; 5g Carbohydrate; 3g Fiber

Strawberry Blackberry Jam

This low carb jam uses gelatin instead of pectin and sugar as the thickening agent. I think that strawberries and blackberries are better blended together then they are on their own in a jam.

1½	lbs	strawberries
1/2	lb	blackberries
1/4	cup	water
1	Tbsp	Splenda®
1	packet	Knox unflavored gelatin
1/3	cup	boiling water

24 Servings
5g Net Carbs

Yes, this recipe calls for 3 times more strawberries than blackberries.

I generally use frozen berries to make jam except when my garden is in the height of production. But even then, I sometimes freeze them so I can make jam when I feel like it instead of when they are ready.

1. Cut the strawberries into quarters or eights depending on their size. If the blackberries are fresh then rinse them well. You should have about 6 cups total of fruit.

2. In a large heavy pot over medium heat, add the 1/4 cup of water and the fruit. Cook until all the fruit has broken up into a mush, stir frequently (~10 minutes).

3. Taste test for sweetness. Be careful not to burn your mouth, the fruit will be very hot - so spoon out just a little and let it cool for a minute. I usually don't need to sweeten this blend of fruits, but every one has their own tastes. Keep adding Splenda a little at a time until the desired sweetness.

4. Dissolve the gelatin in the 1/3 cup of boiling water. Then add this to the fruit and mix thoroughly.

5. Pour into 3-4 jelly canning jars (or recycled jelly jars). Refrigerate for 3 or more hours before using. If you don't think you'll use up the jam within a month, then keep one jar in the refrigerator and put the others in the freezer for future use.

Yields about 3 cups of jam with 2 Tbsps per serving

Per Serving: 26 Calories; trace Fat; trace Protein; 6g Carbohydrate; 1g Fiber

Strawberry Rhubarb Jam

Low carb jam using gelatin instead of pectin as the thickening agent.
Strawberry and rhubarb were made for each other.

1	lb	**strawberries -- fresh or frozen**
1	lb	**rhubarb**
1/4	cup	**water**
1/3	cup	**Splenda®**
1	tsp	**cinnamon**
1	dash	**cloves, ground**
1	dash	**allspice**
1	packet	**Knox unflavored gelatin**
1/3	cup	**boiling water**

> **24 Servings**
> **5g Net Carbs**

1. Cut the strawberries into quarters or eights depending on their size. Slice the rhubarb into 1/4 inch slices. Be sure not to use much close to the leave end of the stack. This part is extremely bitter. (The leaves are poisonous, you know.) You should have about 3 cups each of the chopped fruit.

2. In a large heavy pot over medium heat, add the 1/4 cup of water and the rhubarb. Cover and cook for about 5 minutes, stirring occasionally.

3. Add the cinnamon, cloves and allspice and stir. If you have pumpkin pie spice mix you can substitute 2 tsp of that.

4. Add the strawberries and cook until all the fruit has broken up into a mush, stir frequently.

5. Now start adding the Splenda. Start off with about half of it. Stir well and taste. Be careful not to burn your mouth, the fruit will be very hot - so spoon out just a little and let it cool for a minute. Keep adding more and more Splenda until the desired sweetness. Add more spices now too if you'd like.

6. Dissolve the gelatin in the 1/3 cup of boiling water. Then add this to the fruit and mix thoroughly.

7. Pour into 3-4 jelly canning jars (or recycled jelly jars). Refrigerate for 3 or more hours before using. If you don't think you'll use up the jam within a month then keep one jar in the refrigerator and put the others in the freezer for future use.

Yields about 3 cups of jam with 2 Tbsps per serving

If you are not happy with the color of this jam, feel free to add some red food coloring. Or next time add 1/2 cup of blackberries too.

Per Serving: 22 Calories; trace Fat; 1g Protein; 6g Carbohydrate; 1g Dietary Fiber

Spiced Blueberry Jam

Low carb blueberry jam uses gelatin instead of pectin and sugar as the thickening agent. It is jazzed up with a touch of ground cloves.

4	cups	blueberries
1/4	cup	water
1/8	tsp	cloves
1	Tbsp	Splenda® -- optional
1	packet	Knox unflavored gelatin
1/3	cup	boiling water

16 Servings
9g Net Carbs

1. In a large heavy pot over medium heat, add the 1/4 cup of water, blueberries and cloves. Cook until all the fruit has broken up into a mush, stir frequently.

2. Taste test for sweetness. Be careful not to burn your mouth, the fruit will be very hot - so spoon out just a little taste and let it cool for a minute. I usually only need a scant Tbsp of Splenda, but every one has their own tastes. Keep adding Splenda a little at a time until the desired sweetness.

3. Dissolve the gelatin in the 1/3 cup of boiling water. Then add this to the fruit and mix thoroughly.

4. Pour into 2-3 jelly canning jars (or recycled jelly jars). Refrigerate for 3 or more hours before using. If you don't think you'll use up the jam within a month then keep one jar in the refrigerator and put the others in the freezer for future use.

Yields about 2 cups with 2 Tbsps per serving

Per Serving: 41 Calories; trace Fat; 1g Protein; 10g Carbohydrate; 1g Fiber

Hawaiian Salsa

Papaya, coconut and Maui onion make an outstanding salsa!

1	cup	papaya -- cubed
2/3	cup	red and green bell pepper -- diced
3	Tbsps	unsweetened coconut -- flakes
1/2	cup	Maui onion -- diced
1		lime -- juiced
1	Tbsp	water
1	tsp	Splenda®
1/8	tsp	pepper
	pinch	salt

**4 Servings
6g Net Carbs**

I dedicate this recipe to my friend Debbie who witnessed its creation and provided a validating response of, "Oh wow! This is wonderful!"

Substitute vadalia or red onions if you don't have access to Maui onions.

1.   Juice the lime in a small bowl. Remove any seeds. Add the water, Splenda, salt and pepper and stir. Add the coconut flakes, onion and bell pepper. Stir. Cover and refrigerate for 1 hour.

2.   About 5 minutes before serving, toss with the papaya.

This is great served with the Macadamia Nut Crusted Ahi (page 201) or the Coconut Chicken (page 265). It can also be placed on squares of bell pepper or Belgian endive leaf for a colorful and impressive looking appetizer. Also try topping off a bed of lettuce or arugula for a nice side salad.

Per Serving: 53 Calories; 3g Fat; 1g Protein; 8g Carbohydrate; 2g Dietary Fiber

Jicama Papaya Salsa

A delectable contrast of crunchy and soft as well as spicy and sweet.

1	cup	papaya -- cubed
1/2	cup	jicama -- diced
1/2	cup	onion -- diced
1/2	cup	cilantro leaves, whole
1		jalapeno -- seeded and minced
1		lime -- juiced
1/4	tsp	cumin
1/4	tsp	salt

**4 Servings
5g Net Carbs**

1.   Juice the lime in a small bowl. Remove any seeds. Add the cumin and salt and stir. Add the jicama, onion, cilantro and jalapeno. Cover and refrigerate for 1 hour.

2.   About 5 to 30 minutes before serving, toss with the papaya.

Per Serving: 29 Calories; trace Fat; 1g Protein; 7g Carbohydrate; 2g Dietary Fiber

Mint Cucumber Salsa

This salsa is a natural compliment to your favorite curry dishes.

1		cucumber -- diced
1		scallion -- minced
2	Tbsps	red bell pepper -- minced
2	Tbsps	fresh mint leaves -- minced
1	Tbsp	wine vinegar
1	dash	Tabasco sauce
	pinch	salt

> **4 Servings**
> **2g Net Carbs**

1. In a mixing bowl, add the vinegar, Tabasco sauce, pinch of salt and the minced mint leaves. Stir.

2. Meanwhile, peel and dice the cucumber. Mince the scallion and the red bell pepper. Toss everything together, cover and refrigerate for an hour or more.

Per Serving: 14 Calories; trace Fat; 1g Protein; 3g Carbohydrate; 1g Dietary Fiber

As an Appetizer: Spoon onto Belgium endive leaves or stuff it into tomatoes.

Mint Pesto

This is a wonderful compliment to lamb dishes. It is also good
with fish and tossed with steamed vegetables.

1	cup	fresh mint leaves
1/2	cup	fresh flat-leaf parsley
1/4	cup	walnuts -- roasted
1	clove	garlic -- smashed
1/4	cup	walnut oil
1/4	cup	Romano cheese -- grated

> **8 Servings**
> **1g Net Carbs**

Any type of fresh mint will work well with this recipe. I have some generic mint growing in my backyard which has a spearmint/wintergreen flavor. Towards the end of the season it starts to get a little bitter so then I will add a scant tsp of Splenda to this.

1. In a food processor add the walnuts and chop. Transfer to a bowl.

2. Then add the garlic, parsley and about 1 table of the walnut oil to the food processor. Begin to puree. When well blended add the mint leaves and turn on again slowly drizzling the walnut oil into the food processor until everything is well blended. You may need to stop a couple of times to scrape down the sides.

3. Add the mint puree to the walnuts. Add the cheese and stir well. Taste to see if it needs a pinch of salt (depends on the saltiness of the cheese) or even a bit of Splenda.

Makes almost 1 cup with 2 Tbsps per serving

Try stuffing it into mushrooms, cherry tomatoes or artichoke hearts as delicious appetizers. Also great tossed with veggies, especially roasted turnips with mushrooms.

Per Serving: 104 Calories; 10g Fat; 3g Protein; 2g Carbohydrate; 1g Dietary Fiber

Basil Variation: The classic basil pesto is made in the same manner.
- Substitute basil for the mint and parsley.
- Substitute toasted pine nuts for the walnuts.
- Use 2 cloves of garlic
- Substitute canola oil for the walnut oil.
- I generally use Parmesan cheese, but Romano is just as good.

1g Net Carbs; 101 Calories; 10g Fat; 2g Protein; 1g Carbohydrate; trace Dietary Fiber

Basil pesto is awesome on summer squash. Try this version in the Patty Pan Squash stuffed with Pesto (page 191). It can also be spooned onto mushrooms, tomatoes, etc. as above, to make appetizers. Mix with a bit of cream and pour it over chicken or fish or pasta.

Caramelized Onions

These are great to spoon over grilled meats or chicken
as well as a compliment to vegetables.

2	cups	yellow onion slices
2	Tbsps	butter
1	tsp	balsamic vinegar

> **2 Servings**
> **8g Net Carbs**

- In a sauce pan over medium heat, melt the butter and then add the onion slices. Stir well. Let cook for 10 minutes; stirring occasionally. Add the vinegar and cook another 15 minutes.

This can be served right away on top of meat or veggies or it can be stored in the refrigerator for about 4 days.

Yields about 1/2 cup with 1/4 cup per serving

Per Serving: 147 Calories; 12g Fat; 1g Protein; 10g Carbohydrate; 2g Dietary Fiber

As an Appetizer: Garnish 8 roasted mushroom topped with ½ oz brie cheese each and pop under the broiler for 1 minute. 4 servings of 2 each

6g Net Carbs; 91 Calories; 6g Fat; 2g Protein; 8g Carbohydrate; 2g Dietary Fiber

Ravigote

This is a type of onion and fresh herb relish that goes well with grilled fish.

1/4	cup	red onion -- coarsely chopped
1	Tbsp	capers – drained and rinsed
2	Tbsps	red wine vinegar
4	Tbsps	olive oil
1	Tbsp	fresh parsley -- chopped
1	Tbsp	fresh chives -- chopped
1	Tbsp	fresh tarragon -- chopped
1/2	tsp	black pepper -- freshly ground
1/4	tsp	salt -- to taste

**4 Servings
2g Net Carbs**

Be sure to rinse and drain the capers otherwise they are too salty. I like using the small French type for this recipe.

- Mix together the capers with the chopped onions, parsley, chives, tarragon salt and pepper. Toss. Drizzle the vinegar and oil. Toss. Let it sit for about 30 minutes before serving.

Makes about 1/2 cup with 2 Tbsp per serving

Per Serving: 129 Calories; 14g Fat; trace Protein; 2g Carbs; trace Dietary Fiber

Tapenade

This olive relish is great with grilled fish or chicken or served as an appetizer.
Choose the type of olive that best suits your application.

1	cup	olives -- pitted
2	cloves	garlic
1	Tbsp	capers
1	Tbsp	fresh lemon juice
2	tsps	extra virgin olive oil
1/2	tsp	fresh thyme
1/2	tsp	fresh oregano
1/2	tsp	fresh rosemary

**6 Servings
1g Net Carbs**

Place all ingredients in a food processor and pulse a few times until it is a blended chunky relish. Do not over process to a smooth paste. You are going for the chunky appearance.

Makes a little over 1 cup with 3 Tbsps per serving

Per Serving: 42 Calories; 4g Fat; trace Protein; 2g Carbohydrate; 1g Dietary Fiber

- Use Spanish olives and serve with the Spanish Meat loaf (page 215).
- Use Greek olives and toss with feta cheese to put over grilled fish.
- Use black olives and serve on red bell pepper squares garnished with cilantro or chives as an appetizer.

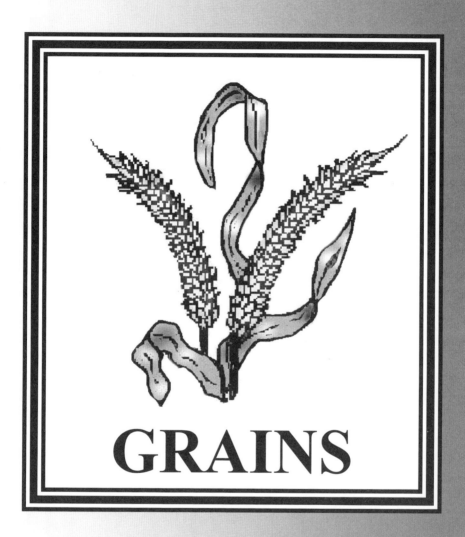

GRAINS

GRAINS

~ Regarding Grains ~

Grains have been sinfully misrepresented by a few people in the low carb world. Some claim that any and all forms of grain products are nothing but starch and will make you fat. At first, I believed this myth too. Although this starts to approach the truth when we look at refined carbohydrates (such as enriched all purpose flour) but it could not be further from the truth for whole grains.

Grain have three parts to them; the bran, which is the fiber packed outer layer; the germ, which is the nutrient-rich inner kernel; and the endosperm which is the middle portion that is primarily composed of starch (carbohydrates) and gluten (protein). All three parts contain B vitamins and other goodies but the majority of whole grains' nutrients are in the germ and the bran. These two components are often used individually or together in many types of "health" foods. And they are indeed healthy and very useful for a low carb diet especially during the weight loss phase. But there is a synergistic effect when all three parts are eaten together in the exact ratio with which they were created. Whole grains have more health benefits than any of the individual grain parts alone. That is why The Atkins group and several other low carb proponents encourage us to include whole grains once we have reached our desired weight. Studies have shown that whole grains will lower our risk of coronary heart disease, diabetes, obesity, stroke, certain cancers and many other ailments. It is unfortunate that some promoters of the low carb diet claim that carbs from all forms of grains are bad. Please understand that it is **refined carbohydrates** (including sugar) that are the real culprits to American's weight and health problems.

One of the reasons that a low carb diet is so effective for some people is that certain individuals are gluten intolerant. By eliminating grains from their diet, they will immediately start feeling better, healthier, more energetic and will start losing weight. Gluten is found in most grains, but particularly in wheat which is utilized in so many processed foods. Gluten is known to cause and aggravate many ailments such as allergies and celiac disease. It is estimated that as many as 15-25% of all Americans have some level of gluten intolerance. Individuals who are sensitive to gluten may need to completely eliminate grains from their diet forever.

For the rest of us, however, introducing whole grains back into our diets is considered an important part of the maintenance program along with incorporating a larger variety of fruits and vegetables. But not all grains are created equal. Although whole grains in general are healthy food sources, some have more nutrients and fiber than others and some have more gluten and other components that some individuals may find difficult to digest. They also have varying concentrations of carbohydrates. For example, oats have 5g of net carbs per ¼ cup serving where as brown rice has 10g.

Most processed foods today do not use many whole grains. They use refined grains stripped of their bran and germ and that is why these foods have been labeled "empty calories" by most nutritionist; they have so few nutrients in them.

A cracker that calls itself a "wheat cracker" might not have any *whole* wheat in it at all. Most are made primarily with refined wheat flour which is indeed made from wheat (so it is not a case of false advertising) however refined flours have only the endosperm which has negligible health benefit and a host of health detriments. So why are refined flours used so abundantly in the food industry? Because they have plenty of wonderful cooking qualities – special powers to make breads, muffins, cakes, to thicken sauces, to bind other ingredients and they have a better shelf life and other manufacturing advantages in addition to tasting so darn good. But health benefits are not on this list. Please beware of prepackaged foods and learn how to read labels. Even crackers that call themselves "whole wheat" or "whole grain crackers" will often have some type of refined flour listed as the first ingredient and will state the specific whole grain somewhere else down the list. These products are still inferior, in my opinion, especially for people living a low carb lifestyle. I get angry at manufacturers who list their refined flour simply as "wheat flour" which is not the same as "*whole* wheat flour" and is purposefully misleading. If you what a healthy whole wheat cracker when you get to maintenance I suggest Ak-Mak (only 3g net carbs per cracker).

All that being said, don't get me wrong: I am not a purist. The convenience of some processed foods are simply too irresistible. I greatly enjoy *La Tortilla Factory*'s low carb tortillas. But I do try to keep processed foods down to a minimum, especially foods that are primarily made from grains. Yet I still use white flour (oh my!) when I make certain type of gravies. I have yet to find a suitable substitute for thickening meat or poultry pan dripping than the classic French roux; which is made using a 1:1 ratio of heated fat or oil (typically butter) and all purpose flour. The outstanding flavor and texture that a roux gives gravy is worth the trade-off for me. Besides, we are not talking about very much white flour – I generally use no more than 2-3 teaspoons per cup of gravy.

During your **induction phase** you will probably need to eliminate every type of grain altogether. One of the primary purposes of the induction phase is to clear your body of starches and sugars especially those from processed foods. The Induction phase will kick start your metabolism by putting you into a state of ketosis. Grains will abate that process lickety-split. However, you may find flaxseed meal to be a very useful product for helping you to stay regular.

For your **weight loss phase**, you would be well advised to include wheat bran, oat bran or rice bran as well as flax seed meal on a regular basis. These grains are packed with nutrients and fiber and are so easy to incorporate into muffins, cookies, waffles, etc. but they can also be sprinkled on steamed vegetables or added to smoothies, salad dressings, casserole, and soups. Sometimes I will mix flax seed meal into almond butter and stuff that into celery stalks for a very healthy, nutritious, high fiber, low carb snack.

Once you have achieved your desired weight, then whole grains should become a part of your **maintenance program**. The thing is this; the size of your portions and the type of grains becomes critical and will require some time and effort to determine what works best for you. Every one is different and there is no magical formula (although experts keep wasting time and resources trying to find one). Some people will do great with several servings per day of all types of whole grains. Others will still need to exercise restrictions with both type and quantities. Chances are, if the low carb diet worked for you in the first place then you will probably be one of those individuals who will need to closely monitor your intake of grains. Ideally, you'll want to start off by adding small portions of whole grains to casseroles, stews or as part of a side dish of veggies. This cookbook contains a jambalaya recipe made with brown rice which is intended to be a side dish and not a main entrée. I have also included several recipes utilizing oatmeal, bulgur, barley and wild rice that you might like to try.

Each person's tolerance for grains is different. You will need to experiment to find out what works best for you. I recommend introducing one specific grain at a time over the course of a week or two and see how it goes. Pay attention to your energy level, headaches, sleep pattern, bloating, skin condition, appetite and of course weight gain. If you feel good it is probably a good grain for you. Most people do fine with oats and so this would be a good place to start, since it is our Champion when it comes to grains. Then it is advisable to eliminate that grain while you test another. This can be a long process, but is worth doing if you know that you have some intolerance to grains in general. Wheat intolerance is very common in our society, although some seem to do better with a few of wheat's less common cousins such as triticale, kamut and spelt. There are many cookbooks on the market that you can acquire to find recipes for these less common whole grains; look for cookbooks in the vegetarian and macrobiotic diet sections of your bookstore or library.

The most useful place to incorporate whole grains into your diet is by having them for breakfast. A bowl of oatmeal or seven grain cereal to start your day is one thing that basically all the nutritional experts are able to agree upon. Having your grains early in the day allows your body to metabolize them more completely and so they will have minimal impact on blood sugar or weight gain. For those of us who are 50+, this is particularly important. Although occasionally we might be able to have a small serving of grains with a very early dinner if we have physical activities scheduled for that evening. If you are quite young and active then this may not be as much of a concern for you. Yet most everyone should be cautious of eating grains at night. In general, our metabolic rate slows in the evenings so the carbohydrates will not be burned for immediate energy use and so they will be converted to fat. But all of us should feel free to have wheat, oat or rice bran as well as flaxseed meal anytime throughout the day.

Oats are the Champion low carb whole grain. Oats are a powerhouse of nutrients and should be included in any healthy diet. They have been shown to lower cholesterol, particularly the LDLs (the bad guys), stabilize blood sugar and reduce the risk of heart disease as well as many types of cancer. Oats are relatively low in carbs, calories and fat yet they are high in fiber, minerals, antioxidants and a host of other impressive phytonutrients. Some researchers claim that oats have many anti-aging properties.

Oats come in several different forms including; steel-cut oats (also known as Irish or Scottish oats); rolled oats (also known as "Old Fashion" oats); quick oats and instant oats. For the sake of nutrition, we only care about steel-cut oats and rolled oats. The steel-cut oats take 20–30 minutes to cook (and benefit from an over night soaking). Rolled oats cook-up in about 5 to 6 minutes - so why the heck would you use nutrient-depleted quick or instant oats that also take about 5 minutes to cook? Steel-cut oats have superior flavor and texture to rolled oats when making oatmeal breakfast cereals or when used in salads and casseroles. But rolled oats are best for baking.

Barley is a nutritious flavorful grain that has been cultivated for centuries. It is low in gluten but high in nutrients and fiber. It comes in several forms. The whole grain form is generally called hulled (as the outer hull has been removed) and is the most nutritious form. Scotch barley is also very nutritious as it is simply coarsely ground hulled barley. I use Scotch barley in my recipes and it can be found at most health food stores. Pearl barley is what you will mostly find at regular grocery stores. It has much few nutrients as the bran has been removed and the polishing process also depletes nutrients (same as with white polished rice). Barley flour and barley meal are typically made from pearl barley.

Bulgur is a specific type of whole wheat that has been parboiled, dried and crushed. It is quick-cooking, but unlike quick oats or barley, bulgur still retains all of its nutrients. It is has all the nutrients of whole wheat as well as the gluten. Although the type of wheat used to make bulgur has a lower gluten content than the type of wheat typically used to make flours and breads. So if you know that you are sensitive to wheat or gluten, then bulgur may not be a good choice for you.

Bulgur is a frequent ingredient to Middle Eastern cuisine and is probably best known in the US as the primary ingredient for tabouli. Bulgur is often confused with cracked wheat, but they are not quite the same. Basically, cracked wheat is to bulgur as steel-cut oats is to rolled oats. However the type of wheat is also somewhat different.

Bulgur is a very useful grain for the low carb diet, second only to oats. Bulgur is relatively low in carbs and high in fiber. It is easy to add bulgur to casseroles or to toss in with vegetables. Just add equal amounts of boiled water to the bulgur and let sit for 10 minutes, stir and then toss it in with a casserole or other recipe.

Corn is actually a grain and can be added back into your maintenance program in moderation. Yellow corn has more nutrients and less sugar than white corn. But it is best to consume very small quantities at a time and preferably early in the day (fresh or frozen kernels of corn make a nice addition to scrambled eggs, omelets and frittatas). With your maintenance program, feel free to sprinkle a few kernels over your salad for dinner especially if you plan a brisk evening walk with the dog. But don't beat yourself up if you indulge in a freshly cooked corn on the cob at a summer holiday cookout. We are human after all! Enjoy it! But eat slowly, thoroughly chewing every delicious bite. But please say "no thanks" to over-cooked or over-processed corn wherever possible (like corn chips) it's just not worth the carbs. If you use canned corn, please do not cook it. Just drain, rinse, strain and eat it as is. So what about popcorn? Well most of the microwave types are a big no-no for many reasons including those nasty trans fatty acids that are used for many of the "butter" flavor as well as a host of other undesirable additives. But if you pop it yourself the old fashion way (or use an air popper) then popcorn isn't a huge problem; you can even use real butter! One cup of popcorn has about 6g of carbs, 2g of fiber for just 4g of net carbs (but one cup of popcorn isn't very much, so be careful).

The following tables show some of the more common grains that are useful to a low carb lifestyle. They are list in order of net carbs. Please note that I use a serving size of just ¼ cup of cooked grains. Except for corn, most grains generally double or triple in size when cooked.

Net Carbs for Common Whole Grains

Whole Grain ¼ cup cooked	Carbs grams	Fiber grams	Net Carbs grams
Oats	6.0	1.0	**5.0**
Bulgur	8.5	1.6	**6.9**
Yellow Corn	8.5	1.0	**7.5**
Wild Rice	8.8	0.8	**8.0**
Barley	11.1	2.6	**8.5**
Brown Rice	11.5	0.9	**10.6**
Millet	14.2	2.9	**11.3**

In my opinion, bread is not the best way to get whole grains into our diets. Commercial whole grain breads often have added extra gluten and other undesirable ingredients. For me, even the low carb breads can set up a pattern of carb cravings where the next thing I know I desire a doughnut or some other equally non-nutritious food. But if you are a sandwich or toast and jam type of person and cannot possibly live without bread, then I highly recommend that you purchase a bread machine and make it yourself using fresh ingredients. Although these machines are relatively expensive they can save you a bundle over the long run. Sorry, but I don't have any bread recipes in this cookbook.

Authentic Oatmeal

This is the real deal made with steel-cut oats that provide
a superior texture and flavor over rolled oats.

1/2	cup	steel-cut oats
2	cups	Carb Countdown™ Milk, 2%
1	dash	salt
1/8	tsp	cinnamon
1/8	tsp	vanilla extract
1	Tbsp	Splenda®

> **Maintenance**
>
> **2 Servings**
> **26g Net Carbs**

I like this best cooked in all milk but you can use 1/2 milk and 1/2 water if you prefer. Sliced apple or 1/2 cup of berries is a delicious addition but be sure to add in the carbs.

1. In a sauce pan, bring the milk just to the boil and add the oats and a dash of salt. Stir and reduce heat to a simmer. Cook (uncovered) for 20-25 minutes stirring occasionally. Taste for preferred level of crunchiness/softness. Remove from heat.

2. Add your own choice of flavoring and sweetener. I like the cinnamon with vanilla as indicated above or cardamom with almond extract. Also consider maple flavoring with cinnamon.

Per Serving: 251 Calories; 7g Fat; 18g Protein; 30g Carbohydrate; 4g Dietary Fiber

Multi-Grain Breakfast Cereal

Bob's Red Mill 5 Grain Cereal is his lowest carb cereal blend.
This recipe jazzes it up for more protein and flavor.

1/4	cup	**Bob's Red Mill 5 Grain Cereal**
2	Tbsps	**Whey protein powder**
1	tsp	**cinnamon**
1	Tbsp	**Splenda®**
1/2	cup	**water**
1/2	cup	**Carb Countdown™ Milk, 2%**
	few	**drops of extract such as almond, vanilla, orange or maple flavor**

Maintenance

1 Servings
19g Net Carbs

I love this whole grain cereal which includes oats, wheat, rye, barley, triticale and flax seed. Soooooooo nutritious! This is a great way to start the day when you can afford the carbs. Consider eating extra low carbs for the rest of the day.

Mix together all ingredients in a large bowl (big enough for handling the boiling bubbles without spilling over) stir well. Zap in the microwave for 1 minute (or until it boils) and stir. Zap for another minute then stir. Let sit for 2 minutes then zap again for about 30 seconds. Let it cool a bit before eating.

Although this is great with fruit, I can't afford that many carbs in one meal. But if you can then go for it!

Per Serving: 264 Calories; 12g Fat; 32g Protein; 24g Carbs; 5g Dietary Fiber

Barley with Mushrooms

Barley is a wonderful grain to include in your low carb maintenance program.
Enjoy this basic recipe as a side dish or add it your favorite
casserole or toss it with vegetables.

1	Tbsp	butter
1	stalk	celery -- minced
1/2		green bell pepper -- minced
1		scallion -- minced
6	ozs	mushrooms -- diced
1/4	cup	Scotch barley
2/3	cup	chicken stock -- or more if needed
1/2	tsp	herbs
		choose herbs that compliment your entrée

Maintenance
2 Servings
19g Net Carbs

1. In a pot with a good fitting lid, melt the butter over medium high heat. Add the celery and peppers and sauté for 1 minute. Add the scallions and sauté another minute. Add the mushrooms and barley, stir and cook for about 3 minutes. Add the chicken stock and herbs. Bring to a boil, then reduce to lowest setting and cover. Cook for 30 minutes. Leave it alone and don't stir it for at least 25 minutes.

2. Check for tenderness of barley. If it is still too crunchy then cook a little longer adding more stock if needed.

Per Serving: 174 Calories; 7g Fat; 5g Protein; 24g Carbohydrate; 5g Dietary Fiber

Chicken Barley Casserole: Preheat oven to 350ºF. Place 20 oz of diced chicken meat (cooked) into a casserole dish. Toss the chicken with the above barley mixture, once it is cooked and tender. Top with 1/2 cup of grated cheddar cheese. Bake in a 350ºF oven for 15 minutes; or until the cheese has melted and started to bubble or brown.
20g net carbs, 705 Calories; 45g Fat; 48g Protein; 25g Carbohydrate; 5g Dietary Fiber

Broccoli & Barley Variation: Once the barley & mushrooms are cooked, toss with 2 cups of steam broccoli and 1 Tbsp of butter
20g net carbs, 245 Calories; 13g Fat; 8g Protein; 28g Carbohydrate; 8g Dietary Fiber

Brown Rice Jambalaya

This low carb interpretation has more meat and less rice
and is wonderful as a side dish for your low carb maintenance plan.

1	lb	smoked sausage
1	lb	chicken breasts – boneless, skinless
4	stalks	celery -- minced
4		scallions -- minced
2	cloves	garlic -- minced
1		green bell pepper -- seeded and diced
1		red bell pepper -- seeded and diced
3/4	cup	brown rice
2	cups	chicken broth
1	Tbsp	Cajun seasoning

Maintenance

6 Servings
23g Net Carbs

Although Jambalaya is typically a main course, for your low-carb lifestyle it is used as a side dish or a light meal served with a salad.

1. Trim the tops of the scallions to remove any bruised ends. Cut off the top 1/3 of the green part, mince and set aside for a garnish. Mince the rest of the scallions and the garlic. Dice the celery and the bell peppers.

2. Cut sausage and chicken into bite sized pieces.

3. In a large heavy pot over medium heat, cook the sausage until brown (about 5 minutes) transfer to a bowl. Add the chicken to the pot and sear on all sides (about 3 minutes), transfer to the bowl.

4. Pour off the fat, except for about 1 Tbsp worth. Add the celery, the white part of the scallions, the garlic and the bell peppers. Sauté for about 5 minutes. Add the chicken stock, the chicken, sausage, rice and Cajun seasoning. Bring to a boil, stir, reduce heat to a simmer, cover and cook for 30 minutes.

5. Check tenderness of the rice. If it is still too crunchy, cook a little longer (adding more stock if needed).

Per Serving: 466 Calories; 19g Fat; 31g Protein; 25g Carbs; 2g Dietary Fiber

Flavor-Packed Brown Rice

This brown rice can be used as a side dish or tossed with steamed veggies or stuffed into Cornish game hens.

1	cup	brown rice
2	cups	chicken stock
2	Tbsps	butter
4		scallions -- minced
4	stalks	celery -- minced
1		green bell pepper -- minced
1/2	tsp	dried herbs
		choose herbs that compliment your entree

Maintenance

6 Servings
25g Net Carbs

1. In a pot with a tight fitting lid, melt the butter over medium high heat. Add the celery and peppers and sauté for 1 minute. Add the scallions and sauté another minute.

2. Add the rice and stir to coat. Add the chicken stock and herbs. Bring to a boil. Then reduce to a simmer, cover and cook for 30 minutes.

Rice does not cook very well in small quantities so don't try to reduce the amounts. Use this when you have enough people to feed or want some left-overs for another recipe. For a smaller quantity try the Barley with Mushrooms instead (page 376).

Per Serving: 168 Calories; 5g Fat; 3g Protein; 27g Carbohydrate; 2g Dietary Fiber

Oat Salad Annie

This salad of oats and veggies has a fresh lemon flavor.
Although there is some chili powder in the recipe it is not spicy.

1/3	cup	steel-cut oats
2/3	cup	water
1/4	tsp	chili powder
1/4	tsp	garlic powder
1/4	tsp	lemon pepper
1/8	tsp	salt

1	stalk	celery -- diced
1/2		cucumber -- diced
1		scallion -- minced
1/3	cup	orange bell pepper -- minced
2	Tbsps	lemon juice
1	Tbsp	extra virgin olive oil

Maintenance

2 Servings
19g Net Carbs

1. In a sauce pan, bring the water to a boil. Add the oats, chili powder, garlic powder, lemon pepper and salt. Bring back to a boil then reduce heat to a simmer. Cook for 20 minutes stirring occasionally.

2. Meanwhile, dice the celery and cucumber and mince the scallion and bell pepper. Toss in a bowl with the lemon juice and olive oil. Let marinate while the oats cook.

3. When the oats are done, drain in a colander and rinse quickly with cool water to wash away a bit of starch but not so much that you wash way nutrients and flavor. Fluff with a fork a few times as it cools. Let cool for about 5 minutes.

4. Add the oats to the veggies and toss well. Cover and refrigerate for 30 minutes.

Serve as a side salad or make several wrap-ups with leaf lettuce for a nutritious lunch. Eat left-overs within 48 hours.

Per Serving: 190 Calories; 9g Fat; 6g Protein; 24g Carbohydrate; 5g Dietary Fiber

Spinach with Bulgur

Spinach mixed with bulgur wheat and lots of Parmesan cheese.

3/4	cup	bulgur
4		scallion -- minced
1	Tbsp	butter
2	Tbsps	dry sherry
1½	cups	chicken stock
10	ozs	spinach, frozen -- block
1/2	Tbsp	lemon pepper
1/2	cup	Parmesan cheese

1. In a sauce pan over medium heat, melt the butter and add the minced scallions and the bulgur. Saute for 1-2 minutes. Stir frequently.

2. Add the sherry and stir. Add the chicken stock and let it slowly come to a boil stirring frequently.

3. Add the frozen spinach and lemon pepper. Cook until spinach has thawed and the liquids come back to the boil (6-10 minutes). Remove from heat. Add the Parmesan cheese and serve. Or cover and keep in a 200°F oven until ready to serve (up to 15 minutes).

Per Serving: 202 Calories; 7g Fat; 10g Protein; 25g Carbohydrate; 7g Dietary Fiber

Tabouli Salad

This nutritious Middle Eastern Salad is wonderful! It is low enough
in carbs to enjoy occasionally during your weight loss phase
and frequently once you get to the maintenance phase.

1/3	cup	**Tabouli - Casbah Brand**
1/3	cup	**boiling water**
1	Tbsp	**lemon juice**
1/4	tsp	**cumin**
1/4	cup	**fresh parsley -- minced**
1/4	cup	**fresh mint leaves -- minced**
1	Tbsp	**olive oil**
1		**cucumber**
1	large	**tomato -- seeded and chopped**
2	cups	**spinach -- or lettuce**

Maintenance
3 Servings
11g Net Carbs

1. In a mixing bowl, add the tabouli mix, the boiling water, lemon juice and cumin. Stir well and cover. Let sit for 10 minutes while you do the following.

2. Remove the stem from the tomato, slice in half and squeeze to remove the seeds (most of them anyway and that's good enough). Dice the tomato. Dice the cucumber. Mince the parsley and mint leaves.

3. Uncover the tabouli and stir. Add the parsley, mint, tomatoes, cucumber and olive oil. Stir well, cover and refrigerate for 1 hour.

4. On 4 salad plates, make a bed of lettuce and then spoon the chilled tabouli into the centers.

Per Serving: 110 Calories; 5g Fat; 3g Protein; 14g Carbohydrate; 3g Dietary Fiber

Wild Rice with Hazelnuts

This is a perfect low carb stuffing for Cornish game hens.
Or you can serve it as a side dish.

3/4	cup	water
1/3	cup	wild rice
1/2		bay leaf
1	tsp	thyme
1/2	tsp	sage
1/4	tsp	salt
1/4	tsp	pepper
1	Tbsp	butter
4		celery rib
1	clove	garlic
1/4	cup	hazelnut, dry-roasted -- chopped
2		scallion -- minced

> **Maintenance**
>
> **4 Servings**
> **11g Net Carbs**

1. Bring the water to a boil and add the rice, bay leaf, thyme, sage and the salt and pepper. Bring back to the boil, cover and reduce heat to a simmer. Cook for 40 minutes if using as a stuffing, and 60 minutes as a side dish. Drain, lightly rinse and remove the bay leaf.

2. Meanwhile, in a sauce pan or small skillet, melt the butter over medium high heat. Add the celery sauté for 1 minute; add the garlic and sauté for another minute.

3. For a stuffing: remove from heat and toss with the rice, hazelnuts and scallions. Taste test before stuffing the bird and add additional thyme, sage or salt and pepper.

    As a side dish: add the scallions and hazelnut to the fry pan and sauté for 1 or 2 minutes then combine with the rice. Taste test and add additional thyme, sage or salt and pepper as needed. Remove from heat and cover. Let stand for a couple of minutes. Serve.

Per Serving: 144 Calories; 9g Fat; 3g Protein; 14g Carbohydrate; 3g Dietary Fiber

DESSERTS

DESSERTS

For a discussion **Regarding Sweeteners** see page 26. During the Induction phase, you are advised to keep your sweet treats to a minimum. But if your sweet tooth gets the best of you, try sticking to very small amounts of the few Induction recipes that I have created – but be mindful of serving sizes. Although some of the store-bought sweet treats claim to be very low in carbs, be cautious of using them during the Induction phase. This is particularly important for those products made with one or more polyol sweeteners as they do have more digestible carbs than the labeling indicates. It would be sad to disrupt your Induction phase over the effects of the polyols. I suggest that you wait two weeks and then experiment with them in during your Weight Loss phase.

~ REGARDING FRUITS & NUTS~

The majority of my dessert recipes contain some amount of fruits, nuts or chocolate (okay, chocolate in neither a fruit nor a nut; but I'm not going to talk about chocolate anyway). You will find fruits and nuts in many of my other recipes too. They can add such a variety of flavor and textures to recipes, besides being nutritiously delicious and full of fiber.

Fruit

Some people think that we can't have fruit on a low carb diet. But there are many fruits that are suitable to the low carb lifestyle, particularly berries.

Berries are the low carb Champions of the fruit world. They are a delicious way to get fiber in your diet, as well as providing a host of disease fighting nutrients such as antioxidants. Many of the nutrients are contained in the seeds, so I generally prefer not to strain a sauce containing berries.

Berries ½ cup	Carbs grams	Fiber grams	Net Carbs grams
Blackberries	9.1	3.9	5.2
Blueberries	10.3	2.0	8.3
Boysenberries	8.0	2.6	5.4
Cranberries	6.0	2.0	4.0
Raspberries	7.4	4.3	3.1
Strawberries	5.1	1.5	3.4

Recent studies are showing that blueberries have more powerful disease-fighting antioxidant activity than any other fruit or vegetable. Truly astonishing health benefits have been contributed to blueberries including lowering the risk for cardiovascular disease, diabetes, cancer, degenerative eye diseases as well as a multitude of anti-aging properties which helps maintain health skin but more importantly seems to reduce the effects of Alzheimer and dementia. But blueberries do not stand on the pedestal alone; all of the berries offer exceptional nutrients and health benefits. Since some of the phytonutrients, particularly the polyphenols, differ amongst the berries it is recommended that we eat a variety of berries everyday. A daily serving of ½ cup of berries consisting of a mixture of blueberry, raspberry and strawberry has approximately 7.6g carbs and 2.7g fiber resulting in ~5g net carbs. It is so easy to work in a serving of berries everyday. This cookbook includes many recipes with berries including jams, muffins, cereals, salads, desserts and sauces.

Raspberries and strawberry have the lowest net carbs, but raspberries have almost three times more fiber as well as more vitamin A and niacin. Where as strawberries have more vitamin C and antioxidants than raspberries. I prefer to purchase raspberries at a farmer's market or frozen, as they spoil quickly. When buying frozen fruit, be sure to check the labels to make sure that they have not been sweetened.

There are several other fruits besides berries that are compatible with the low carb diet, particularly papaya, guava, watermelon and rhubarb. Okay, rhubarb is technically not a fruit it is a vegetable. But it is generally served in similar ways as fruit. I have not yet experimented with recipes for guava, as this fruit is not available in my area. I am quite partial to papaya, mangos, apples and apricots, so you will find a variety of recipes using these delicious fruit too.

Fruit ½ cup	Carbs grams	Fiber grams	Net Carbs grams
Apple, diced	8.4	1.5	6.9
Apple juice	14.5	t	14.5
Apricot, fresh	8.5	1.4	7.1
Apricot, dried	40.2	5.8	34.4
Banana	27.1	2.8	24.3
Cantaloupe	6.7	0.7	6.0
Cherries	8.5	1.3	7.2
Dates	65.1	6.6	58.5
Fig, fresh	19.1	3.3	15.8
Fig, dried	64.9	12.1	52.8
Grapefruit	9.3	1.3	8.0
Grapes	8.2	0.4	7.8
Guava	**9.7**	**4.4**	**5.3**
Honeydew melon	7.7	0.5	7.2
Kiwi	13.1	3.0	10.1
Kumquat	18.1	7.2	10.9
Lemon juice	10.5	0.5	10.0
Lime juice	11.1	0.5	10.6
Mandarin orange	10.9	2.2	8.7
Mango	14.0	1.9	12.1
Nectarine	8.1	1.1	7.0
Orange sections	10.6	2.2	8.4
Orange juice	12.9	0.2	12.7

Fruit cup	Carbs grams	Fiber grams	Net Carbs grams
Papaya	**6.9**	**1.3**	**5.6**
Peach	9.4	1.7	7.7
Pear	12.5	2.0	10.5
Pineapple	9.6	0.9	8.7
Plum	10.7	1.2	9.5
Prune	52.6	5.9	46.7
Raisins	57.4	2.9	54.5
Rhubarb	**2.8**	**1.1**	**1.7**
Tangerine	10.9	2.2	8.7
Watermelon	**5.5**	**0.4**	**5.1**

Nuts

I go nuts for nuts! They are so delicious and so incredibly healthy too (if eaten in moderation). The low-fat craze of the past few decades has given nuts a bum rap. Yes, they contain a high percentage of fats. But for the most part, these are essential fatty acids that we are talking about here. Simply put, nuts are good for you. I've included peanuts (which technical are legumes) in the table below since most people will treat them in the same way as most nuts. A typical serving of nuts in considered as 1 ounce, which isn't very much. That's generally about a small handful or about 2-3 tablespoons depending on the size and shape of the nut. Nuts are great for the low carb diet, because in addition to being low in carbs they are typically high in fiber.

Nuts 1 ounce	Carbs grams	Fiber grams	Net Carbs
Almonds	5.8	3.1	2.7
Brazil nuts	3.6	1.5	2.1
Cashews	8.1	1.7	6.4
Chestnuts	12.9	2.3	10.6
Coconuts	4.3	2.6	1.7
Hazelnuts	2.0	0.8	1.2
Macadamia nuts	3.9	2.6	1.6
Peanuts	4.6	2.4	2.2
Pecans	5.2	2.1	3.1
Pine nuts	3.1	1.0	2.1
Pistachios	3.5	1.5	2.0
Walnuts	3.4	1.4	2.0

There is no clear-cut Champion in the nut category but several nuts are major contenders. Hazelnuts (filberts) have the lowest net carbs, while almonds have the highest fiber content. Macadamia nuts and coconuts are also quite low in carbs and high in fiber. But walnuts are the most nutritious nut overall. So if I needed to single out a specific nut, it would have to be walnuts.

Walnuts are very high in omega-3 fatty acids, vitamin E, vitamins B_1 and B_2, as well as various minerals including manganese, copper and magnesium. Walnuts have been shown to significantly improve cardiovascular function through various mechanisms including lowering cholesterol. Researchers have identified over a dozen different polyphenols which have remarkable antioxidant activity including ellagic and gallic acids. Ellagic acid has been shown to have many anticancer properties and provides general immune system support.

While I was in college, I had read somewhere that walnuts increase brain functioning including memory recall. So I took up the habit of nibbling on walnuts while I studied for exams. I progressed from less than a mediocre student to an "A" student within one year. Some will say that this is a coincident, because this experiment was conducted at the same time as I started engineering school and discovered talents I never imagined that I possessed. So my dramatic improvement in grades may have been fueled by walnuts or by enthusiasm; who is to say for sure. But I like to believe that it was the synergy of them both. For enthusiasm alone generally is not sufficient to create good grades. I continue to employ walnuts when I feel that I need an extra boost with respect to memory. Research studies are indeed showing that walnuts improve various levels of cognitive functioning and some people like to refer to walnuts as "brain food".

Almonds are also much higher in nutrients than most nuts (although they can't compete with walnuts in the area of omega-3). You will notice that I use quite a lot of almond meal. This is ground up almonds (typically blanched first) and is sometimes called almond flour. Not only is it high in fiber and vitamin E, it is also a great substitute for flour and other ingredients for certain types of recipes. Bob's Red Mill® is a quality provider of almond meal and is the brand that I used to develop the recipes in this cookbook, as this product is reliably consistent in quality. It is readily available in both health food stores and many ordinary grocery stores. I personally prefer to use the raw, organic almond meal because it typically includes the skin as well (lots of additional nutrients there). But this product is not readily available and my source delivers inconsistent texture. But you can also grind your own easily enough in a food processor (and from a nutritional point of view, is the preferred approach). Bob's Red Mill® almond meal is very convenient to have on hand (please note that it should be refrigerated if it will not be used up within about 2 months).

You'll find many recipes in this cookbook that utilizes nuts, particularly with the baked goods such as cookies, pie crusts and muffins. But don't forget, nuts are also a great addition to salad and vegetables and are a quick and satisfy snack.

Berry Zinger Gel-O

A perfect low carb gelatin dessert made with
Celestial Seasonings' Wild Berry Zinger herb tea.

10	bags	herbal tea
4	cups	water
4	packets	Knox gelatin -- unsweetened
1/2	cup	Splenda®

Induction

4 Servings
3g Net Carbs

Packaged gelatin desserts are typically sweetened with either sugar or aspartame. So here is a healthier alternative. You can make this with any type of tea that you prefer. Constant Comment Green tea is rather good, but the color is somewhat unappealing so I only make it for myself and never serve it to my guests. All of the Celestial Seasonings Zinger teas are excellent for this recipe; my favorite happens to be the Wild Berry Zinger.

1. In a bowl or mold, add 1 cup of the water and the contents of all four gelatin packets. Stir and let it sit while you brew the tea.

2. In a microwave safe bowl, add the remaining 3 cups of water and the 10 tea bags. Zap it in the microwave until the water comes to a boil (typically 3 minutes). Stir and cover the tea (I cover with plastic wrap and then put a pot holder on top to help keep in the heat). Let the tea steep for 3-5 minutes.

3. Add the Splenda to the tea and stir. Then pour the tea into the dissolved gelatin and stir well. Be sure to get up all those little bits sticking to the sides and bottom of the bowl (otherwise the will form a very rubbery skin). Refrigerated for several hours.

Yields 4 cups with 1 cup per serving

Per Serving: 24 Calories; 0g Fat; 6g Protein; 3g Carbohydrate; 0g Dietary Fiber

Fresh Raspberry Variation: Makes 6 serving. Prepare the gelatin and tea, as above, and mix them together. Place 1/4 cup of fresh or frozen raspberries into 6 wine glasses (total of 1 1/2 cups of berries). Pour the tea/gelatin blend over the berries. Cover each glass with plastic wrap and refrigerator for at least 2 hours. Use one carton (4 oz) of Dannon's Carb Control™ raspberry yogurt and place 1 heaping Tbsp of the yogurt onto each dessert just before serving.
4g net carbs; 42 Calories; 1g Fat; 5g Protein; 6g Carbohydrate; 2g Dietary Fiber;

Lemon Mousse with Strawberries

Sweet and creamy mousse. Very low in carbs and very satisfying.

1	packet	lemon, sugar-free Jell-O®
8	ozs	cream cheese
2	cups	water
4		strawberries – sliced

> **Induction**
>
> **4 Servings**
> **3g Net Carbs**

1. In a sauce pan, add 1 cup of the water and the packet of Jell-O. Bring to a boil, stir well and remove from heat.

2. In a food processor (or a mixing bowl and electric blender) whip the cream cheese. Little by little add some of the Jell-O mixture. Let each batch become fully incorporated before adding more. Scrape down the sides, occasionally. Then add the remaining water, also in batches.

3. Spoon mixture into 4 wine glasses. Cover and refrigerator for 3 hours.

Garnish with sliced strawberries

Per Serving: 210 Calories; 20g Fat; 6g Protein; 3g Carbs; trace Dietary Fiber

Yes, sugar free Jell-O® contains aspartame, but it's just a small deviation to help you through your Induction phase.

Be sure to clean up your food processor and sauce pan right away. Dried gelatin is much harder to clean (use really hot water).

Reduced Carb Variation: Omit the strawberries. You can use any flavor Jell-O that you prefer.
2g Net Carbs; 207 Calories; 20g Fat; 6g Protein; 2g Carbohydrate; 0g Dietary Fiber;

Chocolate Almond Cookies

Yummy low carb cookie at just 3g net carbs each.

1	Tbsp	unsalted butter -- room temperature
3/4	cup	Splenda®
1	cup	almond meal
1/4	cup	unsweetened cocoa powder
1	tsp	vanilla extract
1	tsp	almond extract
2		egg whites -- lightly beaten

Induction
12 Servings
3g Net Carbs

Preheat oven to 375°F

1. Using the back of a wooden spoon or a spatula, cream together the room temperature butter and the Splenda.

2. Then add the almond meal and cocoa powder and blend well. No lumps.

3. Add the beaten egg whites and the extracts and blend well.

4. Drop about a rounded Tbsp of batter onto a cookies sheet lined with parchment paper. The cookies will pretty much hold whatever shape they are when going into the oven, so experiment. I like them in rugged looking drops but sometimes I flatten them more like a cookie. You can even pipe them out with a pastry bag.

5. Bake at 375°F for 8 to 10 minutes. Let cool for a few minutes.

Yields a dozen cookies; just 1 per serving during the induction phase.

Per Serving: 70 Calories; 6g Fat; 3g Protein; 5g Carbohydrate; 2g Dietary Fiber

Sweet Whipped Cream

Almond extract makes whipped cream taste even more heavenly.

1	cups	heavy whipping cream
1	Tbsps	Splenda®
1/8	tsp	almond extract

Induction
4 Servings
2g Net Carbs

In a mixer add the cream, vanilla extract and the Splenda. Whip until soft peaks.

Yields ~2 cups with 1/2 cup per serving

Per Serving: 205 Calories; 22g Fat; 1g Protein; 2g Carbohydrate; 0g Dietary Fiber

Use this to top off a bowl of fruit or other treats. During the Induction phase just have few spoonfuls to satisfy the craving for something sweet and creamy. Add it to the top of sugar-free Jell-O® for a very satisfying dessert.

Almond Coconut Pie Crust

This low carb crust is great for baked pies, refrigerator pies, tarts, etc.

1	cup	almond meal
1/4	cup	butter
1/4	cup	coconut flakes
1/4	cup	Splenda®
2	tsps	Just Whites (powered egg whites)
2	Tbsps	water

Weight Loss

6 Servings
4g Net Carbs

This makes enough for one 9 inch pie or tart pan or 4 individual tart pans. You can use 1 fresh egg white instead of the powdered egg whites if you prefer. It is easier to make a 1/2 batch doing it this way though.

Preheat oven to 350°F

1. Soften the butter and blend with the almond meal, coconut flakes and Splenda.

2. Whisk together the powdered egg whites and water. Be patient, it takes a little while before it dissolves. Add to the almond mixture. Blend well.

3. Press dough into your pan. (I prefer a tart pan with the removable bottom because the crust stays together better that way).

   If it is difficult to shape the crust the way that you want it, then put it in the freezer for 5-10 minutes and then fine-tune the shape.

4. Bake at 350°F for about 8 minutes for a baked pie or 12 minutes for a refrigerator pie. Allow to cool before filling.

1 Pie with 6 servings: Each portion of the crust contains the following
4g Net Carbs; 191 Calories; 18g Fat ; 5g Protein; 6g Carbohydrate; 2g Dietary Fiber

4 Individual Tart pans: The crust portion contains the following
7 Net Carbs; 287 Calories; 27g Fat; 7g Protein; 10g Carbohydrate; 3g Dietary Fiber

Blackberry Peach Yogurt Pie

The combination of peach flavored yogurt with the blackberries
is not only delicious but it is very pretty too.

1	batch	Almond Coconut Pie Crust (page 392)

Filling

2		eggs -- beaten
2	ozs	cream cheese -- softened
1	cup	Dannon's Carb Control™ Yogurt -- Peach
2	Tbsps	Splenda®
1	cup	blackberries -- 3/4 cup if frozen

Weight Loss
6 Servings
8g Net Carbs

This is enough for one 9 inch pie or tart pan or 4 individual tart pans.

Preheat oven to 350°F

1. Make the Almond Coconut Crust. You can use 1 fresh egg white instead of the powdered egg whites if you prefer.

2. Press dough into your pan. (I prefer a tart pan with the removable bottom). Bake at 350°F for about 8 minutes. Allow to cool before filling.

3. Filling: Mix into the soften cream cheese the yogurt and Splenda. Then mix in the beaten eggs.

4. Distribute the berries over the bottom of the pie crust, then pour the yogurt mixture over the berries. Bake for 40 minutes or until firm (no jiggle in the center when you shake it a bit) and the top is slightly brown. Let cool for at least 10 minutes.

5. This can be served warm, at room temperature or chilled.

To garnish: consider using a dollop of fresh peach yogurt or sour cream with a sprig of mint or the zest of a lemon or lime.

Yields 1 pie with 6 servings

Per Serving: 278 Calories; 24g Fat; 9g Protein; 11g Carbohydrate; 3g Dietary Fiber

Reduced Carb Variation: Omit the berries.
6g Net Carbs; 266 Calories; 24g Fat; 9g Protein; 8g Carbohydrate; 2g Dietary Fiber.

Blueberry Variation: Substitute blueberries for the blackberries. You may also want to use the blueberry yogurt instead of the peach.
9 Net Carbs; 279 Calories; 24g Fat; 9g Protein; 12g Carbohydrate; 3g Dietary Fiber.

Induction Variation: Omit berries and crust and pour yogurt mixture into 4 individual ramekins. Bake for about 20 minutes. Makes 4 servings.
3g Net Carbs; 112 Calories; 9g Fat; 6g Protein; 3g Carbohydrate; 0g Dietary Fiber

Grasshopper Pie

This low carb adaptation uses Carb Solutions™ mint chocolate chip ice cream scooped into a chocolate crust.

1	cup	almond meal
1/4	cup	butter
2	Tbsps	cocoa powder
1/2	cup	Splenda®
2	tsps	Just Whites
2	Tbsps	water
4	cups	Carb Solutions™ Mint Ice Cream

Weight Loss
8 Servings
8g Net Carbs

Preheat oven to 350ºF

1. Soften the butter and blend with the almond meal, cocoa powder and Splenda.

2. Whisk together the powdered egg whites and water. Be patient is takes a little while to dissolve. Add to the almond mixture. Blend well.

3. Press dough into a 9 inch pie pan. It will be gooey, but just get a general shape. Then pop it into the freezer for about 5-10 minutes (or the refrigerator for 15-20 minutes) and then remove and finish shaping the crust. It should be much easier to shape now.

4. Bake at 350ºF for about 12 minutes. Allow to cool completely before filling.

5. Pull the ice cream out of the freezer while the pie shell is cooling. Just when soft enough to work with, gently spoon into the crust. Using a spatula, smooth off the top. Cover and freeze for 1 hour or longer.

6. Cut into 8 slices. Serve as it is, or you can add a dollop of Sweet Whipped Cream (page 391) or a bit of the Chocolate Fudge Sauce (page 409)

Per Serving: 285 Calories; 24g Fat; 8g Protein; 20g Carbohydrate; 6g Dietary Fiber; 8g polyols

Each serving includes 8 grams of polyols. Allow 70% (~6g) to be subtracted from the total carbs.

Almond Cookies

These low carb cookies are the perfect dessert to serve after your low carb Chinese dinner. This cookie does not use any wheat flour but instead uses almond meal and chopped almonds as well as whey protein powder.

2/3	cup	almond meal
1/3	cup	Whey protein powder
1½	cups	Splenda®
1	tsp	baking powder -- **see note
1/2	cup	butter
1/2	cup	almonds -- finely chopped
1		egg
1/4	tsp	salt
2	tsps	almond extract

Weight Loss
10 Servings
5g Net Carbs

** High Altitude cooking: use 1/2 tsp baking powder

Pre heat oven to 375°F

1. In a large mixing bowl, mix together the almond meal, whey, Splenda and baking powder.

2. Cut the butter into small pieces and add to the mixing bowl. Using a pastry blender or two knives or your fingers, blend the butter into the dry mixture keeping it light and fluffy. (I prefer using my fingers, smashing the pieces of butter until well incorporated with no noticeable pieces of butter remaining.)

3. You can buy chopped almonds but they are more course than I like for this recipe so run them through the food processor for a minute. I sometimes purchase whole raw almonds (they are usually cheaper) and give them a course grind in the food processor. Add the almonds to the mixture.

4. Lightly beat the egg with the salt and almond extract. Pour into the mixing bowl. Stir until well blended.

5. Using lightly buttered hands, rolls batter into 20 balls each about 2 Tbsps. Place 10 to 12 on a parchment lined cookie sheet. Flatten just slightly. Bake for 10 minutes or until cookies have a golden color and just to turn brown along the edges. Transfer to a cookie rack and then repeat with the remaining batter.

Yields 20 cookies with 2 cookies per serving
If you make more or less cookies then be sure to adjust the carb count.

Per Serving: 205 Calories; 18g Fat; 10g Protein; 7g Carbohydrate; 2g Dietary Fiber

Lime & Coconut Squares

Very tangy, very satisfy sweet treat. These have a pale yellow color, so your mouth will expect a lemon flavor, but they are very distinctively key lime! "Put the lime with the coconut and then you'll feel better."

1	batch	Almond Coconut Pie Crust (page 392)
3		eggs
2	Tbsp	water
	pinch	salt
1/4	cup	cream
1	cup	Splenda®
1/2	cup	Nellie & Joe's Key Lime Juice
1	tsp	guar gum
2	Tbsps	butter

Weight Loss

16 Servings
4g Net Carbs

Topping

1/4	cup	coconut flakes
1	tsp	Splenda® -- optional

This dessert is quite a project. If you want something relatively quick and easy then this is not the one for you right now. But if you have the time to make this dessert then you will be well reward with an awesome treat.

Preheat oven to 350ºF

1. Separate the eggs, setting aside 1 egg white for the pie crust recipe. Beat the remaining egg whites with the water and a pinch of salt, cover and set aside.

2. In a medium to large bowl, beat the egg yolks with the cream and lime juice. Add the Splenda and mix well. Add the guar gum and whisk until completely dissolved and then another 30 seconds or more to be sure it is well distributed. Cover and set aside.

3. Make the crust dough on page 392 using the single egg white that you reserved (instead of the Just Whites and water). Firmly press dough into a lightly butter non-stick 8x8 baking pan. Take your time and make sure it is very flat and even. Bake for 12 minutes at 350ºF or just until the edges start to show a tiny bit of color. Let cool.

4. Meanwhile; toast the coconut for the topping. In a dry fry pan over medium heat add the coconut flakes and stir occasionally until they begin to brown. Transfer to a plate, bowl or paper towel and sprinkle with 1 tsp of Splenda (optional). Set aside.

5. Then in a sauce pan over med-low heat melt the butter.

6. Beat the egg yolk mixture again and then slowly (little by little) pour in the melted butter while whisking. Pour this mixture back into the sauce pan and heat on med-low heat while whisking continuously for about 3 minutes (it seems like forever when you are whisking constantly - but you want to cook

the egg yolk but you don't want scrambled eggs). Slowly add the beaten egg whites, whisking rather fast for 30 second and then normally for another minute or two. It should be quite thick at this point; as thick as mayo and developing an elastic quality to it (you'll see). If not, continue cooking until it thickens.

7. Pour the lime mixture over the cooled crust; spread it out evenly paying attention to the edges. Sprinkle the toasted coconut evenly over the top. Refrigerator for at least 1 hour. (Now clean up the kitchen while you wait. I'm sure that you made a bit of a mess!)

8. Cut into 16 squares. Enjoy!

I hope you have people to help you eat these otherwise they may be too tempting to overeat. If you make a half batch, then use 2 eggs.

Yields 16 squares with 1 square per serving

Per Serving: 114 Calories; 11g Fat; 3g Protein; 5g Carbohydrate; 1g Dietary Fiber

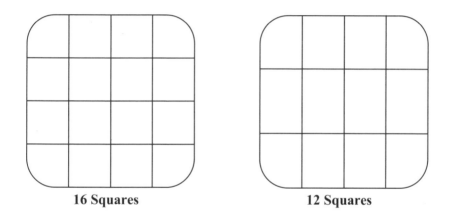

16 Squares   **12 Squares**

Cut into 12 squares; then each square has the following:
6g net carbs; 151 Calories; 14g Fat; 4g Protein; 7g Carbohydrate; 1g Dietary Fiber

Cinnamon Coconut Thins

Crispy, delightful and addictive low carb cookies. I bet you can't eat just one!

1/2	cup	almond meal
1/4	cup	coconut flakes
3	Tbsps	Splenda®
1	tsp	cinnamon
1	tsp	Just Whites
1	Tbsp	water
1/4	tsp	vanilla
2	Tbsps	butter -- melted

Weight Loss
4 Servings
5g Net Carbs

I purposefully made this recipe to yield just 1 batch of 12 cookies because they are so good you may have troubles resisting them. Each cookie is 1.7 g net carbs so a serving of 3 cookies puts you right at 5g net carbs. They are quite delicate so handle with care. They make a nice garnish for other desserts such as a bowl of low carb ice cream topped with fresh berries and then one of these cookies. Oh so yum!

1. Melt the butter and then mix with the almond meal, coconut flakes, Splenda and cinnamon.

2. Whisk together the powdered egg whites, water and vanilla. It will resist at first but keep whisking until it is all dissolved and frothy. Add to the coconut mixture. Blend well.

3. Flatten the dough onto a sheet of parchment paper; then place another sheet on top. Roll out a somewhat rectangular shape (roughly the size of your cookie sheet) and about 1/8 inch thick. Then place the parchment paper and dough onto an upside down cookie sheet and refrigerate for 30 minutes.

4. Remove from refrigerator and preheat oven to 375ºF

5. Carefully loosen and remove the top parchment paper from the dough and place it on your cookie sheet. Using a cookie cutter or scoring with a knife make about 9-11 cookies. (A harlequin diamond shape is nice and has very little waste - but any shape with do). The scraps will be used to fill out the dozen in the next step.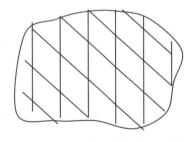

6. Carefully turn the dough and parchment paper over onto the lined cookie sheet. Carefully remove parchment paper. Now gently remove all the "scrap" pieces from around your cookies (save the scraps without deforming them too much) and gently move the cookies apart so that they are at least 1/4 inch apart from each other. If a cookie breaks just fit it back together with a gentle press. Now using the scraps fit together a few interesting shapes forming the last few cookies in the dozen.

7. Bake at 375°F for about 5 or 6 minutes, just until the edges start to brown. Do not over cook.

8. Remove from oven and let cool for 3 or 4 minutes.

Yields 12 cookies with 3 per serving

Per Serving: 157 Calories; 14g Fat; 4g Protein; 7g Carbohydrate; 2g Dietary Fiber

Pecan Drop Cookies

These low carb cookies are so yummy
with only 5g net carbs for a serving of 2 cookies

1/2	cup	**Whey protein powder**
1	cup	**Splenda®**
2	Tbsps	**flax seed meal**
1	tsp	**baking powder -- **see note**
1	tsp	**cinnamon**
1/2	cup	**butter (1 stick)**
1		**egg**
1/2	tsp	**vanilla extract**
1/2	tsp	**maple flavoring**
1	cup	**pecans -- finely chopped**

Weight Loss
9 Servings
5g Net Carbs

** **High Altitude cooking use 1/2 tsp baking powder.**

Preheat oven to 375°F

1. In a large mixing bowl, mix together the whey, Splenda, baking powder and cinnamon.

2. Cut the butter into small pieces and add to the mixing bowl. Using a pastry blender or two knives or your fingers, blend the butter into the dry mixture keeping it light and fluffy. (I prefer using my fingers, smashing the pieces of butter until well incorporated with no noticeable pieces of butter remaining.)

3. Lightly beat the egg with the maple and vanilla extract. Pour into the mixing bowl. Stir until well blended.

4. You can buy chopped pecans but they are more course than I like for this recipe, so run them through the food processor for a minute. Add the chopped pecans and the flax to the mixture.

5. Drop about 1 Tbsp of the batter onto a parchment lined cookie sheet. Bake for 10-12 minutes or until cookies have a golden color and just start to turn brown along the edges. Transfer to a cookie rack and then repeat with the remaining batter.

Yields about 18 cookies with 2 cookies per serving

Per Serving: 244 Calories; 20g Fat; 13g Protein; 7g Carbohydrate; 2g Dietary Fiber

Ginger Pecan Cookies

These low carb cookies are a wonderful cross between a ginger snap and ginger bread cookies. The kids will love them too!

1/2	cup	Whey protein powder
1½	cups	Splenda®
2	Tbsps	flax seed meal
2	tsps	ground ginger
1/2	tsp	baking powder
1/4	cup	butter (1/2 stick)
1	cup	pecan halves -- ground
1		egg
1/4	tsp	salt
1	Tbsp	blackstrap molasses

Weight Loss
10 Servings
6g Net Carbs

Preheat oven to 375°F

1. In a large mixing bowl, mix together the whey, Splenda, flax, ginger and baking powder.

2. Cut the butter into small pieces and add to the mixing bowl. Using a pastry blender or two knives or your fingers, blend the butter into the dry mixture keeping it light and fluffy. (I prefer using my fingers, smashing the pieces of butter until well incorporated until no noticeable pieces of butter are remaining.)

3. Run the pecans through the food processor for a minute to get a medium grind. Add the pecans to the mixture.

4. Lightly beat the egg with the salt and molasses. Pour into the mixing bowl. Stir until well blended.

5. Using lightly buttered hands, rolls batter into 20 balls with each just a bit more than a tablespoon. Place 10 to 12 on a parchment lined cookie sheet. Flatten just slightly. The flatter they are the more crispy they become. Bake for 10 minutes. Transfer to a cookie rack and then repeat with the remaining batter.

Yields 20 cookies, 2 cookies per serving
If you make more or less cookies then be sure to adjust the carb count.

Per Serving: 184 Calories; 13g Fat; 11g Protein; 8g Carbohydrate; 2g Dietary Fiber

Ginger Bread Cookie: If you love ginger bread, then add another Tbsp of molasses. This will give the cookies more of a bread-like texture. However, you will be increasing the carb count to 4 grams per cookie or 8 grams per serving of 2 cookies. This is recommended only during the Maintenance phase.
8g net carbs; 189 Calories; 13g Fat; 11g Protein; 10g Carbohydrate; 2g Dietary Fiber;

Nutty Oatmeal Cookies

Wonderful cookies with almonds, macadamia nuts, coconut and oatmeal.

1/2	cup	Whey protein powder
1/2	cup	almond meal
1	cup	Splenda®
2	Tbsps	flax seed meal
1/2	tsp	baking powder
1	tsp	cinnamon
1/2	cup	butter
3	Tbsps	coconut oil
1		egg
1	tsp	vanilla extract
1/2	cup	macadamia nut -- coarsely chopped
1/2	cup	rolled oats
1/4	cup	coconut flakes

Weight Loss
12 Servings
6g Net Carbs

Preheat oven to 350°F

1. In a large mixing bowl, mix together the whey, almond meal, Splenda, flax, baking powder and cinnamon.

2. Cut the butter into small pieces and add to the mixing bowl along with the coconut oil. Using a pastry blender or two knives or your fingers, blend the butter into the dry mixture keeping it light and fluffy. (I prefer using my fingers, smashing the pieces of butter until well incorporated with no noticeable pieces of butter remaining.)

3. Lightly beat the egg with the vanilla extract. Pour into the mixing bowl. Stir until well blended.

4. It's hard to find unsalted macadamia nuts, so I am assuming that yours are lightly salted, which would be too much for this recipe. However, if yours are unsalted then you'll need to add about 1/2 tsp or salt to the recipe.

    Wet 1 or 2 paper towels and squeeze out all the excess water. Then in batch rub the macadamia nuts in the paper towel to remove some of the salt. Coarsely chop using a good knife. A food processor will chop too finely for this recipe.

5. Drop about 1 rounded tablespoon of the batter onto a parchment lined cookie sheet. Flatten the batter a bit, unless you prefer cake like cookies then leave them mounded. Bake for 8-10 minutes or until cookies have a golden color and just start to turn brown along the edges. Transfer to a cookie rack and then repeat with the remaining batter.

Yields about 2 dozen cookies with 2 cookies per serving

Per Serving: 239 Calories; 19g Fat; 11g Protein; 8g Carbohydrate; 2g Dietary Fiber

Basic Brownies

This is a basic low carb brownie recipe.
There are some days when only a brownie will do!

3	ozs	unsweetened baking chocolate squares
4	Tbsps	butter (1/2 stick)
2		eggs
1½	cups	Splenda®
1	tsp	instant coffee, decaffeinated
1	tsp	vanilla extract
1	cup	almond meal
1	tsp	baking powder
1/2	cup	walnut

Weight Loss
8 Servings
8g Net Carbs

Preheat oven to 350°F

1. In a medium sized bowl, add the chocolate and butter and zap in the microwave for 30 seconds. Stir and repeat until melted.

2. In a bowl, beat the eggs well until they are light and form a ribbon (that is when the eggs form a string shape impression for a moment on top of the beaten eggs when drizzled from a distance of about 1 foot over the bowl). Add the Splenda, coffee crystals and vanilla extract. Stir. Add the almond meal and baking powder, stir. Then stir in the chocolate mixture.

3. Chop the walnuts with a chef's knife or by placing them in a food processor. Add to the mixture.

4. Lightly grease an 8 x 8 baking dish. Pour the batter into the pan and smooth out with a spatula. Bake in the middle of the oven for 12-15 minutes. Do not over bake.

5. Let cool in the pan for at least 10 minutes (or more). Cut into 16 squares (see page 397 for cutting style).

Yields 16 brownies with 2 per serving

Per Serving: 252 Calories; 24g Fat; 7g Protein; 12g Carbohydrate; 4g Dietary Fiber

Chocolate Cupcakes

These are decadent and delicious cupcakes using
Amber Lyn low carb chocolate bars.

4	bars	Amber Lyn low carb chocolate bars
2		eggs
5	Tbsps	unsalted butter
1/2	tsp	vanilla extract
1	tsp	instant coffee, decaffeinated

Weight Loss

5 Servings
4g Net Carbs

I think that the Amber Lyn Chocolates are the best on the market so far. I like to use the dark raspberry bar for this recipe but you can use any of the low carb flavors (the orange is quite wonderful too). Contact them to see where you can purchase these bars (**www.amberlynchocolates.com**). Substitute the chocolate Atkins bars or others as you see fit.

Preheat oven to 325°F

1. Beat the eggs until they form ribbons (that is when the eggs form a string shape impression for a moment on top of the beaten eggs when drizzled from a distance of about 1 foot over the bowl).

2. In a double broiler (or over very low heat stirring constantly) melt the butter and the chocolate bars.

3. Remove the chocolate from the heat and stir in the instant coffee and vanilla.

4. Add about 1 Tbsp of chocolate to the eggs and whisk vigorously. This is tempering the eggs. Add another 2 Tbsps, whisking vigorously. Fold in the remaining chocolate.

5. Pour the batter into 5 cupcake parchment paper cups. Don't worry that this does not look like enough batter per cup cake; it will raise doubling in size.

6. Bake at 325°F for 18-20 minutes or until a tooth pick comes out clean. Don't peak at them cooking for the first 12 minutes.

7. Allow to cool for at least 5 minutes - if you can resist.

Serve as is or with a dollop of Sweet Whipped Cream (page 391). Also consider the Cream Cheese Icing (page 413) or the Raspberry Sauce (page 358) drizzled on top.

Per Serving: 255 Calories; 23g Fat; 4g Protein; 13g Carbohydrate; 2g Dietary Fiber; 12g polyols

These cupcakes include 10g of polyols (sugar alcohol) per serving. Allowing 70% to be subtracted (7g) results in a total net carbs of 4g per cupcake.

Zucchini Cakes with Cream Cheese Icing

Do you like carrot cake? Well this is very similar except it is low carb.
It is cooked in a cupcake shape primarily for portion control.

1	cup	zucchini – grated
1/2	tsp	salt
2	Tbsps	Just Whites
1/4	cup	heavy cream
1/2	tsp	vanilla extract
1	tsp	cinnamon
1	tsp	baking powder
2	Tbsps	wheat bran
1/2	cup	Whey protein powder
1/2	cup	Splenda®
1/2	cup	walnuts -- finely chopped

```
+----------------------+
|    Weight Loss       |
+----------------------+
| 6 Servings           |
| 7g Net Carbs         |
+----------------------+
```

Cream Cheese Icing

4	ozs	cream cheese
1	Tbsp	heavy cream
1/2	tsp	vanilla
1/3	cup	Splenda®

Preheat oven to 350°F

1. Cut off the blossom end of the zucchini. Grate until you have 1 cup worth (loosely packed). Place in a medium sized bowl and add the salt. Toss and let sit for a couple of minutes. Squeeze the zukes to encourage them to give up some of their juices. Add the Just Whites and beat into the liquids with a fork.

2. Add the cream, vanilla extract, cinnamon and baking powder. Blend well.

3. To get 1/2 cup of finely chopped walnuts, put about 2/3 cup of walnut pieces into a food processor until about 1/3 of the walnuts are almost flour and the rest are no bigger than about this - O.

4. Add the wheat bran, whey powder, Splenda and walnuts. Stir well.

5. Insert 6 parchment paper baking cups into a muffin tin. Spoon batter into the cups dividing evenly (each about 3/4 full). Bake at 350°F for 15-20 minutes until tops start to brown. Cool for 5-10 minutes before adding the icing.

   Alternatively, pour the batter into a small bread loaf pan and bake for 20-30 minutes.

6. Meanwhile, make the icing. Soften the cream cheese by zapping it in the microwave for about 30 seconds. Stir in the cream, vanilla and Splenda. Stir until smooth. Ice the cupcakes once they have cooled. I like to keep them in the paper because the stay moist longer.

Store extras in Tupperware in the refrigerator

Yields 6 cupcakes with 1 per serving

Per Serving: 266 Calories; 18g Fat; 21g Protein; 8g Carbohydrate; 1g Dietary Fiber

Reduced Carb Variation: Omit icing
5g net carbs; 190 Calories; 11g Fat; 19g Protein; 6g Carbohydrate; 1g Dietary Fiber;

Ginger Pumpkin Custard

This stove-top custard is soft and creamy and a great alternative to pumpkin pie.

1	cup	canned pumpkin
2		egg yolk
1	cup	heavy cream
1/2	cup	Splenda®
1	tsp	fresh ginger -- grated
1/2	tsp	orange extract

Weight Loss
4 Servings
8g Net Carbs

Sometimes there is so much holiday cooking going on that it requires a master planning session to see who gets oven space and when. This custard requires only a few minutes of stove top time.

You will need a double broiler or a stainless steel mixing bowl that fits nicely over one of your pans. The water should not touch the bowl and should be just below the boiling point. Bring the water to a boil then turn to low (or medium low).

Finely grate the fresh ginger so that it is basically a paste. You can use a tsp of ground ginger but it will have a different taste.

1. In the stainless steel mixing bowl, beat the eggs. Add the cream, Splenda, ginger and orange extract. Mix well. Place bowl over the pan or double boiler with simmering water and whisk continuously until the custard thickens (about 5 minutes).

2. Remove from heat and whisk in the pumpkin. Keep stirring for 1 or 2 minutes. Let cool to room temperature then spoon into ramekins or wine glasses. Cover with plastic wrap and refrigerate for two hours before serving.

Per Serving: 257 Calories; 25g Fat; 3g Protein; 10g Carbohydrate; 2g Dietary Fiber

Mousse Variation: Serves 6. You can turn this into a mousse by folding in Sweet Whipped Cream (page 391) into the custard after it has cooled but before refrigerating. Now this fluffy version is enough for 6 servings.

7g net carbs; 308 Calories; 31g Fat; 3g Protein; 8g Carbohydrate; 1g Dietary Fiber

Pumpkin Pudding

Baked pumpkin pudding is an autumn favorite. Deliciously low carb.

15	ozs	canned pumpkin
4	ozs	cream cheese
1	cup	heavy cream
2		eggs
3/4	cup	Splenda®
1	tsp	maple flavoring -- or vanilla
1	tsp	cinnamon
1/2	tsp	ground ginger
1/2	tsp	salt
1/4	tsp	ground allspice -- optional
1/4	tsp	ground clove -- optional

Weight Loss

8 Servings
6g Net Carbs

Preheat oven to 350°F

1. Soften cream cheese in a small bowl by zapping in the microwave for about 30 seconds.

2. In a large bowl, beat the eggs and cream. Add the Splenda, maple flavoring, cinnamon, ginger, salt, allspice and cloves. Mix well. Add the pumpkin and mix until well blended.

3. Pour batter into a casserole dish and bake for about 40 minutes. The center may still be a tiny bit wiggly, but this will set with the residual heat. Cool at room temperature for 30 minutes.

Serve slightly warm or at room temperature or refrigerate and serve chilled. I prefer it warm with a scoop of low carb vanilla ice cream with it (oh so yum!).

Per Serving: 188 Calories; 17g Fat; 4g Protein; 8g Carbohydrate; 2g Dietary Fiber

Ricotta Pudding with Strawberries

This is a great low carb treat that is quick and easy!

1	cup	ricotta cheese
2	Tbsps	Carb Countdown™ Milk, 2%
1	Tbsp	Splenda®
1/4	tsp	cardamom
1/4	cup	strawberries -- thinly sliced

Weight Loss

2 Servings
6g Net Carbs

1. In a small bowl, mix together the ricotta cheese, milk, Splenda, and the cardamom. Mix until blended then continue to mix until it becomes very smooth (another minute or so).

2. I like to cut the strawberries in half and then slice them thin. They can be used to line a wine glass for a beautiful presentation, then carefully spoon in

the ricotta mixture. But if I'm in more of a hurry then I just cut the strawberries into tiny bites and stir them into the pudding.

3. Refrigerate for 30 minutes or more. Or serve it right away.

Per Serving: 226 Calories; 16g Fat; 15g Protein; 6g Carbs; trace Dietary Fiber

Blueberry Variation: Replace strawberries with ¼ cup of blueberries.
6g net carbs; 231 Calories; 16g Fat; 15g Protein; 7g Carbohydrate; 1g Dietary Fiber

Maple Walnut Pudding: Omit the cardamom and the strawberries. Add 1/4 tsp cinnamon and 1/2 tsp of maple flavoring in step 1. Then stir in 1/4 cup of chopped, toasted walnuts. (If your walnuts are raw, then toast them in a non-stick skillet for a minute or so. If your walnuts are toasted but they are salted, then rub them with a damp paper towel to remove the salt.)
6g net carbs; 316 Calories; 25g Fat; 18g Protein; 7g Carbohydrate; 1g Dietary Fiber

Raspberries with Cinnamon Ricotta Cheese

Whipped ricotta and cream cheese flavored with cinnamon topped with fresh raspberries presented in a wine glass.

10	ozs	ricotta cheese
4	ozs	cream cheese
3	Tbsps	Splenda®
1/2	tsp	vanilla extract
1/2	tsp	cinnamon
1	pint	raspberries
1	Tbsp	Splenda®
1/2	tsp	cinnamon

Weight Loss

4 Servings
7g Net Carbs

This is similar to the preceding recipe but different enough not to be just a "variation". The cream cheese makes this pudding much more rich and creamy. Your cream cheese should be room temperature.

1. Mix together the cream cheese, ricotta cheese, Splenda, vanilla extract and cinnamon. This can be done by hand, processor or mixer. Cover the bowl with plastic wrap and refrigerate for a couple of hours or a day or two in advanced.

2. When ready to serve. Rinse the berries with cold water and place in a bowl. Sprinkle 1 Tbsp of Splenda over the berries and lightly toss.

3. Then remove the ricotta mixture from the refrigerator. Stir well. Loosely spoon the mixture into 4 wine glasses. Add the berries to the top and serve.

If you like, you can garnish with a twist of lemon zest or a sprig of mint.

Per Serving: 256 Calories; 19g Fat; 11g Protein; 12g Carbohydrate; 5g Fiber

Strawberry Crepes with Chocolate Sauce

Perfect for that special occasion! This low carb adaptation is a lot of work but you can make the crepes, filling and the sauce ahead of time and then the assembly is easy.

Crepes

1		egg
2	Tbsps	Carb Countdown™ Milk, 2%
1	tsp	Splenda®
2	drops	vanilla extract
4	Tbsps	Whey protein powder
1/4	Tbsp	butter

Filling

2	Tbsps	Dannon's Carb Control™ Yogurt -- Strawberry
4	Tbsps	ricotta cheese
1	tsp	Splenda®
1/2	cup	strawberries -- quartered
4	Tbsps	Chocolate Fudge Sauce (next page)

1. Make the chocolate fudge sauce. Set aside.

2. Crepes: This takes a little bit of practice, if you are not already familiar with the technique. If this is your first time at making crepes then perhaps you might want to make a double batch of the crepe mix so that you can screw up one or two of them. In a small bowl, beat the egg. Add the milk, Splenda and extract and beat again. Then beat in the whey powder, mix well. It may be a little lumpy but that's okay.

3. Heat a crepe pan or a small non-stick skillet over medium-high heat. Once it is hot, melt a tiny bit of butter and spread it around. Add 1/2 of the egg mixture and immediately tilt the pan around so that the batter evenly covers the bottom of the pan. Set back on the heat and let it cook for about 20 or 30 seconds. Carefully lift up an edge to see if it has begun to brown. When it is a nice golden brown, carefully flip it over and cook another 30 seconds. Remove to a paper towel or parchment paper. Repeat with a tiny bit of butter and the remaining batter.

4. If you are not using the crepes right away layer parchment paper between them and slip into a large baggie or place on a plate and cover with plastic. Refrigerate up to two days.

5. Filling: The strawberries can be fresh or frozen. You may want to slice 1 strawberry into several very thin slices and reserve as a garnish (this is not easy with frozen berries). If frozen then let thaw until they are soft enough to cut. Cut into quarters or smaller if they are large berries. In a bowl, mix together the yogurt, ricotta cheese and Splenda. Fold in the strawberries.

6. To assemble: Place a crepe on a flat surface and heap 1/2 of the filling across the lower third of the crepe and then carefully roll up. Transfer to dessert plate with the seam side down. Repeat for the other crepe. Heat the chocolate sauce in the microwave for a few seconds and pour over the crepes.

Serve garnished with the reserved strawberry. A sprig of mint is also an attractive garnish.

Per Serving: 330 Calories; 19g Fat; 32g Protein; 10g Carbohydrate; 3g Fiber

Chocolate Fudge Sauce

This low carb adaptation is semi sweet, simple and delicious.

2		baking chocolate square
1	Tbsp	butter
6	Tbsps	Carb Countdown™ Milk, 2%
1/4	tsp	vanilla extract
1/2	cup	Splenda®

Weight Loss
5 Servings
4g Net Carbs

1. In a microwave safe bowl add the chocolate squares and butter. Zap for 30 seconds and stir for 30 seconds. Zap for 30 seconds and stir for 30 seconds. Continue until melted. The pauses are important so that the chocolate does not get too hot and burn.

2. Mix together the milk, extract and Splenda. Add to the chocolate. Stir well. You may need to zap it again if it is too thick to stir.

Store left overs in the refrigerator tightly covered, for up to a week.

Yields 10 Tbsps (just less that 2/3 cup) with 2 Tbsps per serving

Per Serving: 88 Calories; 9g Fat; 2g Protein; 6g Carbohydrate; 2g Dietary Fiber

Orange Decadent Chocolate Sauce: Use only 5 T milk, add 1T Grand Marnier, and use orange extract instead of the vanilla.
4g net carbs; 97 Calories; 9g Fat; 2g Protein; 6g Carbohydrate; 2g Dietary Fiber

Pavlova

This light and colorful pie consists of a meringue shell
filled with whipped cream and topped with an assortment of fresh fruit.

5		egg whites (~1/2 cup)
1/8	tsp	cream of tartar
1	cup	Splenda®
1/4	tsp	guar gum
1	Tbsp	raspberry vinegar
		(or apple cider vinegar plus one
		drop of raspberry extract)
1/2	tsp	vanilla extract
2		kiwi fruit -- peeled and sliced
2/3	cup	fresh strawberries -- sliced thin
2/3	cup	fresh blackberries
1½	cups	heavy whipping cream
2	Tbsps	Splenda®
1/2	tsp	almond extract

Weight Loss

8 Servings
8g Net Carbs

Preheat oven to 325°F

1. In a small bowl mix together the Splenda and the guar gum. Set aside.

2. In a clean dry bowl, whip the egg whites with the cream of tartar until soft peaks. Add the vinegar and vanilla and beat until blended. While whipping, gradually add the Splenda. Whip until stiff peaks (the peaks on the beaters stay straight even when turned completely upright).

3. Line a cookie sheet with parchment paper. Pour out the meringue in the center forming a small circle (about 10 inches in diameter). Use a spatula to form even sides and to smooth the top flat forming an even disk. Bake at 325°F for 10-15 minutes. Reduce heat to 300°F and bake another 40-50 minutes until the meringue just starts to pick up some color. Turn off heat and leave in the oven with the door ajar for 30-60 minutes until completely cooled. Transfer to a round platter or a very flat dinner plate.

4. Meanwhile, prepare your fruit. Slice the kiwi as thin as you can with a serrated knife. Then put the point of the knife between the peel and flesh and turn the slice, removing the peel without losing any of the yummy flesh. Then cut each slice in halves or quarters. Trim and slice strawberries thinly. Leave the blackberries whole. Refrigerate until needed.

5. Whipped cream: In a mixer add the cream, vanilla extract and the Splenda. Whip until soft peaks.

6. Spread the whipped cream on top of the meringue almost to the edge. Along the edge of the whipped cream, alternately place a piece of kiwi and then a

slice of strawberry until completing the circle. Sprinkle the remaining kiwi and strawberry evenly inside the circle. Then add the blackberries evenly within the circle. Bring to the table whole. Then using a serrated knife cut into 8 slices and serve.

Per Serving: 188 Calories; 17g Fat; 3g Protein; 10g Carbohydrate; 2g Dietary Fiber

I wish that I was able to include some photography in this cookbook, especially for recipes such as this one. The presentation can be quite remarkable.

Raspberry Yogurt Crisp

Sweet, crunchy and creamy; that's what I'm talking about! Frozen raspberries are actually better than fresh, as they help chill the yogurt even more. Notice that this dessert has 6 grams of fiber per serving!

4	ozs	Dannon's Carb Control™ Yogurt raspberry flavored
1/2	cup	raspberries
1/4	cup	Atkins Morning Start Almond Crisp

Weight Loss

1 Serving
7g Net Carbs

Use any flavor yogurt that you choose (they all have the same nutritional values).

1. Pour Atkins cereal into a bowl and crush (or use a mortar and pestle)
2. In a serving bowl, stir together the raspberries and yogurt. Top with the crushed cereal. Enjoy!

Per Serving: 129 Calories; 4g Fat; 11g Protein; 13g Carbohydrate; 6g Dietary Fiber

Apricot Variation: Use fresh apricots instead of the raspberry and substitute the peach yogurt for the raspberry flavored one.
11g net carbs; 134 Calories; 4g Fat; 12g Protein; 14g Carbohydrate; 3g Dietary Fiber

Strawberry Variation: Use strawberries instead of the raspberries and substitute the strawberry yogurt for the raspberry flavored one.
7g net carbs; 120 Calories; 4g Fat; 11g Protein; 11g Carbohydrate; 4g Dietary Fiber

Blueberry Variation: Use blueberries instead of the raspberries and substitute the blueberry yogurt for the raspberry flavored one.
12g net carbs; 138 Calories; 4g Fat; 11g Protein; 16g Carbohydrate; 4g Dietary Fiber

Pecan Cups

This yummy low carb dessert is similar to a crustless pecan pie
but prepared in individual cups to make this recipe quick and easy.
Substitute walnuts and subtract 1 gram carbs per serving.

3/4	cup	pecans -- chopped
2		eggs
1/2	cup	Joseph's Sugar Free Maple Syrup
3	Tbsps	butter
1	Tbsp	blackstrap molasses
1	tsp	vanilla extract

> **Weight Loss**
>
> **4 Servings**
> **7g Net Carbs**

Maltitol (see page 29) is the primary ingredient in the Joseph's Maple Syrup. If you are not accustom to it, be cautious not to have more than one serving in a 24 hour period and test how your system does. DO NOT try this recipe with the Atkins' Syrup - it will be a disaster. But if you have a source for another, sugar-fee syrup made primarily from maltitol then that product should work okay.

Preheat oven to 375°F. You'll need 4 custard cups (5 or 6 oz size).

1. Melt the butter in one of the custard cups by putting it in the microwave for 20-30 seconds.

2. In a small mixing bowl, add the eggs and beat well with a whisk. Before measuring the Sugar Free Maple Syrup, pour the melted butter into the measuring cup and then back into the custard cup. This will make it easier to get the syrup out of the measuring cup. Add the syrup to the egg mixture. Then before more measuring the molasses, dip the Tbsp into the melted butter and coat it well. Add the molasses to the egg mixture. Now add the vanilla extract. Mix well.

3. Pour the melted butter into each custard cup to coat them. Then add the melted butter to the egg mixture. Mix.

4. Rough chop the pecan. This is easily done with a good knife. If using walnuts, a food processor may work better for you. But do not grind. Reserve 4 nut halves to place in the center of each cup if you'd like. Distribute the nuts to the 4 custard cups evenly.

5. Pour the egg mixture evenly between the 4 cups. Place the custard cups on a cookie sheet and bake at 375°F for 12 to 15 minutes. They will rise a little in the center of each cup when they are done.

Serve hot, at room temperature or cold. Try adding a dollop of Sweet Whipped Cream (page 391) or low carb ice cream. These pecan cups are fantastic with low carb butter pecan ice cream. Good brand choices are Carb Solutions™ and Keto.

Per Serving: 259 Calories; 25g Fat; 4g Protein; 12g Carbohydrate; 2g Dietary Fiber; 5g maltitol
Each serving has 4.5g of maltitol; allow 70% (3g) to be subtracted from the total carbs.

Cream Cheese Icing

Turn your favorite muffin into a cupcake with this classic icing.
This makes enough icing for 8 cupcakes.

6	ozs	cream cheese
1	Tbsp	heavy cream
1/2	tsp	vanilla
1/2	cup	Splenda®

Weight Loss

8 Servings
2g Net Carbs

Soften the cream cheese by zapping it in the microwave for about 30 seconds. Stir in the cream, vanilla and Splenda. Stir until smooth.

Per Serving: 81 Calories; 8g Fat; 2g Protein; 2g Carbohydrate; 0g Dietary Fiber

Pecan Cream Cheese Icing: Add 1/2 cup finely chopped pecans
2g net carbs; 126 Calories; 13g Fat; 2g Protein; 3g Carbohydrate; 1g Dietary Fiber

Coconut Cream Cheese Icing: Add 1/2 cup unsweetened coconut flakes
3g net carbs; 99 Calories; 10g Fat; 2g Protein; 3g Carbohydrate; trace Dietary Fiber

Pecan & Coconut Cream Cheese Icing: Add both the pecans and coconut
3g net carbs; 144 Calories; 14g Fat; 2g Protein; 4g Carbohydrate; 1g Dietary Fiber

Warm Spiced Milk

Warmed sweet milk with plenty of spices is my favorite treat just before bedtime.

1	cup	Carb Countdown™ Milk, 2%
2	tsp	Splenda®
1/4	tsp	cardamom
pinch		cinnamon
pinch		ground ginger
3	drops	almond extract

Weight Loss

1 Servings
4g Net Carbs

Although technically not a dessert, I didn't know where else to put this treat. The calcium in milk is a very good sleep aid. Do you need to take any herbs or medicines just before bed? Well for me, generally this milk is enough to keep me from getting an upset stomach (especially if I have one low carb cookie along with it – tee, hee).

1. Place in a microwave safe mug, 1/2 cup of the milk, the Splenda, cardamom, cinnamon, ginger and almond extract. Zap until it comes to a boil (~30 seconds). Remove and stir well.

2. Add the remaining milk and stir. Depending on how warm you want your milk, you can zap it again for another 30 seconds.

I like my milk just luke warm in the summer and quite hot in the winter.

Per Serving: 100 Calories; 4g Fat; 12g Protein; 4g Carbs; trace Dietary Fiber

Peanut Butter Cookies

Smooth or crunchy peanut butter works fine here;
just be sure it is a good quality natural brand with no additives.

1	cup	peanut butter
2		eggs
1	cup	Splenda®
1/4	cup	whey protein powder

Maintenance
6 Servings
10g Net Carbs

Preheat oven to 350°F

1. Beat the eggs in a mixing bowl. Add the Splenda and the whey protein powder and mix. Add the peanut butter and mix well. Since peanut butter is not so easy to measure just estimate it. Set your measuring cup near the mixing bowl and just guess at a cup's worth.

2. Use a nonstick cookie sheet or better yet, line a cookie sheet with parchment paper. Spoon out a rounded Tbsp worth and roll it into a ball. Then flatten it out on the cookie sheet. After 12 cookies have been made, take a fork and score the top of each cookie (this is for decoration only).

3. Bake for 12 minutes. Remove from oven and let cool before eating.

Yields 12 cookies with 2 cookie per serving

Per Serving: 346 Calories; 24g Fat; 20g Protein; 13g Carbohydrate; 3g Dietary Fiber

Triple Goddess Brownies

Three layers of decadence; a low carb brownie base with a thin,
mint cream cheese layer and then topped with chocolate fudge.

First Layer
1	batch	Basic Brownies, page 402

<table>
<tr><td colspan="2">Maintenance</td></tr>
<tr><td>8 Servings</td></tr>
<tr><td>13g Net Carbs</td></tr>
</table>

Second Layer
8	ozs	cream cheese
1	cup	Splenda®
1	tsp	mint extract
1/2	tsp	vanilla extract
3	drops	green food coloring -- optional

Third Layer
1		baking chocolate square -- unsweetened
1/2	Tbsp	butter
3	Tbsps	Carb Countdown™ Milk, 2%
1/4	tsp	vanilla extract
1/2	cup	Splenda®

1. Make a batch of Basic Brownies page 402. Do not cut and let cool completely before adding the next layer.

2. Second Layer: Zap the cream cheese in the microwave for about 30 seconds to soften it. Add the Splenda, mint extract and vanilla extract. If you want it to be a bit green add a couple of drops of green food color. Careful a little goes a long way. Evenly spread the cream cheese over the brownies. Pop in the freezer while you make the top layer.

3. Third layer. In a microwave safe bowl add 1 chocolate square and 1/2 Tbsp butter. Zap for 30 seconds and stir for 30 seconds. Zap for 30 seconds and stir for 30 seconds. Continue until melted. The pauses are important so that the chocolate does not get too hot and burn.

4. Mix together the milk, extract and Splenda. Add to the chocolate. Stir well. It resists at first put then stirs in just fine. You may need to zap it again if it is too thick. Pour evenly over the cream cheese layer tipping the pan to spread evenly.

5. Cover and refrigerator for 3 hours. These are best when they are served quite cold. They are just so-so when eaten before they are fully chilled. Cut into 16 brownies (see page 397 for cutting style).

Yields 16 brownies with 2 squares per serving

Per Serving: 379 Calories; 37g Fat; 10g Protein; 18g Carbs; 5g Dietary Fiber

Apple Crumble

Apple and pecans smothered in a cinnamon, sour cream sauce
with a crumble topping.

1		**Granny Smith apple**
1/4	**cup**	**water**
1/4	**cup**	**Splenda®**
1/2	**tsp**	**cinnamon**
1/4	**tsp**	**allspice**
1/4	**tsp**	**vanilla extract**
1/4	**cup**	**sour cream**
1/4	**cup**	**pecans -- chopped**

Maintenance
2 Servings
16g Net Carbs

CrumbleTopping

1/4	**cup**	**almond meal**
1	**Tbsp**	**rolled oats**
1	**Tbsp**	**Splenda®**
1/4	**tsp**	**cinnamon**
1	**Tbsp**	**butter -- room temp**

I use two ramekins (1 cup size) to make this dessert. But it can be made in a small casserole dish.

Preheat oven to 375ºF

1. Prepare the topping first. In a mixing bowl, add the almond meal, rolled oats, Splenda and cinnamon. Stir until blended. Add the soften butter and cut through forming a crumble about the size of peas or smaller. Place in the refrigerator while you prepare the apples.

2. I like to leave the skin on the apple, but I think many people will want to peel their apple (to each their own). Cut the apple into cubes. Place in the mixing bowl with the pecan.

3. In a sauce pan over high heat, add the water, Splenda, cinnamon, allspice and vanilla. Bring to a boil. Pour over the apples and pecans and stir. Let sit for 1-2 minutes.

4. Stir in the sour cream. Stir until incorporated.

5. Divide apple mixture between the two ramekins (or place in a single casserole dish). Crumble the topping over each and bake in a 375ºF oven for 30 minutes. Remove from oven and let cool for 5 or 10 minutes before serving.

Per Serving: 328 Calories; 28g Fat; 6g Protein; 21g Carbohydrate; 5g Dietary Fiber

Noodle Kugel

Baked low carb pasta in a sweet creamy sauce.

1	cup	low carb pasta -- rotini
1/2	cup	ricotta cheese
1/2	cup	sour cream
8	ozs	cream cheese -- softened
1		egg
1/2	cup	Splenda®
1	tsp	vanilla extract
1/2	tsp	cinnamon -- ground
1/2	tsp	cardamom -- ground
2	tsps	blackstrap molasses -- optional

Maintenance
4 Servings
12g Net Carbs

This recipe was formulated with the soy-based low carb pasta (CarbFit – rotini style). I must admit that this dessert is just so-so, at best. But if you use the DreamFields low carb pasta, then it becomes outstanding (and then you can also eliminate the molasses which I included to help mask the soy pasta flavor). However, I'm not convinced about DreamFields' story yet (see page 22), so I can not recommend their product at this time, as part of a carb conscious lifestyle.

1. Boil the noodles according to the directions on the packet except reduce the time by about 2 minutes. Low carb noodles are awful when they are overcooked and you'll be baking the kugel so you want the noodles still firm.

Preheat oven to 350°F

2. Beat the egg thoroughly. Add the Splenda and stir. Then add the ricotta, sour cream, cream cheese, cinnamon, cardamom, vanilla extract and molasses and blend well until very creamy.

3. Gently fold the noodles into the mixture. Pour into a greased 8x8 casserole dish.

4. Bake at 350°F for about 35 minutes. Serve warm.

Per Serving: 392 Calories; 32g Fat; 17g Protein; 14g Carbs; 2g Dietary Fiber

Sweet Egg Cake with Boysenberry Sauce

This is similar to a dessert soufflé but without all the effort.

4		eggs
1	cup	heavy cream
1/2	cup	whey protein powder
1/2	cup	almond meal
1/2	tsp	almond extract
1	Tbsp	butter

1½	cups	boysenberries – fresh or frozen
1/3	cup	Splenda®
1/4	tsp	guar gum
	pinch	ground cloves -- optional

Preheat oven to 350ºF

1. In a mixing bowl, beat the eggs. Add the cream, whey, almond meal and almond extract. Beat well.

2. Butter 4 large ramekins. Divide the batter evenly between the ramekins. Place on a cookie sheet and bake for 25 minutes or until the tops are puffed up and beginning to brown. Remove and let cool for at least 10 minutes.

3. In a small bowl mix together the Splenda, cloves and the guar gum. Set aside

4. Meanwhile, make the boysenberry sauce. You may want to set aside a few of the most perfect berries as a garnish. In a sauce pan over medium-high heat, cook the boysenberries until they have completely broken up. You can strain the sauce at this point to remove the seeds if you wish, but you will be removing a source of nutrients. Gradually add the Splenda mixture, whisking constantly so that the guar gum doesn't lump. Carefully taste test (careful, it is VERY hot) to see if it needs more Splenda. Add more as needed.

5. Pour sauce over the cakes and serve.

I like to serve this in the ramekin. You can try to remove the cake from the ramekin, but I've not had much luck with that. If you want the cakes to be free standing, then I suggest lining the ramekins with parchment to facilitate removing the cakes.

Per Serving: 520 Calories; 38g Fat; 32g Protein; 14g Carbs; 4g Dietary Fiber

A

Order Additional Copies of this Cookbook

LOW CARB CREATIONS from Lauri's Kitchen

Return an order form and your
check or money order to:

Avalon Enterprises, Inc.
Re: Low Carb Creations
P.O. Box 1044
Golden, CO 80402-1044

Includes **free shipping & handling** via US Media Mail (expect delivery in ~2 weeks after Avalon's receipt of check). Or add $5 per book for US Priority Mail (expect delivery 4-5 business day after receipt of check).

Please send _____ copies of **Low Carb Creations from Lauri's Kitchen** at $18.95 per copy. Please send via ____ US Media Mail (free shipping) or via ____ US Priority Mail (include an additional $5 per book).

Mail books to:

Name _____

Address _____

City _____ State _____ Zip _____

Please send _____ copies of **Low Carb Creations from Lauri's Kitchen** at $18.95 per copy. Please send via ____ US Media Mail (free shipping) or via ____ US Priority Mail (include an additional $5 per book).

Mail books to:

Name _____

Address _____

City _____ State _____ Zip _____

PUBLISHERS SPECIAL

LAURI'S LOW-CARB COOKBOOK

**Overstock clearance of 2nd Edition copies with
<u>minor blemishes on the cover</u>
lightly scuffed during shipping or handling.**

**40% Off
only $12^{00}**

Return an order form and your
check or money order to:

**Avalon Enterprises, Inc.
Re: Lauri's Cookbook
P.O. Box 1044
Golden, CO 80402-1044**

Includes **free shipping & handling** via US Media Mail (expect delivery
in ~2 weeks after Avalon's receipt of check). Or add $5 per book for US
Priority Mail (expect delivery 4-5 business day after receipt of check).

Please send _____ copies of **Lauri's Low-Carb Cookbook, 2nd Edition,
lightly scuffed** at Publisher's Special price of $12 per copy.

Mail books to:

Name _____

Address _____

City _____ State _____ Zip _____

Please send _____ copies of **Lauri's Low-Carb Cookbook, 2nd Edition,
lightly scuffed** at Publisher's Special price of $12 per copy.

Mail books to:

Name _____

Address _____

City _____ State _____ Zip _____